James
BALDWIN
a reference guide

A
Reference
Publication
in
Literature

Ronald Gottesman
Editor

James
BALDWIN,
a reference guide

FRED L. STANDLEY
AND
NANCY V. STANDLEY

(G.K.HALL&CO. 1980

70 LINCOLN STREET, BOSTON, MASS.

Library of Congress Cataloging in Publication Data

Standley, Fred L
    James Baldwin, a reference guide.

    (A Reference publication in literature)
    Includes index.
    1. Baldwin, James 1924-   —Bibliography.
I. Standley, Nancy V., joint author. II. Title.
III. Series: Reference publication in literature.
Z8068.74.S72   [PS3552.A45]   016.818′5′409
ISBN 0-8161-7844-5   79-19992

This publication is printed on permanent/durable acid-free paper
MANUFACTURED IN THE UNITED STATES OF AMERICA

For
BETTY FLORY PHIFER
(1930 - 1978)
Who personified
"love . . . in the tough and universal
sense of quest and daring and growth."
The Fire Next Time

Contents

Preface

The career of James Baldwin (b. 1924) as an American man of letters has spanned three decades. Since his early book reviews of 1947 in New Leader, Baldwin has published eighteen books, including six novels, two dramas, six collections of essays, one edition of short stories, two series of dialogues, and one text accompanying a collection of photographs; additionally, he has produced countless shorter pieces--articles, interviews, recordings. Throughout this corpus there echoes in prophetic tone and moral concern, in intense language and poignant sincerity, a passionate and perceptive exploration of a broad spectrum of themes: the intertwining of love and power in the universal scheme of existence and in society's structure; the misplaced emphasis in the value systems of the United States; the necessity for the indivisibility of the private life and the public life; the past historical significance and the potential explosiveness of the continuing racial crisis between blacks and whites; the essential need to develop sexual and psychological consciousness and identity; and the responsibility of the artist to promote and contribute to the evolution of the individual and society.

The criticism elicited by the volume and magnitude of this literary output and its thematic interests has been constant and prodigious; and it divides readily into three discernible periods equivalent to the three decades of the primary works. In the first decade --the fifties--the principal responses were in the form of reviews of Baldwin's books and commentary on the author as spokesman for his race, with little attention afforded the literary artistry. The decade of the sixties saw the continuation of extensive book reviews, a decided change of emphasis to Baldwin's role as a civil rights advocate, and increasing attention to his artistic achievement in literature. The third decade--the seventies--has witnessed the prolongation of interest on the part of reviewers, an attenuation of concern with his participation in the civil rights movement, and a definite enlargement in the consideration of his literary and aesthetic accomplishments, and, indeed, an overall assessment of his proper place in the pantheon of American literary figures. Specific evidence for such a pronounced shift toward critical evaluation of Baldwin's literary merit is readily observable in the fact that within the five-year period from 1973 to 1978, three book-length critical

studies and two anthologies of critical essays appeared in print
(1973.27; 1974.29; 1977.39; 1977.52; 1978.12). Thus, from the earliest point of external recognition of his promise as a novelist by being awarded a Saxton Fellowship (1946.1) to the more recent lavish
praise of him as belonging "in an extremely select group . . . the
few genuinely indispensable American writers" (1972.29), Baldwin has
been in the public eye, endeavoring to fulfill his vocational credo
expressed in "Autobiographical Notes" (Notes of a Native Son): "I
consider that I have many responsibilities but none greater than this:
to last, as Hemingway says, and get my work done. I want to be an
honest man and a good writer."

Although this Reference Guide contains initially a list of primary works by Baldwin, the principal value of the volume consists in
its being a chronological, annotated survey of reviews, commentaries,
and interpretations about his works as well as its containing significant references to him found in books, periodicals, newspapers,
monographs, and dissertations both in English and in several foreign
languages. The Guide covers the period from the publication of his
first important book, Go Tell It on the Mountain, 1953, to the end of
1978. However, the listing for the latter is only preliminary because
the traditional bibliographic data were not yet available for many
sources at the time this Guide was being finished. Whenever possible
the methodology used for each entry involved a combination of quota-
tion and paraphrase in an effort to construct an annotation in the
format of precis or abstract that would reflect the writer's own
points of emphasis and evaluation. We hope, then, the Guide will contribute to the furthering of interest in and examination of the work
of James Baldwin, who is the first black American "to achieve international status as a masterful creative artist" (1964.68).

Fred L. Standley
Florida State University

Nancy V. Standley
Florida A&M University

Acknowledgments

We are grateful to several people for aiding in the completion of this bibliographic guide. Our colleagues Joseph R. McElrath, Jr., and R. Bruce Bickley, Jr., provided advice and encouragement. Bonnie Braendlin translated several items from German into English. Paula Sewell rendered secretarial assistance. Nancy Matthews arranged schedules, made travel plans, and performed numerous other services that resulted in the freeing of time to devote to this project.

Additionally, we are indebted to the following universities for allowing us the use of their library facilities: Atlanta University, Duke University, Emory University, Florida A&M University, Florida State University, Howard University, New York University, University of California at Berkeley, University of Colorado, University of Denver, University of North Carolina at Chapel Hill, and University of Tennessee at Knoxville. And we are also appreciative of the opportunities for using the New York Public Library, the Library of Congress, and the State Library of Florida.

List of Periodical Abbreviations

BA Rev	Black Academy Review
BALF	Black American Literature Forum
BB	Bulletin of Bibliography
Cath W	Catholic World
CCC	College Composition and Communication
CLAJ	College Language Association Journal
Col Q	Colorado Quarterly
EJ	English Journal
Harper's	Harper's Magazine
Hud R	Hudson Review
JNH	Journal of Negro History
LJ	Library Journal
NALF	Negro American Literature Forum
PR	Partisan Review
Players	Players: Magazine of American Theatre
PMLA	Publications of Modern Language Association
Sat R	Saturday Review
Sat R/W	Saturday Review World
SAQ	South Atlantic Quarterly
TLS	Times Literary Supplement

List of Short-Titles

Writings by James Baldwin

BOOKS

Novels

Another Country. New York: Dial Press, 1962.

Giovanni's Room. New York: Dial Press, 1956.

Go Tell It on the Mountain. New York: Alfred A. Knopf, 1953.

If Beale Street Could Talk. New York: Dial Press, 1974.

Little Man, Little Man. A Story of Childhood. Illustrated by Yoran Cazac. New York: Dial Press, 1976.

Tell Me How Long the Train's Been Gone. New York: Dial Press, 1968.

Dramas

The Amen Corner. New York: Dial Press, 1968.

Blues for Mister Charlie. New York: Dial Press, 1964.

Essays

The Devil Finds Work. An Essay. New York: Dial Press, 1976.

The Fire Next Time. New York: Dial Press, 1963.

No Name in the Street. New York: Dial Press, 1972.

Nobody Knows My Name: More Notes of a Native Son. New York: Dial Press, 1961.

Notes of a Native Son. Boston: Beacon Press, 1955.

Nothing Personal. Photographs by Richard Avedon and text by James Baldwin. New York: Atheneum Publishers, 1964.

Books

Short Stories

Going to Meet the Man. New York: Dial Press, 1965.

Dialogues

A Dialogue. James Baldwin and Nikki Giovanni. Philadelphia: J. B. Lippincott, 1973.

A Rap on Race. Margaret Mead and James Baldwin. Philadelphia: J. B. Lippincott, 1971.

Scenario

One Day, When I Was Lost. A Scenario Based on Alex Haley's "The Autobiography of Malcolm X." London: Michael Joseph, 1972.

OTHER WORKS

Essays, Reviews, Letters

"Among the Recent Letters to the Editor." New York Times Book Review (26 February 1961), pp. 52-53.

"Anti-Semitism and Black Power." Freedomways, 7 (Winter 1967), 75-77.

"The Artist's Struggle for Integrity." Liberation, 8 (March 1963), 9-11.

"As Much Truth as One Can Bear." New York Times Book Review (14 January 1962), pp. 1, 38.

"At the Root of the Negro Problem." Time, 17 May 1963, pp. 26-27.

"Baldwin Excoriates Church for Hypocritical Stance." Afro-American (16 July 1968).

"Battle Hymn." New Leader, 30 (29 November 1947), 10.

"The Black Boy Looks at the White Boy Norman Mailer." Esquire, 55 (May 1961), 102-106. Rptd. in Nobody Knows.

"Bright World Darkened." New Leader, 31 (24 January 1948), 11.

"Charge within a Channel." New Leader, 31 (24 April 1948), 11.

"Color." Esquire, 58 (December 1962), 225, 252.

"Compressions: L'Homme et La Machine." In Cesar: Compressions d'or by Cesar Baldaccini. Paris: Hachette, 1973, pp. 9-16.

2

"The Creative Dilemma: 'The War of an Artist with His Society Is a Lover's War.'" Sat R, 47 (8 February 1964), 14-15, 18.

"The Creative Process." In Creative America. The National Cultural Center. New York: Ridge Press, 1962, pp. 17-21.

"The Crusade of Indignation." Nation, 183 (7 July 1956), 18-22.

"The Dangerous Road before Martin Luther King." Harper's, 222 (February 1961), 33-42.

"Dead Hand of Caldwell." New Leader, 30 (6 December 1947), 10.

"Dear Sister . . ." Manchester Guardian Weekly (27 December 1970), p. 31.

"The Discovery of What It Means to Be an American." New York Times Book Review (25 January 1959), p. 4. Rptd. in Nobody Knows.

"Envoi." In A Quarter Century of Unamericana 1938-1963; A Tragico-Comical Memorabilia of HUAC. Edited by Charlotte Pomerantz. Nieuw Amsterdam: Marzani and Munsell, 1963.

"Equal in Paris." PR, 16 (1949), 578-85. Rptd. in Notes.

"Everybody's Protest Novel," Zero, 1 (Spring 1949), 54-58. See also, PR, 16 (June 1949), 578-85. Rptd. in Notes.

"The Exile." Prevue (February 1961). Rptd. in Nobody Knows.

"Faulkner and Desegregation." PR, 23 (Winter 1956), 568-73. Rptd. in Nobody Knows.

"Fifth Avenue, Uptown: A Letter from Harlem." Esquire, 52 (July 1960), 70-76. Rptd. in Nobody Knows.

"From Dreams of Love to Dreams of Terror." In Natural Enemies? Youth and the Clash of Generations. Edited by Alexander Klein. Philadelphia: Lippincott, 1969, pp. 274-79. Rptd. from The Los Angeles Free Press.

"Gide as Husband and Homosexual." New Leader, 37 (13 December 1954), 18-20. Rptd. in Nobody Knows as "The Male Prison."

"God's Country." The New York Review of Books, 8 (23 March 1967), 20.

"The Hard Kind of Courage." Harper's, 217 (October 1958), 61-65. Rptd. in Nobody Knows as "A Fly in Buttermilk."

"The Harlem Ghetto: Winter 1948." Commentary, (February 1948), 165-70.

"History as Nightmare." New Leader, 30 (25 October 1947), 11, 15.

"If They Take You in the Morning." Excerpt from "Dear Sister. . .," Manchester Guardian Weekly (27 December 1970), p. 31.

Other Works

"The Image of the Negro." Commentary, 5 (April 1948), 378-80.

"In Search of a Basis for Mutual Understanding and Racial Harmony."
In The Nature of a Humane Society. Edited by H. Ober Hesse. Philadelphia: Fortress Press, 1976-1977, pp. 231-40.

"James Baldwin on the Negro Actor." Urbanite (April 1961). Rptd. in
Anthology of the American Negro in the Theatre. Edited by Lindsay
Patterson. New York: Publishers Company, 1967, pp. 127-30.

"Journey to Atlanta." New Leader, 31 (9 October 1948), 8-9. Rptd.
in Notes.

"A Letter from the South: Nobody Knows My Name." PR, 26 (Winter
1959), 72-82. Rptd. in Nobody Knows as "Nobody Knows My Name: A
Letter from the South."

"A Letter to Americans." Freedomways, 8 (Spring 1968), 112-16.

"A Letter to My Nephew." Progressive, 26 (December 1962), 19-20.
Rptd. in The Fire as "My Dungeon Shook."

"Letters from a Journey." Harper's, 226 (May 1963), 48-52.

"Letters from a Region in My Mind." New Yorker, 38 (17 November
1962), 59-144. Rptd. in The Fire as "Down at the Cross."

"Life Straight in De Eye." Commentary, 19 (January 1955), 74-77.
Rptd. in Notes as "Carmen Jones."

"Literary Grab Bag." New Leader, 31 (28 February 1948), 11.

"Lockridge: The American Myth." New Leader, 31 (10 April 1948), 10,
14.

Los Negros en U.S.A. Cuba: Lunes de Revolucion, July 1960. 39 pp.

"Malcolm and Martin; Excerpt from No Name in the Street." Esquire,
77 (April 1977), 94.

"ManyThousands Gone." PR, 18 (November/December 1951), 665-80.
Rptd. in Notes.

"Mass Culture and the Creative Artist: Some Personal Notes," in
Culture for the Millions. Taiment Institute. Princeton: Van Nos-
trand, 1959, pp. 120-23, 176-87.

"Maxim Gorki as Artist." Nation, 164 (12 April 1947), 427-28.

"Me and My Home . . ." Harper's, 211 (November 1955), 54-61. Rptd.
in Notes as "Notes of a Native Son."

"Modern River Boys." New Leader, 31 (14 August 1948), 12.

"A Negro Assays the Negro Mood." New York Times Magazine (12 March
1961), pp. 25, 103-104. Rptd. in Nobody Knows as "East River Down-
town: Postscript to a Letter from Harlem."

Writings by James Baldwin

Other Works

"The Negro at Home and Abroad." Reporter, 5 (27 November 1951), 36-37.

"The Negro in Paris." Reporter, 2 (6 June 1950), 34-36. Rptd. in Notes as "Encounter on the Seine."

"The Negro Writer in America: A Symposium." Negro Digest, 12 (June 1963), 54-65.

"Negroes Are Anti-Semitic Because They're Anti-White." New York Times Magazine (9 April 1967), pp. 26-27, 135-40. Rptd. in Black Anti-Semitism and Jewish Racism. Introduction by Nat Hentoff. New York: Baron, 1969, pp. 3-14.

"The Negro's Role in American Culture; Symposium," Negro Digest, 11 (March 1962), 80-98.

"The New Lost Generation." Esquire, 56 (July 1961), 113-15.

"The Nigger We Invent." Integrated Education, 7 (March/April 1969), 15-23.

"Notes for a Hypothetical Novel." Address at the Third Annual Esquire Magazine Symposium on "The Role of the Writer in America" at San Francisco State College, October 22, 1960. Rptd. in Nobody Knows.

"On an Author: Excerpts from Letters." New York Herald Tribune Book Review, 29 (31 May 1953), 3.

"On Catfish Row: Porgy and Bess in the Movies." Commentary, 28 (September 1959), 246-48.

"An Open Letter to My Sister, Miss Angela Davis." The New York Times (7 January 1971), p. 15.

"Our Divided Society: A Challenge to Religious Education." Religious Education, 64 (September/October 1969), 342-46.

"Paris Letter: A Question of Identity." PR, 21 (July/August 1954), 402-10.

"'Pour Libérer les Blancs . . .' (Propos Recueillis par François Bondy)." Prévues, 152 (1963), 3-17.

"The Precarious Vogue of Ingmar Bergman." Esquire, 53 (April 1960), 128-32. Rptd. in Nobody Knows as "The Northern Protestant."

"Present and Future." New Leader, 31 (13 March 1948), 11.

"Preservation of Innocence." Zero, 1 (Summer 1949), 14-22.

"Princes and Powers." Encounter, 8 (January 1957), 52-60. Rptd. in Nobody Knows.

"A Question of Identity." PR, 21 (July/August 1954), 402-10. Rptd. in Notes.

5

Other Works

"A Report from Occupied Territory." Nation, 203 (11 July 1966), 39-43.

"Richard Wright." Encounter, 16 (April 1961), 58-60. Rptd. in Nobody Knows as "The Exile."

"Roots: The Saga of an American Family," Unique, 1 (1976), 31-32.

"The Search for Identity." In American Principles and Issues. Edited by Oscar Handlin. New York: Holt, Rinehart and Winston 1961, pp. 459-67. Rpt. of "Stranger in the Village."

"Sermons and Blues." New York Times Book Review (29 March 1959), p. 6.

"Sidney Poitier." Look, 23 July 1968, pp. 50-58.

"Smaller than Life." Nation, 165 (19 July 1947), 78-79.

"Stranger in the Village." Harper's, 207 (October 1953), 42-48. Rptd. in Notes.

"The Survival of Richard Wright." Reporter, 24 (16 March 1961), 52-55. Rptd. in Nobody Knows as "Eight Men."

"Sweet Lorraine." Esquire, 122 (November 1969), 139-40.

"A Talk to Harlem Teachers." In Harlem, U.S.A., rev. ed. Edited by John Henrik Clarke. New York: Collier Books, 1971, pp. 171-80.

"Talk to Teachers (The Negro Child--His Self Image)." Sat R, 46 (21 December 1963), 42-44.

"Theatre: The Negro In and Out." Negro Digest, 15 (October 1966), 37-44.

"There's a Bill Due That Has to Be Paid." Life, 24 May 1963, pp. 81-84.

"They Can't Turn Back." Mademoiselle, 51 (August 1960), 324-26, 351-58.

"They Will Wait No More." Negro Digest, 10 (July 1961), 77-82.

"To Whom It May Concern: Report from Occupied Territory." Nation, 203 (11 July 1966), 39-43.

"Too Late, Too Late." Commentary, 7 (January 1949), 96-99.

"Two Protests against Protest." Perspectives USA, 2 (Winter 1953), 89-100.

"Unnameable Objects, Unspeakable Crimes," in The White Problem in America. Edited by Ebony. Chicago: Johnson Publishing Company, 1966, pp. 173-81. Rpt. of "The White Man's Guilt."

"The Uses of the Blues." Playboy, 11 (January 1964), 131-32, 240-41.

Dialogues, Debates, Discussions

"The War Crimes Tribunal." Freedomways, 7 (Summer 1967), 242-44.

"We Can Change the Country." Liberation, 8 (October 1963), 7-8.

"What Kind of Men Cry?" (James Baldwin, Harry Belafonte, Sidney Poitier, et al.). Ebony, 20 (June 1965), 47.

"What Price Freedom?" Freedomways, 4 (Spring 1964), 191-95.

"When the War Hit Brownsville." New Leader, 30 (17 May 1947), 12.

"The White Man's Guilt." Ebony, 20 (August 1965), 47-48.

"White Racism or World Community?" Ecumenical Review, 20 (October 1968), 371-76.

"Without Grisly Gaiety." New Leader, 30 (20 September 1947), 12.

"Why a Stokely?" St. Petersburg Times (3 March 1968), p. 1D.

"A Word from Writer Directly to Reader." Fiction of the Fifties. Edited by Herbert Gold. New York: Doubleday, 1959, pp. 18-19.

Dialogues, Debates, Discussions

"The American Dream and the American Negro." With William F. Buckley, Jr., New York Times Magazine (7 March 1965), pp. 32-33, 87-89.

"Dialog in Black and White: James Baldwin and Budd Schulberg." Playboy, 13 (December 1966), 33-36, 282-87.

"The Image: Three Views, from Messrs. Shahn, Milhoud, Baldwin; Three Creative Artists Debate the Meaning of a Fashionable Term," Opera News, 27 (8 December 1962), 8-13.

"'Let me finish, let me finish . . .,' a Television Conversation." With Peregine Worsthorne and Bryan Magee. Encounter, 39 (September 1972), 27-33.

"Liberalism and the Negro: A Round-Table Discussion (James Baldwin, Nathan Glazer, Sidney Hook, and Gunnar Myrdal)." Commentary, 37 (March 1964), 25-42.

Nationalism, Colonialism and the United States, One Minute to Twelve: A Forum. New York: Liberation Committee for Africa on Its First Anniversary Celebration, June 2, 1961, pp. 23-27.

"The Negro in American Culture." Discussion by James Baldwin, Lorraine Hansberry, Langston Hughes, Alfred Kazin, and Emile Capouya; moderated by Nat Hentoff, on Pacifica Radio, WBAI-FM, New York, 1961. See also, Cross Currents, 11 (Summer 1961), 205-24; Negro Digest, 11 (March 1962), 80-98.

"Of Angela Davis and 'the Jewish Housewife Headed for Dachau': An Exchange--James Baldwin and Shloma Katz." Midstream, 17 (June/July 1971), 3-7.

Dialogues, Debates, Discussions

"Race, Hate, Sex and Colour: A Conversation." With James Mossman and Colin MacInnes. Encounter, 25 (July 1975), 55-60.

"A Rap on Race: Mead and Baldwin." McCall's, 98 (June 1971), 84-85, 142-54.

"What's the Reason Why: A Symposium by Best Selling Authors." New York Times Book Review (2 December 1962), p. 3.

Short Stories, Excerpts

"The Amen Corner." Zero, 2 (July 1954), 4-8, 11-13. Excerpt (Act I) from The Amen Corner.

"Any Day Now." PR, 27 (Spring 1960), 282-94. Excerpt from Another Country.

"Come Out the Wilderness." Mademoiselle, 46 (March 1958), 102. Rptd. in Going to Meet.

"The Death of the Prophet." Commentary, 9 (March 1950), 257-61.

"Easy Rider." The Dial: An Annual of Fiction. New York: Dial Press, 1962, pp. 3-26. Excerpt from Another Country.

"Elizabeth's Prayer." In Blackamerican Literature: 1760-Present. Edited by Ruth Miller. Beverly Hills, Calif.: Glencoe Press, 1971, pp. 511-44. Excerpt from Go Tell It.

"Exodus." American Mercury, 75 (August 1952), 97-103. Excerpt from Go Tell It.

"Gabriel's Prayer." In Black Insights: Significant Literature by Black Americans--1760 to the Present. Edited by Nick Aaron Ford. Waltham, Mass.: Ginn and Company, 1971, pp. 196-219. Excerpt from Go Tell It.

"Go Tell It on the Mountain; Excerpt." Wilson Library Bulletin, 42 (June 1968), 984-85.

"Going to Meet the Man." Status, 1 (October 1965), 47-49, 69-72. Rptd. from Going to Meet.

"The Man Child." Playboy, 13 (January 1966), 101-102, 211-14. Rptd. from Going to Meet.

"The Outing." New Story, no. 2 (April 1951), pp. 52-81. Rptd. in Going to Meet.

"Previous Condition." Commentary, 6 (October 1948), 334-42. Rptd. in Going to Meet.

"Roy's Wound." New World Writing, vol. 2. New York: New American Library, 1952, pp. 109-16. Excerpt from Go Tell It.

"Sonny's Blues." PR, 24 (Summer 1957), 327-58. Rptd. in Going to Meet.

"Tell Me How Long the Train's Been Gone." McCall's, 94 (February 1967), 118-19, 154, 156, 158-60, 162, 164, 166.

"This Morning, This Evening, So Soon." Atlantic Monthly, 206 (September 1960), 34-52. Rptd. in Going to Meet.

"The Threshing Floor." In Cavalcade: Negro American Writing from 1760 to the Present. Edited by Arthur P. Davis and Saunders Redding. Boston: Houghton Mifflin Company, 1971, pp. 572-83. Excerpt from Go Tell It.

Interviews

"Are We on the Edge of Civil War?" In The Americans. Interviews by David Frost. New York: Stein and Day Publishers, 1970, pp. 145-50.

"At a Crucial Time a Negro Talks Tough: 'There's a bill due that has to be paid.'" Life, 24 May 1963, pp. 81-86A.

"The Author Speaks." New York Herald Tribune Books (17 June 1962), p. 3.

"Black Man in America; an Interview by Studs Terkel." WFMT Perspectives, 10 (December 1961), 28-39.

"The Black Scholar Interviews: James Baldwin." Black Scholar, 5 (1973), 33-42.

"A Conversation with James Baldwin." Interview by Kenneth B. Clark. Freedomways, 3 (Summer 1963), 361-68.

"Disturber of the Peace: James Baldwin." Interview by Eve Auchincloss and Nancy Lynch, in The Black American Writer, Vol. I. Edited by C.W.E. Bigsby. Deland, Florida: Everett/Edwards, 1969, pp. 199-216.

"Exclusive Interview with James Baldwin." Interview by Joe Walker. Muhammad Speaks (8, 15, 22, 29 September 1972).

Gesprache mit James Baldwin, Carl J. Burckhardt, Mary McCarthy, et al. Interviews by François Bondy. Vienna, Munich, Zurich: Europaverlag, 1972.

"How Can We Get the Black People to Cool It? Interview." Esquire, 70 (July 1968), 49-53.

"Incontro con Baldwin." La Trappola e la Nudita. Milan: Rizzoli, 1974.

"Incontro con Baldwin a Napoli." Interview by Piero Mandrillo. Gazzettino della Jonio (18 December 1965).

"Incontro con James Baldwin." Interview by Marisa Bulgheroni. Il Nuovo Romanzo Americano, 1945-1959. Milan: Schwarz, 1960.

Interviews

"An Interview with a Negro Intellectual," in The Negro Protest: Talks with James Baldwin, Malcolm X, Martin Luther King. Edited by Kenneth B. Clark. Boston: Beacon Press, 1963, pp. 1-14, 49.

"It's Hard to Be James Baldwin." Black Times 2 (1972), 10.

"It's Hard to Be James Baldwin: An Interview." Interview by Herbert R. Lottman. Intellectual Digest, 2 (July 1972), 67-68.

"James Baldwin." Television interview with Dick Cavett. September 5, 1973.

"James Baldwin Breaks His Silence." Atlas, 13 (March 1967), 47-49.

"James Baldwin Comes Home." Interview by Jewell Hardy Gresham. Essence, 7 (June 1976), 54-55, 80, 82, 85.

"James Baldwin . . . in Conversation." Interview by Dan Georgakas, in Black Voices: An Anthology of Afro-American Literature. Edited by Abraham Chapman. New York: New American Library, 1968, pp. 660-668. Rptd. from Arts in Society (Summer, 1966).

"James Baldwin, the Renowned Black American Novelist, Talks to Godwin Matatu." Africa: International Business, Economic and Political Monthly, 37 (1974), 68-69.

"James Baldwin: Une Interview Exclusive." Interview by Nobile Fares. Jeune Afrique, 1 (September 1970), 20-24.

"James Baldwin: Une Interview par Guy Le Clec'h." Le Figaro Littéraire, 19 (23-30 September 1964), 4-5.

"New York and Negroes and Bobby--Both Shocked." Interview with Kenneth Clark and James Baldwin by Sue Solet. New York Herald Tribune (29 May 1963), pp. 1, 31.

"'The News from All the Northern Cities Is, to Understate It, Grim; the State of the Union is Catastrophic.'" The New York Times (5 April 1978), p. A29.

"Pour Libérer les Blancs . . ." Interview by François Bondy. Prévues, 152 (1963), 3-17.

"T.V. and Radio: An Interview with James Baldwin." Interview by Robert Lewis Shayon. Sat R, 45 (24 February 1962), 35.

"Una Conversazione di James Baldwin." Interview by Furio Colombo. Libreria Feltrinelli. Milan, 1963.

"Une Rencontre avec James Baldwin." L'Afrique Littéraire et Artistique, 38 (1975), 51-54.

"'We Are All the Viet Cong!': An Interview with James Baldwin." Interview by Karen Wald. Nickel Review, 4 (27 February 1970), 5.

"Why I left America. Conversation: Ida Lewis and James Baldwin." New Black Voices. Edited by Abraham Chapman. New York: New American Library, 1972, pp. 409-19. Rptd. from Essence (October 1970).

"Writer Foresees Collision Course." Interview by Nick Ludington, The Washington Post (14 December 1969), p. E8.

Recordings, Films

"Black Man in America; An Interview by Studs Terkel." Recorded at WFMT, Chicago's Fine Art Station for the program 'Almanac.' Chicago: Credo I, 1961. Phonodisc. Credo No. 8P-63-96-6367.

"James Baldwin Discusses Tell Me How Long the Train's Been Gone with Columnist Robert Cromie." Tuscon, Arizona: Motivational Program Corporation, c. 1969.

"James Baldwin Reading from Another Country." Boston: Caliope Records, 1963. 15 minutes. CAL. 18.

"James Baldwin Reading from Giovanni's Room." Boston: Calliope Records, 1963. CAL.11.

"James Baldwin Reading from Giovanni's Room and Another Country." CMS (517) Records, 1967.

"Malcolm X. Black Muslim Debates James Baldwin, C. Eve Lincoln, Eric Goldman." N. Hollywood, Calif.: The Center for Cassette Studies, c. 1971. 55 minutes.

"My Childhood." James Baldwin's Harlem, Part II. Benchmark Film, 1964.

Writings about James Baldwin
1946-1978

1946

1 ANON. "Three Writers Receive Eugene Saxton Fellowships."
   Publishers Weekly, 129 (19 January), 308-309.
      Announces Baldwin as one of three recipients of the sec-
   ond annual Saxton Memorial Trust Fellowships, "to enable
   new and unrecognized authors to complete books."

1953

1 ANON. "Go Tell It on the Mountain." Kirkus, 21 (1 April),
   231-32.
      Gives a very brief plot summary of Go Tell It, and as-
   serts that the novel is "a powerful instrumentation of passion and protest" and "a first novel of considerable distinction as well as feeling."

2 ANON. "Lord, Hold My Hand." Time, 18 May, pp. 126-27.
      Holds that Go Tell It is written with "the powerful rhy-
   thm of a storefront church meeting" and that God's presence
   sometimes seems to live on the page. While revealing the
   secret sufferings of a dozen characters, the book also
   evokes a sense of compassion toward the sufferings of a
   race.

3 ANON. "A Negro Family." Nation, 176 (6 June), 488.
      Briefly describes Go Tell It as a story of the tangled
   histories and "somewhat morbid relationships" of a Negro
   family cast down by sin but determined on salvation in a
   religious sect.

4 ANON. "Novels and Tales." United States Quarterly Book Review, 9 (September), 297.
      Presents Go Tell It as a "forceful poem in prose" stres-
   sing the realistic awakening of young John Grimes to a
   sense of sin, the contrast between worldly and otherworldly,
   and the difference between the Negro and the white. The

novel also creates the myth of the natural man in Gabriel
Grimes, who is driven equally by the flesh to lust and anger, and by religious outbursts of abasement and ecstasy
into a morality that is alternately violent and tender.

*5 ANON. "Review of Go Tell It on the Mountain." Springfield
   Republican (19 July), p. 70.
      Cited in Fischer, 1965.31.

6 ANON. "Reviews of Forthcoming Books." Booklist, 49 (15
   March), 229.
      Contends that Go Tell It, dealing with religious rival-
   ism among Harlem Negroes, compares to a spiritual in emotional intensity and to the King James Bible in its rhyth-
   mic language. The surface story of John Grimes has deeper
   meanings indicated by the biblical names of characters, the
   apocalyptic language, and the vision of the New Testament's
   Last Judgment. The simple dignity of the characters and
   the impassioned writing remind one of Paton's Cry the Beloved Country.

7 Barksdale, Richard K. "Temple of the Fire Baptised." Phylon,
   14 (Third Quarter), 326-27.
      Reviews Baldwin's first work as a religious novel con-
   cerned with ethical values and patterns of conduct rather
   than race relations or the sociology of the Negro. The
   stress is on character analysis and reaction--especially in
   the protagonist John Grimes. The "message to sophisticated,
   skeptical, utilitarian America is that such a religion is
   part of the American scene and that it merits quiet acceptance, not patronizing tolerance."

8 Barr, Donald. "Guilt Was Everywhere." New York Times Book
   Review (17 May), p. 5.
      Discusses Go Tell It as a "beautiful, furious first no-
   vel" about pietism that "makes its utterance by tension and
   friction." Guilt is a major motif of the novel, which has
   its setting in Harlem, "the metropolis of grief." Guilt
   can be removed only by conversion, "by being born again al-
   together, as in baptism, but with huge pangs and convul-
   sions"; thus John Grimes is saved, and the notion of sin,
   central and inclusive, all the way back to slave days, justifies the need for salvation.

9 Bingham, Robert K. "Two American Writers: I. Baldwin."
   Reporter, 8 (23 June), 38-39.
      Emphasizes the religious conversion of John Grimes in
   Go Tell It as an act in which the boy finds himself against

his will, "invaded, set in naught, possessed." The story
suggests that the past "must be accepted, and that in the
things which hurt can often be found the things which help."

10 Breit, Harvey. "Durability." New York Times Book Review
     (24 May), p. 8.
         Agrees with Baldwin's contention that the greatest re-
     sponsibility of the writer is "to last, as Hemingway says,
     and get my work done," and that the greatest theme for a
     novel to contain is "how a man lasts and how a man gets his
     work done. The modus vivendi and the modus operandi."

11 Brunn, Robert R. "About People Who Are Also Negroes." Chris-
     tian Science Monitor (28 May), p. 13.
         Describes Go Tell It as a novel without joy and with lit-
     tle hope of either progress or self-realization for the Har-
     lem Negroes who struggle with poverty, sensualism, each
     other, and whites, and how they turn to religion to "escape
     the cheerless world."

12 Byam, Milton S. "Fiction." LJ, 78 (15 May), 916.
         Maintains that Go Tell It presents alternately a photo-
     graphic and surrealistic picture of a Negro family in Har-
     lem and does not shirk truth for prettiness.

13 Cassidy, T.E. "The Long Struggle." Commonweal, 58 (22 May),
     186.
         Advocates that the outstanding dimension of Go Tell It
     is the presentation of "a sometimes majestic sense of the
     failings of men and their ability to work through their
     misery to some kind of peaceful salvation." The book does
     not embody the author's intention of wanting his "people to
     be people first, Negroes almost incidentally," because there
     is always present "the absolute feeling of injustice toward a
     people, not as people, but as a race of people."

14 E.B. "Go Tell It on the Mountain." San Francisco Chronicle:
     World (5 July), p. 18.
         Views Go Tell It as a perceptive, brutal, objective, and
     compassionate novel focusing on the members of a Harlem
     storefront church who face "constant discrimination" and on
     "the guilt and confusion felt by people in whom the old
     deep drives of Africa are overlaid with a stern Calvinism."

15 Hicks, Granville. "James Baldwin's Promising First Novel, Go
     Tell It on the Mountain." New Leader, 36 (1 June), 21-22.
         Asserts that Go Tell It is not a novel of protest, for
     "it neither expresses indignation nor seeks to arouse it."

1953

As in much of the world's greatest literature, the theme of
the book is "the strange fatal conflict between the ideal
and reality." The principal characters are sustained by
"their peculiarly dogmatic and violent interpretation of
Christianity." The book makes one clearly aware of the
meaning of religion and morality in their lives, with the
climax and ending centering on the conversion of John
Grimes; it is a novel of "phenomenal maturity."

16 Hobson, Susan, comp. "New Creative Writers: 42 Novelists
Whose First Work Appears This Season." LJ, 78 (15 February), 364-70.
     Presents Go Tell It as among the forty-two first novels
and gives a thumbnail biographical sketch of Baldwin.

17 Hughes, Riley. "Novels Reviewed." Cath W, 177 (August), 393.
     Argues that Go Tell It is a "portrayal, not protest" in
which the characters are "less conscious of race than of
God and of the daily problem of survival." The focus of
the story is the storefront church, "The Temple of the Fire
Baptised." The chief technical fault of the novel is "its
striving after 'poetic effect' when the language of revival-
ism is not everybody's language."

18 Hutchens, John K. "On an Author." New York Herald Tribune
Book Review, 29 (31 May), 3.
     Presents excerpts from letters from Baldwin to reveal in-
formation about, ideas of, and points of view of the author.
Three major influences on his writing are specified: the
King James Bible, the rhetoric of the storefront church,
Dickens' love for bravura. Baldwin states "that the truth
about white and black men in America is so terrible that it
cannot really be told," yet that truth about the past is
the only guide in the present; it includes both a "cause
for shame" and "equally, cause for pride."

19 Marcus, Steven. "The American Negro in Search of Identity."
Commentary, 16 (November), 456-63.
     Reviews three novels: Wright's The Outsider, Ellison's
Invisible Man, and Baldwin's Go Tell it. All three deal
primarily with "the city Negro in the North," employ similar
devices, and treat "their subject as a problem in personal
identity." Wright refused to consider "the fact of being a
Negro"; Ellison assumes it but does not consider it necessary to discuss; Baldwin tries "to define precisely what it
is like." Baldwin shows that religion is the main refuge
from "the outrageously narrow range" and "inflexibility" of
American Negro life. John Grimes, the fourteen-year-old

protagonist, chooses conversion not revolt, thereby avoid-
ing death and trying to escape the fate of the modern Negro:
"the endurance of calamity, the renunciation of earthly
pleasure, and the acceptance of no fulfillment." Baldwin's
novel captures "all the uniqueness, foreignness, and exoti-
cism of Negro life." Religion allows the Negro to have a
sense of coherence and allows him to live without destroying himself.

20 Monas, Disney. "Fiction Chronicle: 'No Mommy and No Daddy.'"
    Hud R, 6 (Autumn), 466-70.
        Reviews Go Tell It as one of five recently published
    books and "a first novel of unusual promise." Using bibli-
    cal phraseology, cliché, and parody, and with a keen sense
    of place and objects, the author recreates "a desperate re-
    ligious culture--a prism as well as a fortress." The only
    weakness is the incompletely drawn character, John Grimes,
    who barely begins "to realize the bitterness of his posi-
    tion in a crushing and hateful white world."

21 Ottley, Roi. "The Negro Seeks a Way Out." Chicago Sunday
    Tribune Magazine of Books (12 July), p. 7.
        Asserts that Go Tell It is primarily a religious novel
    but it also treats violence, lust, and compassion in real-
    istic and brutal details. Three generations of the Grimes
    family are seen in their emotional wandering and search
    for Jesus with the focus on the storefront church as a
    transmission between the rural life of their ancestral
    South and the alien tenements of the North.

22 Pickrel, Paul. "Outstanding Novels." YR, 42, no. 3 (March),
    x.
        Notes briefly that Go Tell It is a novel of "great force
    and vigor" using flashback techniques to study the primi-
    tive religious experiences of the Harlem storefront
    churches.

23 Prescott, Orville. "Books of the Times." The New York Times
    (19 May), p. 27.
        Treats Go Tell It as a novel about religion and sex
    whose "elaborate, cadenced prose reflects the biblical
    language that constantly runs through the minds of the
    saints in the Temple of the Fire Baptised." With vivid
    imgery, the book explores eloquently "the role of a primi-
    tive, naive and frequently hysterical variety of religion"
    in the lives of American blacks--both in "the nameless com-
    munity of their origin somewhere in the South" and in their
    current condition of ghetto life in the North.

1953

24 Raleigh, John Henry. "Messages and Sagas." New Republic, 128
    (22 June), 21.
         Views Go Tell It as impressive for its blending of psy-
    chology and saga, its construction--a skillful timeshift--
    and "a style rich in metaphor and sad eloquence." As a
    background for developing a consciousness of John Grimes,
    "the great grim saga, guilt ridden and blood stained,
    whose end is not yet written but whose horror, pathos and
    muffled triumphs" are elements of "the national conscious-
    ness," is presented: slavery days, postbellum South, clas-
    sic ghetto of the North, religion and sexuality in Harlem.

25 Redding, J. Saunders. "Sensitive Portrait of a Lonely Boy."
    New York Herald Tribune Book Review, 29 (17 May), 5.
         Suggests that Go Tell It shows the influence of Faulkner,
    Wright, and Dostoevski, and uses as its principal technique
    the familiar story within a story. The theme of the expo-
    sitory narratives within is frustration while the novel's
    theme is "the search for a father." John Grimes and the
    other characters seem to illustrate that "the human being's
    need for identification with others is one of the major
    drives in life."

26 Walters, Raymond. "The Critics Separate Wheat from Chaff."
    Sat R, 36 (20 June), 12-13, 38-40.
         Lists Go Tell It as one of the ten works most frequently
    recommended in a poll of twenty-seven literary editors who
    were asked to name ten books that they believed merited the
    attention of discriminating readers.

27 Webster, Harvey Curtis. "Community of Pride." Sat R, 36
    (16 May), 14.
         Contends that Go Tell It presents a protagonist, John
    Grimes, as "not just a victim of underprivilege, segrega-
    tion, and unreasoning violence" but a Negro enmeshed in the
    human dilemma. Baldwin's handling of the flashbacks, pene-
    tration of the protagonist's mind, and presentation of the
    past "makes plausibly sympathetic the Holy Roller religion"
    and reveals something about "the mystical basis for even
    sophisticated religion."

28 West, Anthony. "Books: Sorry Lives." New Yorker, 19 (20
    June), 93.
         Maintains that Go Tell It is "a first novel of quite ex-
    ceptional promise" that gives a vivid picture of the "in-
    tellectual seediness and poverty" of the religious behavior
    of a Harlem "Bible-thumping tabernacle" and the secular
    life that produces it. Compared to Ellison's Invisible Man

with its rich comic invention relative to religion, and to
Dostoevski's The Brothers Karamazov "with its broad farce
effects treating religious behavior," Baldwin's novel is
"humorless" and therefore less penetrating because it fails
"to give a rounded picture of the business of being a man."

29 Winslow, Henry F. "Church Sermon." The Crisis, 60 (December),
637-38.
   Suggests that Go Tell It is an "extended and polished
storefront church sermon." The novel endeavors "to invest
the religious experience of Negroes with a significance
which supposedly links them with a peculiar 'tradition' or
'past,'" viz., by tracing the origins of the "Harlem holy-
rollers" back to the South.

1955

1 ANON. "In the Castle of My Skin." Time, 5 December, 112,
114, 117.
   Interprets the purpose of the personal essays in Notes
as an effort to "retrieve the Negro from the abstractions
of the do-gooders and the no-goods." The essays, "written
with bitter clarity and uncommon grace," treat significant facets of being black: 1) the dilemma of Western nations with their legacy of white supremacy and democratic
ideal of equality and brotherhood; 2) the inherent failure
of the protest novel because it reinforces the white world's
stereotype of the black experience; 3) the contradictions
inherent to living as a black in Paris; 4) the author's insistence on the right to criticize America because of his
love for it.

2 ANON. "Notes of a Native Son." Kirkus, 23 (1 October), 777.
   Asserts that the collection of essays expresses many insights relative to the Negro search for identity both in
America and Europe: that black is "devil color"; that the
ghetto has both churches and hatred, especially of the Jewish face; that to be black and treated in a Swiss village
as a "living wonder" is unique, etc.

3 Brunn, Robert R. "In a Negro's Shoes." Christian Science
Monitor (16 December), p. 13.
   Affirms that Notes expresses precisely "the Negro problem" from the Negro side and "its emotional core" while representing a swing by Baldwin from "an early harshness and
uncompromising anger and frustration toward a willingness
to recognize that it is not the American character that

causes 'the Negro problem,' but human nature." The essay,
"Stranger in the Village," about living in a Swiss village
whose people had never seen a Negro, is the climax.

4 Byam, Milton S. "Too Late For Last Issue." <u>LJ</u>, 80 (15 November), 2602.
      Asserts that <u>Notes</u> shows vision, objectivity, and detachment that force the reader to look at "the mess that no
one really looks at"--black and white relations; praises
the essays as being written from a point of view neither of
attack nor defense.

<u>1956</u>

1 Algren, Nelson. "Lost Man." <u>Nation</u>, 183 (1 December), 484.
      Sees <u>Giovanni's Room</u> as more than just "another report
on homosexuality"; it is the story of David, an American of
thirty, who could not make up his mind, "who could not say
yes to life." Told with a driving intensity and a sustained
horror, "it is a glimpse into the special Hell of Genet."

2 ANON. "Briefly Noted." <u>New Yorker</u>, 32 (7 April), 162.
      Describes <u>Notes</u> as a short collection of essays treating
Carmen Jones, the protest novel, Harlem, life in a Paris
jail, and the author's own past in "a good jaunty, metaphorical prose" best seen in the autobiographical pieces.

3 ANON. "Classified Books." <u>Booklist</u>, 52 (1 January), 179.
      Treats <u>Notes</u> as a "clear-sighted view of an unhappy, complex situation"--the color problem in the U.S. Baldwin examines with honesty and fairness the painful emotions,
mixed feelings, and equivocal attitudes and actions of both
black and white Americans toward each other.

4 ANON. "Essays." <u>United States Quarterly Book Review</u>, 12 (March), 35-36.
      Posits that <u>Notes</u> is characterized "by a literary style
of complexity and power" in its analysis of "the Negro and
white mentalities in various contexts." Baldwin believes
that the problem of the American Negro is alienation both
from his African tradition and from the American white
world, and he compares the Negro's religious expression and
its fusion with the Old Testament position of the Jews.
Ultimately recognizing that hatred is self-destructive, he
stresses that human, not American, nature must be evaluated.

5 ANON. "Fiction." Booklist, 53 (1 December), 174.
    Describes Giovanni's Room as a "delicate handling of an
unconventional triangle," which involves the homosexual relationship between David and Giovanni.

6 ANON. "Two Arts Groups Make 24 Awards." The New York Times
    (24 May), p. 25.
    Records that Baldwin was among seven recipients of
$1,000 grants from the National Institute of Arts and Let-
ters at its fifteenth annual ceremony; others receiving
awards were: John Cheever, Josephine Miles, Frank Rooney,
Henry Russell Hitchcock, and Joseph Kerman.

7 Butcher, Margaret J. "The Negro in Modern American Fiction,"
    in her The Negro in American Culture. New York: Alfred A.
    Knopf, 180-81.
    Recalls that Go Tell It was acclaimed one of the finest
novels written by a Negro author. The work deals primarily
with aspects of Negro life in a moving and sensitive way.
It is noted that not all Negro writers are depending upon
"Negro themes"; today, the Negro author is moving more and
more toward the problems of individuals--their experiences,
their aspirations as well as conflicts and defeats--the universal concerns rather than the racially provincial ones.

8 D.B. "Giovanni's Room." San Francisco Chronicle: World
    (2 December), p. 24.
    Proclaims that Giovanni's Room has some of "the violent
excruciating beauty of a late Beethoven quartet." The
homosexual struggle has "dignity and compassion" that
raises it above just some sordid relationship.

9 Esty, William. "The Cities of the Plain." New Republic, 135
    (17 December), 26.
    Contends that Giovanni's Room is the best American novel
dealing with homosexuality that he has read, in spite of
its being "a painful novel" that does not deal "cheaply or
too simply" with its subject. The basic theme is "Europe-
versus-America" expressed in summations of individual and
national character, but "in the end neither Europe nor
America is 'right.'" The "void of mutual lovelessness" is
the central pain of the homosexual relation between David
and Giovanni; the problem of love is not resolved at the
end because they fail each other "as each seeks to become
strong through the imagined strength of the other."

1956

10 Fielder, Leslie A. "A Homosexual Dilemma." New Leader, 39
     (10 December), 16-17.
          Affirms that Giovanni's Room represents Baldwin's attempt
     to be more than just a Negro writer. The work does not fo-
     cus upon any Negro problems; in fact, there are no Negroes
     even present. The main character encounters no black faces
     as he moves through Paris and the south of France. Beneath
     the unfolding drama of homosexuality lies the tragic theme:
     "the loss of the last American innocence"--"Americans
     should never come to Europe . . . . It means they never
     can be happy again."

11 Fielder, Leslie A. "Some Footnotes on the Fiction of '56."
     Reporter, 15 (13 December), 46.
          Sees "the authority of terror" that distinguishes Bald-
     win from the "current run-of-the-mill novelists." Gio-
     vanni's Room is an "old fashioned moral story . . . told
     with a kind of painful honesty."

12 Flint, Robert W. "Not Ideas But Life: Review of Notes of a
     Native Son." Commentary, 21 (May), 494-95.
          Maintains that Notes is a collection of essays, "all
     bearing on the Negro question," which is an example "of
     honest, perceptive, dramatic reporting." Although the
     book's real quality is "essentially novelistic--dramatic,
     dense, bitter, swift, and self-absorbed," its chief fault
     is that the "political and social opinions, however just,
     are uniquely private and . . . frustratingly circular." In
     spite of this equivocation, however, Baldwin presents "not
     ideas but life, not opinion but art"; this is "autobiography
     that future readers of his novels return to with more than
     curiosity, and an important chapter in our cultural history."

13 Hicks, Granville. "Tormented Triangle." New York Times Book
     Review (14 October), p. 5.
          Views Giovanni's Room as dealing with "the rareness and
     difficulty of love" in words that have both "boldness and
     rightness." The author treats the involvement of David
     with a man and a woman with candor, dignity, and intensity
     but not sensationalism.

14 Hughes, Langston. "From Harlem to Paris." New York Times
     Book Review (26 February), p. 26.
          Views Notes as a survey in "pungent commentary" of cer-
     tain phases of contemporary America as related to its
     citizenry, especially Negroes: Harlem, the protest novel,
     the press, bigoted religion, Jews and Negroes, etc. As an
     essayist, Baldwin is "thought-provoking, tantalizing, irri-
     tating, abusing, and amusing."

22

15 Jackson, Blyden. "The Continuing Strain: Resumé of Negro
        Literature in 1955." Phylon, 17 (First Quarter), 35-40.
            Cites Baldwin as the "finest writer of the year." He
        has "applied his mind honestly to ideas and human exper-
        iences . . . and conveys his prose with suppleness of
        thought and . . . acuity of vision." His observations are
        based on literal facts but are presented in metaphorical
        truth where Negroes and whites have "bound themselves to
        each other in establishing their American heritage." Bald-
        win takes heart in America's future; his book "ends on the
        note of hope."

16 Jarrett, Thomas D. "Search for Identity." Phylon, 17 (First
        Quarter), 87-88.
            Reviews Go Tell It within the context of major works
        written on the "Negro in America and abroad." Notes is
        looked at within the framework of the Negro as writer and
        actor, race relations in America, and the Negro abroad.
        All emphasize "the Negro's search for identity." Most
        readers will find the essays "electrifying," and the volume
        is an example of "fine writing" with "penetrating realism."

17 Karp, David. "A Squalid World." Sat R, 39 (1 December), 34.
            Asserts that Giovanni's Room treats "the special, tor-
        tured world of the homosexual" with "great artistry and re-
        straint." The room is used as "a symbol of David's fear
        and distaste and fascination with homosexuality as a way of
        life." Baldwin's emphasis on the loss of "sexual authority"
        may refer to "the general erosion of personal identity
        which has been working on modern man since the emergence of
        the machine and the big State."

18 Rainer, Dachine. "Rage into Order." Commonweal, 63 (13
        January), 384-86.
            Argues that Notes proves Baldwin to be "the most elo-
        quent . . . the most perceptive Negro writing today."
        These essays "portray in lyrical, passionate, sometimes
        violent prose the complex, oblique, endless outrages by
        which a man, particularly a black man, can be made to feel
        outside the established social order"--the anti-Negro mani-
        festations of Hollywood, the opportunism of political
        groups, Negro anti-Semitism, isolation of the Negro
        intellectual.

19 Redding, J. Saunders. "James Baldwin Miscellany." New York
        Herald Tribune Book Review (26 February), p. 4.
            Proclaims that Notes is concerned with "the same ques-
        tion of identity that burdened" Go Tell It. Some of the
        essays included are irrelevant to the question, and others

argue in a nonsensical way that the Negro American is "by
the nature of his being and his experience disqualified to
find and even unlicensed to seek his identity in the very
environment which he helped to create." If Baldwin can set-
tle his own question of identity, he will become "either a
contributor to the magazines not intended for ladies from
Dubuque, or one of the best writers of his generation."

20 Rolo, Charles J. "Other Voices, Other Rooms." Atlantic
    Monthly, 198 (December), 98.
        Affirms that Giovanni's Room belongs in "the top rank of
    fiction concerned with homosexuality" and that Baldwin is
    endowed with "exceptional narrative skill, poetic intensity
    of feeling, and a sensitive command of language."

21 Spingarn, Arthur B. "Notes of a Native Son." Crisis, 63
    (February), 87.
        Summarizes briefly Go Tell It as a collection of ten
    autobiographical essays that are of "uneven merit but the
    best ones are outstanding."

22 Sullivan, John F. "Fatal Ambiguity." Commonweal, 65 (21 De-
    cember), 318.
        Sees Giovanni's Room as raising the "prudential problem
    of whether raw sincerity and seriousness of purpose can
    justify this explicit treatment of a homosexual tragedy."
    There is no doubt that this book has merit as a "work of
    art." It is constructed with economy and an inherently
    powerful technique. Yet, throughout the pages there is "a
    fatal ambiguity" about what sin has been committed and by
    whom. The ending is reminiscent of Graham Greene's novels
    in which the grace of God reconciles man.

23 West, Anthony. "Books: At Home and Abroad." New Yorker,
    32 (10 November), 220-22.
        Suggests that Giovanni's Room is less successful than
    Baldwin's earlier works because it describes a passage, a
    ripple on the surface of life "that completely lacks the
    validity of actual experience." Although the problem of
    the homosexual, caught in the conflict "between his instinc-
    tive desires and his moral sense, is a real one and legiti-
    mate subject for a psychological novel," Baldwin fails to
    create the frame of reference to give the conflict meaning.
    The dilemma that the book presents is really that of the
    expatriate writer inevitably cut off by a barrier of lang-
    uage and experience from the texture of life as it is being
    lived around him.

24 Winslow, Henry F. "They Speak of Brotherhood." Crisis, 63
    (June/July), 376.
        Sees Notes as one of the recent books dealing with
    "brotherhood." Yet, within this context and "for all the
    high sound," Baldwin gives only half-truths in his presen-
    tation about man's search for identity and his tortured
    self-alienation.

1957

1 Flint, Robert W. "The Undying Apocalypse." PR, 24 (Winter),
   139-45.
        Praises Giovanni's Room as "a compelling book, unmis-
   takably alive" in its details, bitterness, and perversion
   but "at cross purposes with itself" because of its willingness to throw the reader "the sop of a tepid heterosexual
   tragedy" in the thin character of Hella. What could have
   been a masterful novella of "the modern Parisian underworld"
   is nearly lost by the author's "special pleading of a psy-
   chiatric case history."

2 Ivy, James W. "The Fairie Queenes." Crisis, 64 (February),
   123.
        Views Giovanni's Room as treating "the scabrous subject
   of homosexual love" in a scene that resembles the "brutal
   world of Jean Genet." Though frustration, despair, and
   death are usually tragic, here they strike the reader as
   incongruous and therefore comic.

3 Lash, John. "A Long, Hard Look at the Ghetto: A Critical
   Summary of Literature by and about Negroes in 1956."
   Phylon, 18 (First Quarter), 7-24.
        Asserts that neither of the two novels that received
   widespread recognition in 1956 was distinguished for its
   craftsmanship or theme: Yerby's Captain Rebel and Baldwin's Giovanni's Room. The former consists of "slickly
   written phrases that skim the surface of the subject"--
   Southern history; the latter treats homosexuality as an increasingly common experience that is as yet "uncomprehended
   in sensitive, rather than sympathetic, reactions."

4 Nichols, Charles H. "The New Calvinism." Commentary, 23
   (January), 94-96.
        Summarizes the author's theology in Giovanni's Room as
   consisting of "a sense of human depravity, a deterministic
   view of the universe, a hopeless search for salvation, and

a conviction that unregenerate, alienated modern man is
doomed." The characters are pursued by loneliness, fear,
desperation, and a sense of sin, and exist on the peri-
phery of society. Though some phrases are close to sensa-
tionalism and melodrama, the work has an intense emotional
quality. Compared to Hawthorne's Calvinism, which was al-
leviated by a healthiness of mind and spirit, Baldwin's
view is permeated by doom, depravity, and damnation. Compared to Harriet Beecher Stowe, whose theology at least allowed a hope of redemption and a social gospel, Baldwin
"accepts a theology which denies him life"; furthermore,
his complicity in the racism that accepts the damnation of
the black man makes him a spiritual cousin of Stowe because
he believes the black can survive only by "the incessant
mortification of the flesh."

1958

1 MacDonald, Dwight. "The Bright Young Man in the Arts."
    Esquire, 50 (September), 38-40.
        Responds to the question "Who are the brightest young
    men of 1958, the potential leaders of tomorrow?" The selec-
    tions in prose are Baldwin and Mailer: the former because
    his essays and short stories combine intelligence and emo-
    tion, and his other fiction has subtly explored race and
    lucidly expressed passion.

1959

1 ANON. "Ford Fund Gives Writers $150,000." The New York Times
    (16 February), p. 31.
        Reports that eleven American novelists and poets (inclu-
    ding Baldwin, Bellow, Cummings, Malamud, O'Connor, Roethke)
    were selected from 220 nominations as the first recipients
    of Ford Foundation grants because "their talents give pro-
    mise of major contributions to their artistic development
    and to contemporary American art."

2 ANON. "James Baldwin." Current Biography Yearbook, 1959.
    Edited by Charles Moritz. New York: H. W. Wilson, pp.
    21-22.
        Gives a biographical account of Baldwin, citing his
    major works: Go Tell It, a "realistic, yet poetic story of
    religious experience in Harlem"; Notes, his "most widely
    acclaimed book," a collection of personal essays; Giovanni's
    Room, his second novel, about homosexuality.

1960

3 Mailer, Norman. <u>Advertisements for Myself</u>. New York: Putnam,
   pp. 471-72.
        Argues that <u>Notes</u> and <u>Giovanni's Room</u> exhibit Baldwin as
   having "a sense of moral nuance" and courage but they are
   unrealistically "sprayed with perfume"; by them he is
   "doomed to be minor."

4 Ulman, Ruth. "James Baldwin." <u>Wilson Library Bulletin</u>, 33
   (February), 392.
        Presents chiefly biographical data about "one of today's
   outstanding young writers" who compares his own vocation to
   that of his father: "I still try to write as he preached,
   that is, in the sight of God."

1960

1 Brooks, Hallie B. "Baldwin in Paperback." <u>Phylon</u>, 21 (Fall),
   296-97.
        Advertises <u>Notes</u> as appearing in a paperback edition.

2 Clark, Edward. "Images of the Negro in the American Novel."
   <u>Jahrbuch für Amerikastudien</u> (Heidelburg), 5: 175-84.
        Examines the Negro in major American novels including <u>Go
   Tell It</u> in which the hero is "fully alive" in his "arduous
   search for himself."

3 Curley, Thomas F. "The Quarrel with Time in American Fiction."
   <u>American Scholar</u>, 29 (Autumn), 558.
        Asserts that <u>Giovanni's Room</u> concerns David, a young
   American in Paris, on his way from "a precarious bisexuality
   to complete homosexuality"; that the main problem posed is
   not sexual ambivalence but "a crucial lack of sexual authority"; and that the events presented reveal David's servi-
   tude to sensation, to time itself."

4 Fiedler, Leslie A. "Development and Frustration," in his <u>Love
   and Death in the American Novel</u>. New York: Criterion
   Books, p. 470.
        Mentions <u>Go Tell It</u> as having the freshness and direct-
   ness but lacking the madness that gives <u>Invisible Man</u> "a
   special kind of conviction."

5 Isaacs, Harold R. "Five Writers and Their African Ancestors."
   <u>Phylon</u>, 21 (Fourth Quarter), 322-29.
        Poses a question to Baldwin: "If a man from Mars ap-
   peared suddenly before you and asked 'what are you?' what
   would you say?" Baldwin's response would probably be:

27

1960

"I'm a writer with a lot of work to do and wondering if I
can do it." Even while in exile in France, Baldwin realized
that the key to his identity had to be found in America, so
he returned to the American South to begin his "journey."
He sought a clearer view of American culture, and "a more
inclusive view of human culture and his place in it." He
came to see that his "sense of lostness" made him kin with
white Americans who were no different than he; they were
just as "lost and alienated as he was," and that "depthless
alienation from oneself and one's people is, in sum, the
American experience." Baldwin also resolved his sense of
"divorcement from the stream of culture. 'No matter where
our fathers had been born, or what they endured, the fact
of Europe had formed us both, was part of our identity,
part of our inheritance.'" Thus Baldwin has regained his
sense of American identity. Yet throughout Go Tell It,
Notes, and Giovanni's Room, there runs "a dark little African thread."

6 Redding, J. Saunders. "The Negro Writer and His Relationship
    to His Roots," in The American Negro Writer and His Roots.
    New York: American Society of African Culture, pp. 1-8.
        Argues that the themes of identity and community as a
    human being are inherent to Go Tell It and Notes.

                            1961

1 ANON. "Book of the Week: Nobody Knows My Name." Jet, 20
        (3 August), 26.
            Sees a "cult" of Baldwin "devotees" growing since the
        publication of Go Tell It. Nobody Knows is a "sort of se-
        quel" to Notes; although it lacks the same "freshness and
        intensity" of the latter, it is a "provocative outpouring
        of the thoughts and feelings of a restless and troubled
        American."

2 ANON. "Classified Book." Booklist, 57 (15 July), 687.
            States briefly that Nobody Knows is a compilation of
        "powerful first-person essays" that deal "astutely and can-
        didly" with the relationship between black and white, and
        between the writer and society.

3 ANON. "Intelligent Cat." Time, 30 June, p. 71.
            Contends that although Nobody Knows shares the obsession
        of most black authors--"the Negro's relationship to the
        white world"--Baldwin expresses it with passion, candor,
        and intelligence. He writes with a balanced and perceptive

grace and insight whether the subject be Faulkner's ambiguous stand on the Negro problem, an interview with film di-
rector Ingmar Bergman, reports on journeys to the South,
the relation with Mailer, or his unhappy friendship with
Richard Wright.

4   ANON. "Mboya Cautions Commonwealth." The New York Times
    (18 April), 6.
        Presents an interview with Tom Mboya, African national-
    ist leader of Kenya, concerning independence movements for
    several African nations and the racial policies of South
    Africa. Mboya had appeared at an African Freedom Day rally
    at Hunter College, sharing the platform with Kenneth Kaunda
    of Northern Rhodesia, Senator Hubert Humphrey, and James
    Baldwin.

5   Finn, James. "Critic's Choice for Christmas." Commonweal,
    65 (8 December), 288-90.
        Praises Nobody Knows as a prose collection written "with
    a combination of passions, insight and intelligence" and
    showing Baldwin as "an unproclaimed moralist whose argu-
    ments and insights rest on traditional, conventional
    values."

6   Fulford, Robert. "Facing Up to the Masses." Exchange, 1 (No-
    vember), 5-6, 67.
        Recognizes a difference in the American writers' pro-
    tests and criticisms of the present and those of the recent
    past as a direct result of the mass media and the condition-
    ing of mass culture. The postwar writers were the first to
    react and to "define themselves" in terms of it; sometimes
    in "weird celebration of the grotesque." Among these books
    presenting "personalities confronting America" is Baldwin's
    Nobody Knows, which is an indictment of mass society and
    mass media by their efforts to generalize, categorize, de-
    clare, and move on. Instead, Baldwin faithfully depicts
    and records specific aspects of Negro life in America,
    from Harlem housing projects to whites who favor integration
    always elsewhere, and exposes the unrealistic quasi-reli-
    gious beliefs of society and the media--especially the be-
    lief in progress, and the American fear of experience.

7   Gerard, Albert. "James Baldwin et la Religiosité Noire."
    Revue Nouvelle, 33 (February), 177-86.
        Points out that the Negro, according to Booker T. Wash-
    ington, "is the only immigrant who has to be invited to
    live in America." Black Americans are without a doubt de-
    prived of their human dignity. But the blacks have not

adopted a passive posture like the "catechism" (teachings) of Christianity, which is what many whites wish they would inculcate. This religious stance is often manifested in the literature written by blacks. One such writer is James Baldwin, whose novel, Go Tell It, has not received the attention it deserves. The subject of the novel is the religious crisis that confronts John Grimes on the day of his fourteenth birthday; he is faced with contradictory aspirations. The theme of Go Tell It centers on the choices that man must make when he accepts personal responsibility for his actions. The extraordinary intensity of emotions and convictions of Baldwin's characters are like those of Dostoevski. Although the emotional religious aspects of the work may seem "primitive," they are "essentially human," and the moral problems facing man are timeless. It is good that Baldwin enlightens himself and his readers about the nature of the problems confronting man today.

8 Gleason, Ralph J. "The Painful Voice of Desperate Sanity in a World Hiding." San Francisco Chronicle: This Week (2 July), p. 20.
    Describes Notes as an expression of the "real attitudes of Negroes toward whites in this country." In addition, Nobody Knows shows Baldwin to be more than a Negro writer, but to be the "most important American essayist--the man who is discussing with agonizing and terrible clarity the basic problem of American society for black and white alike." His use of "we" and "our country" in his essays is very significant because it reveals Baldwin to be as "American as any Texas GI." His role as a writer is "to describe things" that other Americans cannot.

9 Hassan, Ihab. Radical Innocence: Studies in the Contemporary American Novel. Princeton, N.J.: Princeton University Press, pp. 77, 81, 83.
    Calls Giovanni's Room a "tighter and more nervous novel." The true heroes are the "martyrs"; the "secret quest of the soul ends in quiet or blazing defeat." Notes centers upon the "necessity of the American white man to find a way of living with the Negro in order to be able to live with himself." Go Tell It focuses upon a "world swollen with the power of God, howling with sin, in which good and evil clash with apocalyptic fury."

10 Hicks, Granville. "Commitment without Compromise." Sat R, 44 (1 July), 9.
    Describes the essays of Nobody Knows as sometimes pedestrian and sometimes exciting but never lacking in

conviction, determination, and boldness. Two main subjects
are stressed: the situation of the Negro, primarily in
America; and artistic matters, conjoining Baldwin's views
of other writers with statements about "the functions and
problems of the man of letters in contemporary society."
The major premise posited is the fact that "Negroes want to
be treated like men" and must be.

11 Howe, Irving. "A Protest of His Own." New York Times Book
    Review (2 July), p. 4.
        Argues that the personal essay form of Nobody Knows
    combines "vivid reporting, personal recollection and specu-
    lative thought" to present the author's own protest--"non-
    political in character, spoken more in the voice of anguish
    than revolt, and concerned less with the melodrama of dis-
    crimination than the moral consequences of living under an
    irremovable stigma," viz., skin color. Baldwin's honesty
    is stressed, showing his doubts and aggressions and his re-
    cording of the "tortuous efforts" to establish peace be-
    tween the sense of being both a lonely writer and a suffer-
    ing Negro.

12 Hyman, Stanley Edgar. "Blacks, Whites, and Grays." New Leader
    (31 July/7 August), pp. 21-22.
        Describes the jacket design of the Dial edition of No-
    body Knows, which reveals Baldwin through a broken window
    with a look of "infinite sadness." This cover strikes "the
    perfect note for this collection" of essays, which are di-
    vided into two groups: those dealing with the Negro ques-
    tion; and those largely literary. Throughout the book,
    Baldwin projects himself onto the scene, but usually it
    comes through as the "artificial persona or mask" found in
    the blues. He seems less frank here than in Notes. Nobody
    Knows's racial message is "ultimately simple"--white Ameri-
    ca, stop making him a "mammy or a eunuch and recognize him
    as a man." The literary message is more complicated, for
    it involves his "coming to terms with Richard Wright."

13 Ivy, James W. "Book Reviews--Nobody Knows My Name." Crisis,
    68 (October), 522.
        Calls Nobody Knows a "grave commentary on men and af-
    fairs, on life and literature" that is vibrant with the
    author's personality and written in a beautiful and poetic
    prose. The work reveals that Baldwin has learned to accept
    his origins--Negro and American--and to evaluate men--Mai-
    ler, Gide, etc.; the best piece, however, is "The Discovery
    of What It Means to Be an American."

1961

14 Jacobson, Daniel. "James Baldwin as Spokesman." Commentary,
    32 (December), 497-502.
        Depicts Notes as Baldwin's attempt to "fix within him-
    self an area of experience which he could feel was truly
    his own." He has "hacked away desperately at every possible
    demand or insistence which might be made upon him by his
    public." Notes remains his "best book"; it is more force-
    ful than any of his other works. Nobody Knows, subtitled
    More Notes of a Native Son, is directed intimately to his
    fellow Americans. He writes about both white and black
    Americans, yet his summing up is: "Negroes are . . . ig-
    nored in the North and are under surveillance in the South
    and suffer hideously in both places." He profoundly hopes
    that the American Negro will be able to win for himself a
    place other than the one he now occupies.

15 Kazin, Alfred. "Close to Us." Reporter, 25 (17 August),
    58-60.
        Contends that Baldwin is a "good novelist and is likely
    to become an even better one," but he strains "pretty hard"
    in Giovanni's Room. Notes reveals a "first class essayist,
    reporter, and social critic," and the work is "one of the
    two or three best books ever written about the Negro in
    America."

16 McDonnell, Thomas. "The Emergence of the Negro in Literature."
    Critic, 20 (December 1961/January 1962), 31-34.
        Sees the Negro writer as "adding a unique dimension to
    the national experience," especially the "continual search
    for an identity which is continually denied." The voice of
    Baldwin "is one of the authentic voices" of the times. No-
    body Knows has brought the emergence of Negro American
    literature to "its fullest possibility at this state of our
    cultural relationship." There is the "ultimate reconcilia-
    tion" not of opposites, but of "mutual worth and awareness"
    --in Europe, in Africa, in America--"in the abolition of
    the 'no-man's land between the black world and the white.'"

17 Malcolm, Donald. "Books: The Author in Search of Himself."
    New Yorker, 37 (25 November), 233-38.
        Cites the "problem of identity" as a "solemn preoccupa-
    tion of contemporary literature." The essays of Nobody
    Knows can be divided into two groups: observations on a
    series of events sometimes not intimately connected with
    Baldwin's search for his own identity; and "direct as-
    saults on the problem of identity." The latter reflects a
    strong personal tone but contains "paragraphs of harmless
    tosh" and "unilluminating details." His true character

appears more distinctly when he "stops pecking around for
it and turns to other things." Also, his "pungent good
sense of his social criticism is not easily matched," especially when he deals with the "two most powerful movements among Negroes in this country today:" the Negro
student movement and the Black Muslim movement. When Baldwin writes in this vein, "he finds access to as much solid
character as any man can reasonably require."

18 Mayfield, Julian. "A Love Affair with the United States."
    New Republic, 145 (7 August), 25.
         Suggests that Nobody Knows exemplifies a wide range of
    interests and an intensely personal view "from a native
    artist seriously concerned with the fate of the country to
    which he has finally returned after a long and anguished
    exile." Some of the essays are uneven and even pedestrian;
    nevertheless, they grapple with the problems of race rela-
    tions with an honesty and irreverence that "are his [Bald-
    win's] most maddening qualities as a writer and a human
    being." "East River Downtown" is especially significant,
    for it explodes the idea that Communists inspired the Negro
    demonstration after the death of Patrice Lumumba and re-
    veals that the riot clearly suggests that something is
    wrong in the Negro community.

*19 Miller, Albert H. [Review of Nobody Knows My Name]. Perspec-
     tives, 6 (September/October), 25-27.
          Cited in Fischer, 1965.31.

20 Moon, Eric. "Biography--Personal Narrative." LJ, 86 (Septem-
    ber), 2792.
         Contends that Nobody Knows fuses intellect and feeling
    in exploring the same theme as Ellison's Invisible Man,
    viz., the search for identity as a man; and that the essays
    are an account of the impact of places--Europe, the South,
    Harlem--and of people--Faulkner, Gide, Wright, Bergman,
    Mailer--upon the author.

21 Morrison, Allan. "The Angriest Young Man." Ebony, 16 (Octo-
    ber), 23-30.
         Sees Baldwin as a "spokesman of his generation." In
    both Go Tell It and Notes, he speaks with a "controlled
    anger modulating from a restrained dissent to a reverbera-
    ting roar." The "chief incendiary" behind his rage is
    "America's historical conspiracy" to deprive Negroes of
    real humanity. The rise of Africa and black consciousness
    means an end to Negro subservience; the American Negro "can
    no longer, nor will he ever again be controlled by white
    America's image of him."

1961

22 Nichols, Charles H. "Color, Conscience and Crucifixion: A
    Study of Racial Attitudes in American Literature and Criti-
    cism." Jahrbuch für Amerikanstudien (Heidelburg), 6: 73-77.
        Explores the contributions of various authors to the un-
    derstanding of the "Negro character." Go Tell It, Invisible
    Man, and Black Boy present the "great human possibilities
    of character" as seen from the Negro's perspective, yet
    there is much that is "universal" in these works. There
    are distinctive aspects of experience and outlook in the
    Negro characters, and the old image of the Negro is being
    "replaced by a consciousness of the variety and subtlety
    of every human group." The novel's function is to "inte-
    grate us all into the realities of our time and place" and
    to unite individuals by a "sense of our common humanity."

23 Nyren, Dorothy, ed. "James Baldwin," in A Library of Literary
    Criticism. New York: Frederick Ungar Publishing Company,
    32-33, 555-56.
        Quotes from selected excerpts of reviews of works by
    Baldwin.

24 Poore, Charles. "Books of the Times." The New York Times
    (15 July), p. 17.
        Maintains that Nobody Knows is a collection of essays
    1) showing the "crucial points of stress and turbulence"
    in being "a writer, an American, a Negro in this century";
    2) dissecting the strengths and limitations of other wri-
    ters--Gide, Wright, Mailer; and 3) analyzing bigotry and
    "the varieties of fear--born inhumanity."

25 Redding, J. Saunders. "In His Native Land." New York Herald
    Tribune Books (25 June), p. 36.
        Advocates that the essays in Nobody Knows mix personal
    honesty, intellectual integrity, and extravagant opinions;
    and that the emotional quality of the author as man is im-
    portant, especially "his carefully controlled excitement of
    ideas, and a quivering responsiveness to the experiences
    that make being Negro in America so strange and incredible
    to non-Negroes everywhere."

26 Rolo, Charles. "Questions of Color." Atlantic Monthly, 208
    (July), 126-28.
        Describes Nobody Knows as a "passionate, probing, con-
    troversial book which is outstandingly well written." One
    can hear in its pages the "voice of a new generation of
    Negroes, fortified by the conviction that the white man's
    power to mold their identity and control their fate is
    rapidly crumbling." The work is informed by "deep serious-
    ness" and a "major literary talent." He acts as a "witness"

who seeks to "convey in human terms the truth," as he sees
it, about "a terrible injustice."

27 R.W. "Nobody Knows My Name." Tamarack Review, 21 (Autumn),
     86.
          Asserts that Go Tell It has established Baldwin "as one
     of the most talented of the postwar writers in America."
     Notes reveals his own feelings and his own history, and No-
     body Knows is a "book of essays that no other writer in
     America is likely to outpace this year."

28 Sullivan, Richard. "A Negro Examines His Native Land in Love
     and Anger." Chicago Sunday Tribune Magazine of Books
     (25 June), p. 4.
          Presents briefly Nobody Knows as an analysis of the
     Negro's position in American society: his grief, love,
     anger.

                              1962

1 Abels, Cyrilly. "To the Editor." New York Times Book Review
     (5 August), p. 24.
          Argues that Paul Goodman's review of Another Country on
     June 24 misses the poetic beauty and power and the acute
     insights of the novel.

2 Adams, Donald J. "Speaking of Books." New York Times Book
     Review (28 January), p. 2.
          Contends that Baldwin's statements in Book Review (14
     January) are the most challenging expressed by a young wri-
     ter. He has "set the course of American literature during
     the remainder of this century" by challenging Americans to
     see themselves as they are and by reminding writers that it
     is important to "reveal a people to itself," i.e., to take
     a "sufficiently hard look" at private selves and to ask a
     host of questions. Baldwin seeks answers to these
     questions.

3 ANON. "Another Country." Kirkus, 30 (1 June), 478.
          Describes the novel as a "curiously juvenile book" that
     nevertheless has "emotional power" in its treatment of "tor-
     mented love" among men and women in various relationships.
     The ending is "a tragic and inconclusive general dissolu-
     tion in which truth destroys love" though it does express
     an honest and "despairing conviction of reality."

4 ANON. "Another Country." Negro Digest, 11 (August), 51-52.
          Recognizes Baldwin as the "most gifted of all Negro

1962

writers," and "one of the finest writers of this generation." Previous works all attest to the talent of this
young man with "audacious, probing, lilting prose," with
"needle sharp intelligence" and "savage groping beyond
images." Another Country is a novel "about the many faces
of love." All of the characters are joined in "subtle and
painful ways," but it is with the two Negro characters,
Rufus and Ida, that Baldwin "flirts with failure." They
are the least sympathetic, the least developed. This may
have been intentional--deliberate thwarting of their development, the incomplete "fruits of denial."

5 ANON. "Baldwin." PMLA, 77 (May), 231.
   Presents annual secondary bibliography for 1961.

6 ANON. "New York Cacophony." Time, 29 June, p. 76.
   Characterizes Baldwin as "one of the brashest, brightest,
   most promising young writers in America." He has proved
   himself willing to step on anyone's toes--black or white--
   to say what he feels. Yet, his new novel, Another Country,
   proves a failure because he has tried to "unburden" himself of all his feelings about racism and homosexuality,
   about the "cacophony of despair and misunderstanding that
   he believes America to be." The inadequate fictional frame
   is incapable of maneuvering the complex array of characters.
   The dialogue is sometimes wooden and comic, the action
   drags, the characters' inner soul searchings lapse into interior recollections carried on not by individuals, but by
   the author. In an earlier essay, "Everybody's Protest
   Novel," he insisted that the novelist had no excuse for bad
   writing or the "use of sociological stick figures," but he
   falls into the very errors he deplores.

7 ANON. "On the Scene." Playboy, 9 (December), 126.
   Blends some biographical facts and quotations in a brief
   overview of Baldwin as writer and as campaigner for civil
   rights with a concern for both moral and aesthetic reforms.

8 ANON. "Ralph Ellison Talks about James Baldwin." Negro
   Digest, 11 (September), 61.
   Cites quotations from 1962 that refer to Baldwin.

9 ANON. "Saul Bellow and Ralph Ellison: Two Authors in Search
   of a Chance to Write a Novel." University of Chicago Magazine, 53/54 (April), 6-8.
   Quotes Ellison that "writing is a discipline which involves the deepest levels of the psyche" and that "the process
   of learning to write is a process of discovery of oneself and

one's values." Ellison defends Baldwin's concern with the
Negro experience as "one of the major facts of our time,"
especially his focus on "the impact of race upon personality," which is rendered artistically with skill and passion.

10 ANON. "Tragedy in the Village." Newsweek, 25 June, p. 91.
    Asserts that Baldwin "writes with a plain, sturdy narra-
tive force" reminiscent of Dreiser and Farrell. Another
Country portrays people living in and around Greenwich Village. The characters are not "beatniks," rather they are
individuals immersed in "desperate emotions and dilemmas."
Baldwin treats explicitly many passions and situations previously seen as taboo in fiction--miscegenation, homosexuality, bisexuality. His power as a writer moves the characters not through a "maze of immorality" but a labyrinth
of "tragic anguish." His characters are "crying for a
sense of human significance." This novel is "harsh and
painful," but its people are seen with an "ardent imagination" that deems their perversities "ordeals of the spirit."

11 Balliett, Whitney. "Wrong Pulpit." New Yorker, 38 (4 August),
    69-71.
    Describes Another Country in Baldwin's own dialogue when
Vivaldo talks of his own novel: "He did not seem to know
enough about the people in his novel." The novel is primarily a "turbid melodrama," continually "checked by novel-
istic fatigue." One has the feeling of reading at the book,
rather than in it. Occasionally, Baldwin the polemicist-
moralist-essayist comes through, revealing the gifted quality for which he has become celebrated.

12 Bardeen, Constance L. "Love and Hate." Crisis, 69 (November),
    567-68.
    Attests that Another Country has elicited strong reac-
tions and a storm of controversy. More than a novel about
love, hate, and sexual aberrations, it graphically treats
the lack of communication among Negroes and whites, both
within and between the races as well as sexes. The suicide
of Rufus permeates the novel, exhibiting the price exacted
by the white world's doctrine of superiority as well as exposing the debilitating effect of racism on the development
and structure of personality.

13 Barrett, William. "Weight of the City." Atlantic Monthly,
    210 (July), 110-11.
    Sees Another Country as a "powerful and disturbing novel
by one of the most talented of our young writers." The
book is "stark, relentless, unpleasant," but has at times a

1962

"faulknerian surge of power and violence." Nevertheless,
the white characters are blank and boring. Baldwin himself
seems bored by them and "uses them only as fillers." It is
the enormous and heavy presence of the city that is, indeed,
the impressive character of the book.

14 Beck, Warren. "Irony and Compassion for Atypical Americans Be-
    set by Self and Society." Chicago Sunday Tribune Magazine
    of Books (24 June), p. 3.
        Views Another Country as a novel of irony and compassion
    in which paradox abounds for the group of atypical American
    characters struggling to avoid "an aimless, defeated and de-
    fensive bohemia." Sharing uncertainty, instability, and
    loneliness, the characters are tortured by self-generated
    conflicts and the ills of society while becoming increas-
    ingly conscious of color in their quest for reality both in
    sexual and racial relations.

15 Bloomfield, Caroline. "Religion and Alienation in James Bald-
    win, Bernard Malamud, and James F. Powers." Religious Edu-
    cation, 57 (March/April), 97-102, 158.
        Discusses Baldwin, Malamud, and Powers in terms of a re-
    ligious attitude regarding man's alienation. The three
    are "second-layer" Americans, which is to say they are de-
    scendants of post-Civil War immigrants and freed slaves;
    their writings reflect the impact of a minority group. The
    problem of Negro alienation is terribly complicated with a
    multitude of causes, including irrational behaviors stem-
    ming from fear and hatred of the white oppressor as well as
    the Negro himself. Notes and Go Tell It are two works that
    prescribe for the "alleviation of the pain" of the hero's
    alienation, the "opiate" of the people. The hero in Bald-
    win's novel as well as that of Malamud's The Assistant re-
    sist and suffer reversals, and accept their own limitations;
    both embrace the difficulties of life with joy and exalta-
    tion, "which the power of their religious inspiration" has
    created. Both Malamud's and Baldwin's characters are the
    renegades of society "seeking themselves" and some structure
    for their lives. Powers' characters are structured; they
    are curates, pastors, and parishioners who have embraced
    the church, but still face the problem of alienation. Thus,
    the three writers are joined together, for they see that
    the problem of finding values and a structured existence
    can only be dealt with by a religious commitment. Their
    characters are not just priests or Jews or Negroes--they
    are "Americans in search of self, pursuing purpose, in
    need of faith."

16   Bonosky, Phillip. "The Negro Writer and Commitment." <u>Main-</u>
       <u>stream</u>, 15 (February), 16-22.
            Criticizes <u>Nobody Knows</u> as being "abruptly banal"--con-
       cerned more with the melodrama of discrimination than with
       the moral consequences of it. Baldwin is accused of empty-
       ing all history out of the Negro question and substituting
       a doctrine that places the Negro problem on a plane of uni-
       versal evil--man's loss of vision and descent to doom.
       Baldwin is a Negro whose theories about art cannot change
       the color of his skin; he is himself a target of discrimi-
       nation. Yet, in his belief that all writers must first of
       all accept the reality of this universal evil, he offers
       only pessimism to the "American Eden."

17   Brooks, A. Russell. "The Comic Spirit and the Negro's New
       Look." <u>CLAJ</u>, 6 (September), 35-43.
            Implies that the "comic spirit is alive among Negroes in
       America," and that it is presenting itself to the world.
       This humor can be found in abundance in "folk expressions"
       and even in "certain spirituals"--a buoyancy and "charming
       good nature" have been found in Negro expressions in all
       generations. Yet, the "bulk of Negro writing . . . has
       been in the area of protest against discrimination and
       other forms of injustice"; therefore, much of the comic
       is coupled with the tragic. Works by William Demby, Wright,
       Ellison, Baldwin, etc., reveal the "lurking tragedy beneath
       the laughing surface," with an image of "confusion, inse-
       curity and tentative existence." To Baldwin, the Negro is
       a "series of shadows, self-created, intertwining, which
       other Americans are helplessly battling." Negro humor,
       seen in relation to the Negro's condition is "authentic"
       and can be classified under three principal headings: 1) ob-
       jective, involving the faithful representation of situations
       as they occur in real life; 2) interpretation, seeking de-
       liberately to suggest unapparent meaning; and 3) evaluation,
       encompassing favorable or sometimes unfavorable judgments.

18   Campbell, Finley. "More Notes of a Native Son." <u>Phylon</u>, 23
       (Spring), 96-97.
            Sees the rise of "Negro Militancy" as "shaking America
       with her first social revolution since the industrial wars
       of the thirties." The essays in <u>Nobody Knows</u> portray a
       "Negro's humanism," the awareness of man's quest to be a
       man. The sensitive and intelligent expressions of the "ar-
       tist-as-humanist" are lucid, imaginative, and kaleidoscopic.

*19 Cook, Bruce A. [Review of <u>Another Country</u>]. <u>Perspectives</u>, 7
       (September/October), 154-55.
            Cited in Fischer, 1965.31.

1962

20 Cruttwell, Patrick. "Fiction Chronicle." Hud R, 15 (Winter),
    593-98.
        Examines Another Country from the main theme: "racial-
    ism, black against white." Also, the sexual obsession in
    the book has the "effect of a disastrous narrowing of in-
    terest." People are reduced to nothing more than some par-
    ticular aspects of their sexual behavior. A subtheme is
    "anti-success"--the man who is about to become a success--
    a protest against the whole scale of values of Western
    success.

21 Curley, Thomas F. "Critic's Choice for Christmas." Common-
    weal, 77 (7 December), 286.
        Asserts briefly that anyone who wants to understand pre-
    sent day America must read Another Country.

22 Davenport, Guy. "Magic Realism in Prose." National Review,
    13 (28 August), 153-54.
        Discusses a new realism in the art of the novel "so in-
    timate of detail and so pathetic of impact that the critic
    feels like a trespasser saying anything at all." This new
    "Magic Realism" demands total illusion and exploits visual
    and verbal diction. Like Dickens, Baldwin demonstrates a
    capacity for understanding divergent types of people. Ano-
    ther Country stages it scenes with the "hard focus of a
    newsreel camera," showing the interrelated problems of his
    characters. He does not act as analyst so much as "accu-
    rate observer" of "domestic life in the Cold War."

23 Dobbs, Kildare. "Lighten Our Darkness." Saturday Night, 77
    (7 July), 27-28.
        Insists that "whatever is unspeakable" is "what the
    novelist who aspires to greatness must find courage to
    say." It is this "bringing up" of the unspeakable into
    consciousness and art form that is the very essence of fic-
    tion--"it is a heroic task." Such a view is inherent in
    Another Country. The work may shock, hurt, and "ravage"
    many readers; it may be misunderstood, hated, and the tar-
    get of censors, yet it presents Baldwin's "apocalyptic
    vision of America": "Terrible and beautiful in black elo-
    quence." It is because he has found the courage to tell so
    much that "Another Country may be a great novel." The uni-
    versal theme of isolation and loneliness of modern man per-
    meates the work, and, like Dante's Divine Comedy, concludes
    on a note of irony.

24 Ellsworth, Roy. "To the Editor." New York Times Book Review
    (5 August), p. 24.

Argues that Paul Goodman's review on June 24 of <u>Another Country</u> as "mediocre" shows the lack of talent in the post-war group of American novelists.

25 Evanier, David. "The Identity of James Baldwin." <u>Commonweal</u>, 77 (28 December), 365.
    Begins with a quote from Baldwin regarding the depiction of human beings: "In overlooking, denying, evading his complexity . . . we are diminished and we perish . . .; only within this web of ambiguity, paradox, . . . danger, darkness, can we find at once ourselves and the power that will free us from ourselves." Unfortunately, this is what Baldwin has not done in <u>Another Country</u>. He is too emotionally involved with his characters, and he imposes his own needs in place of his art. It seems as if he has "not yet come to grips with the materials in novel form" that he treats with "such eloquence in the essay and short story."

26 Fear, Leonard. "Another Country." <u>Downbeat</u>, 29 (25 October), 46.
    Cites two previous works as being "explosively eloquent" and praises <u>Another Country</u> as a "documentary of this century" even with a few minor deficiencies.

27 Finn, James. "The Author Replies." <u>Commonweal</u>, 77 (28 December), 365-66.
    Agrees that <u>Another Country</u> is not "wholly successful"; there is too much treatment of Baldwin's feelings about the characters rather than the characters themselves. He is too emotionally involved with them; only Rufus is a "real, moving, breathing person."

28 Finn, James. "The Identity of James Baldwin." <u>Commonweal</u>, 77 (26 October), 113-16.
    Considers <u>Another Country</u> within the context of Baldwin's accomplishments to date. He is a "fine and imaginative writer," but the real question yet to be answered is whether he belongs to that small group of writers "who affect . . . the life of our Country." Baldwin has a "rare combination of intelligence, passion, and talent," and he has the ability to focus them on significant aspects of contemporary life. <u>Go Tell It</u> gives a sharp, clear impression of life, not a cry of protest. <u>Notes</u> confirms the brilliance of Baldwin's "poise, determination, and incisive intelligence." <u>Giovanni's Room</u> takes the "battered theme" of homosexuality and explores what it means to be an American man. <u>Nobody Knows</u> explores the various aspects of Negro life in Western society with Baldwin relying on his search

1962

for identity. The most recent work, <u>Another Country</u>, seems
to be incomplete; it fails to "press the right nerve." He
contrives passages so that large portions have escaped his
"imaginative control." The characters sometimes seem dead,
unreal, unbelievable, and even wooden. Despite these
shortcomings, there are parts of "such a high order . . .
that we will not find their counterpart in American writing." The great reason to trust in the future of Baldwin
is "that in addition to his evident talent, he has immense
moral energy." He is concerned with the ethical spirit
that undergirds all actions and "wells up to reveal . . .
the unpredictable, irreducible creatures of freedom" that
humans are.

29 Fontinell, Eugene. "The Identity of James Baldwin." <u>Inter-
racial Review</u>, 35 (September), 194-99.
    Begins by asking the question, "Who am I?" It is under-
standable that this "big question" has left its distinctive
mark on present day man. Baldwin has been labeled a Negro
writer who specializes in questions concerning race. This
is true, but it is also true that he is "the most promising
young writer, Negro or otherwise, who specializes in questions concerning man." <u>Nobody Knows</u> not only supplies information, but it gives "new and deeper insight" into human
understanding. He "makes us weep a little and thrill a
little at this reality called man"; he explores his quest
for identity as a Negro, an American, and a man. Baldwin
has struggled with his personal acceptance and has realized
a degree of his humanity; he cannot be dismissed as an extremist or a disgruntled Negro. "His writings . . . establish him as a man of depth, sensibility, and insight."

30 Ford, Nick Aaron. "Search for Identity: A Critical Survey of
Significant <u>Belles-Lettres</u> by and about Negroes Published
in 1961." <u>Phylon</u>, 23 (Summer), 128-38.
    Proclaims <u>Nobody Knows</u> as the "most significant literary
work by or about Negroes published in 1961," and Baldwin as
the "most distinguished contemporary Negro writer." The
thirteen essays are bound together by the theme of man's
search for identity. Although there are some minor weak-
nesses--gullibility, faulty logic--"Americans everywhere
and of all shades of color and creed should be proud that
James Baldwin is one of them."

31 Friedenberg, Edgar Z. "Another Country for an Arkansas Trave-
ler." <u>New Republic</u>, 147 (27 August), 23-26.
    Sees <u>Another Country</u> as an extension of reality that
makes the work a "moral problem for a Southern reader."

Segregation and racial oppression are not the crux of the
moral problem, rather the emphasis is upon the need for
"roots." There is the constant assertion that continuity
is basic in human relations. Another Country is about a
"peer group," all of whose members are "trying to make it."
Yet, "making it" is never just status-seeking; it is an
effort "to confront and dominate the crushing reality of
poverty and anonymity." One of Baldwin's great strengths is
that he does not "disparage" the material consequences of
success. He raises a crucial issue: "just how high do
justice and equality rank among the social virtues when a
choice among virtues must be made?" All persons have the
right of claiming their heritage, if and wherever it can be
found.

32 Gerard, Albert. "Humanism and Negritude: Notes on the Con-
    temporary Afro-American Novel." Trans. S. Alexander.
    Diogenes, 37 (Spring), 115-33.
        Explores the positive contributions that black people,
    isolated until now from the main current of history, might
    furnish "toward future humanist orientations." Here is
    where literature becomes important, for it can help men
    understand each other by the "power of imagination and sen-
    sitivity" rather than by "the coldness of abstraction."
    The Negro experience in America has produced a "distinctive
    minority culture not completely separate from it." The
    Negro novel, like Negro life, "is at once alike and dif-
    ferent from the novels of white Americans." The Afro-
    American novel thus offers a key to the secrets of negri-
    tude, "destined to bear an important contribution toward
    the evolution of civilization during the next few centur-
    ies." This type of novel can be divided into two currents:
    protest and expression. Both currents reveal a genuine
    Negro humanism. Go Tell It is a "classical work" with ele-
    ments of romantic enchantment and journalistic exoticism.
    The characters may appear "primitive to the Western reader
    trained to the doctrines of self control, concealment of
    passions, restraint and skepticism," but they exemplify an
    exceptional integration of the "emotional, moral, physical
    elements of their personality." They do not "suffer from
    any dissociation of self." The interest of Baldwin's novel
    "resides in the fact that it established in the eyes of the
    imagination the concrete, physical, and emotional reality"
    of his observations. He gives "life to men and women."
    This "emotional personalism," a type of "natural integra-
    tion" of the personality, offers in action "a series of
    values which the white world has long yearned for."

1962

33 Goodman, Paul. "Not Enough of a World to Grow In." New York
    Times Book Review (24 June), p. 5.
        Describes the persons of Another Country as existing "in
    a kind of vacuum"; they do not have "enough world to grow
    in." There is not much reality presented so that a serious
    novel can be constructed; a work like this, therefore, has
    a "fictitious texture." Its structure has evolved only be-
    cause "there is a climate of publishing--for a bad (and big)
    audience--that demands these yarns." The book is "medio-
    cre"; it is "unworthy of its author's lovely abilities."

34 Hagopian, John V. "This Morning, This Evening, So Soon." In
    Insight I: Analyses of American Literature. Edited by
    John V. Hagopian and Martin Dolch. Frankfurt: Hirschgra-
    ben, pp. 14-22.
        The commentary on Baldwin is identical to 1963.38.

35 Hardwick, Elizabeth. "All About Love." Harper's, 225 (July),
    90-92.
        Admits that Baldwin is a very important American writer
    of "great courage and originality," but sees Another Coun-
    try as just a "hard-boiled novel of love and sex." The
    novel is written competently but in an "uninspired realistic
    manner" lacking humor and the typical "true wildness" of
    Baldwin. These defects seem to be linked to his turning
    away from his "own powers of mind" to get "down to the
    body." Another criticism is that the novel is too long.
    Length appears to have become "an aesthetic principle,"
    but frequently it is due to the author's lack of plot se-
    curity and the loss of ability to create "significant
    forms."

36 Hentoff, Nat. "Baldwin and His Critics." Village Voice,
    2 August, pp. 6, 8.
        Criticizes Baldwin the man rather than the author of
    Another Country and refers to other critics of Baldwin's
    life. He seems too occupied with sex, including the love
    of men for other men. The crucial question is does he
    really understand the nature of love, for his characters
    seem desperate in the "explosion of unsafe emotions." It
    seems that Baldwin lacks social insights to accurately
    judge public life.

37 Hicks, Granville. "Outcasts in a Caldron of Hate." Sat R,
    45 (7 July), 21.
        Alleges that Another Country is a novel about love and
    hate, and "more about hate than love." Although there are
    occasional weaknesses, it is "one of the most powerful

novels of our time." The complexities of love and the terrifying forces of hate are presented with great depth. The
hatred is not limited to the resentment of Negroes toward
whites; rather, Baldwin presents American life as a "terrifying barbarism." The very violence of the language is itself an expression of horror. He compels one to participate
in a kind of life that is horrible and "important because
it is horrible." The novel is "an explosion," yet it is
not uncontrolled or artless; it is "shaped with rigorous
care." Baldwin is a "skilled craftsman" with a great gift
as a novelist.

38 Hogan, William. "Baldwin's Comment on a 'Sub-culture.'" San
Francisco Chronicle (28 June), p. 35.
    Declares that Another Country in "its preoccupation with
totally destructive sex" within one segment of a subculture
is a savage, ruthless, irritating, and disappointing "may-
pole dance of bitterness" in which love is ironically "a
record of mass hate."

39 Holman, Ben. "The Importance of Being Earnest--Though Black."
Community, 21 (February), 8-9.
    Uses brief references to Notes to focus on Baldwin's
realistic assessment of the Negro's plight in the United
States compared to the Black Muslims' unrealistic stress
on separatism.

40 Hyman, Stanley Edgar. "No Country for Young Men." New Leader,
45 (25 June), 22-23.
    Admires Another Country, but finds parts of it weak and
unconvincing, a "very mixed bundle." The most powerful and
convincing aspects of the book are those that deal with
"Negro consciousness," which "seethes with bitterness and
race hate." Rufus' neurotic self-destructiveness manifests
a "working of raw hatred, a turning of it not against true
enemies but against friends and against the self." Many
parts of the book are weak, merely decorative, confusing,
slipshod, sentimental, and exceptionally bad by Baldwin's
own high standards. One can only conclude that he has
changed his writing style in order to create a bestseller,
which he surely will do. One cannot call Another Country a
success, "but it has considerable successes in it."

41 Johnson, Lucy. "Love and Hate." Progressive, 26 (August), 34.
    Describes Another Country as Baldwin's attempt to synthe-
size all the elements in himself that he has expressed in
his other works--"trying to impose his secrets on the world
and make them a part of the world's experience." In his

1962

struggle to do this, he ends up with a "ragged novel," in
part "fascinating, strong and tremendously moving."

42 Kazin, Alfred. "The Essays of James Baldwin." In his <u>Con-</u>
<u>temporaries</u>. Boston: Little, Brown, pp. 254-58.
Reprint of 1961.15.

43 Klein, Marcus. "James Baldwin: A Question of Identity." In
his <u>After Alienation: American Novels in Mid-Century</u>. New
York: World Publishing Company, pp. 147-95.
Asserts that the "invisibility of the Negro in America
has in fact been James Baldwin's underlying metaphor."
What seemed to have been a "dramatic recognition" of the
actual conditions of invisibility in <u>Go Tell It</u> also developed a "rhetoric of private alienation." The plight in
this invisibility manifests itself in the characters who
are "victims caught between despair and spite." They are
heroes who "cannot make themselves felt in the world"; they
have no clear, felt identity. <u>Giovanni's Room</u> argues that
the hero cannot love; he faces a nonexistence, a kind of
invisibility. And "it is the loneliness in invisibility
that is the affective basis" of the "constant story" found
in Baldwin's writings; everywhere there are characters dispossessed of their places, robbed of their identities in
the world, and who are therefore lonely. Thus, "the re-
covery of identity" becomes an all-pervasive theme, and
"the drama is in the hero's loneliness and the injustice
of his having to strive for identity in the world that
would make him invisible." Pity with some sarcasm is the
primary mode of Baldwin's indignation; his use of self-pity
might be the means of revealing his perceptions, "a special-
ty of the informal essay." In his essays, he creates a
series of images of himself that is "the chief function of
his rhetoric."
Baldwin uses the music of Negro folk tradition as an
"expression of identity"; the music projects a style that
contains a specific character, and this provides a tone for
attaining an identity. The "story of the Negro that the
music tells is of ancient sorrows . . . borne . . . in a
world that still confers suffering; that is what Negro-ness
is." <u>Go Tell It</u> was written "out of a completeness of experience"; it showed what it "is to become a Negro in
America, to accept the conditions that create identity."
<u>Another Country</u> is a novel of "insistent shrillness, a
greater howling for the communion of innocence, and the
sacrifice inevitably of plot, character, and the strong
sense of persons achieving identity by moving through their
circumstanced lives."

46

44 Luce, Phillip Abbot. "Communications on James Baldwin."
     Mainstream, 15 (May), 45-48.
         Attacks Bonosky's criticism of Baldwin's Nobody Knows
     and charges Bonosky with "anti-intellectualism and shoddy
     research." There is no doubt that Baldwin "fails to ful-
     fill the promise" that was hoped for among America's con-
     temporary writers, but Bonosky is callous in his contention
     that Baldwin's "victory lies in defeat." Bonosky takes
     quotations of Baldwin out of context, which does a "dis-
     honor" to both of them. Whether Bonosky likes it or not,
     Baldwin is a "fighter for the freedom of Negro people" and
     is "not content with his place in society."

45 McReynolds, David. "Baldwin Versus the White Negro." *Village
     Voice*, 29 March, pp. 9, 16.
         Suggests that the most energetic note in the thirteen
     essays of Nobody Knows is the focus on the Negro minority.
     Baldwin debunks the myth of the sexually unique Negro by
     emphasizing the white middle class's romantic fantasy of
     his élan vital and primitive nature, and its alternate envy
     and fear of blacks. Two problems that receive special
     attention: 1) the Negro's greater sense of community and
     social belonging compared to the white's emphasis on in-
     dividuality--life may be hell but without shame, guilt, or
     sense of failure; 2) the desire to become white psycholo-
     gically and physically by living down African roots and
     assimilating white language, culture, and religion. The
     tone exhibits the author's love of his country.

46 Maloff, Saul. "The Two Baldwins." *Nation*, 195 (14 July),
     15-16.
         Sees two Baldwins--the novelist and the essayist. In
     the latter, he is a witness and prophet. His testimony
     serves as a reproach, and his prophecy as a lesson--all
     done with clarity and "reverberant feeling." As a novelist,
     he lacks the precision, the control of form, language,
     moral content, and theme. Another Country is a "big"
     novel that seems to lose control in terms of moral and
     aesthetic failure. The language is without energy, the
     tempo flags, scenes lose their force, the point of view
     shifts erratically, the dialogue is wooden. Yet Baldwin is
     an "authentic" and gifted writer, whose novel Go Tell It is
     a "fine and sensitive work." Still, it is his essays that
     demonstrate his exemplary moral and literary achievement.

47 Moon, Eric. "Fiction." *LJ*, 87 (1 June), 2154.
         Describes Another Country as "a problem book" and "very
     sad," coming from the writer "who is one of the most gifted
     crystallizers of pain, and the social forces which create
     it in our society."

1962

48 Moten, Etta. "Another Country: Review." Muhammad Speaks
    (17 July), p. 23.
        Affirms that Another Country treats in "a most explicit
    and penetrating way" a group of intellectuals and artists
    who are "interracial and international, homosexual and
    bisexual."

49 Murray, Michele. "To the Editor." New York Times Book Review
    (5 August), p. 24.
        Argues that Paul Goodman's review of Another Country on
    June 24 fails to show reasons for his dislike of the novel.

50 Nordell, Roderick. "Old and New Novels on Racial Themes."
    Christian Science Monitor (19 July), p. 11.
        Argues that this "obscene book" (Another Country) with
    its "sordid story of whites and Negroes, bohemiams, homo-
    sexuality and miscegenation" is not equal to the eloquence
    of the author's essays. Baldwin belabors a psychologically
    plausible relationship between racial and sexual themes "to
    the point of nausea and absurdity," merges one character
    into another, and offers no moral condemnation, which the
    conduct of the characters merits.

51 Podhoretz, Norman. "In Defense of a Maltreated Best Seller."
    Show, 2 (October), 91-92.
        Defends Another Country against the "maltreatment" by a
    number of reviewers. The work "is informed by a remorse-
    less insistence on a truth which . . . is . . . compelling
    as a perspective on the way we live now." This is a "cruel
    truth" and a "demanding one," but it is "not without an
    element of sweet spiritual generosity." The work will come
    to be seen as the book in which, for the first time, the
    "superb intelligence of Baldwin the essayist became fully
    available to Baldwin the novelist."

52 Poore, Charles. "Books of the Times." The New York Times
    (26 June), p. 31.
        Contends that Another Country is a "sad story, brilliant-
    ly and fiercely told." Focusing on the central event of
    Rufus Scott's suicide and its repercussions on his friends
    and family, Baldwin reveals "endless cavities of depravity"
    in an "angrily taut" narrative that involves dramatic con-
    frontations among all the leading characters and that rests
    squarely in "the gritty squalor of the modern naturalistic
    tradition."

53 Root, Robert. "It's a Wasteland." Christian Century, 79
    (7 November), 1354-55.

1962

Calls <u>Another Country</u> a "wasteland"--a novel without
honor, loyalty, honesty, purity, diligence, virtue, or love.
Baldwin seems to have opened up an "overflowing Garbage Can
School of Writing." The characters seek love but cannot
find it; they cannot even find themselves--life is a
"bitch." No religion illumines this wasteland--Negro re-
ligiosity is undermined. In addition, there is an absence
of intellectuality among the "arty types"; no theology or
philosophy is noted. The book is "sex-obsessed," with the
characters acting as if sex, natural or unnatural, will
somehow give them meaningful relations with others. The
author's style is more than vigorous; it is "red raw";
there is a continuous "torrent of gutter words." The biggest disappointment of the book is the treatment of race;
racism emerges as "brutally absurd"; an artistic failure.

54 Simmons, Charles. "Square Dance of Love." <u>Village Voice</u>,
28 June, pp. 9-11.
Condemns <u>Another Country</u> as a "tortuous square dance of
love" in which almost all combinations of sex and color
pair off; the novel is "didactic, therapeutic, overfelt
and under-thought." The characters lack true concern for
each other's well-being and exemplify hate; the viewpoint
shifts amateurishly; the dialogue is flat and lengthy.

55 Southern, Terry. "When Film Get Good . . ." <u>Nation</u>, 195
(17 November), 331-32.
Suggests that the quality of fiction has improved in recent years--it more "fully exploits the known . . . potentials of the medium." At the same time, only a handful of
these books can compete aesthetically, psychologically, or
in any other way, with a "good" film. Film, by its very
nature, "more closely approximates first hand experiences
than does print." It seems "wasteful, pointless," and in
terms of art, "inexcusable, to write a novel which could
. . . have been a film." The recent improvement in the
quality of fiction can be attributed to recent court de-
cisions (e.g., <u>Lady Chatterly's Lover</u>) that have allowed
publishers and writers to become bolder. <u>Another Country</u>
is a "lulu" of a "protest novel," for it depicts not
"ideal truth" but one man's truth with suggestions that
"it may be a general truth." In essence it is this: "that
if a person . . . has been severely mistreated, there is no
immediate redress--that even when mistreatment ends, hatred
for the oppressor remains." The book by virtue of its in-
trospection, detail, and dialogue falls outside the current
limitations of film.

1962

56 Spector, Robert D. "Everybody Knows His Name." New York
    Herald Tribune Books (17 June), pp. 2-3.
         Contends that Another Country does more than depict the
    plight of the Negro, but rather shows what man has made of
    man. The relationships between the races provide the pri-
    mary means by which Baldwin "dramatizes the human condi-
    tion," but the problems are by no means restricted to race
    relations. Each character is faced with his inability to
    comprehend the motives not only of others but of himself.
    The people are seen in conflict with the forces of the lar-
    ger society that contribute to the loneliness in their own
    struggles. "Torment and anguish infect the hearts" of the
    characters. And love, the only solace, is often limited by
    the individual ego. Baldwin is a "hip writer," and to ap-
    preciate him, one "must willingly suspend his moral judg-
    ments." For some, his novel will "seem too far out."

57 Strong, Augusta. "Another Country." Freedomways, 2 (Fall),
    500-503.
         Sees some basic truths about life in Another Country--
    race, personal freedom, self-searching. Cynicism, despair,
    self-torment, and predestined agony permeate the work mak-
    ing it "bafflingly inexpert and disappointing." This novel
    has none of the sense of reality and conviction of his ear-
    lier works. Each of the characters, through whom the au-
    thor speaks, has "buried his nose in his own novel." Al-
    though white and black America must live together, this
    mingling leads to grief and destruction. His aim is to be
    an "honest writer," and the novel is written "honestly" out
    of Baldwin's personal preoccupations and uncertainties.
    But the message fails in the "dreary, sordid stretches of
    this book." It would have been wonderful if this could
    have been his best book, but Another Country is the "worst"
    of this genre.

58 Strong, Augusta. "Notes on James Baldwin." Freedomways, 2
    (Spring), 167-71.
         Praises Baldwin's work in generalizations: its honesty
    and perspicacity; its faithful reproduction of Negro per-
    ceptions; its expression of the "rage in the blood" as re-
    action to discrimination; its recurring themes--the strug-
    gle for survival, the search for identity, the efforts to
    escape oppression, the ties between whites and blacks. His
    writings reflect "the dimensions and complexity of the Ne-
    gro problem" and reveal that the myth of white supremacy is
    exploding from the Congo to New Orleans. They are charac-
    terized by clarity, honesty, and humility as well as ego-
    tism, vacillation, and disputable assertions.

59 Taubmann, Robert. "Early Sartre." New Statesman, 64 (13
     July), 53.
          Includes comments about Another Country in a review of
     five novels and says that it focuses on the characters'
     "search for a means of putting up with the horror of their
     lives" in which the "unrelenting consciousness of sex" and
     the failure of sexual relations follow them around. Sar-
     tre's Nausea is recalled, in that jazz in this novel is the
     only "firm reference" as a general therapeutic device.

60 Walker, Gerald. "Reviewing Nat Hentoff." Village Voice,
     9 August, p. 4.
          Responds to Hentoff's claims that critics and reviewers
     mistreated Baldwin and Another Country with questions as to
     why the book was too "disappointingly shockingly bad" es-
     pecially in its flat characters--a clumsy effort to show
     sterility of city life--and its structure--suffering from
     "naturalistic elephantiasis."

61 W.R. "Another Country." Tamarack Review, 24 (Summer), 108.
          Describes Another Country as a "big, rough, courageous
     book," which presents "rage and agony, and . . . a perva-
     sive consciousness of race." It is a "great novel in that
     major American tradition that includes Melville, Dreiser,
     Faulkner, and Wolfe."

                              1963

1 Adams, Robert Martin. "Fashions in Fiction." PR, 30 (Spring),
     128-33.
          Reviews Salinger's Raise High the Roof Beam, Carpenters
     and Seymour, and Introduction; Fiedler's first novel,
     Second Stone; and Baldwin's Another Country, the "big novel
     everyone has thought for years he had in him." This latter
     novel is a work of "great integrity" and great "occasional
     power," but also it is an "impressive failure." Spiritual-
     ly, the novel is pure and noble, but the "hipster" charac-
     ters are "dull and uninventive." Despite its shortcomings,
     Another Country is the "sort of failure" that does the
     author enormous credit.

2 ANON. "At a Crucial Time a Negro Talks Tough: There's a Bill
     Due That Has to Be Paid." Life, 24 May, pp. 81-90.
          Begins with a quote from Baldwin speaking from a church
     pulpit: "I represent sin, love, death, sex, hell, terror
     and other things too frightening for you to recognize."
     This is a new role for the author who has "found himself a

1963

celebrity overnight." He contends that "there's a Bill Due
That Has to Be Paid," and now with Birmingham, "it's come
in and it's got to be paid." His outspoken convictions are
presented in a "dazzling, fluent rhetoric drawn from the
stately cadences of the Old Testament, the glib breathless-
ness of postgraduate cocktail parties and the funk argot
of Harlem." He has made people mad, but he has never failed
in "shaking them up, disturbing their peace, getting them
to ask real questions."

3 ANON. "At the Root of the Negro Problem." Time, 17 May,
    pp. 26-27.
       Views Baldwin as the preeminent writer expressing with
    "poignancy and abrasiveness the dark realities of the
    racial ferment" and as a reluctant lecturer exhorting both
    blacks and whites. The latter focuses on these points:
    1) the need for a realistic view of American history to
    overcome the white man's delusions and terror and the Ne-
    gro's demoralization and rage; 2) the need for a change in
    the presumed superiority of whites and their image of the
    blacks; 3) the need to change the fact that Negroes are ig-
    nored in the North and under surveillance in the South;
    4) the need to see that the price of the liberation of
    whites is the liberation of blacks.

4 ANON. "Baldwin." PMLA, 77 (May), 190.
       Presents the annual secondary bibliography for 1962.

5 ANON. "Baldwin: Grey Flannel Muslim?" Christian Century, 80
    (12 June), 791.
       Asserts that Martin Luther King, Jr., is the prophet of
    black experience exposing the hopes of Negroes to public
    view while Baldwin is the poet exposing the Negroes' pri-
    vate vision to public view. The Fire presents hope, pro-
    vided that compassion survives and man accepts man in spite
    of Christianity or racial memory.

6 ANON. "Black Man's Burden." TLS (6 September), p. 672.
       Explains that Baldwin's creative work is closely linked
    with "intellectual and sociological formulations" expressed
    in his other works, yet finds his forte not in social pro-
    test--either racial or sexual--but "in the concocting of
    beautifully elaborate sentences and thoughts and stories
    which give off an aromatic hint of decadence." Go Tell It
    treats a crisis that is "sexual in essence and religious in
    expression" and presages the development of a homosexual.
    Giovanni's Room ends in death, and "nobody gains anything--
    not even an insight into their own true nature."

1963

7 ANON. "The Fire Next Time." Best Sellers, 23 (15 April), 38.
       Discusses in The Fire the desperate position of the
   Negro citizen faced with the unreasoning fear and hatred of
   his white countrymen.

8 ANON. "Kennedy and Baldwin: The Gulf." Newsweek, 3 June,
       p. 19.
       Reports on a meeting between Attorney General Robert
   Kennedy and a group of blacks led by Baldwin and emphasizes
   the differences between living in Harlem and McLean, Virginia. Kennedy was surprised and confounded by "a message
   of anger of quickening urgency, of deepening alienation"
   and by the question: "How many Negroes would fight to free
   Cuba when they can't be free themselves?"

9 ANON. "The Racial Nightmare." Newsweek, 4 February, p. 81.
       Conceives of Baldwin as a latter-day Stephen Dedalus
   trying to forge the uncreated conscience of his race, but
   his devils are white institutions, values, and gods. The
   Fire offers a kind of final plea and warning "to end the
   racial nightmare . . . and change the history of the
   world."

10 ANON. "The Rainbow Sign." Time, 4 January, pp. 18-19.
       Maintains that The Fire shows Baldwin as "the most bit-
   terly eloquent voice of the American Negro" who speaks com-
   pellingly to the whites about being black in a white world,
   the inadequacy of the Black Muslims, the refusal of whites
   to confront the reality of their history, and the delusion
   of value placed on skin color.

11 ANON. "State of the Negro." TLS (26 July), p. 537.
       Reviews The Fire as an energetic, compassionate, and
   autobiographical expression of "the dilemma of the American
   Negro" deprived of pride in race, created unfree, and
   scorned as inferior. It is suggested that the work be read
   with Bettelheim's The Informed Heart as an example of the
   ways men can be deprived of their manhood so that killing
   them is "a mere mechanical action which puts them out of
   their misery rather than a willed act which could occasion
   feelings of guilt."

12 ANON. "Too Much Fire?" Economist, 208 (3 August), 444.
       Praises The Fire for portraying what it is like "to be
   an American Negro intellectual in the nineteen-sixties"
   but condemns its exaggerations, hostilities, generalities,
   and lack of proportion and objectivity.

1963

13 Barrett, William. "Reader's Choice." Atlantic Monthly, 206
   (March), 156.
      Praises The Fire as a manifestation "eloquent in its
   passion and scorching in its candor" on what it means to be
   "branded from the start with the mark of inferiority" in
   the United States, and as offering hope for reconciliation
   if the Negro forgives and the white examines what he wants
   to vilify in himself by seeing another as inferior.

14 Binn, Sheldon. "Books of the Times." The New York Times
   (31 January), p. 7.
      Contends that Baldwin's "translation" of what it means
   to be a Negro in America in The Fire is "masterful." The
   reader can be "transformed, as far as words will take him,
   into the skin of the teller." Out of his own pain and despair and hope, Baldwin has "fashioned such a transformation."

15 Bond, Jean Carey. "The Fire Next Time." Freedomways (Spring),
   pp. 235-37.
      Recalls that The Fire was originally printed in the New
   Yorker under the title, "Letter from a Region in My Mind."
   It is impossible to evaluate The Fire since it is "almost
   without organization, occasionally incoherent and contradictory." The work's "biggest problem" is "superficiality,"
   and this tends to give support to the claim that Baldwin
   "is primarily concerned with the white reading public and
   is covetous of their attention and praise." It appears
   that he is in an "advanced state of excitement not anger,"
   which would account for his "undisciplined puddle-jumping
   from one idea to another."

16 Breit, Harvey. "James Baldwin and Two Footnotes." In The
   Creative Present: Notes on Contemporary American Fiction.
   Edited by Nona Balakian and Charles Simmons. New York:
   Doubleday, pp. 1-23.
      Begins with a quote from Fred Dupee regarding Baldwin
   as a writer of polemical essays on the Negro question who
   has no equal, in fact, he probably has "no real competi-
   tors." His "dark passion and lighted language have proved
   a unique description of the Negro's situation in America."
   Go Tell It is his "most free" and most creative work; Notes
   is his most "natural and graceful one" with its candor, its
   search for truth. Giovanni's Room is concerned with homosexuality, and "deflection takes on its first disguise" in
   this work, "an entirely personal mask." Nobody Knows is a
   "rare and great book" with a sense of tragedy, but it is
   also a "constricting book" with a narrow perspective.
   Another Country "fails him a little" because "it has been

inspired by the essays in the wrong way"; the social, political, and moral issues of the essays "rush" into the novel.
The Fire is "too prophetic," a mixture of the gospel preacher and the political activist. Baldwin, like Ellison, is
in the vanguard of American fiction.

17 Buckley, W.F., Jr. "The Call to Color Blindness." National
    Review, 14 (18 June), 488. Reply by Marcella Whalen, 14
    (13 August), 120.
        Portrays Baldwin as a catalyst of the policy of "uncon-
    ditional surrender"--whites give up their poor to the Ne-
    groes, renounce their civilization, despise their god.
    Baldwin's "crushing hortatory eloquence" (which no writer
    living today can imitate) calls for the total liberation of
    the Negro. What he asks for is "nothing less than the
    evanescence of color"--the disappearance of color-conscious-
    ness. He wants a mobilized Negro community to view life as
    he does, to be 110 percent black. The job at hand is not
    to obliterate differences, but to "stimulate man's capacity
    for love, and his toleration, understanding and respect for
    others, different people."

18 Bulman, Leonard T. "Books for Young Adults." LJ, 88 (July),
    2784.
        Lists The Fire as among the titles especially recommended
    for young people of high-school age.

19 Charney, M. "James Baldwin's Quarrel with Richard Wright."
    American Quarterly, 15 (Spring), 65-75.
        Cites Baldwin's review of The Selected Poems of Langston
    Hughes as "one of the best statements . . . of the dilemma
    of the Negro writer in America." The inability of a writer
    to reconcile his social and artistic responsibilities is
    also the basis of Baldwin's "quarrel" with Wright who he
    believes "distorted artistic truth into protest and propa-
    ganda." The issues of "intention, aim, and values" of the
    writer were central to his criticism of Wright. The quar-
    rel emerged in 1949, when Baldwin's essay, "Everybody's
    Protest Novel," appeared, and Wright felt "betrayed by his
    spiritual son." Although Baldwin witnessed to Wright's
    power as a novelist and as a spokesman for the Negro, he
    felt that Wright had failed to "deal with man in his whole-
    ness and complexity"; he had been "content to create stereo-
    types with carefully defined social roles." Hence Native
    Son was a failure even as a social protest novel, for it
    gave the impression that "the Negro has no real society and
    tradition about which one can write." In some ways Baldwin
    allies himself with Ellison--neither is a writer of despair.
    Tragic paradox may appear, but hope and love define the
    characters' being and make "war on the chaos of despair."

1963

20 Ciardi, John. "Manner of Speaking: Black Man in America."
    Sat R, 57 (6 July), 13.
        Bases some observations on a recording, Black Man in
    America--an interview with Baldwin. The price the American
    Negro "has paid for existence is something more than reason
    and moderation will assess." The cry of agony may not be
    heard or answered in time to avert the violence that may
    result from a far too slow march of "do gooders." The
    trouble is that "prejudice makes the Negro invisible--No-
    body knows my name." White men do not see the black man,
    they only see what they have invested--danger, torment,
    passion--a level of existence they deny. The denial of
    the Negro's rights of humanity can only drive all to self-
    hatred and defeat.

21 Clancy, T.H. "Of Fire, the French, and Fiction." America,
    108 (16 March), 376-77.
        Compares The Fire and The Diary of Anne Frank as a means
    for teaching people about horror, hate, and inhumanity.
    The essays have a "clean and honest quality" filled with
    "fierce pride and dogged hope."

22 Collinson, Laurence. "Another Country." Overland, 27/28
    (July/September), 23.
        Defends Another Country, encourages adults to read it,
    and deplores the censorship of it as "a moral outrage."
    The "frankness and the fury and the skill" with which the
    three themes (heterosexual relationships, homosexual re-
    lationships, racial obsessions) are treated make the work
    one of the "most impressive, exciting, and powerful novels"
    published that year. It gives the non-Negro reader a deep
    and unequivocal understanding of the minds and feelings of
    blacks within the domination of a white society.

23 Cook, Bruce. "Writers in Midstream: John Williams and James
    Baldwin." Critic, 21 (February/March), 35-40.
        Cites the fact that of the sixty-two Negro novelists
    writing between 1853 and 1952, forty have published only
    one novel. After an account of the Negro writer's plight--
    lack of recognition and just rewards--Baldwin is discussed
    as having a "prominent though somewhat ambiguous position
    in the American establishment." He is the white man's pro-
    fessional "gadfly" whose function is "to sting and irritate"
    and be seen always "as the Negro." Most of his articles
    and essays are "intensely concrete and personal--often em-
    barrassingly so." This intense subjectivity was originally
    "the major virtue" of his writing and is now "its major
    fault." Go Tell It is the "most perfect Negro novel

1963

published in America"; but Nobody Knows is marred by an ex-
cess of self-pity; Giovanni's Room fails to establish contact with real life; Another Country is an old-fashioned
social protest novel. Baldwin is "somewhere in midstream"
as a writer; if he doesn't start swimming, he may drown.

24 Dupee, F.W. "James Baldwin and the 'Man.'" New York Review
    of Books, 1 (February), 1-2.
       Views Baldwin as "the negro in extremis, a virtuoso of
    ethnic suffering, defiance and aspiration" strongly influ-
    enced by existentialism and expressing "a condition of
    spirit" in formal prose with a syntax that "mounts through
    clearly articulated stages to a resounding and clarifying
    climax" and suggests "the ideal prose of an ideal literary
    community." In The Fire, prophecy has been exchanged for
    criticism and exhortation for analysis; the subjects lack
    definition and specificity except for "the cruel paradoxes"
    of the Negro's life, the failures of Christianity, and the
    relations of Negro and Jew.

25 Dwyer, R.J. "I Know about the Negroes and the Poor." National
    Review, 15 (17 December), 517-21.
       Submits the thesis that poor people in America are poor
    because they want to be; they are lazy, uneducated, unde-
    pendable. The problems presented by Baldwin are not the
    Negro's problems but his problems. He misses the point
    when he says America has forgotten the poor, especially the
    urban poor. They are poor because they are dirty, uneduca-
    ted, and dependent upon others. This dependence induces a
    "spiritual and moral disintegration fundamentally destruc-
    tive to the moral fiber." They have resigned from the
    struggle for self-improvement. Baldwin's cries are touch-
    ing, but he fails to recognize that the "average man is,
    and always will be, a slob," regardless of the level of in-
    struction. True, his writings show a tremendous pride in
    his race, and this is to be commended, but why should he
    despair so when "more progress has been made in the past
    generation than in all the past history?"

26 Ellison, Ralph. "The World and the Jug." New Leader, 46
    (9 December), 22-26.
       Begins with three essential questions: 1) Why is it
    that critics drop their "advanced critical armament" when
    looking at works by American Negroes and revert to "primi-
    tive modes of analysis?" 2) Why is it that "sociology-
    oriented critics seem to rate literature so far below poli-
    tics and ideology?" 3) Why is it that so many critics talk
    about the "meaning of Negro life" but never bother to learn

1963

how varied it really is? Ellison analyzes at length Irving
Howe's essay, "Black Boys and Native Sons," which is written "with something of an Olympian authority." Howe attacks Baldwin's rejection of so-called "protest literature"
and sees "Everybody's Protest Novel" as Baldwin's declara-
tion to "transcend the sterile categories of Negro-ness."
While Howe agrees with Baldwin that "literature and sociology are not . . . the same," he feels it is important to
understand how a writer's own experience affects how he represents "human affairs in a work of fiction." But evident-
ly, Howe believes that "unrelieved suffering is the only
real Negro experience"; thus the "true Negro writer must be
ferocious." Howe does not seem to consider that Negro life
is a "discipline," with its own fullness and richness. The
Negro, like any other human being, must consciously grasp
the complexities of his life--he is not an abstraction in
someone's head. Yet, in his loyalty to Richard Wright,
Howe considers "Ellison and Baldwin guilty of filial betrayal" because they have rejected the path for "black boys"
and "pretend to be . . . American writers." Howe seems too
committed to a "sociological vision of society"; he cannot
understand that no matter how strictly Negroes are segregated socially and politically, on the "level of the imagination, their ability to achieve freedom is limited only by
individual aspiration, insight, energy and will." Howe
sees segregation as "an opaque steel jug" with the Negroes
inside "waiting for some black Messiah to come along and
blow the cork." Ellison attests that if he were in a jug,
it would be transparent not opaque, and he would be able to
see, read, and make identifications as to "values and human
quality." He has released himself from "whatever segregated idea" he had of his human possibilities, and he has
rejected Wright's Bigger Thomas as any "final image of
Negro personality."

27 English, Charles. "Another Viewpoint." Jubilee (September),
    pp. 43-46.
      Recalls a conversation with a French friend who had re-
    marked that he thought of Baldwin as being "fierce," yet
    basically he was no different than any white American--
    black and white Americans are "generous, curious, . . . and
    possessors of great potential." The Frenchman had made the
    same discovery as Baldwin: "Americans, black and white,
    . . . differ only in color, they share everything else,
    . . . their destiny is that of lovers who need one another."
    Baldwin, of all the young American writers, demands of his
    readers a sense of history--an involvement and identifica-
    tion. Notes and The Fire contain some of the most

accomplished essays of the decade; Go Tell It presents the
artistic depth of his art. Giovanni's Room and Another
Country symbolically portray man's alienation.

28 Finn, James. "James Baldwin's Vision." Commonweal, 78
     (26 July), 447-49.
     Describes the presence of racism as a "festering evil,"
     which "oozes its poison" into society. The Fire has
     served as a "convenient lightning rod" to the present con-
     fusion. "Logic and internal consistency" are not the vir-
     tues that lend power to this work, which is "full of con-
     tradictory statements and isolated insights." He has con-
     fused his vision of man with his vision of the white man;
     thus, he "cannot separate the problem of being a man."
     Podhoretz's essay, "My Negro Problem--and Ours," is a sub-
     tle and sensitive response to The Fire.

29 Foote, Dorothy. "James Baldwin's 'Holler Books.'" The CEA
     Critic, 25 (May), 8, 11.
     Defines The Fire as a "holler book" of unreliable socio-
     logy that arrogates for blacks what is denied to whites.
     "Reversed stereotyped beliefs" abound in the work: the
     Negro is a sexual giant; he is a jazz giant; only a black
     can have/soul; only a black loves children; only the Negro
     sees reality and has no self-delusions.

30 Ford, Nick Aaron. "Walls Do a Prison Make: A Critical Survey
     of Significant Belles-Lettres by and about Negroes Published
     in 1962." Phylon, 24 (Summer), 123-34.
     Describes Baldwin as "one of the most talented novelists
     alive today" and Another Country as a "powerful pessimistic
     vision of life"--a prison where "those who seek to escape
     are doomed to everlasting suffering for their failure to
     understand that there is no escape." His tremendous talent
     for fiction writing is evident in this book; his characters
     speak naturally; he creates suspense compelling the reader
     on; he constructs memorable scenes; he grapples with the
     here-and-now; he expresses passion--hate, anger, love, sor-
     row. Yet in spite of these "virtues," he misses the "quali-
     ties of greatness." His vision is negative; his language
     succumbs to meaningless obscenities; he fails to "satisfy
     reasonable curiosity" about the final actions of his charac-
     ters. Despite these shortcomings, Another Country is "an
     enlightening and stirring experience to anyone who will
     read it with an open mind."

31 Fulford, Robert. "On Books: The Black Nationalism of the New
     James Baldwin." Maclean's Review, 76, no. 14 (27 July),
     45-46.

1963

Calls Baldwin a "major spokesman for American Negroes." He
writes and speaks with "eloquent passion" on behalf of the
new generation of Negroes; he has become one of the "most
exciting and compelling figures on the American scene."
This social prophet of 1963 is the same "brilliant intellectual" who was trying hard <u>not</u> to be a "Negro writer" but
to be a writer instead. <u>Go Tell It</u>, <u>Another Country</u>, <u>Gio-
vanni's Room</u>, <u>Notes</u>, <u>Nobody Knows</u>, <u>The Fire</u> all deal with
more than the discontents and aspirations of blacks. He
writes as though there were two Americas, separate in beliefs and attitudes yet united by the suffering that mass
society produces. It is when Baldwin joins earlier Negro
writers who have expressed a form of "racial self-satisfac-
tion" that he becomes "trapped in his own rhetoric." The
contention that Negroes have developed special resources of
character because of their decades of mistreatment has no
proof to support it. <u>The Fire</u> has a central theme that ap-
peals to a certain "literary masochism"--things are rotten
and are getting worse; the content is "the least coherent,
the least intelligent" of his works.

32 Geller, Allen. "An Interview with Ralph Ellison." <u>Tamarack
    Review</u>, 32 (Summer), 3-24.
        Interviews Ellison regarding his work, <u>Invisible Man</u>, as
    well as other pertinent experiences and ideas, e.g., secur-
    ing a publisher for his book, obtaining equal rights for
    Negroes now, analyzing Baldwin's role as writer and Negro
    spokesman. Concerning this last area, Ellison believes
    that the only way to deal with political power is to have
    "some structure" behind a person, and Baldwin does not have
    it; "he has no way of imposing his will." In terms of his
    quality as a spokesman and as a novelist, Ellison "prefers"
    Baldwin's essays to his novels; and if people can be moved
    by changing their views then this is "all to the good."
    Ellison considers himself both a Negro and an American wri-
    ter, but when one looks at Baldwin, it seems as if "he is
    not writing in the Negro idiom"; he is writing a "mandarin
    prose, a Jamesian prose," which gives an indication of
    "where he really comes from." Yet, Baldwin does not use
    "an imposed style," rather the "emphasis upon the Negroness
    is an imposition"; he is, after all, a Negro as well as an
    American. Thus, he can draw upon his uniqueness as a Negro
    and as an American, and add something to the general quality
    of American literature.

33 Godsell, Geoffrey. "Baldwin: 'I'm Not Mad . . . I Am Wor-
    ried.'" <u>Christian Science Monitor</u> (21 February), p. 11.
        Suggests that Baldwin's stress on achieving the well-
    being of American society distinguishes <u>The Fire</u> from

earlier essays on the racial theme. Rejecting solutions
offered by the Black Muslims and organized churches to the
problem of the white's stereotype of the black as inherently
inferior, he preaches the need for love in "the tough and
universal sense of quest and daring and growth."

34 Golden, Harry. "A Comment on James Baldwin's Letter." Crisis,
70 (March), 145-46.
Contends that a letter by Baldwin in The New Yorker describing the American Negro as "forever consigned to the
margins of the most affluent society ever invented" expresses torment, betrays self-pity, pleads for love, and
portends a symbolic doom.

35 Greeley, Andrew M. "The Fire Next Time." Critic, 21 (April),
72.
Describes Baldwin as part of "the new Negro intelligen-
sia," which is restless, critical, dissatisfied, and eager
for change. While The Fire reveals the author's own prejudice and ignorance about many subjects, it also correctly
analyzes the nature of hatred and the victimization of
blacks and issues a warning about the future.

36 Gross, John. "Day of Wrath." New Statesman, 66 (19 July),
79-80.
Shows that Baldwin "knows how to probe the liberal conscience at its tenderest spots," how to create a "panicky
feeling" in white readers so that whatever their sentiments
are, they will realize that perhaps they never have "really
looked a coloured man full in the face before." He has
been transformed into a "spokesman and a culture-hero," a
major celebrity. His novels reveal a "true gift of forcing
the reader back on his own life by involving him with lives
of others." In addition to establishing himself as a novelist, Baldwin has made a name for himself "as a social critic, with a succession of mordant essays on the Negro's
situation and the ways in which he copes with the White
Problem." As long as he is "trying to blast open the doors
of complacency" and alert others to the urgency of the present racial situation, he can be applauded. But when he
moves on to "dubious ground," dwelling on an "extremist
group like the Muslims," he does not "pay himself a compli-
ment." Much of Baldwin's forcefulness as a writer comes
from "a religious sensibility." He "exults, laments, pours
out his wrath," and then summons the "nations to repentance."

37 Gross, John. "Disorganization Men." New Statesman, 65
(8 February), 202-204.

1963

Contends that Norman Mailer, William Burroughs, and
Baldwin write "out of boredom or disgust with American
liberalism," and that The Fire, while alternating between
the points of view of the liberal and the absolute pessi-
mist, embodies the white idea of "the Negro as a victim or
a symbol, but not as a man."

38 Hagopian, John V. "James Baldwin: The Black and the Red-
      White-and-Blue." CLAJ, 7 (December), 133-40.
        Contends that Baldwin "is one of the most accomplished
    and sophisticated American writers of today." It is unfor-
    tunate from a literary standpoint that he expends so much of
    his energy on nonfiction. He says that he does not want to
    be a Negro, but rather a writer, and then he spends most of
    his creative energies on the protest essay, which is "a way
    of being a Negro rather than a writer." His short story,
    "This Morning, This Evening, So Soon," deserves "to take
    its place as one of the most important short stories writ-
    ten since the war" not just because of the theme--the Negro
    taking his rightful place in American society--but because
    as literature, it is a very fine piece of work. The story
    falls into three sections: family, friends, strangers.
    The "I" narrator tells the story, which moves from the "in-
    timate center of unnamed narrative experiences outward into
    public life and society."

39 Haselden, Kyle. "Reverberating Explosion." Christian Century,
      80 (1 May), 582-83.
        Confesses the need to probe the "seminal depths and mea-
    sure the social impact of Baldwin's soulburst," The Fire.
    It is a "baffling book, a haunting riddle, demanding solu-
    tion but remaining insoluble, a literary gadfly stinging
    the soul and pestering the mind." The book is a candid
    confession of an angry young Negro man undressing his soul
    and allowing "peepers at the window."

40 Hentoff, Nat. "It's Terrifying." New York Herald Tribune
      Books (16 June), pp. 1, 6.
        Interviews Baldwin and tells what it's like now to be
    him. For Baldwin, the act of writing continues to be an
    obsessive need, a meaningful way in which he can speak for
    himself. Blues represents his third play; the others are
    Amen Corner and a dramatization of Giovanni's Room. He
    confesses that Another Country is in his own eyes his best
    novel. He is working on a long novel, Tomorrow Brought Us
    Pain, that starts when the Negroes began to realize they
    were free. Another project is a book of essays, The Beast
    in the Playground, that will include views on housing, edu-
    cation, sex, as well as profiles of a few key Negro figures,

e.g., Martin Luther King, Jr. Although Baldwin has traveled in Africa, he does not plan a book on Africa; he may
do an article on Sierra Leone called, "The Price of
Diamonds."

41 Hodges, Louis W. "The Fire Next Time." Shenandoah, 14
    (Summer), 65-68.
        Analyzes Baldwin's explanation of the behavior of the
    "innocents" as being "trapped in a history which they do
    not understand and from which they cannot be released so
    long as they do not understand," and in which color is a
    "political reality." The result in the Negro is the "dis-
    enchantment with the white man's world and the scoffing
    ridicule of his alleged good will." The only hope for
    restoration and for the survival of humanity is love as a
    "state of being or a state of grace." The special value
    of The Fire consists not in what is being said, but in the
    person saying it, and the greatness of the book is that "it
    speaks prophetically."

42 Hoffman, Frederick J. "Marginal Societies and the Novel." In
    his The Modern Novel in America, rev. ed. Chicago: Henry
    Regnery Company, pp. 246-55.
        Differentiates between the "comic" or "pathetic lesson"
    of the American Jew in literature and the Negro role in
    fiction. The Negro fiction of the twentieth century owes
    "its strength . . . to the genuine opportunities for pro-
    test" that exist in a race with a long history of oppres-
    sion. Some protest exists in all Negro fiction, the dif-
    ference lies in the use to which the black-white conflict
    is put. Baldwin wants to break through the conflicts and
    agonies "to a point where self-discovery may properly be-
    gin"; that is what distinguishes him from Wright and Elli-
    son. Nobody Knows, The Fire, Go Tell It, and Another
    Country contribute to "clarifying the question of the
    racial impact upon American self-identity." Another Coun-
    try goes further, for it includes whites in the desperate
    struggle of "going the whole way toward seeing and knowing
    and loving"; thus, humanness matters above all else.

43 Howard, Jane. "Doom and Glory of Knowing Who You Are." Life,
    24 May, pp. 86B, 88-90.
        Describes several of Baldwin's personal habits and be-
    haviors and reports on interviewing him about biography,
    fiction, lecturing, etc. He talks about the influence of
    Dostoevski and Dickens.

44 Howe, Irving. "Black Boys and Native Sons." Dissent, 10
    (Autumn), 353-68.

Cites Baldwin's essay, "Everybody's Protest Novel," as
the start of his literary career. His criticism of the
conventional Negro novel expounded his polemic against
Wright and the "school of naturalistic protest fiction."
Years later, he wrote that he hoped to prevent himself from
becoming "merely a Negro or even, merely a Negro writer."
In Notes, Baldwin's position "evades, through rhetorical
sweep, the genuinely difficult issue of the relationship
between social experience and literature"; yet he does
profess that "one writes out of one thing only--one's own
experience." Go Tell It shows the Negro world in its diversity and richness, not as a "mere spectre of protest."
Giovanni's Room seems to be a "flat failure"; it abandons
Negro life and focuses upon the problem of homosexuality
with a "disconcerting kind of sentimentalism." Another
Country is a "protest novel"; the material is handled in a
manner reminiscent of "Wright's naturalism"; the narrative
voice is one of anger. The Fire has reached "heights of
passionate exhortation unmatched in modern American writing." He has "secured his place as one of the two or
three greatest essayists this country has ever produced."

45 Howe, Irving. "Black Boys and Native Sons." In his A World
    More Attractive. New York: Horizon, pp. 98-122.
        Reprint of 1963.44.

46 Howe, Irving. "The Writer and the Critic--An Exchange: A
    Reply to Ralph Ellison." New Leader, 47 (3 February),
    12-14.
        Argues that the differences described by Ellison in "The
    World and the Jug" are not what he makes them out to be.
    Howe contends that Ellison has "wildly twisted the meaning"
    of what he wrote, but he does not impute "malice to him."
    Howe's central theme of the essay, "Black Boys and Native
    Sons," was this: Baldwin rebelled against Wright's protest
    stance and insisted that Negro life "could be portrayed
    with greater richness and affection." Baldwin's claim to
    humanity was through "an act of personal realization";
    Wright insisted upon struggle and militancy. Howe then
    tried to show the "literary consequences" of each writer's
    views; his approach was "analytic, not exhoratory; descrip-
    tive, not prescriptive." Howe charges Ellison with "making
    up" certain statements without precise quotations to back
    up the allegations, e.g., Howe has "urged Negro writers not
    to become too interested in the problems of literature."
    Howe further points out a serious misrepresentation by
    Ellison regarding the nature of the "real Negro experience"
    as being "unrelieved suffering"; Howe cites his original
    quote, which states that "plight and protest are insepa-
    rable from Negro experience, not the whole of it." Elli-

son seems to fear that calling his novel a "protest novel"
(which in part it is) is somehow denigrating. To say that
Invisible Man is a "notable protest novel" is far from saying that is all it is; it ranks with the most honorable of
company--Dickens, Dreiser, Melville, and even Wright.

47   Jackson, Katherine G.   "Books in Brief."   Harper's, 226
     (March), 118.
         Praises The Fire as a "compassionate and eloquent ser-
     mon for our time" that explains in passion, poetry, hate,
     and love what it means to be a Negro in America.

48   La Farge, John.   "Freedom Is an Unfinished Business."   Sat R,
     46 (2 February), 28-29.
         Observes that it is difficult for white Americans to
     divest themselves of a notion that somehow they are in pos-
     session of some intrinsic value that blacks need, or want.
     It is this idea that makes the "solution to the Negro
     problem" dependent upon how fast Negroes accept and adopt
     white standards.   It was the treatment Negroes received
     during World War II that marked the turning point in the
     Negro's relation to Americans.   Simply speaking, a feeling
     for white Americans faded; they began to be pitied or hated.
     What about the black man, fighting for the defense of his
     country, yet called "nigger" by his comrades?   What about
     prisoners of war being treated with more human dignity than
     the black American?   What happens to this black citizen
     when he returns home and sees the segregated buses, rest
     rooms?   Baldwin expresses in "downright, earthy language"
     what it means to be an American Negro in a white society
     that only vaguely grasps the meaning of the Emancipation
     Proclamation.

49   Lamming, G.   "The Dark Challenge."   Spectator, 211 (12 July),
     58-59.
         Compares the American Negro's plight to the Cold War--
     the "unholy reign of ice where tensions reverberate," and
     where the specific person-enemy may be absent but all the
     events are proof of his existence.   The Fire makes these
     events more vivid; yet there is an insistence that the
     country is capable of achieving a change "which is neces-
     sary for its liberation from the racial myths which still
     obscure and limit its vision of a creative freedom for all
     its citizens."   This is an enormous challenge, but it can
     also offer an opportunity for unique, self-renewal.

50   Leaks, Sylvester.   "James Baldwin--I Know His Name."   Freedom-
     ways, 3 (Winter), 102-105.
         Criticizes Baldwin for failing to "seriously come to
     grips with 'the Negro question' in his writings."   Notes is

1963

an especially revealing work, for it shows that Baldwin has
"effected a truce" with "those forces that Afro-Americans
have been fighting all their lives." Is a truce the best
thing blacks can hope for? Does the word struggle have any
meaning for him as a black writer? The "resistance to oppression" is something that he refuses to see in his Negro
characters; this is genuinely evident in Go Tell It and
Another Country. It is in his novels that he "fails most";
he seems to have "studied too much English and not enough
people--especially black people."

51 Levant, Howard. "Aspiraling We Should Go." Midcontinent
American Studies Journal, 4 (Fall), 3-20.
        Questions whether or not it is as easy "to spiral" as it
used to be. The spirit of the age is ambiguous, and American selfness has retained "sanity by achieving non-involve-
ment." Americans seem "unwilling" to engage in political,
social, or economic experiments; thus their lives are full
of despair. The implications of this condition are overwhelming to the Negro problem, discouraging to the Negro
finding a way to create himself. The literature that Negroes have been producing in the past few years "reflects
and clarifies the situation." Two of the more significant
writers are Baldwin and Ellison--"makers of prose, the har-
sher, cruder harmony." The essays of Baldwin are more impressive than his novels; his treatment is analytical,
whereas Ellison's is "pictorial." Baldwin's style is "con-
voluted" given to "backtracking, qualifying phrases," while
Ellison's is "precise and unencumbered." Baldwin's "moral
force" of having identified himself permits him to see
everyman--he deals with the human condition. Perhaps he
has "won an insight" that even few whites have gained about
themselves. His moral force refuses to allow him to accept
hopelessness. Notes advances his definition of identity by
using precise language and objectivity; there is the freeing from the "distortion of propaganda." He makes the artistic assumption that lines of communication must exist;
therefore, the "masterful rhetoric," the "tightly parallel
clauses," permit the logic of the work aesthetically to
"break through." If there is any spiral, onward and up-
ward, in an age that has achieved a seemingly ultimate barbarism, "it is alive in Baldwin's implicit belief that
white people are worth bothering with."

52 McCudden, John. "James Baldwin's Vision." Commonweal
(11 October), pp. 75-76.
        Accuses James Finn, in his recent article on Baldwin's
vision, "of missing the point and misrepresenting Baldwin's

thoughts." Finn's reproach of Baldwin for turning the white
man into "the invisible man," not seeing who he really is,
lacks credibility. He fails to see that the question is:
Who or what is the white man, really? For Baldwin, he is
the man who has mistreated Negroes throughout history. If
Finn does not like the picture, "let him blame the white
man, not Baldwin." Also, Finn criticizes Baldwin for not
writing on the race problem as he (Finn) would: calmly,
judiciously, objectively. Perhaps this is a subject on
which Finn can "afford to be calm and judicious; Baldwin
cannot." He does say over and over that there can be no
separation from the problems of growing up black and growing up to be a man. He believes that white and black men
must build the future of the country/together; this is his
compassionate response to the race question, and it certainly is not lacking in "idealism" as Finn accuses him.

53 MacInnes, Colin. "Dark Angel: The Writings of James Baldwin." Encounter, 21 (August), 22-33.
    Predicts that even a century from now, Baldwin's works
will be discussed since his style is classic and his theme
"one of the most relevant." His "life-death-passion-honour-
beauty-horror" theme has been central since the Greeks. He
has written both novels and essays; he is a "premonitory
prophet, . . . a soothsayer, a bardic voice falling on deaf
and delighted ears." These qualities seem to emerge more
in his essays than in his novels. Go Tell It is a "densely
packed, ominous, sensual, doom ridden story," with a language that is "marvellously economical, accurate, and revealing." Giovanni's Room portrays whites so "successfully"
that one might say it was written by a white, yet it seems
to be a "melodrama." This defect may arise from Baldwin's
own ambiguity in his attitude about homosexuality. Another
Country is the least overtly personal novel, and perhaps
the "least successful." The worthy theme centers on the
uniting of blacks and whites, but the book is "much too
bulky for what it has to say." The "immense amount of
dialogue" is simply "dull." Notes, Nobody Knows, and The
Fire have a recurrent theme--race. The tone of the essays
is "taut, ironic, authoritative and double edged" with "a
natural dignity, a sadly acid wit, and an enormous . . .
humanity."

54 McNabb, Jim. "Baldwin and Friends." National Review, 15
(16 July), 31.
    States that Garry Wills (author of "What Color Is God?")
is another defender of Baldwin.

1963

55 Mailer, Norman. "Norman Mailer vs. Nine Writers." Esquire,
     60 (July), 63-69.
         Praises Baldwin as an essayist because "not one of us
     hasn't learned something about the art of the essay from
     him," but calls Another Country, with its protagonist of
     sex, "closest to the mood of New York in our time" and
     "almost a major novel and yet it is far and away the weak-
     est and worst near-major novel one has finished." The
     directness and urgency of the essays will not substitute
     as "characters, milieu, and mood for the revelation of im-
     portant complexities" in fiction; the novel is an amateur
     expedition "into the privacy of the Self."

56 Maloff, Saul. "Love: The Movement Within." Nation, 196
     (2 March), 181-82.
         Indicates that although The Fire is only "one hundred
     small pages," its intrinsic and singular value "triumphant-
     ly justified its publication"--it is a "document in the
     chronicle of the human spirit." The work serves as a sum-
     mation of much of the writer's thoughts fused violently to-
     gether into a single statement--a credo, a manifesto; Bald-
     win seems to say "here is where I stand." There is no
     analysis of the Negro question, for he is a novelist, not
     a sociologist. He seeks to analyze an internal state of
     feeling, the "furious conviction, the indignities and
     humiliations" of what it is like to be a Negro. The Fire
     is a "tract-for-the-times," not an agreement in the usual
     sense.

57 Mayfield, Julian. "And Then Came Baldwin." Freedomways, 3
     (Spring), 143-55.
         Analyzes some of the comments about Baldwin especially
     from various "black intellectuals." Much of the reaction
     has been negative, sometimes "couched in extreme, almost
     violent language." The two topics frequently used "as wea-
     pons" by his detractors are "his critical and commercial
     success, and the use of the homosexual theme." Many mili-
     tant black intellectuals assert that he is ignorant of eco-
     nomics, history, and politics, but for the most part these
     are superficial views of Baldwin and the society in which
     he functions. He has raised vital social issues since he
     returned from Europe even though he has also made a point
     of disavowing protest writing. His outstanding achievement
     can best be summed up in saying that he has captured, in
     "beautiful, passionate, and persuasive prose the essence of
     Negro determination to live in the American house as a free
     man. . . ." He, almost alone, still talks to whites with
     "love and compassion," offering them "a way out, if only
     they will listen."

58 Mergen, Bernard. "James Baldwin and the American Conundrum."
    Moderna Sprak, 57 (December), 397-405.
        Recounts some biographical events of Baldwin's life be-
    fore entering on a discussion of him. Notes attempts to
    define the "nature of Negro-white relations in the United
    States without resorting to popular myths or platitudes."
    The Fire employs terms more familiar to an American anthro-
    pologist than to a literary critic. He resembles the his-
    torian and autobiographer, Henry Adams; both have been con-
    cerned with "the acquisition and the use of power," and
    both have been "aware of the importance of the past in shap-
    ing the present." At first glance, Go Tell It seems to
    have little in common with the essays, but it is concerned
    with the nature of "religious experience" and is linked
    with the ever-present theme of "prediction and control."
    Both Giovanni's Room and Another Country attempt "to define
    and measure the nature and intensity of love." Baldwin's
    place in contemporary literature is "unique"; his assault
    on the "status quo through his novels" and essays "is
    vigorous and profound."

59 Merideth, Robert. "The Revival of Uncle Tom's Cabin." Phylon
    (Fall), pp. 300-302.
        Sees a revival in the reading of Uncle Tom's Cabin, but
    claims it is still "universally misunderstood." The Negro
    revolt that began in the 1950s has "forced a revaluation of
    the Negro as a human being." Baldwin's essay, "Everybody's
    Protest Novel," calls Uncle Tom's Cabin a "very bad novel,"
    having as the mark of its "dishonesty" a "self-righteous,
    virtuous sentimentality." Mrs. Stowe is seen as "over-
    looking, denying, evading" the complexity of Negroes. But
    perhaps Baldwin has misread the book and does not realize
    the "true message" and purpose of the book. The revival of
    the novel can also be attributed to the Civil War Centen-
    nial and a new interest in slavery and abolition. Also,
    the revival may be related to the "attack on liberalism"
    and the new movement for liberals to unite. Finally, the
    book is being revived because of a positive interest in
    American literature, especially before World War II.

60 Meriwether, L. M. "James Baldwin: Fiery Voice of the Negro
    Revolt." Negro Digest, 12 (August), 3-7.
        Quotes from a statement by Baldwin that eventually
    everyone must pay his dues, but that does not mean that the
    Negro must continue to pay the white man's dues. The Fire
    "entrenched him firmly as the angry young voice of the New
    Negro." For him society is made by man and can be remade
    by man, but the price is high. Both blacks and whites will
    have to move "toward maturity," an embrace "based on mutual

love and respect," and upon the "true history of the Negro's
role in America and not upon myth."

61 Merton, Thomas. "The Negro Revolt." Jubilee (September),
    pp. 39-43.
       Cites the works of William Melvin Kelley, Jonathan Wil-
    liams, and Baldwin to illustrate the message of American
    Negro writers today--the Negro needs to recover his belief
    in his own autonomous reality; he needs to get the "white
    man, spritually and psychologically, off his back." The
    Negro revolution is real; it is ultimately part of man's
    salvation. There is one Kairos for everybody, and if the
    white man can open his heart to listen to what the Negro is
    now hearing, he too will be called to freedom. The real
    tragedy is that the white man does not recognize that he is
    actually "the victim of the same servitude" he has imposed
    on the Negro. The Fire carries the message that it is the
    Negro who hears the "true voice of God in history . . .,"
    and that his days of tragedy are over. "He has awakened
    and taken his destiny into his own hands."

62 Moon, Eric. "Social Science." LJ, 88 (15 February), 787.
       Praises the essay "Down at the Cross" in The Fire as
    "part autobiographical, part philosophical--Baldwin's best
    blend"--and exhibiting the belief in the futility of a
    complete separation of the races.

63 Nichols, Charles H. "James Baldwin: A Skillful Executioner."
    Studies on the Left, 2 (Winter), 74-79.
       Quotes a reviewer who had written that a reader of
    Baldwin has as much "choice about how to respond as he
    would to a skillful executioner." The emotional intensity
    of Baldwin's writing is the direct result of his calculated
    effect. His "bitter honesty" and "truth" are a pose, in-
    volving considerable art. This pose is especially apparent
    in Another Country, where his "favorite themes" are pre-
    sented with less "brash assault" than in Go Tell It or
    Giovanni's Room. His novels seem to grow out of a "smoul-
    dering rage, an hysterical sensitivity, a fear so unbear-
    able it clutches at destruction, and a guilt that begs for
    doom." The apocalyptic vision in Go Tell It has the trauma
    of a bad dream, but the work manifests "discriminating in-
    telligence" as well as an artful form of expression where
    "every detail is invested with immediacy and life." Gio-
    vanni's Room is also "a bad dream" of anguished recollec-
    tions; it lacks a sense of "social reality." Notes and
    Nobody Knows are writings of an "uncanny and disturbing
    intelligence"; his personal accounts of racial discrimina-
    tion are unsurpassed in literature.

64 O'Daniel, Therman. "James Baldwin: An Interpretive Study."
    <u>CLAJ</u>, 7 (September), 37-47.
       States that although Baldwin has written a book with the
"deceptive title, <u>Nobody Knows</u>, his name is widely known
and highly respected." He has produced six successful
works: <u>Go Tell It</u>, <u>Notes</u>, <u>Giovanni's Room</u>, <u>Nobody Knows</u>,
<u>Another Country</u>, and <u>The Fire</u>. All of these works reveal
the talent and versatility of this remarkable author. He
is a very intelligent and deeply perceptive observer of
contemporary society, and he presents these observations
in a penetrating and dynamic manner. Also, he is a bold
and courageous writer who is unafraid "to search into the
dark corner" of society; he refuses to shy away from frank
discussions. His literary style consists of a crystal
clear and "passionately poetic rhythm." Although he states
to the contrary, Baldwin belongs to the same "school" as
Richard Wright, and is like him, in another way, in being
a "writer of protest."

65 Opton, Edward. "Baldwin and Friends." <u>National Review</u>, 15
    (16 July), 31.
       Notes that Wills ("What Color Is God?") criticizes Bald-
win's willingness to "scuttle the Constitution" yet misses
the point, which is that American Negroes do not enjoy the
benefits of the Constitution. "Whites read the words of
the Constitution; Negroes smell the practice of it," e.g.,
uncollected garbage, unpaved streets, wretched housing.
Saying "it could be worse" is no comfort to American
Negroes.

66 Plummer, Kenneth. "Baldwin's Burden." <u>Christian Century</u>, 80
    (28 August), 1057.
       Writes in a letter that Baldwin is correct to be in-
terested in the problems of man, not in the problems of
civil rights as such. Baldwin's rejection of Christianity
appears rooted in his anger at the "church's distortion of
perception and communication, and therefore, its irrele-
vance." His commitment is to the realization of artistic
integrity, which is sidetracked by a commitment to racial
justice. Perhaps he does not ask the right question: "How
to understand the active power of God's grace in our
times."

67 Redding, J. Saunders. "Fiery Style But with It, Confusion."
    <u>New York Herald Tribune Books</u> (7 April), p. 7.
       Reviews <u>The Fire</u> in totality rather than as a "dozen
desperate theses" and posits its themes as 1) "if you want
to know what hell is, wake up black some morning," and 2)
"the Negro will endure if . . . he resists the awful

1963

temptation to return hate for hate." This has been said
many times before; the "brilliant display of stylistic
virtuosity" of The Fire needs "less manner and more matter."

68 Simmons, H. G. "James Baldwin and the Negro Conundrum."
    Antioch Review, 23 (Summer), 250-55.
        Examines some of the basic themes found in The Fire:
    acceptance of the proposition that life is dangerous; un-
    willingness of white Americans to accept the existence of
    evil; the masking of evil with a type of "peculiar inno-
    cence." Baldwin maintains that the Negro is a "key figure"
    in America; he criticizes the characterization of the Negro
    in Uncle Tom's Cabin and Native Son as either "super or
    sub-human," not as an American man. The problem of iden-
    tity, as well as the process of love, becomes central to
    his work--"love is the catalyst which precipitates and
    helps to reintegrate the shattered fragments of personality
    of those who are torn between detesting themselves because
    society tells them they are detestable. . . ." The only
    solution to the problem of identity then is love, for one-
    self and for others. The theme that Negroes are Americans
    runs through his work, and it is only when the Negro has
    confronted and accepted his past that he can know who he is
    and where he is going. Baldwin is one of the first to say
    that there is no easy way to do this, and this is the black
    man's dilemma.

69 Spender, Stephen. "James Baldwin: Voice of a Revolution."
    PR, 30 (Summer), 256-60.
        Affirms that Baldwin is more than the voice of American
    Negroes; he is also the "voice of an American consciousness
    (conscience) which is not Negro." As a writer, he has no
    color, but only "mind and feelings as they are realized in
    words." His power lies in his ability to express situa-
    tions--being a Negro, being a white, being a human. At
    times he is "too impatient" to be a good novelist, and of-
    ten his essays are "so colored with feelings" that he seems
    unable to relate the thoughts to other situations. Yet, he
    has made tremendous contributions as an American writer by
    finding "words to express what one knows to be true."
    Within his own work, "he has solved the problem of inte-
    gration; not by love, but by imagination using words which
    know no class nor color bars."

70 Stevenson, David L. "The Activist." Daedalus, 92 (Spring),
    238-49.
        Sees a special kind of novel having emerged in American
    fiction since the war with a "distinct and definable

identity of its own." The outlines of this new fiction
were first sketched in Bellow's Notes of a Dangling Man,
which is representative of the works of Walker Percy, Herbert Gold, Bernard Malamud, Monroe Engel, Philip Roth, and
Baldwin. Characteristically, this new fiction has little
of the formal structure associated with the American novel
of the first half of the century--no central character moving in a prescribed fashion, no sense that one episode in
time has a relationship to the next one, no attempt to create a "highly idiosyncratic rhetoric." This "activist fiction" is almost wholly concerned with the details of an
"energetic quest," an "aimless search through the endless
clutter of everyday existence for a sense of a privately
satisfying identity . . ." Another Country is written
within this "activist framework"; the heart of the novel is
the battle between the "active, eager self, Negro or white,
and its environment." The activists of Another Country are
not "solvers of their momentary problems, but men and women
solved by them."

71 Wakefield, Dan. "Disturbing Letters from a Native Son." New
    York Times Book Review (7 April), pp. 2-3.
        Describes the book, The Fire, as containing the elements
    of sermon, ultimatum, confession, deposition, testament,
    and chronicle, all in a "searing, brilliant prose"--a fit-
    ting work for the centennial of the Emancipation Proclama-
    tion. The work is comprised of two letters that are "de-
    signed to disturb as well as to engage and inform, and in
    all these respects, they succeed."

72 Whalen, Marcella, "Dear James Baldwin." National Review
    (13 August), p. 120.
        Cites Buckley's article, "Baldwin's Call to Color Blind-
    ness," as the stimulus for writing an open letter to Bald-
    win. The repeated harsh criticisms of New York have chal-
    lenged his "old English teacher" to remind him of the
    "happy experiences" at De Witt Clinton High School. Facul-
    ty members at the school wrote very positive "character
    cards" about him; surely not all of New York is completely
    hostile.

73 Williams, John A. "Problems of the Negro Writer: The Liter-
    ary Ghetto." Sat R, 20 (3 April), 21, 40.
        Contends that the labels used to describe a novel by a
    Negro (e.g., anger, hatred, rage, or protest) deprive the
    work of its concern for humankind. Labeling limits the ex-
    pansion of the talents of Negro writers and confines them
    to a "literary ghetto" from which only one name at a time

1963

may emerge. Today, it is Baldwin, and "Negro stuff is selling well!" This trend has been beneficial, but there is
still the comparison of their works, e.g., "he is in the
view of . . . and achieves a similar power." Such "bigo-
try" tells more about the reviewer than it does about the
book being reviewed.

74 Wills, Garry. "What Color Is God?" National Review, 14
(21 May), 408-17.
Presents Baldwin as "the most sensitive and discrimina-
ting articulator of Negro suffering" who also constructs an
intricate sympathy for the crudest kind of Negro racism
. . ." His indictment of Western civilization's religion
(of the "white God") is "carefully and consciously outrageous." The Fire falls into three major sections: 1) the
story of his struggle with his father, with God, and with
the white man; 2) his interview with Muhammad; 3) the
"parading" of all the "liberal clichés in their pristine
naiveté." Despite all the contrived effects and stridency,
Notes is intensely moving, having a "seismic effect whose
tremors are not even beginning to subside." Go Tell It,
Giovanni's Room, and Another Country have an "uncanny"
background of music transmitted along with the words, a
"moaning and keening of spirituals." In an interview in
the New Yorker, Baldwin has accused white Americans of not
believing in the things their religion, civilization, and
country stand for; they have been living an elaborate life.
Christianity has done nothing for the Negro; yet (according
to Wills) it is the only thing that can "keep the Negro,
and the white man as well, from despairing." Granted that
the Christian ethic can be used to deceive man; the "church
rackets" can "steal food from the body," but when the test
is applied over and over to Christianity, it emerges victorious. "God is colorless, no matter how many Christians
are white."

1964

1 Allen, Walter. "War and Post War: America." In his The
Modern Novel in Britain and the United States. New York:
E. P. Dutton, pp. 320-21.
Lauds Go Tell It as concentrating on the religious aspect of Negro experience, rather than racial, against a
historical background emerging from the experience of slavery and injustice.

2 ANON. "American Gothic." Time, 6 November, pp. 108-10.

Indicates why photographer Richard Avedon collaborated with his old high-school classmate to "expose the corruption in American life" (Nothing Personal). Although the pictures are a "chilling, engrossing display of ferocity," Baldwin's brief text is "oddly irrelevant, obviously hasty, too often drawn on by his sheer flow of language into shrill overstatement."

3 ANON. "Anger and Guilt." Newsweek, 4 May, p. 46.
Categorizes Baldwin as "a hero, a prophet, a great essayist, a routine novelist, and an inept playwright." Although the play Blues seemed to be a "liberating act for its creator," it is an "imprisoning one" for the audience; it is "crude, belligerent, naive, constructed out of unassimilated grievances and untransformed pain." He has taken "abstractions of interracial situations" and has thrown a "net of quarter-truths and outright myths."

4 ANON. "Baldwin." PMLA, 79 (May), 202.
Presents annual secondary bibliography for 1963.

5 ANON. "Baldwin Hits Mallory Case." Muhammad Speaks, (31 January), p. 2.
Reports on Baldwin's efforts to raise money for the Monroe (N.C.) Non-Violent Action Committee in its defense of four individuals (including Mae Mallory) accused of kidnaping in a civil rights case but never brought to trial.

6 ANON. "Blues for Mister Charlie: Baldwin's Drama Roars with a Spirit of Negro Revolt." Ebony, 19 (June), 188-93.
Qualifies Baldwin's dramatic efforts of "eloquence and outrage" by indicating some of the "inevitable shortcomings" of Blues, a "first try." Yet he has accomplished what he intended--to "electrify his audiences, outrage them, and create controversy." Some critics have called the play a "hymn of hate" making unfair stereotypes of whites and magnifying the wrongs done to the American Negro. Generally, however, such contentions have been confined to white observers. Negroes, as well as many whites, have been unanimous in their praise.

7 ANON. "Dark Exposure." TLS (10 December), p. 1122.
Describes Nothing Personal as a "terrifying and deeply moving book." Part of the work consists of Avedon's photographs; the other part consists of Baldwin's "prose sermons." The result is "obscene"; a set of pictures, "immediate in their impact," that make the reader feel like a "voyeur catching glimpses of some peculiarly intense hell." The

1964

text documents the pictures with a claim that "America is
a land where 'no one is happy.'" Yet, despite the stirring
text and powerful glossy pictures, it seems to be a "dishonest work." It is dishonest to perpetuate "long exploded
myths" and to have onesided "representations of euphoric
affluence against which it protests so vehemently."

8 ANON. "James Baldwin." In Current Biography Yearbook, 1964.
Edited by Charles Moritz. New York: H. W. Wilson, pp.
22-24.
Begins the biographical sketch with the statement: "The
American Negro revolution claims as perhaps its most artic-
ulate spokesman the writer James Baldwin . . ." His main
thesis is that "what happens to the Negro, happens also to
everyone else in a society and that the victims of segregation are the white people because the myth of white supremacy prevents them from facing their own weaknesses." He
has the ability to "put the white man in the shoes of the
colored man," and this ability has been recognized as one
of the outstanding merits of his novels and his plays.

9 ANON. "James Baldwin Book Should Be Dropped: School Aide."
Chicago Daily News (21 December), p. 33.
Reports on the request by the Chicago Board of Education
to remove Another Country from the required reading list of
a literature course at Wright Junior College. The dean of
the college upheld the teacher's right to select the in-
structional material for his class. He declined to remove
it from the list even though "parts of the book deal with
homosexuality and interracial relationships."

10 ANON. "Of Hurt and Hate." Time, 1 May, p. 50.
Contends that Blues "sabotages most of its own good purposes." It means to be an "eloquent cry from the heart of
the Negro's hurt" but "spends itself showering rhetorical
spleen on the white man." Instead of seizing the playgoer's
conscience, it only grabs his lapel. It strives to be new
and fresh, but its story is overly familiar. Baldwin is
capable of far more intelligent reflections on the racial
question and the "universal fate of being human."

11 ANON. "Racial Issues in U.S. Drama through Negro Eyes: Broadway View of the South." Time, 9 June, p. 14.
Asserts that Blues is "more a lesson than a drama" that
oversimplifies the racist Southern white and uses superficial dramatic techniques in order to indict Negro-white
relations in the South, and that resembles closely Sartre's
The Respected Prostitute.

12 ANON. "Richard Avedon and James Baldwin." <u>Newsweek</u>,
   26 October, p. 122.
    Shows the intense and sensitive relationship between the
   "chic, diamond-brilliant fashion photographer," Avedon, and
   the "bitterly passionate rhapsodist," Baldwin. <u>Nothing
   Personal</u> presents their shared sensitivity to "the masks
   and gestures, the public charades, which mask the private
   person."

13 ANON. "Sisters under Their Skins." <u>Time</u>, 5 June, p. 96.
    Describes <u>Blues</u> as a hard play for a white man to take.
   "Brutally and sometimes eloquently, it tells every white
   man how much every Negro hates him . . ." Two young sisters saw the play, both daughters of Governor Nelson Rocke-
   feller, and they donated $5,000 apiece to keep the play go-
   ing. What probably moved the sisters was a "raging solilo-
   quy" by Diana Sands.

14 Beja, Morris. "It Must Be Important: Negroes in Contemporary
   American Fiction." <u>Antioch Review</u>, 24 (Fall), 333-36.
    Recounts a statement by Sterling Brown in 1937: "the
   treatment of the Negro in American fiction, since it parallels his treatment in American life, has naturally been
   noted for injustice." A quarter of a century later, this is
   still an accurate picture; the stereotypes are all too
   familiar. There has been an increased tendency of current
   writers to suggest the plight of American Negro through
   "the image of emasculation." Baldwin's use of this image
   is likely to be ambiguous. <u>Blues</u> and <u>Another Country</u> have
   the black man reflecting "how nice it would be to go 'where
   a man could be treated like a man.'"

15 Blaisdel, Gus. "A Literary Assessment: James Baldwin, the
   Writer." <u>Negro Digest</u>, 13 (January), 61-68.
    Begins with a quote from Whitman, "I am the man, I suf-
   fered, I was there." Baldwin has had the "audacious tena-
   city" to explore and attack two very sacred "totems," sex
   and color, with a "revolutionary attitude" and with the
   "tenderness, integrity, love and courage" befitting his
   care for America. For him, the unexamined life is not
   worth living; he seeks to reevaluate the institutions of
   America in terms of <u>himself</u>, not in the terms laid down by
   society as constituting his <u>self</u>. <u>Giovanni's Room</u> and
   <u>Another Country</u> explore the problems of color and sex; <u>The
   Fire</u> is a "tough, grim book" with a message of love. His
   works embody the dilemmas of people the same way Camus'
   have done. "Perhaps, in the future, America will be very
   proud of having produced a black replica of Camus."

1964

16 Boyle, Kay. "Introducing James Baldwin." In <u>Contemporary</u>
    <u>American Novelists</u>. Edited by Harry T. Moore. Carbondale,
    Ill.: Southern Illinois University Press, pp. 155-57.
        Introduces Baldwin by recalling his own introduction
    when he said that "at the root of the American Negro prob-
    lem is the necessity of the American white man to find a
    way of living with the Negro in order to be able to live
    with himself." His artistic struggle for integrity "must
    be considered as a kind of metaphor for the struggle which
    is universal and daily in the lives of all human beings on
    the face of the globe to become and remain human beings."
    His writing has brought a "new climate, a new element, a
    new season" to the foreground of America's awareness. "The
    breadth of his vision and the tenacity of his belief in man
    offer . . . a far better national reality" than has ever
    been known.

17 Brower, Brock. "Of Nothing But Facts." <u>American Scholar</u>, 33
    (Autumn), 613.
        Starts with a quote from a Dickens novel: "In this life,
    we want nothing but Facts." It is an increasingly factual
    existence that permeates today's "Hard Times"; and now, a
    type of "literature of fact" has emerged. <u>The Fire</u> is not
    just <u>about</u> facts; it is <u>with</u> facts. This approach may have
    opened the doors for a "false literature" to be let loose,
    written by hacks with a killing touch. Facts may be forced
    into a "put-up literary job for the sake of melodrama, in-
    stead of enlightenment." This nonsense has no place in any
    sound literature of fact, but is important to understand
    why such "odd trash" (instant biography, nonfiction novels)
    is now appearing. Present society has contributed to this
    move: "a society of manners has given way to a society of
    procedures." Hence the fictional world of manners has been
    transformed to the more decisive world of procedures in
    "fixing the fate of men in a functional society."

18 Brustein, Robert. "Everybody Knows My Name." <u>New York Review</u>
    <u>of Books</u>, 3 (17 December), 10-11.
        Condemns <u>Nothing Personal</u>, photography by Avedon and
    text by Baldwin, as a superfluous nonbook exhibiting "an
    honorable tradition of revolt gone sour." Baldwin's prose
    signifies "the further degeneration of a once courageous
    and beautiful dissent" because of its rage inspired by op-
    portunism, its ambiguous use of "we," its contorted grammar,
    its "incredible self-inflation," its opiates and clichés.
    The author is "merely a self-constituted Symbol, bucking
    hard for the rank of Legend."

19 Brustein, Robert. "Everybody's Protest Play." New Republic,
      150 (16 May), 35-37.
          Plays on Baldwin's essay, "Everybody's Protest Novel,"
      and shows how Blues is the "embodiment of everything he
      once professed to deplore." The play is a work of "'notori-
      ously bloodthirsty' propaganda of the crudest sort, with
      little existence either as truth, literature, or life." It
      is a play to "gouge the eyes of the audience." Over the
      years Baldwin has changed his concept of himself so that
      now he has become "an Official Spokesman for a Cause." No
      doubt the material for Blues (the Emmett Till case) is al-
      most "automatically destined to be a melodrama." The most
      disappointing thing about the play appears to be its "moral
      and intellectual deficiency" as well as its "aesthetic
      flatness."

20 Cassidy, Claudia. "Baldwin's New Play: Abuse with Tom-Toms."
      Books Today, Chicago Sunday Tribune, 10 May, p. 5.
          Begins with a poignant statement regarding Blues:
      "Strange that from so tragic a mask, confronted by so
      hideous a spectacle, should come so hollow an oracle." The
      play is "little more than a torrent of abuse, obsessed, in-
      coherent, and obscene." There is a sense of unreality
      throughout the play, and the characters are mere carica-
      tures.

21 Ciardi, John. "Choose Something Like a Star." Sat R, 47
      (11 January), 16.
          Poses a series of questions about Another Country, e.g.,
      do any of the characters like one another? does everyone
      lust for the bodies of Negroes? is love always "tooth-and-
      claw" warfare? Although the critics have tended to be "es-
      pecially generous" to Baldwin, is this praise a "Whole
      praise"? An artist, whatever his color or creed, must be
      "committed to all men."

22 Clarke, John Henrik. "The Alienation of James Baldwin."
      Journal of Human Relations, 12 (First/Quarter), 30-33.
          Sees The Fire as Baldwin's success in "restoring the per-
      sonal essay to its place as a form of creative literature."
      From his "narrow vantage point of personal grievance, he
      has opened a window on the world." He is highly regarded
      as an intellectual and as the "most honored Negro writer
      since Richard Wright." Yet he has not created a single
      Negro character "who attains stature in a fight against
      his condition." There is also no evidence of his aware-
      ness of the economic base for oppression. These are

1964

"serious limitations in a man hailed by many as the spokesman for his people."

23 Clurman, Harold. "Blues for Mister Charlie." Nation, 198
    (1 May), 495-96.
        Contends that the plot of Blues is "somewhat novelistic
    or Faulknerian" in fashion. The thematic material is com-
    posed of many of Baldwin's thoughts on this country's in-
    terracial problems. Although the play has much "crude
    propaganda," it still has "the Baldwin touch," and the ex-
    cellent acting gives "value" to the text.

24 Cohen, Nathan, "A Flawed Talent." National Review, 16
    (8 September), 780-81.
        Contends that only "someone with an undisputed and high
    literary talent could write a play as nearly worthless, and
    yet as important" as Blues. Baldwin has no sense of thea-
    trical character; his characters are stereotypes. He is
    insensitive to the demands of construction, modulation,
    pace, and climax; time is "hopelessly jumbled." Yet, in
    spite of the absurdities and flaws, in his command of lang-
    uage Baldwin is telling white people what Negroes think of
    them, and "what he says is a desperate, frustrated, angry
    message."

25 Coles, Robert. "Baldwin's Burden." PR, 31 (Summer), 409-16.
        Argues that many novelists of today might be called
    "literary social scientists" since they spend so much ener-
    gy on descriptions of social struggles, cultural changes,
    or "clinical psychopathology." Characters tend to be il-
    lustrative of social conditions; they are used as a way for
    a "meticulous study" of various groups and problems. Bald-
    win "translates his own adolescent agony into the hate in
    all Negroes for whites" and then predicts the "white man's
    inevitable doom unless he learns . . . a new way of getting
    along with the Negro." He tends to portray the Negro as a
    kind of "natural man," an outsider; he simultaneously wants
    civil rights for this "natural man." His dilemma, then, is
    that he is demanding acceptance by a country denounced as
    worthless.

26 Collier, Eugenia W. "The Phrase Unbearably Repeated." Phy-
    lon, 25 (Fall), 288-96.
        Attests to the fact that Another Country has something
    "offensive" for everyone; it is brutal and violent, but be-
    neath the violence and brutality there is a tenderness--"a
    hurting compassion." It is not just about race or sex, "it
    is a novel about the individual's lonely and futile quest

for love." Each character has lost his "sense of self,"
and seeks to remedy this situation in the arms of another.
However, the characters remain essentially isolated for the
contemporary mores make their relationships unacceptable,
e.g., black-white, homosexual. Thus, the isolation becomes
a devastating loneliness, a theme ever-pervasive in the novel. From the cold, hostile New York landscape to the "low-
down blues" crying from a saxophone, Baldwin presents man's
desperate need for love. The question repeated throughout
the novel is: "Do you love me?" And the answer is, "I
can't!" The profound suffering revealed in blues music
gives significance to one's basic emotions--those fundamental feelings that are buried deep, not remembered, until a
strain of music releases them. These same blues give "eco-
nomy and realism" to the character's language and actions,
for the music presents the desolation of a situation, the
emptiness of a relationship, the agony of silence, and the
tragedy of a futile quest. Thus, "it is largely through
the medium of music" that Baldwin reveals the victimizing
of personal and social forces that one cannot control.

27 Cooley, Margaret. "Social Science." LJ, 89 (15 December),
    4925.
        Denounces Nothing Personal as an "exploitative work" of
    "the stupidities, miseries, and sorrows of this world" es-
    pecially the United States. Baldwin's text is a "bitter,
    scornful and hating . . . compendium of beautifully phrased
    clichés, pompous pronouncements and . . . outrageous gene-
    ralizations." Avedon's photographs are generally "beauti-
    ful, cynical and invasive" and most pander to "our preju-
    dices or commitments."

28 Cox, C. B. and A. R. Jones. "After the Tranquillized Fifties:
    Notes on Sylvia Plath and James Baldwin." Critical Quar-
    terly, 6 (Summer), 107-22.
        Comments on the poetry of Sylvia Plath and compares her
    process of "moving into new and disturbingly unusual terri-
    tories of the mind" to Baldwin's in Another Country. There
    is a concern with violence and neurotic breakdown as well
    as new areas of experience that makes Another Country very
    different from the literature of the 1950s. It is sugges-
    ted that security, order, and common sense are illusions,
    and only those who submit themselves to "the mystery and
    chaos of their emotions are truly alive." Sex involves an
    "entry into an unknown violent country"; thus, to live and
    to perceive reality means submission to suffering and chaos
    --a universal condition. Only a few have the courage to
    face their own identities. It may be that this "return to

1964

violence and perversity" is reminiscent of romanticism in
its sub-literary Gothic phase (e.g., Frankenstein, Udolpho).
Novelists whose main concern is violence and morbidity
"mirror an age in which the predominant feeling is one of
being overwhelmed by irrational forces." The irrationality
that seems to overwhelm man comes "not from without but
from within"--the individual, "the urge toward order" in
direct conflict with the individual subconsciousness.

29 Driver, Tom F. "Blues for Mister Charlie: The Review That
    Was Too True to Be Published." Negro Digest, 13
    (September), 34-40.
        Reprints a review that The Reporter refused to publish
    and that subsequently led to Driver's resignation. Blues
    is praised for its acting, production, and content. Bald-
    win has stepped outside of the usual context in which most
    Americans see the racial struggle as a constitutional ques-
    tion of civil rights and has taken what may seem like a re-
    actionary step. He describes racial strife as being rooted
    in the separate ways people experience life, "the differ-
    ence symbolized in their sexuality." Thus, he opened him-
    self to the attacks that he has "swallowed the myth of Ne-
    gro sexual superiority, and his characters are caricatures."
    Yet his portrayal of small-town Southern whites is the
    "most accurate" ever seen in America. "What the play sins
    against is not the reality down South but the social (hence
    aesthetic) myths up North." Although Baldwin is no Brecht,
    "the temper of the play is Brechtian but not Marxist"; it
    avoids both comedy and tragedy; it is a call to action ra-
    ther than an imitation of action. The social significance
    of Blues lies in what it reveals about one's fear of fear:
    "Those who cannot risk when they are afraid . . . will be
    made impotent by their fear."

30 Elkoff, Marvin. "Everybody Knows His Name." Esquire, 62
    (August), 59-64, 120-23.
        Reports on meetings and conversations with and among
    Baldwin, his family, and friends, and affords excellent
    glimpses of the author as conversationalist, writer, drama-
    tist, and civil rights activist during the time of the re-
    hearsals for the play, Blues. In spite of describing Bald-
    win as "a truth-teller, not a truth-seeker" who asserts his
    point of view "emotionally, like a prophet," the essay ac-
    knowledges Baldwin as the person who has had the greatest
    "impact on the entire white liberal world."

31 Ellison, Ralph. "The World and the Jug." In his Shadow and
    Act. New York: Random House, pp. 107-43.
        Reprint of 1963.26 and 1964.32.

82

32 Ellison, Ralph. "The Writer and the Critic--An Exchange: A
    Rejoinder." New Leader, 47 (3 February), 15-22.
        Apologizes to Howe for getting the impression that "bean-
    balls" were being thrown at him, when only "hyperbole" was
    meant. Ellison still feels, though, that Howe approves of
    "angry Negro writers only until one positions his ideas;
    then he reaches for his honor" and uses such terms as "mis-
    representation" and "distortions." Ellison contends that
    Howe's essay, "Black Boys and Native Sons," is not just a
    "collection of thematically related fragments" but a "lite-
    rary exposition" of a person's point of view. Thus, Elli-
    son tried to interpret the essay in terms of the impact it
    had upon his sense of life and literature. It is evident
    that Howe is interested in "militant confrontation and suf-
    fering," yet he fails to recognize either when it involves
    some act of his own. Many who write of Negro life today
    seem to assume that "as long as their hearts are in the
    right place, they can be as arbitrary as they wish in their
    formulations." Others feel they can vent their "most pri-
    vate Freudian fantasies." Thus "prefabricated Negroes are
    sketched on sheets of paper and superimposed upon the Negro
    community." But if someone thrusts his head through the
    page and yells, "Watch out . . . there're people living
    here," these writers are shocked and indignant. The intent
    of Ellison's original reply to Howe was to question his pre-
    sumptions regarding American social reality. As a writer,
    Ellison also was conscious of the need to maintain a "cer-
    tain level of precision in language, a maximum correspon-
    dence between . . . a piece of writing and its content, and
    between word and ideas and the thing and processes of the
    world." Howe apparently does not see that "the meaning
    which emerges from his essay is not determined by isolated
    statements." Perhaps he needs to examine some of the mean-
    ings he gives to the word "Negro," e.g., "stigma," "sterile
    category." Howe makes of "Negroness" a "metaphysical con-
    dition, one that is a state of irremediable agony which all
    but engulfs the mind." It appears that Howe's strategy of
    bringing Ellison into the "public quarrel between Baldwin
    and Wright was inept."

33 Ford, Nick Aaron. "The Fire Next Time? A Critical Survey of
    Belles-Lettres by and about Negroes Published in 1963."
    Phylon, 25 (Summer), 123-34.
        Critiques the 1963 survey and laments that "most of the
    books covered by this survey lack the creative force to set
    the imagination aflame and make the reading experience an
    exciting adventure." The last two years Baldwin has led
    the list of the "most significant books by and about Ne-
    groes" (i.e., Nobody Knows, Another Country). This year

1964

The Fire is acclaimed the "most artistically satisfying contribution to belles-lettres." The key word in the work is love; it is a "beautiful, . . . challenging, and powerful book." It is profoundly philosophical, but it offers "no new solution to the problem of race relations . . . Its solution is as old as the Bible and as simple as the Ten Commandments: Love."

34 Fuller, Hoyt W. "Ivory Towerist vs. Activist: The Role of the Negro Writer in an Era of Struggle." Negro Digest, 13 (June), 62-66.
    Contends that "the most successful polemicist of this generation is a bug-eyed, boy-sized Negro named James Baldwin" who has demonstrated what is the black writer's role in this era of struggle--a role that follows the patterns of other great activist writers such as Voltaire and Paine. He serves as "disturber of that spurious peace which is arrived at through the degradation of some men," tries to move the uncommitted to positive action, and seeks to open the eyes of people blinded too long by bigotry. Some critics, e.g., William Buckley, "the darling of the Right-Wing," see Baldwin as "an eloquent menace," but "no self-respecting black man could desire the approval of such a man."

35 Geismar, Maxwell. "The American Short Story Today." Studies on the Left, 4 (Spring), 21-27.
    Sees the American short story as "flourishing" but raises some questions about its range of talent and the nature of its literary content. It is flourishing at a time when the novel is in a "state of relative decline." Writers who employ both literary forms seem to excel in the short story, e.g., Updike, Malamud, Salinger, Roth, Wright. These writers became spokesmen for particular causes--the cult of family, the hypocrisy of academe, the "hodge-podge" of religiosity. Now, Baldwin, "who opened his career with an indictment of the 'social protest' novel . . . has become a leading spokesman on the race issue itself"; although he has "yet to fuse" this aspect of his "temperament into significant fiction."

36 Graves, Wallace. "The Question of Moral Energy in James Baldwin's Go Tell It on the Mountain." CLAJ, 7 (March), 215-23.
    Questions whether Baldwin is a major novelist "whose creations will continue to live beyond the essays, beyond the local conditions which created them" or whether he is popular because as an intelligent Negro he has captured

the current events of the time and has presented them to a
curious audience. In other words, does the writer present
human life in such a way as to move the reader's emotions,
or is one moved simply because experience is lacking in the
area of Negro life depicted? The first novel, Go Tell It,
was praised by most critics, but were these praises "clouded
by a politeness engendered by Caucasian guilt," or by an
"experiential void in Negro life?" From the outset he
wanted equal treatment as an artist, irrespective of his
race, but did he get it? Two more novels and three books
of essays have been published since then; it should be time
to "separate the educator from the artist." The criticisms
of these later novels were not kind; many felt that the
characters were dead and unreal, with wooden conversation.
One critic stated that Baldwin had yet to find the artistic
form that would reveal life's mystery and truth he knew was
there. If this is part of the current consensus, then Baldwin's promise as a novelist has certainly flagged.

37 Gresset, Michel. "Sur James Baldwin." Mercure de France, 350
    (April), 653-55.
        Begins with a quote from Nobody Knows in which Baldwin
    described himself: "I was then (and I have scarcely
    changed) a bohemian, a raw-boned black, hungry, very stiff
    and very aggressive." He presents an analysis of the
    "hideous relations" between whites and blacks that is lu-
    cid, passionate, penetrating, and sometimes violent. What
    is remarkable about him is that he goes beyond the immedi-
    ate terms of the race problem; through blackness, "which he
    surmounts," he comes to the essential question: What con-
    stitutes the American identity? In The Fire, he reminds
    his "racial brothers" that in the "white universe, the
    black fills the function of a fixed star . . . If he aban-
    dons his place, Heaven and Earth will tremble to their
    foundations."

38 Gross, Theodore L. "The World of James Baldwin." Critique, 7
    (Winter), 139-49.
        Refers to Baldwin's role as literary spokesman for the
    Negro as "precarious." He has created the "Negro for his
    white audience" just as "Hawthorne . . . created and de-
    fined the Puritan world for his audience." This is a "re-
    markable achievement, the dramatic assertion of a way of
    life that is only vaguely felt and understood by most peo-
    ple," and then it becomes more than literary for the author
    himself; there is always peril. Go Tell It is impressive
    in recounting Baldwin's early Harlem days, but Giovanni's
    Room does not succeed in its depiction of a young American

1964

seeking his sexual and national identity. Another Country censures white America because of its refusal to believe in reality, in death. Notes and Nobody Knows are dominated by acts of dehumanization. The Fire presents his widening scope of vision; both essays are written "superbly, prophetically and self consciously--a full awareness of the maturity of his career."

39 Harper, Howard M., Jr. "Concepts of Destiny in Five American
   Novelists: Bellows, Salinger, Mailer, Baldwin, Updike."
   Ph.D. dissertation, Pennsylvania State University.
      Considers the attitudes of five contemporary novelists
   toward the concept of human destiny, especially in the context of post-World War II pessimism about the doctrine of
   progress and the increase of irrationality and violence.
   Baldwin's view is influenced by existentialism--the struggle against nothingness in which certain "given characteristics" are discerned in man's inner nature; transforming
   the social reality requires mutual involvement of these inner natures.

40 Heermance, J. Noel. "A White Critic's Viewpoint: The Modern
   Negro Novel." Negro Digest, 13 (May), 66-76.
      Traces the "long, bitter, but essentially rich and re-
   warding journey of the Negro novel." Baldwin examines himself as a man, an American, and as a Negro, and examines
   America from a "more assured and detached point of view,"
   not from the "emotional position of achingly desiring mem-
   bership in it." Although Baldwin is concerned with the
   social problems of the Negro in a "white world," he also
   asks his Negro characters to "set their houses in order before they go out to eradicate the larger social evils of
   the world." His essential contribution to American and
   Negro literature is the portrayal of the "white world
   trapped within its past history and its preconceptions."

41 Hewes, Henry. "A Change of Tune." Sat R, 47 (9 May), 36.
      States that seeing Blues makes for a "confusing evening,"
   but one cannot but "respect its attempts to paint the country's current racial strife with contemporaneity and with
   new departures from the well-worn formula of just showing
   the horror of racial discrimination and bemoaning its existence." The play's pattern is "erratic" and "unexplained";
   perhaps these imperfections are the glimpses of the spirit
   that "moves militant young Negroes to assert their individual rights and let Mister Charlie--the white man--sing
   the blues for a change."

42 Hicks, Granville. "A Gun in the Hand of a Hater." Sat R, 47
    (2 May), 27-28.
        Recalls that Baldwin once wrote that Negro writers did
    not have to write about Negroes or the Negro problem. Yet
    his first novel, Go Tell It, is about Negroes and their pre-
    dicament (with "no obvious message"). His essays show him
    to be more and more explicitly "a spokesman for the Negro
    people." Another Country tackles the race problem in rela-
    tion to other problems, and in The Fire, he tried to show
    his readers what Negroes are thinking and feeling. Blues
    shows that the patience of Negroes is wearing thin, and
    Mister Charlie must change.

43 Hoffman, Stanton. "The Cities of Night: John Rechy's City
    of Night and the American Literature of Homosexuality."
    Chicago Review, 17, nos. 2 and 3; 195-202.
        Indicates that recent American literature of homosexual-
    ity can be characterized by two poles: the image of the
    "gay world"; and the image of personal homosexual relation-
    ships. The connection between the two is society, which
    conforms to the stereotypes of homosexual life, poses a
    threat to individual homosexuals, and makes love an impos-
    sibility. Baldwin sees the "gay world" as a type of "under-
    world" in which homosexuals are prisoners, "where the possi-
    bility of genuine human involvement has altogether ceased."
    Vidal's The City and the Pillar, John Rechy's City of Night,
    and Baldwin's Giovanni's Room all depict the overwhelming
    aspects of the "gay world" which make the possibility of
    human relationships a "vast hell."

44 Jourdain, M. "For the Liberal Coffee-Table." Economist, 213
    (26 December), 437.
        Singles out Nothing Personal as a book not just for any
    old coffee table, but for the "thinking person's table."
    The pictures "work through a crescendo of misery to a brief
    coda of bliss," and the text, by a "good novelist shoved by
    history . . . into the unbecoming role of a propagandist"
    is a sermon.

45 Kattan, Naim. Deux Ecrivains Américains." Ecrits du Canada
    Français, 17: 87-135.
        Analyzes the writing of Malamud and Baldwin, and affirms
    that no other black novelist is "so successful" as Baldwin,
    who has confronted the moral crisis of black and white re-
    lations. He writes with real precision about the black ex-
    perience in the United States, for he sees that his mission
    is "to lay bare the face" of the Negro who has been

1964

misrepresented and rendered unrecognizable. He says that
he wants to be an honest and good writer, and he is already
acclaimed as a "good" essayist and novelist. Go Tell It is,
without doubt, one of the best novels he has written. Giovanni's Room focuses upon two whites faced with the problem
of sexual identity. The latest novel, Another Country, reveals in his own way the process whereby one raises the
mask of life and fabricates another one in its place. It
is an effective and powerful novel, full of violence, rage,
and anger.

46 Kent, George E. "Baldwin and the Problem of Being." CLAJ, 7
      (March), 202-14.
        Cites a statement by Baldwin that to become a great
      novelist, one must attempt to present the truth even if it
      means attacking much that Americans hold sacred. This
      means being devoted to human freedom and fulfillment--
      "freedom which cannot be legislated; fulfillment which
      cannot be charted." He has rejected the tradition of the
      protest novel which he feels denies life, the human being.
      Instead, he has tried to write in the same way a musician
      reflects his innermost feelings and compassion. He relies
      on "Negro folk tradition," e.g., blues, jazz, spirituals,
      and folk literature, as well as on "experimental practi-
      tioners of modernistic fiction, with special emphasis upon
      Henry James." The moral vision in his works is concerned
      with man as he relates to good and evil and to society.
      The evil in human nature is confronted by love and involve-
      ment, and, in the process, a person achieves "functional
      being." This is the major issue in Go Tell It; Giovanni's
      Room and Another Country are "preoccupied with sex and
      love as instruments in the achievement of full being."

47 Kirstein, Lincoln. "Art Books of 1964." Nation, 199
      (14 December), 471.
        Contends that "the prize of unworthiness is won . . . by
      Nothing Personal, the coffee-table horror supreme." This
      work is the creation of "two great American artists," and
      celebrates "Way-Out America."

48 Kluger, Richard. "Shame May Scorch What Fury Singes." Book
      Week, 31 May, pp. 5, 10.
        Ranks Baldwin as the "most relevant man of letters" and
      "the most artful." But as a black man, he is "full of fury
      at what . . . has been done to black men" since they were
      shipped as cargo. The tone and intent are "blatant"; they
      are not subtle nor meant to be; and they do not constitute
      art, though perhaps they are meant to. The worst flaws of

1964

Blues are: tempo--fury is flung into the viewers' face;
exposition--"ham-handed"; dialogue--often stilted or gro-
tesquely overstated; characterization--unconvincing and
against the white man. Martin Duberman (In White America)
shames the white man; this strategy may be more effective.
Perhaps Duberman's work is a good place to start "understanding what makes Baldwin run."

49 Lash, John. "Baldwin beside Himself: A Study in Modern Phal-
    licism." CLAJ, 8 (December), 132-40.
        Affirms Baldwin's position as a "major contemporary
    writer." The Fire is a "succinct and brilliant analysis of
    America's malignant racism." Another Country, praised by
    popular critics and readers, is "something of an event in
    modern American novelism." Beside the "Negro in Baldwin is
    another man, a surprisingly devout and hopefully persuasive
    religionist." Even when he denounces Christianity, it is
    evident in both the titles and content of Go Tell It and
    The Fire that he seeks "a value system that can transfigure
    the self." This value system, he thinks, can be found in
    "a modern cult of phallicism, the fear and admiration and
    worship of the male sex organ." Both Giovanni's Room and
    Another Country reveal this "current religious faith." One
    problem for Baldwin is that he cannot recognize his own re-
    jection of a religion even if that religion be phallicism.

50 Levin, David. "Baldwin's Autobiographical Essays: The Prob-
    lem of Negro Identity." Massachusetts Review, 5 (Winter),
    239-47.
        Calls Baldwin an "eloquent, indignant prophet of an
    oppressed people," who demands that there be a stop to
    viewing the Negro "as an abstraction, an invisible man."
    The Negro must be recognized in "his full weight and com-
    plexity as a human being." This message forms the core of
    his autobiographical writings, Notes, Nobody Knows, and
    The Fire. The word "identity" occurs over and over again
    in these writings, and the essential question is: "Who am
    I?" or "How can I be myself?" His strength is in the an-
    swers, which make the essays "among the best in American
    literature" in spite of several inconsistencies in his
    works. At times, he writes of Negroes "as if they were
    all of one mind and culture, and of whites . . . as if they
    belonged uniformly to another." This problem is most ser-
    ious in his discussions of the past.

51 Lewis, Theophilus. "Blues for Mister Charlie." America, 110
    (30 May), 776-77.

1964

Views Blues as having "latched on" to an area of conflict that Miller, Williams, and other dramatists have ignored. Baldwin's view of life reflects a burning social
issue, the interracial problem, while "it is red hot." The
subject is charged with his "fervid treatment"; the plan is
exciting. But as drama, it "resembles a casserole of all
meat and no potatoes." It is in creating characters that
he is at his best, and Parnell and Reverend Henry are
"vividly human as perplexed men of good will." Blues is
"topical drama, tied to one aspect of a continuing social
problem," but it is also the "most challenging play of the
season."

52 McCarten, John. "Grim Stuff." New Yorker, 40 (9 May), 143.
Sees Blues as a "highly polemical drama," which has a
contrived plot and "pasteboard" characters. Although there
is considerable melodrama, special praise goes to the
actors.

53 Merton, Thomas. "La Révolution Noire." La Revue Nouvelle, 39
(15 February), 113-22.
Contends that the profound movements that have led to
social transformations began in the "hearts of men" who
had ideas which until recently have been unspoken. Many of
these ideas have never been heard because there appeared
to be no need; they were ignored, repressed, treated as if
they did not exist. The black revolution is not without
its symbols and prophecies; these form a basis from which
the voices of black America can be heard. The black novelists and essayists play an important role in arousing the
"sentiment of Kairos which is behind the treatment of Freedom now." One cannot forget Richard Wright, who spoke to
his disciples with zeal, and there is James Baldwin, who,
with Martin Luther King, Jr., is one of the influential
black orators. Go Tell It is Baldwin's first novel, and it
carries with it the "spirit of the black revolution in
America."

54 Miller, Karl. "America." New Statesman, 68 (4 December), 891.
Condemns Nothing Personal--"wild diatribe against America"--whose principal episode is "a selection of slumped and
staring lunatics" interlaced with a sermon by Baldwin on
the "awfulness of American life."

*55 Mohrt, Michel. "James Baldwin, ce Combattant Noir." Le
Figaro Littéraire, 19 (1-15 January), 3.
Cited in Rosa, 1976.53.

1964

56 Moon, Eric. "Theatre." LJ, 89 (15 May), 2112-13.
        Expresses a Baldwin admirer's disappointment in Blues
    because it is "a set of stock characters speaking stock
    dialogue in a stock situation."

57 O'Brien, Conor Cruse. "White Gods and Black Americans." New
        Statesman, 67 (1 May), 681-82.
        Refers to a Nigerian production of Amos Tutuola's The
    Palm-Wine Drunkard, which presented a European couple, "the
    White Gods," dancing; the predominantly black audience
    laughed in "spontaneous recognition." This scene is com-
    pared to one in Baldwin's Another Country where a white man
    dances with a black girl, but laughter of the black reader
    has a tone of "cold contempt." It is not surprising that a
    West African and an American Negro should react to these
    scenes with quite different emotions; the American Negro's
    experience "has been far more bitter." One thing Baldwin
    has done is to convince his white countrymen that "he is
    here." He has made them see him, and even more important,
    he has "made them see how he sees them."

58 Patterson, H. Orlando. "The Essays of James Baldwin." New
        Left Review, 26 (Summer), 31-38.
        Confesses that, as a black, reading Baldwin has been a
    "strange, complex experience, a mixture of agony, pride,
    . . . displeasure, envy, admiration, and profound disagree-
    ment." There is the paradoxical feeling that somehow the
    reader is informed yet "betrayed." There exists a problem
    of "Negro-White relations," and if one wants to understand
    this problem, he must recognize two alternatives to four
    possible points of view: 1) white talking to white, per-
    haps the most "sophisticated expression" in sociological
    terms dealing with a generally ethical framework of equal-
    ity and democracy; 2) outsider looking in, genuine attempts
    of whites to identify with the Negro community, e.g., Mail-
    er's view in the essay, "The White Negro"; 3) insider look-
    ing in, Negro writer addressing his own audience (Baldwin
    seems to let his readers down here); 4) insider looking
    out, a viewpoint "most Negro writers have . . . adopted"
    (Notes in this respect is "artistically disastrous"). Bald-
    win's works are an "unsuccessful attempt to transcend the
    limitations of . . . these four points of view." The "hope-
    less confusion" comes from the fact that instead of trans-
    cending them, he ends up by trying to use more than one
    point of view at the same time and neglects the most impor-
    tant fact of his minority status. In The Fire, his crafts-
    manship emerges in a "controlled yet spontaneous vigor of

the prose" as a literary counterpart to the "music of the
Modern Jazz Quartet"; the "persuasive power" is outdone
only by the "second book of Isaiah."

59 Peden, William. "Of War and Peace and Other Matters." In his
    The American Short Story: Front Line in the National De-
    fense of Literature. Boston: Houghton Mifflin, pp. 159-60.
        Lauds "This Morning, This Evening, So Soon" as among the
    really good recent stories by and about American Negroes
    that "survive their social and ethical climate."

60 Podhoretz, Norman. "The Article as Art." In his Doings and
    Undoings: The Fifties and After in American Writing. New
    York: Farrar, Straus and Company, pp. 126-42.
        Describes postwar American novelists as doing reviews,
    criticism, memoirs, etc., while frequently expressing con-
    tempt for the discursive prose they write; yet it turns out
    to be better than their fiction--interesting, lively, force-
    ful, and original. Baldwin exemplifies the pattern. Go
    Tell It and Giovanni's Room are fairly conventional; the
    essays in Notes "make up the best book . . . about the
    American Negro" and convey "a phenomenally keen sense of
    the special quality of Negro experience today." The dis-
    cursive prose is more imaginative and honest than his
    novels or short stories.

61 Podhoretz, Norman. "In Defense of a Maltreated Best Seller."
    In his Doings and Undoings: The Fifties and After in Ameri-
    can Writing. New York: Farrar, Straus and Company, pp.
    244-50.
        Reprint of 1962.51.

62 Popkin, Henry. "Blues for Mister Charlie, Dramatic Journal-
    ism." Vogue, 144 (July), 32.
        Describes Blues as "an effective but conventional piece
    of dramatic journalism." It combines in "dramatic form
    both a news column and an editorial," but what it does not
    have is an "intricate, personally meaningful human situa-
    tion." In this "simplistic drama," complications are "ar-
    tificially imposed from outside upon the form of the play."
    In short, Blues would make a better essay than a play.

63 Redding, J. Saunders. "The Problems of the Negro Writer."
    Massachusetts Review, 6 (Autumn/Winter), 57-70.
        Contends that Langston Hughes is the "dean of American
    Negro letters," and his pronouncements about the Negro wri-
    ter have been important. But Hughes and others have not
    explored the critical proposition of the Negro's literary

identity. The Negro, and especially the Negro writer, "has
always known who he is" and has been forced to live in "constant tense awareness of it." It is the problem of identification, distinct from the problem of identity, that
plagues Negro writers. Few black writers presently living
are included in recent anthologies of American literature.
Occasionally there are works by Hughes, Wright, Jones, and
Baldwin. All this has to do with more than the lack of
identification; it has to do with more than "lumping Negro
writers and comparing them to one another rather than to
white writers." It has to do with what Baldwin eloquently
stated in one of his early essays: "the difficulty . . .
of being a Negro writer was the fact that I was, in effect,
prohibited from examining my own experience too closely by
the tremendous demands and the very real dangers of my social situation." The second aspect of this problem of identification rests in the nature of the audience the Negro
writer wishes to attract, and that which he is "obligated
to attract and must attract if he is to be effective."
Typically, this audience is white and middle-class, reluctant or incapable of sharing the experience of being black.
Yet "it is this experience that is the Negro writer's responsibility and--if he is serious--his commitment to depict." Baldwin declares that what he wants to be is an
"honest man and a good writer," yet in Another Country he,
too, succumbs to the problem of identification and fails to
lead his audience to understanding the Negro. In his essays, his "creative integrity" is readily apparent.

64 Rogoff, Gordon. "Muddy Blues." Commonweal, 80 (29 May),
    299-300.
       Describes Baldwin as "muddling" two vital issues in
    Blues: the "art of dramatic writing and the responsibility
    of polemics." Shaw demonstrated how the two could be com-
    patible; preaching was an art in which forensic techniques
    could be used. Within this context, Baldwin's polemics
    meet all the essential needs of dramatic art, yet one
    "guiding element is missing: he preaches, but he doesn't
    argue . . . Inspired plots do not forge drama." For his
    lack of argument, he resorts to assertions that lead to
    "fringe areas of truth while leaving center depths un-
    plumbed." Also, these assertions often emerge not from
    life, but from a "tangled network of banalities, clichés,
    and stereotypes." His play is like a Hollywood novel,
    accurate in sight, touch, and sound, but very distant from
    persuasive truth; Blues is a "succession of appearances
    without reality."

1964

65 Roth, Philip. "Channel X: Two Plays on the Race Conflict,"
    New York Review of Books (28 May), 10-11.
         Cites from the introduction to Blues the need to under-
    stand the main characters of the play and then fails to do
    this. A conflict of impulses--duty toward causes, duty
    toward art--prevents Baldwin from inspiring understanding,
    his or others. The deficiency is not just in failing an
    intention, but in the failure to be true to those "numer-
    ous intentions apparent in the first act, all most worthy,
    but none able to survive." In acts two and three, all the
    purposes of the first act collapse; in fact "everything col-
    lapses, sense, craft, and feeling." The duty to understand
    is replaced by the passion to propagandize.

66 Roy, Gregor. "Blues for Mister Charlie." Cath W, 149 (July),
    263-64.
         Discusses how Blues fails in the fulfillment of Baldwin's
    artistic duty. The play's "theatrical movement is tedious,
    its thematic steps jarring and confused, and its emotional
    highlights disjointed and uncontrolled." His art seems to
    have been "bruised by the grim gauntlet of hatred's ghastly
    reality."

67 Sayre, Robert F. "James Baldwin's Other Country." In Con-
    temporary American Novelists. Edited by Harry T. Moore.
    Carbondale, Ill.: Southern Illinois University Press, pp.
    158-69.
         Affirms that Baldwin "has been exceptional among modern
    American writers by being both a novelist and . . . very
    compelling popular essayist." He has also attained promi-
    nence as a lecturer, panelist, and magazine and television
    interviewee. He has become a "kind of prophet, a man who
    has been able to give a public issue all its deeper moral,
    historical and personal significance." He is one contempo-
    rary writer who is "most beset with a vision, his vision
    being the great urgency and revolutionary implications of
    the race issue"; the vision is in almost everything he
    writes. His reputation as prophet is based primarily on
    three works--Notes, Nobody Knows, The Fire. The two most
    striking features of these works are: the "re-introduction
    of personal experience into what has become a mainly imper-
    sonal form"; and the "presentation of a great deal of hatred
    and despair in a very elegant, graceful style." The major
    defect in his essays is a "dishonest intimacy and an ela-
    borate, pointless self-consciousness." Go Tell It is his
    "best book"; Another Country is not economical, with people
    "endlessly . . . babbling bland inanities," and in Gio-
    vanni's Room, the "background is sometimes just theatrical."

94

Baldwin, as a writer, is a pilgrim on a continuing journey;
whether he can keep a sense of distance from his fictional
other countries remains to be seen. He has a "big job, and
the challenge of his art is every bit as great as the challenge of his materials, which is a very serious challenge
indeed."

68 Schroth, Raymond A. "James Baldwin's Search." Cath W, 198
    (February), 288-94.
        Begins with Baldwin's statement: "I want to be an hon-
    est man and a good writer," and then looks at his present
    actions in the "hate war on the side of Malcolm X." The
    "smoke and confusion of the fifties" seem to have blurred
    the vision of the artist. Still, he is the first American
    Negro writer to achieve international status as a "master-
    ful creative artist and as an intellectual spokesman for
    his race." His ascendancy into this superior position has
    coincided with a real Negro revolt, and "he has become its
    prophet." The Fire is Baldwin's "angriest" book; while Go
    Tell It recreates the "sordid heritage" of his family life.
    Another Country is a "nightmarish round of miscegenation
    and sexual deviation"; Giovanni's Room is a "romantic jus-
    tification of homosexuality as a way of life" full of fire
    "and soot." Inherent in all of his work is the "mystery
    of evil, the realization that man has fallen and that life
    is tragic." His stature as a writer will grow but only in
    proportion to how well he can treat his individual and per-
    sonal resentment in universal terms.

69 Simon, John. "Theatre Chronicle." Hud R, 17 (Autumn), 421-24.
        Sees Blues as a "protest play" that "follows fiction at
    a respectful distance." Unfortunately, "protest plays" al-
    ways have a hard time artistically, and Blues "doth protest
    too much." Baldwin is one of the ablest essayists today,
    but as a novelist he is a "failure, and a progressively
    worse one, at that." The most serious flaw in Blues is
    that the "play pretends to be about racial injustice and
    the Negro's struggle for his human rights, while it is ac-
    tually about something else." There is no deliberate de-
    ception, but Baldwin is deceiving himself, which is artis-
    tically worse. In his fiction there is the suggestion that
    "normal sexuality is found wanting," thus the "superiority
    of inversion over heterosexuality"--the theme disguised in
    this drama. Out of this comes the "most monumental falsi-
    fication of all: the myth of Negro supremacy." The play
    is "preposterous" on the literal level, and for allegory or
    symbolism to be effective, there must be a genuine literal
    level. Blues, then, is merely propaganda, "which can add

some fuel to a sometimes necessary fire"; it is not truth, which is the only element which can rid society of its eternal enemy, ignorance.

70 Sontag, Susan. "Going to Theater, Etc." PR, 31 (Summer), 389-94.
    Describes drama as a personification device for "defining virtue and vice." The American theater has always had a "streak of moralism, or preachiness," and Baldwin's Blues is a sermon of militancy. In this "new post-liberal morality play," it is essential that virtue is defeated, yet as art and as propaganda, the play "stalls." Blues gets bogged down in "repetitions, incoherence, and in all sorts of loose ends of plot and motive"; furthermore, there is a complex displacement of the play's true subject. Race conflict is what the play is supposed to be about, but the problem is drawn mainly in terms of sexual attitudes. Thus it is not about what it claims to be about; it is not about racial strife but about the "anguish of tabooed sexual longing, about the crisis of identity . . . and about the rage and destructiveness . . . by which one tries to surmount this crisis."

71 Steinem, Gloria. "James Baldwin, an Original: A Sharpened View of Him." Vogue, 144 (July), 78-79, 129, 138.
    Calls Baldwin a "Presence" who views the theater as a "series of timid, commercial speculations on-or-off-Broadway." Despite this opinion, he felt Blues had to be written. The theme of death or spiritual death of the young and talented is vividly portrayed in the play as well as in other works. Many of his friends had died before they were thirty, and Baldwin seems to have "an obsession" with this theme. Also, somewhere in all of these "walk recognizable figures of his family," and of the people who have influenced him in the four stages of his life: "Harlem, the Village, Paris, and now, the struggle for civil rights."

72 Taubman, Howard. "Common Burden." New York Times Theater Reviews (3 May), p. 11.
    Describes Baldwin as "a preacher and a rhapsodist," and Blues is an "angry sermon" drawing upon the "humiliation, degradation, frustration, and resentment felt by millions relegated to second-class citizenship." It is not a "trim, well-made play," but it fervidly depicts the Negro's "anguish and passion," which cannot go unheeded.

73 Taubman, Howard. "James Baldwin's Play Opens at the ANTA." New York Times Theater Reviews (24 April), p. 24.

Contends that <u>Blues</u> is "like a thunderous battle cry"
summoning this generation to the burning cause--"the establishment in this country of the Negro's full manhood with
all the perquisites of that simple and lofty station."

74 Van Sickle, Milton. "James Baldwin in Black and White."
<u>Trace</u>, 54 (Autumn), 222-25.
Contends that for a novel to be popular today, it must
be concerned with "communism, sexual oddities, or race relations." Baldwin has dealt with the latter two and has
become a "leading Negro writer." <u>Another Country</u> is a "confused muddle of interweaving loves and hates without symme-
try or meaning." <u>Giovanni's Room</u> is a "successful existential endeavor" that approaches the "compelling simplicity
of Camus, but is more simple than compelling." The earliest novel, <u>Go Tell It</u>, "combines terrifying magnificence
with brooding malevolence" in the Dostoevski tradition. He
has written one really good novel, a good play, and a group
of good essays (<u>Go Tell It</u>, <u>Amen Corner</u>, and <u>Notes</u>).

1965

1 Abdul, Raoul. "Negro Artists, Writers Using Talents to Spur
the Struggle for Liberation." <u>Muhammad Speaks</u> (19 November), p. 22.
Asserts that the idea that artists live in a "hybrid
world removed from reality is being shattered forever" and
cites participants in the civil rights movement (Dick Gregory, Langston Hughes, and LeRoi Jones) as knowing they can
shape public opinion and therefore accepting their moral
responsibility. <u>The Fire</u> continues a line of thought
traceable to DuBois: "the problem of the twentieth century
is the problem of the color line." <u>Blues</u> is viewed as a
drama about the struggle for human dignity.

2 ANON. "Amen." <u>Newsweek</u>, 26 April, p. 90.
Views <u>Amen Corner</u> as inept and tedious in its "clumsy,
groping exposition," irrelevant details, "lifeless movement," and speeches of proclamation relieved only at moments by the double themes of the father freeing the son
from domination by the mother and converting the mother to
"the acceptance of the joy and pain of being human."

3 ANON. "<u>The Amen Corner</u>: A Play." <u>Booklist</u>, 65 (1 February),
630.
Calls <u>Amen Corner</u>, written in 1952, a religious and
highly personal play taken from the author's experience

within the church and examining "the conflict between religious dogmatism and individual responsibility" in the character of preacher Sister Margaret.

4 ANON. "Author! Author!" Newsweek, 1 March, p. 52.
Captures the essence of the Baldwin-Buckley debate at
England's Cambridge University. Baldwin won the debate by
a vote of 544 to 164 including a standing ovation.

5 ANON. "Baldwin." PMLA, 80 (May), 169-70.
Presents annual secondary bibliography for 1964.

6 ANON. "Baldwin Play Wins Acclaim in Tel Aviv." New York
Times Theater Reviews (9 August), p. 19.
Announces the opening of Amen Corner at the Israel Fes-
tival in Tel Aviv. Baldwin, who appeared in Israel, "received warm applause."

7 ANON. "Chicago City Council Delays Action on Novel by Baldwin." The New York Times (16 January), p. 24.
Reports on the Chicago City Council's condemnation of
the required reading of Baldwin's Another Country at Wright
Junior College on the grounds that its language is "vulgar"
and "revolting."

8 ANON. "Chicago School Panel Sets Hearing on Baldwin Book."
The New York Times (6 January), p. 36.
Announces the meeting of the Chicago City Council Com-
mittee on Schools to discuss the banning of Baldwin's
Another Country from the required reading list at Wright
Junior College.

9 ANON. "Going to Meet the Man." Tablet, 219 (11 December),
1390.
Reviews briefly Going to Meet as tales having a mixture
of "the sentimental and the savage," the fantasies of childhood with the pains of growing up, and the "pain of
pigmentation."

10 ANON. "Love, Oh Sweet Self-Love." TLS (28 October), 953.
Describes Going to Meet as a "powerful and persuasive"
work of fiction. The book is saved from "vulgarity" by
Baldwin's gift for narrative, but there are "signs that
the creative intelligence is being corrupted by the sweet-
ness of a purpose that is not properly creative, that is
spiritually self-congratulatory." Still, the achievements
of his work can teach readers to see and to understand
dimensions of life.

11 ANON. "Play by Baldwin Opens in Vienna." <u>The New York Times</u>
<u>Theater Reviews</u> (9 June), p. 42.
    Announces the opening of <u>Amen Corner</u> in Vienna where
even the difficult Harlem "speechways . . . could not muf-
fle the ovation that followed Monday's premiere."

12 ANON. "Tardy Rainbow." <u>Time</u>, 23 April, p. 59.
    Reviews <u>Amen Corner</u> in relation to <u>Blues</u>; the former is
"not a strident, vulgar, melodramatic polemic on the race
question."

13 ANON. "This Week." <u>Christian Century</u>, 82 (10 November),
1385.
    Asks "where's the fire of Baldwin's <u>The Fire</u>?" The
author is more "believable" in nonfiction because the reader has to come to terms with the "fantastic"; in the fiction there is only "fancy," and it can be dismissed.

14 ANON. "Tortured Voice." <u>Newsweek</u>, 8 November, p. 114.
    Shows that in its "justness and virulence," <u>Going To</u>
<u>Meet</u> has become largely a sentimental, gratingly reiterated
polemic from a tortured voice. At the core of the work is
Baldwin's anger--the understanding of "natural man's" agony
as he struggled beneath "both white boot and black breast."
At the same time, there is an overabundance of sentimentality, which turns Baldwin's power and sensitivity "into a
travesty of sentimental hysteria."

15 ANON. "Vestal, N.Y., School Board President H.C. May Urges
Books by J. D. Salinger, J. Baldwin, and E. Hemingway Be
Banned from High School Libraries." <u>The New York Times</u>
(7 March), p. 75.
    Presents the view of Mr. Harold May, president of the
Vestal, N.Y., School Board, that "some works of J.D. Salinger, James Baldwin and Ernest Hemingway do not belong in
high school libraries" because the minds of children "are
being molded" and their "ideas, principles and values are
in a developmental stage."

16 Battacharya, Lokenath. "James Baldwin." <u>Quest</u>, 44 (January/
March), 78-83.
    Describes Baldwin as having a "demon living" under the
"skin of his castle." As a novelist, essayist, playwright,
and Negro spokesman, he is a "literary sensation," whose
name is not confined to literary circles alone; he is a
"public celebrity." His latest work, <u>The Fire</u>, "speaks for
an American Negro to all American whites." The American
Negro is a unique phenomenon having no counterpart anywhere;

he bears a "pathetic untold tale of lost identity." To
discover who <u>he</u> is, is the first task to which Baldwin has
set himself, body and soul. The six outstanding works to-
day are: <u>Go Tell It</u>, <u>Giovanni's Room</u>, <u>Another Country</u>,
<u>Notes</u>, <u>Nobody Knows</u>, and <u>The Fire</u>. His novels present as
"true a definition as possible of the American character,"
and the essays "bring into focus a peculiarly American aspect of Negro suffering." He sees the white American's dilemma as being caught between his European legacy of white
supremacy and the "American Dream" of equality and justice.
Blacks and whites deeply need each other if America is to
achieve unity, maturity, and honor.

17 Bone, Robert. "The Novels of James Baldwin." <u>Tri-Quarterly</u>,
2 (Winter), 3-20.
        Calls Baldwin "the most important Negro writer" of the
last decade, yet sees him as "an uneven writer" whose quality cannot be taken for granted. He is strongest as an
essayist, weakest as a playwright, and successful as a
novelist. <u>Notes</u>, <u>Nobody Knows</u>, and <u>The Fire</u> are outstanding. <u>Amen Corner</u> is a "competent apprentice play," and
<u>Blues</u> is an "unspeakably bad propaganda piece." <u>Go Tell It</u>
is an "impressive achievement" not to be matched by <u>Giovan-
ni's Room</u> and <u>Another Country</u>. His career can be divided
into two distinct thematic periods: 1) flight from self,
quest for identity, and the "sophisticated acceptance of
one's blackness"; 2) "apocalyptic vision" of racial and
sexual oppression. The first period is concerned with the
emotion of shame; the second with the emotion of rage.
Baldwin, like Whitman, his "spiritual progenitor," endows
his diffuse treatment of sexuality with "mythic significance" and on these mythic foundations constructs a theory
of personality: one must face his own "formlessness" before one can "hope to achieve form." At the core of his
fiction is "an existentialist psychology"; all identity
"emerges from the void." Man, "the sole creator of himself,
moves alone upon the face of the waters." It is when Baldwin uses the "hipster idiom," as in <u>Another Country</u>, that
he reaches a "dead end." If he is to prevail, he must
recognize that "his hipster phase is coming to a close";
his future depends on his "ability to transcend the emotional reflexes of his adolescence. So extraordinary a
talent requires of him no less an effort."

18 Bone, Robert. "The Novels of James Baldwin." In his <u>The
Negro Novel in America</u>, rev. ed. New Haven: Yale University Press, pp. 215-39.
        Reprint of 1965.17.

19 Brustein, Robert. "Everybody's Protest Play." In his Seasons
    of Discontent: Dramatic Opinions, 1959-1965. New York:
    Simon and Schuster, pp. 161-65.
        Reprint of 1964.19.

20 Bryden, Ronald. "Protestants." New Statesman, 69 (7 May),
    737-38.
        Analyzes two protest plays: Blues and Shaw's Mrs. War-
    ren's Profession; sees the limitations of the former as
    cardboard characters, banal dialogue, crude flashbacks,
    flat exposition, clichés, and sermonizing. The best mo-
    ments of Baldwin's play are those employing "the imagery
    of oppression." The drama has an anger that is the central
    element and central pleasure, but that inaccurately re-
    flects the self-conscious new dignity that America is find-
    ing in its self-struggle.

21 Buckley, W. F., Jr. "The Negro and the American Dream."
    National Review, 17 (6 April), 273.
        Argues that Baldwin's position in the recent debate with
    him at Cambridge University was "preposterous." Even
    though the vote was "3-1" in Baldwin's favor, there is no
    credence to the view that the American dream is realized
    only at the expense of the American Negro. The audience
    wanted an excuse "to rebuke the United States" for its
    treatment of the Negro and used this debate as a way to
    "censure America." The young men of Cambridge, who reflect
    "the heart of the regnant prejudices of their society," do
    not seem to understand the nature of the American problems.

22 Burgess, Anthony. "The Postwar American Novel: A View from
    the Periphery." American Scholar, 36 (Winter), 150-56.
        Contends that just because England is on the "periphery
    of world power," there is no reason for it to regard it-
    self as being on "the artistic periphery" as well. Yet
    American novelists seem to possess the courage to deal with
    "big themes;" whereas English writers tend to be satisfied
    with "provincial subjects," e.g., class, suburban adultery.
    World War II saw the emergence of some great American
    novels (The Naked and the Dead, Williwaw, Catch 22); only
    Waugh's Sword of Honour trilogy recorded the conflict at
    any length. Some of these American writers continue to
    interest British readers with their daring themes of the
    "male community," homosexual power struggle, racial con-
    sciousness, etc. Baldwin's novels vigorously examine
    this latter theme. The American novel is characterized by
    its "massiveness, the panoramic vision, a sense of history
    and (perhaps most of all) a powerful national awareness."

1965

23 Burgess, Anthony. "These Canapés Are Great." <u>Spectator</u>
    (26 November), p. 706.
        Contends that sometimes the "publishing of fiction is
    more religion than commerce" whether there is a congrega-
    tion or not. <u>Going to Meet</u> presents the "monolithic fact
    of injustice to Negroes"; the reader must "rest between
    blows" so that "each new impact can have full weight be-
    hind it."

24 Clurman, Harold. "The Amen Corner." <u>Nation</u>, 200 (10 May),
    514-15.
        Gives a personal reaction to <u>Amen Corner</u>, which was a
    "pleasure" in spite of its "crudities, banalities, <u>lon-
    gueurs</u>, etc." The text and production are "marred" by some
    "blemishes," but the total effect is "touching and valu-
    able." The weakest points are the "conventionally comic
    and the factually satiric ones." The play is not "propa-
    ganda," and the "religiosity" does not turn the characters
    away from reality.

25 Donoghue, Denis. "Blues for Mr. Baldwin." <u>New York Review of
    Books</u>, 5 (9 December), 6-7.
        Lauds the "high-pressure rhetoric closely related to old-
    style preaching" of Baldwin's essays, fiction, and autobio-
    graphical recording and reporting but faults the novels and
    short stories as "weak on invention"--the ability to imagine
    things different from his own. Baldwin is credited with
    introducing "the nuptial image" of "a Negro of homosexual
    and heterosexual capacities who marries in the white world."
    The themes found in <u>Going to Meet</u> typify Baldwin: hatred
    between father and mother, homosexual love, black married
    to white, etc. "This Morning, This Evening, So Soon" is
    viewed as his best work of fiction because it embodies mea-
    sure, scale, tact, and control.

26 Downes, Bruce. "On Avedon's Controversial Book." <u>Popular
    Photography</u>, 56 (March), 24.
        Praises the photographic work of Richard Avedon, and
    commends <u>Nothing Personal</u> as a "tremendously shocking in-
    dictment" of a segregated society. Baldwin's powerful
    prose "lays bare the inner agonies of the essential modern
    tragedy," and Avedon gives "visual form to the shock that
    lies at the center of the book." The result is a tremen-
    dously successful work.

27 Dupee, F. W. "James Baldwin and 'the Man.'" In his <u>The King
    of the Cats and Other Remarks on Writers and Writing</u>. New
    York: Farrar, Straus and Giroux, pp. 208-14.
        Reprint of 1963.24.

28 Featherstone, J. "Blues for Mister Baldwin." New Republic,
     153 (27 November), 34-36.
       Defines "blues" as "an attempt to retain the memory of
     pain, to transcend catastrophe . . . by an attitude, a
     nearly comic, nearly tragic lyricism." Going to Meet con-
     tains blues, "fragments of his [Baldwin's] vast and cure-
     less sorrow": it gives the reader a series of problematic
     conditions (urban desolation, spurious religiosity) that
     have no resolutions, no new departures. Baldwin's greatest
     strength lies in his ability to "endow his experience, his
     feelings, with universal significance." He is weakest when
     he presents his characters "through the distorted lenses of
     his self-pity and self-love."

29 Feron, James. "'Charlie' Scored by London Critics." New York
     Times Theater Reviews (5 May), p. 52.
       Points out that the London production of Blues "drew a
     hostile reaction from . . . critics." Some praised Bald-
     win's prose, but the majority said that "his drama . . .
     was so full of hatred that it overrode the message."

30 Finkelstein, S. W. "Existentialism and Social Demands: Nor-
     man Mailer and James Baldwin." In his Existentialism and
     Alienation in American Literature. New York: International
     Publishers, pp. 276-84.
       States that Go Tell It represents a "new stage in the
     literary depiction of the American Negro." Baldwin's sub-
     sequent writings show a "diminution in breadth of charac-
     terization, along with a turn to existentialism." Yet in
     all his works, except Giovanni's Room, he expresses "power-
     fully the temper of the struggle for equal rights and Negro
     liberation in the 1960's." He sees that the liberation of
     Negroes is not a necessity just for them, but is equally
     necessary to save white people from their own degradation,
     the loss of whatever freedom they possess. The existential-
     ist quality is manifested in his "dissociation of truth
     from the class forces in society that are an integral part
     of it, the lack of faith that the masses of people, as
     history presents them with its inexorable questions, will
     find the right answers, the tendency to seek a solution
     from the enlightened few." The Fire is an embodiment of
     this theme, and Another Country is full of partially unre-
     solved human conflicts; there is the "existentialist death-
     hauntedness" throughout the work.

31 Fischer, Russell G. "James Baldwin: A Bibliography, 1947-
     1962." BB, 24 (January/April), 127-30.
       Presents primary and secondary bibliography for the
     years specified.

1965

32 Foote, F. G. "Therapeutique de la Haine." Prévues, no. 167,
    pp. 70-73.
        Describes Baldwin's premiere work, Blues, as opening
    with a "Bang! Bang!" The type of confrontation featured in
    the play is violent and brutal. He sees man's misfortune
    within a context of "gross" realities. Blues demonstrates
    the underlying problems of the blacks in the United States;
    Baldwin gives an ultimatum with persuasive force. Blacks
    and whites are presented with lucidity similar to the
    characterization of "Jason Compson in Faulkner's book, The
    Sound and the Fury," having great similarity with real-life
    circumstances. Certainly, Baldwin is a person of "amazing
    complexity and brilliance." As a writer he engages in the
    analysis of psychological literature, sometimes being pre-
    sumptuous and simplistic.

33 Fuller, Hoyt W. "Contemporary Negro Fiction." Southwest Re-
    view, 50 (Autumn), 321-35.
        Argues that World War II symbolizes a change in the
    world, viz., that "the white masters of the West" lost for-
    ever their grip over nonwhite people and that "not being
    white would not automatically doom a man to subordinate
    status." In America, postwar Negro authors became deter-
    mined "to destroy the power of white-perpetuated myths over
    their lives." However, to dismiss their works as "protest
    literature" because it is "accusatory" toward white people
    who have disowned the basic principles of humanity, justice,
    and love is to fail to understand as Ellison phrases it,
    that there is "no dichotomy between art and protest . . .
    Don Quixote, Man's Fate, Oedipus Rex, The Trial--all of
    these embody protest even against the human limitation of
    life itself." In commenting on a multiplicity of writers--
    Wright, Ellison, Ann Petry, John Williams, Chester Harris,
    Ernest Gaines, LeRoi Jones, Julian Mayfield--Another Coun-
    try is praised not as a cry against white oppression, but
    because it deals "with the absence--or the failure--of love
    in the great American metropolis and in the lives of some
    of the people who inhabit it." It is a plea for a return
    to the nation's basic principles for moral and spiritual
    strength.

34 Fuller, Hoyt W. "Reverberations from a Writers' Conference."
    African Forum, 1 (Fall), 78-85.
        Reports on a conference sponsored by the Harlem Writers'
    Guild and The New School for Social Research for which
    Baldwin delivered the keynote address contending that the
    falsehood and myths of history held by "white, Anglo-Saxon
    Americans" had to be confronted and that all writers, black

and white, had two options: "to be immoral and uphold the
status quo or to be moral and try to change the world."
Also, Fuller tells of an attack on Baldwin by a staff writer for the National Review, who called Baldwin "a literary
prostitute."

35 Gilliatt, Penelope. "Actors Studio in London, Or the Broadway
    Boiler-house Abroad." Harper's, 231 (September), 32-36.
    Criticizes the Actors Studio participants who performed
    in London's annual World Theatre Season. Other participants
    were the Théâtre de France, Rome's Compagnia dei Giovani,
    Greek Art Theater, and Israel's Habimah Theater. Blues was
    one of the plays performed; it is not a "good play," but it
    possesses a "bold arc of oratory" which the Actors Studio
    could not "fill in."

*36 Glazier, Lyle. "Suffering Doesn't Have a Color." Litera, 8:
    91-98.
    Cited in O'Daniel, 1977.39.

37 Gray, Simon. "Whose Little Boy?" Delta, 35 (Spring), 2-8.
    Recognizes the rhetorical and prophetic elements in
    Baldwin but stresses his real gift as a novelist who wants
    to "make us see what he has seen, is to make us feel what
    he has felt." Another Country is praised as his major work
    on the theme of the struggle to find love and to find in
    oneself the courage to love. However, Gray finds this novel
    as well as Go Tell It and Giovanni's Room flawed by a "kind
    of collapse" before the end "in the form of a strained and
    constricting plot."

38 Hamilton, Alex. "Headliner: A Survey of the Month." Books
    and Bookmen, 10 (February), 29.
    Mentions Go Tell It briefly, as a fictionalized auto-
    biography of a ghetto youth's religious conversion; Gio-
    vanni's Room is a melodramatic treatment of a homosexual
    affair; and The Fire is an agonized personal statement of
    the need to live nobly in spite of white civilization.

39 Handlin, Oscar. "Bookshelf." Atlantic Monthly, 216 (Novem-
    ber), 191.
    Charges that Going to Meet is a "disappointing indica-
    tion of the deterioration of a writer of genuine ability."
    None of the stories in the work show the "sharp perceptions,
    the economy of language, and the tightly knit structure of
    Baldwin's first novel."

1965

40 Hassan, Ihab. "The Novel of Outrage: A Minority Voice in
    Postwar American Fiction." American Scholar, 34 (Spring),
    239-53.
        States that outrage is thought both "fashionable and
    tedious" nowadays. This is due to the inclination to de-
    precate an idea; it is either dismissed as "faddish," or
    it is ignored as "antique." Yet "modern outrage" means a
    "radical threat to man's nature"; it exists as assault,
    protest, force, and counterforce, and it is both the "final
    threat to being" and the "response to it." Outrage in
    Another Country is "an erotic metaphor which attempts to
    embrace victims and tormentors as lovers embrace in bed."
    The work identifies outrage with chaos, which "it miti-
    gates with the rhetoric of protest and the poetry of love."

41 Heiberg, Inger. "James Baldwin--Negerforfatter or Dikter."
    Samtiden, 74: 28-87.
        Begins with a sketch of Baldwin's situation as a black
    writer, indicating that he is opposed to the racism of the
    white society as well as parts of the civil rights movement.
    He went to Europe to discover that America was truly his
    home. Thus, when he returned home, he had a better under-
    standing of the forces that had driven him away. There is
    considerable discussion of Baldwin's "problems," especially
    his relations to his father, which are reflected in much of
    his works. Religion and the church of his youth have been
    influencing factors in his background and form the basis of
    Go Tell It and Amen Corner. He is continually concerned
    not just with the problems of black people in America but
    with the problems of mankind.

42 Hentoff, Nat. "Uninventing the Negro." Evergreen Review, 9
    (November), 34-36, 66.
        Reports on a conference held in April 1965, on "The
    Negro Writer's Vision of America" involving Baldwin, LeRoi
    Jones, Sterling Brown, Sylvester Leaks (who proposed to
    "uninvent the Negro" by using "Afro-American"), et al.
    Baldwin said in the keynote speech: "My models, my private
    standards of what excellence are are not Hemingway or Faulk-
    ner or Dos Passos. I model myself on jazz musicians, black
    dancers, a couple of whores and a few junkies. Billie Holi-
    day was one of the witnesses to the spiritual state of this
    country, and Ray Charles is being driven down the same path.
    What is important to remember is that the word doesn't come
    from the artist; it comes from the street. All the artist
    is trying to do is make 'you remember who you are.'"

1965

43 Hewes, Henry. "The Gospel Untruth." Sat R, 48 (1 May), 49.
        Contends that Amen Corner does not deal with racial dis-
    crimination, but with the universal problems of man. The
    play appears to be a "more timelessly true story" than
    Baldwin's "more temporal and more categorically unforgiving
    Blues."

44 Kauffman, Stanley. "Another Baldwin." New York Times Book
        Review (12 December), p. 5.
        Argues that the stories in Going to Meet reinforce the
    notion of the superiority of Baldwin's essays with their
    incisiveness of phrase, rhythmic control, and dramatic
    structure while the former are encrusted with clichés and
    triteness "cloaked by social urgency and sexual detail."

45 Killens, John Oliver. "Broadway in Black and White." African
        Forum, 1 (Winter), 66-76.
        Reviews some of the outstanding achievements by American
    Negroes in the media of theater, film, and television, e.g.,
    Ruby Dee, Sidney Poitier, Louis Gossett, Harry Belafonte,
    Ossie Davis, etc. Baldwin had two plays on Broadway within
    two years, Amen Corner and Blues. Both plays received
    "splendid reviews," but "since the New York audiences failed
    to follow the enthusiasm of the critics, both plays had re-
    latively short runs."

46 Kindt, Kathleen A. "James Baldwin, A Checklist: 1947-1962."
        BB, 24 (January/April), 123-36.
        Presents primary and secondary bibliography for the
    years specified.

47 Krim, Seymour. "The Troubles He's Seen." Book Week
        (7 November), pp. 5, 19-20.
        Affirms that Going to Meet is an impressive work of
    which Baldwin can be proud. The stories testify that he
    has dug in the "humbling soil of the Negro, the expatriate,
    the homosexual," and has come out with "uneasy and disturb-
    ing truths" that linger even after the story ends. Even
    when his writing occasionally falls into "platitude," he is
    "intuitive and courageous" enough to turn to his chief
    strength--"common experience uncommonly probed." His im-
    pact has caused "tremendous reverberations" for many peo-
    ple "caught in the black-white impasse." His pride of be-
    ing attests to the fact that he is someone who "survived an
    inhuman situation" and is going to make certain that those
    "who put him there know his name."

1965

48 Levensohn, Alan. "The Artist Must Outwit the Celebrity."
      Christian Science Monitor (18 November), p. 15.
          Asserts that two James Baldwins live and struggle within
      the same black skin--the artist and the celebrity--"anato-
      mizing the world through the same black bitterly observant
      eyes." Going to Meet is an expression of the artist;
      "Sonny's Blues" is praised as the best of the eight stories
      because of its honesty, emotional strength, and depth of
      insight.

49 Lewis, Allan. "Trends of the Decade." In his American Plays
      and Playwrights of the Contemporary Theatre. New York:
      Crown Publishers, pp. 254-57.
          Describes Blues as being an expression of polemics and
      hate rather than drama.

50 Lewis, Theophilus. "The Amen Corner." America, 112 (8 May),
      690.
          Compares Amen Corner with Blues, and sees the former as
      a drama "without the extraneous excitement of controversy."
      It rates "more respect than his more pretentious" Blues.

51 Littlejohn, David. "Exemplary and Other Baldwins." Nation
      (13 December), pp. 478-80.
          Advocates that there are a "number" of Baldwins "who
      write with varying degrees of honesty, relevance, humility,
      precision, and style," and all of them can be found in
      Going to Meet, e.g., the "autobiographizing lyricist, the
      taut-strung neurotic, the truth teller, . . .the celebrated
      bully." He is not just a "stylist bestseller"; he is be-
      coming an "exemplary Man." Going to Meet should not be
      read alone, for it depends on "interreflections" with ear-
      lier works--voice and setting of Go Tell It, "jagged, brit-
      tle tones" of Another Country, "whining, bullying rant" of
      The Fire, the "flip self-importance" of Nothing Personal.

52 Lucas, Lawrence E. "The Amen Corner." Cath W, 201 (June),
      215-16.
          Argues that Amen Corner does not deal only with "the
      things that hurt." In spite of the "speech-making" style,
      the play moves along more rapidly than Baldwin's recent
      work, Blues. In Amen Corner there is also a lack of "un-
      necessary vulgar expression" so typical of his later works.
      The main thesis, that "religion is an escape from the re-
      alities of life," is poignantly presented.

53 McCarten, John. "Tabernacle Blues." New Yorker, 41 (24
      April), 85.

Discloses that <u>Amen Corner</u> forecast some of Baldwin's
"virtues and vices" as a playwright that are displayed in
<u>Blues</u>. In the earlier work, he proved that he could put
the "Negro vernacular to eloquent prose," and that he could
create "cleverly assorted sad and funny vignettes." The
weakness is that "his dialogue is all too often plethoric,"
and his theme "too discursive to command undivided attention" from a three-act play.

54 Mayne, Richard. "Suitable Sermons." <u>New Statesman</u>, 70
(12 November), 740.
Lists several books as being "suitable sermons" including <u>Going to Meet</u>, and compares Baldwin with John Osborne.
Both have been involved in "public controversy" and both
made cautious beginnings and then moved to almost "crip-
pling celebrity" status. <u>Going to Meet</u> includes themes
from most of Baldwin's novels, from the "careful documen-
tary protest of 'Previous Condition' to frenzied . . . outbursts like 'Sonny's Blues.'"

55 Meriwether, L. M. "Broadway Hit for Baldwin: <u>The Amen Cor-
ner</u>." <u>Negro Digest</u>, 14 (January), 40-47.
Thinks that <u>Amen Corner</u>, which opened off-Broadway "has
all the ingredients for making the journey uptown to the
Broadway stage." Some reviews call the play "important
. . . a smash hit," which marks Baldwin as "the top Negro
dramatist," ranking with Tennessee Williams and Arthur
Miller. The play is "shattering" because "it allows a being to be, and being is what the Negro has been denied."
The universality of <u>Amen Corner</u> can best be explained by
that of its author who admits that "the facts of life are
the same for everyone."

56 Minerof, Arthur. "Fiction." <u>LJ</u>, 90 (1 November), 4804.
Points out the familiar Baldwin themes in the short
story collection, <u>Going to Meet</u>: Negro-white relations,
role of religion, conflict between the generations, interracial love, homosexuality. It is suggested that the con-
necting idea among all the stories is the individual's isolation and alienation. The following stories are praised:
"The Rockpile," "The Outing," and "Going to Meet the Man";
the latter from a white man's point of view--his fear,
loneliness, insecurity, and inadequacy.

57 Moore, John R. "An Embarrassment of Riches: Baldwin's <u>Going
to Meet the Man</u>." <u>The Hollins Critic</u>, 2 (December), 1-12.
Gives brief bibliographic data about first editions;
interprets the meaning of stories in <u>Going to Meet</u>,

1965

comments on <u>Go Tell It</u>, <u>Giovanni's Room</u>, and <u>Another Coun-
try</u>. Baldwin thinks that art should "make us change our
lives," to show us that "the public life and the private
life are an indivisible whole," to portray how "love and
power are fatally intertwined" in the scheme of things.
His characters are lonely, frustrated, fearful, angry, and
lovelorn; lovers "believe in love with a primitive intensity that civilization cannot destroy"; they carry the
"burden of racial consciousness, of revolt against social
convention, of a guilt that self-righteousness cannot ab-
solve them from."

58 Morris, Ivan. "<u>The Amen Corner</u>: Shamelessly Maudlin."
<u>Vogue</u>, 145 (June), 68.
Describes <u>Amen Corner</u> as "plodding, banal, and shamelessly maudlin" except for one scene towards the end,
which gives a "glimpse of the effective play it might have
been."

59 Nye, Robert. "Graves in His Anecdotage." <u>Manchester Guardian
Weekly</u>, (2 December), p. 12.
Reviews <u>Going to Meet</u> and Robert Graves's <u>Collected
Short Stories</u> and lauds the former for its "sensitivity
toward other people which amounts . . . to an almost mythic
courtesy towards life" in stories that spring from "moments
of crisis." <u>Going to Meet</u> rejects disgust, despair, fear,
hate, and horror in the "natural exercise of a compassion
disturbing for its very kindness."

60 O'Brien, Conor Cruse. "White Gods and Black Americans." In
his <u>Writers and Politics</u>. New York: Pantheon, pp. 17-22.
Reprint of 1964.57.

61 Pakrasi, B. "<u>The Fire Next Time</u>." <u>JNH</u>, 50 (January), 60-62.
Views <u>The Fire</u> as a "perceptive commentary on race relations" not only by a Negro, but by one "having a deep insight into human psychology." Baldwin sees "the seeds of
hatred and acrimony embedded in the dogma of Christianity
perpetuating the belief in a white god," and as a reaction
to this, the Black Muslims created a black god. Apparently,
he has no faith in either extreme, rather he seeks to assert the "dignity of the human race."

62 Potter, Vilma. "Baldwin and Odets: The High Cost of 'Cross-
ing.'" <u>California English Journal</u>, 1, no. 3 (Fall), 37.
Describes some of the "melodramatic clichés found in
<u>Amen Corner</u>. The play is a reenactment of "an old song,"
yet it has "peculiar relevance to American audiences."

1965

Thirty years ago Clifford Odets was saying the same thing
only his characters were New York Jews and Italians (Awake
and Sing, Golden Boy); now in the 1960s Baldwin is writing
about New York Negroes. The "theme and the formulation of
the struggle" seem so similar; the struggle is between
"powerful adversaries." In both, one adversary is the
"voice of the sub-culture, the parent-voice" who is a
"teacher of survival values." This "Culture-parent's" adversary is the "World-as-parent," who violates the culture's
unity, and whose values are alien and threatening. This
"World-as-parent" becomes more vivid in Baldwin's Blues,
where its force is "dramatized as the play's central problem"--Meredith is the "Culture-parent," and Richard is the
"World-as-parent," the play's "true protagonist." Within
this play pattern, an "interchangeability" of casts is entirely possible: "Golden Boy is not essentially Italian
any more than Amen Corner is essentially Negro."

63 Raddatz, Fritz. "Schwarz Ist die Farbe der Einsamkeit: Skizze
   zu einer Portrat James Baldwin." Frankfurter Hefte, 20:
   44-52.
      Argues that readers do not readily see the "protest au-
   thor" in Baldwin, but even Go Tell It, a novel in the European school of "interior (psychological) novel," was a step
   away from the tradition of American Negro literature. The
   central theme in his works is the interweaving of isolation,
   self-alienation, and self-hatred. He presents no "white-
   wash" of the Negro, nor does he believe in "negritude"--
   the presupposed unity and understanding among all Negroes
   in the world. This attitude led to his break with Richard
   Wright. Baldwin's works are free of sentimentality; he believes that the Negro's self-hatred is a reverse racial
   hatred, and he continually depicts the destructive schizo-
   phrenia of the Negro. In his works, one sees a close connection among religion, angst, love, and fear of love. Man
   becomes clearly conscious of his isolation when he tries to
   escape it, namely in sex; but the homosexual element (a symbol of loneliness) indicates that true friendship, which
   fights loneliness, is possible. Whites are terrified of
   black skin because it reminds them of the Negro's consciousness of death; such an attitude can lead to the Negro's
   annihilation. Baldwin believes that black is beautiful,
   not because it is loved, but because it is feared.

64 Schlesinger, Arthur M., Jr. "The Negro Revolution." In his
   A Thousand Days: John F. Kennedy in the White House.
   Boston: Houghton Mifflin, pp. 957-63.

1965

Reports on Baldwin's The Fire as an attack on the moral confusion and shame of white America, and his meeting with Robert Kennedy in May 1963.

65 Sheed, Wilfrid. "The Stage: Amen, Amen." Commonweal, 82 (7 May), 221-22.
    Sees Amen Corner as coming on like a "cloche hat or a feather boa," out of fashion, out of date. Written in 1953, the "heyday of the tense-family-drama," it was a "sentimental mishmash" even then. It might have brought the author "personal relief," but "it solved no real problems."

66 Smart, William. "James Baldwin." In his Eight Modern Essayists. New York: St. Martin's Press, pp. 298-300.
    Presents brief comments about Baldwin as an author, primarily of a biographical nature, as well as reprints of three essays.

67 Southwick, A. B. "James Baldwin's Jeremiad." Christian Century, 82 (24 March), 363-64.
    Asserts that Baldwin "has had more influence on the thinking of white Americans in regard to black Americans than any other man living." Someday The Fire may be ranked as a "landmark in race relations." But he is "short on both theory and hope" when it comes to really facing the "color line dilemma." His is a "jeremiad of despair, a chronicle of outrage," but not much of a "guide for those seeking a way to higher ground." His eloquence is unquestioned, but his indictments of the Christian church cannot go without protest. There are just reasons to "prick the conscience of white America," to arouse a "sense of guilt for the wrongs that have been done," but there must be "constructive channels" whereby people can see their "moral responsibilities." It is time for Baldwin to put away "his whiplash and join hands with the rest of us sinners."

68 Stern, Daniel. "A Special Corner on Truth." Sat R, 48 (6 November), 32.
    Contends that Going to Meet is more in the tradition of Baldwin's best critical works than it is in his "sensational" fiction. The stories are "beautifully made to frame genuine experience in a lyrical language." They are free from the "intellectual sin" of confusing the Negro's tragedy with the "homosexual's psychic deformity" (which is what happened in Another Country). Going to Meet demonstrates effectively that Baldwin has "no need of racial or sexual special pleading; free of these, at his best he is a rare creature."

69 Straumann, Heinrich. "The Power of Reality." In his American
   Literature in the Twentieth Century, 3rd ed., rev. New
   York: Harper and Row, pp. 39-41.
      Identifies a strong deterministic element in Baldwin's
   work embodied in his Harlem boyhood experiences, which
   assume "the character of a metaphor" for the predicament of
   the ambivalence between accepted social standards and moral
   values, on one hand, and the personal doubts of the lonely
   individual on the other. There is a detachment about the
   race question, although in Giovanni's Room there is a frank
   and tactful treatment of the tender and ghastly aspects of
   homosexuality. Baldwin also points out the symbolism inherent in the loneliness of the Negro, the American, and
   modern man--all in search of identity.

70 Taubman, Howard. "Frank Silvera and Bea Richards Head Cast."
   New York Times Theater Reviews (16 April), p. 35.
      Reviews the "notable performances" of the actors of
   Amen Corner. The most memorable ones come near the end
   when "Sister Margaret . . . comes truly alive." The per-
   formers lift the play "far above the commonplace."

71 Taubman, Howard. "Jones and Baldwin." New York Times Theater
   Reviews (25 April), p. 11.
      Sees a "good deal of platform rhetoric" in Baldwin's
   Blues. This is not the case in Amen Corner, which reveals
   "nothing of the pamphleteer and polemicist." In the latter
   play, the structure is "elementary," and the characters are
   "simple and undimensional," but the theme is "meaningful":
   "religion is used as an escape by impoverished and emotionally troubled Negroes."

72 Thompson, Thomas. "Magical Eleventh-hour Save." Life, 14 May,
   p. 16.
      Expresses the position that Blues was saved at the "11th
   hour" when a lovely actress, Diana Sands, mourned for her
   slain lover. Her words "burned into every corner of the
   theater." Now, Amen Corner, written some years before, has
   appeared on Broadway, and it is only in the third act (the
   so-called 11th hour) that it comes alive.

73 Warren, Robert Penn. Who Speaks for the Negro? New York:
   Random House, pp. 160-61, 277-92, 295-98, 323-24.
      Transcribes conversations and interviews, along with
   settings and commentaries, of Negroes from many social
   strata; contains numerous quotations from references and
   allusions to Baldwin's works and activities, including
   interviews. Several facets of Baldwin's life and actions
   are used. A number of black leaders as well as Warren

113

1965

respond to comments by him: on the notion of the Negro as
redeemer; on his message of "redemptive sensuality" and
"redemptive love"; on his view of cosmic vengeance. Warren
analyzes Baldwin's written and spoken utterances as being
characterized by "a tendency to pull away from the specific
issue which might provoke analysis, toward one more general
in which, in a shadowy depth, the emotion coils." Baldwin's great strength consists "in the constantly presented
drama of the interpenetration of his personal story with
the race issue" whereby he gives the issue "a frightening--
and fascinating--immediacy . . . complexity of precise and
shocking image, and shadowy allusiveness." Warren also compares the affinities shared by Baldwin and Faulkner.

74 Watson, Edward A. "The Novels and Essays of James Baldwin:
Case-Book of a Lover's War with the United States." Queen's
Quarterly, 72 (Summer), 385-402.
    Cites a Time article (1963) that linked Baldwin with
"the national racial crisis" and called him "one of the
leaders of the Negro in his search for first-class citizen-
ship." Prior to this, he had received "sporadic attention
and praise" for over a decade. Go Tell It showed his ability to make "the experiences of the story immediate and
definitive." Notes came in 1955 and represented the emergence of his own conflict between race and nationality;
each essay was a "triumph or failure in understanding himself as a Negro and as an American." Giovanni's Room was
not a particularly successful work, but it possessed "real
beauty of language." Nobody Knows was a collection of
essays written between 1954 and 1961, and presented a new
man, "more certain of himself as a Negro, as an American,
and as an author." His next novel, Another Country, explored the "intense relations" of Negroes and whites in New
York. This work was not a convincing novel because it
lacked "any recognizable standards of value." Baldwin's
real popularity emerged with The Fire, which was merely a
"reaffirmation of a moral stand taken several years before."
He has worked consistently well with the essay as a literary form, and he has continued to point out "the necessity
for the artist to be involved with the life of the society
in order to arrive at a better understanding of humanity."
His fame today must be judged only through "his masterful
employment of the essay as a means of examining his own
soul and that of the country he loves."

75 Wüstenhagen, Heinz. "James Baldwin's Essays und Romane:
Versuch einer ersten Einschätzung." Zeitschrift für Ang-
listik und Amerikanistik, 13: 117-47.

114

Argues that superlative evaluations of Baldwin as "the most important Negro author of our times" are premature. His commercial success is largely due to the "titillation of the sexuality" in which his "nonconformity" or "apparent radicalism" is clothed. The depiction of sexuality (including homosexuality) in his novels does have an inherent element of rebellion, but sexuality in literature is no longer an acceptable nor effective means of expressing protest; it serves as an outer sign of "decadent art." It is to be hoped that Baldwin will one day place his glittering talent unmistakably in the service of the Negro people battling for a just cause.

1966

1   Aldridge, John W. "The 'Establishment' Chart." In his Time to Murder and Create. New York: David McKay Company, pp. 68-75.
    Argues that Baldwin enjoys prominence as a public figure, "as a professional Negro and Negro polemicist," not as an author and writer of novels. His opinions and not his novels receive the important publicity.

2   Alexander, Charlotte. Baldwin's "Go Tell It on the Mountain," and "Another Country," "The Fire Next Time," "Giovanni's Room," "Notes of a Native Son." New York: Monarch Press, 59 pp.
    Attempts to provide students with a general introduction to Baldwin and his works as part of "Monarch Notes" series. The booklet contains sections on "The Author: James Baldwin"--about his life and writings; "The Works"--with detailed critical commentary and character analyses; "Commentary"-- a survey of criticism; "Test Questions"--with sample essay questions and answers; and "Further Reading"--a highly selective bibliography.

3   ANON. "Baldwin." PMLA, 81 (May), 186-87.
    Presents annual secondary bibliography for 1965.

4   ANON. "Going to Meet the Man." Choice, 3 (April), 118.
    Believes that the collection of short stories in Going to Meet expresses "authentic anguish" and one theme--the "Negro's impotent rage and hatred in a white man's world." Baldwin is praised for his treatment of the feelings of aloneness and estrangement in the young, e.g., "The Outing"; but he is seen as sometimes falling into "a patterned response of anger and self-pity."

1966

5   ANON. "Paperbacks." <u>Best Sellers</u>, 26 (15 December), 354.
      Notes that <u>Going to Meet</u> is "strong worded, full of
      awareness of race controversy and vitally alive."

6   Arana, Gregorio. "The Baffling Creator--A Study of the Writ-
      ing of James Baldwin." <u>Caribbean Quarterly</u>, 12, no. 3
      (September), 3-23.
         Argues that "the cult of James Baldwin has threatened
      to go beyond reasonable bounds," but does not disparage
      his achievement, nor his fame as a writer. Reviewers and
      critics seem to be making him a "phenomenon" by their use
      of "extravagant adjectives" to describe his writings.
      <u>Notes</u> sets the context for his writing, the importance to
      his writing for having been born a Negro, and the love he
      has for America. Both <u>Another Country</u> and <u>Giovanni's Room</u>
      are deeply concerned with homosexuality as well as the
      "pathos and pity of life." <u>Blues</u> is a "revelation of the
      whole Southern white attitude to the Negro," full of rage
      and fury. His literary achievements rank him as one of the
      "most relevant men of letters."

7   Barksdale, Richard, K. "Alienation and the Anti-Hero in Recent
      American Fiction." <u>CLAJ</u>, 10 (September), 1-10.
         Presents some reservations about the topic for two rea-
      sons: the critical approach being used "ignores the art,
      technique, and general creative" skill of a writer and
      focuses only on the "moral and social meanings"; and skep-
      ticism emanates from the concept of the "alienated anti-
      hero," merely provokes "tautological confusion." There is
      and has been considerable discussions of man's alienation,
      a "syndrome which has afflicted the entire Western World."
      Yet there are certain "alienating conditions" that are
      uniquely American: 1) the "unbridgeable gap between the
      beautiful American dream and the early historical facts";
      2) power and glory belonging to the machine; 3) threat to
      the "great society" by mass annihilation through nuclear
      war; 4) "Madison-avenueism," dressing society's wounds in
      "sparkling cellophane" and hiding its "evils with dollar
      bills." There are many other conditions, but these seem to
      form the bases for the "articulate artist's vigorous dis-
      sent." And out of the "rich diversity of American fiction"
      today, there are numerous types of antiheroes "depicted in
      reaction to the alienating conditions" of society.   The
      male homosexual is one such antihero; he is the "non-man
      rebel-victim." <u>Giovanni's Room</u> presents him "sacrificed on
      the altar of a pretentious and overly self-assertive eroti-
      cism." In an aggressively heterosexual society, the homo-
      sexual "has no identity, no psychological roots, no

meaning." Another antihero is the Negro--he, too, is in
search of an elusive identity. Go Tell It and The Fire reveal that belonging to a "highly emotional Negro church is
no fit substitute for belonging to society." In the rituals
of the church there are grief, anger, joy, "the hedonistic
release of jazz rhythms," and the "epicurean splendor" of
collards and cornbread, but there is always the bitter reality of "isolation and hopelessness."

8 Berry, Boyd M. "Another Man Done Gone: Self-Pity in Baldwin's
   Another Country." Michigan Quarterly Review, 5 (Fall),
   285-90.
       Expects to hear more than man's inhumanity to the Negro
   in the works of Wright, Ellison, Kelley, or Baldwin. There
   is a need to form new opinions about Negro characters as
   men first and as Negroes second; and there must be a disre-
   garding of the novelist's race. An excellent example of
   this is Baldwin's Another Country; although he is a Negro,
   he does not automatically share the views of his Negro
   characters. These characters are "men not Negroes"; thus,
   he can criticize them "insofar as they are human failures."
   In the midst of the highly praised qualities of this work,
   there are numerous faults. He shows the reader sin, but
   never redemption. The characters become mechanical; the
   ideas line up at two poles; the focus on self-pity allows
   the characters to abdicate moral responsibility.

9 Bier, Jesse. "Recent American Literature: The Great Debate."
   Bucknell Review, 14, no. 2 (May), 98-105.
       Begins with a review of Trilling's The Liberal Imagina-
   tion and Cozzen's By Love Possessed. The first is a collection of essays on literary and cultural criticism of
   liberal analysis of such tenets as "environmentalism";
   these essays question the view of reality held by "liberal
   men of good will." The second is a novel about a conser-
   vative whose value system is "not merely a little wrong
   but entirely unavailing." In this tradition, the "cru-
   sader" Baldwin finds his real impact--a "fundamental attack
   upon the whole philosophy of naturalistic determinism" that
   extends to a "depth analysis of the entire national psyche."
   His prose pieces are "products of great control and insight"; his characters struggle to find their "true selves
   and thus avoid being used or abused by others."

10 Blount, Trevor. "A Slight Error in Continuity in James Bald-
    win's Another Country." Notes and Queries, 13 (March),
    102-103.

1966

        Calls Another Country Baldwin's "most ambitious" work.
It is therefore a pity that "small slips" mar the overall
quality of the novel.

11 Bone, Robert. "The Novels of James Baldwin." In Images of
the Negro in American Literature. Edited by Seymour Gross
and John Edward Hardy. Chicago: University of Chicago
Press, pp. 265-99.
    Reprint of 1965.17.

12 Bradford, Melvin E. "Faulkner, James Baldwin, and the South."
Georgia Review, 20 (Winter), 431-43.
    Cites Baldwin's essay, "Faulkner and Desegregation,"
which questions how a person like Faulkner could respond
the way he did on the problems of a multiracial society.
Baldwin is criticized as a "Negro novelist" not too "perceptive in his comments on the squire of Oxford"; after
all, his fiction and essays suffer from a "suffocating nar-
cissism." Faulkner was most at home where he was born, and
his view of "community" presupposes a hierarchy, a "definite
order of status, function, and place." He always spoke
from a Southern framework, and he was well aware of how
much the "future of his people depended upon their ability
to meet and endure new circumstances" and their attempts to
frustrate outside interference. He insisted that the "responsibility for the stewardship of the Southern community
must ultimately fall upon the white Southerner." Ironically, when Baldwin is not playing the role of "militant
Negro intellectual" or proving his social relevance, he,
too, recognizes the "importance of status and place . . .
in an orderly and civilized society."

13 Brown, Sterling A. "A Century of Negro Portraiture in American Literature." The Massachusetts Review, 7 (Winter),
73-96.
    Argues that Baldwin is "today the best known Negro wri-
ter" because of his perceptive essays and "probably the
best known American Negro writer in history" because of
the paperback revolution." Go Tell It and Another Country
are rich in emotion and understanding and are heavily autobiographical. The Fire is a prophetic voice of young mili-
tants in SNCC and CORE.

14 Cartey, Wilfred. "I've Been Reading: The Realities of Four
Negro Writers." Columbia University Forum, 9 (Summer),
34-42.
    Quotes from the African poet Senghor concerning "lone-
liness and the night," which beats in the "very views" of

the black man. The four novels discussed are: Mphahlele's
Down Second Avenue, Lamming's In the Castle of My Skin,
deJesus' Child of the Dark, and Baldwin's Go Tell It. Each
work consists of a personal environment, a "personal hell,"
in which "the present is pain and the future menacing."
Go Tell It utilizes a water image to describe outer reality
--"the water ran in the gutter," "the water traveled paper
. . . moved slowly . . . to the river." There is also a
"keen relish for a bourgeois propriety"--Grimes's mother
has a "prized parlor." Although the lives of the Negro
characters are "symptomatic of the way Negroes live," the
heroes are more than a general statement about the realities of the Negro's lot; they represent the author's vivid
interest in and involvement with the personal aspects of
circumstance.

15 Cleaver, Eldridge. "Notes on a Native Son." Ramparts, 5
      (June), 51-56.
        Includes an introduction of Cleaver as a person "ready
      to be judged as a writer--not as a prison writer or a wri-
      ter about prisons," but an "authentic voice." He comments
      on Baldwin as a writer who has a "talent capable of pene-
      trating so profoundly into one's own little world that one
      knows oneself to have been unalterably changed and libera-
      ted." There is something disturbing in Baldwin: his "arro-
      gant repudiation" of some important expressions, e.g.,
      Mailer's The White Negro; a "grueling, agonizing, total ha-
      tred of the blacks particularly of himself"; and a "shame-
      ful, fanatical, fawning . . . love of whites" that cannot
      be found in any black. Nobody Knows is convincing in its
      black hatred and his confession for abandoning his African
      heritage. From Go Tell It to The Fire, there is a "deci-
      sive quirk in Baldwin's vision which corresponds to his re-
      lationship to blacks and masculinity"--the slandering of
      Rufus in Another Country, the venerating of André Gide, the
      repudiating of The White Negro, and the stabbing of Richard
      Wright.

16 Clurman, Harold. The Naked Image: Observations on the Modern
      Theatre. New York: The Macmillan Company, pp. 37-39.
        Reprint of 1964.23.

17 Dane, Peter. "Baldwin's Other Country." Transition: A Jour-
      nal of the Arts, Culture and Society, 5, no. 24, pp. 38-40.
        Quotes Baldwin that "it is impossible to be a writer and
      be a public spokesman . . . You cannot talk in terms of
      black and white as a writer." In contrast to Leslie Fied-
      ler's view that only Baldwin's essays are great, Dane sees

the novels as "his supreme achievement" and thinks <u>Another Country</u> is not only his "most ambitious book but also his best." Baldwin is not concerned with the sociology of his characters, but rather with what "lies behind the schemata and the stereotypes in terms of human joy and suffering, human hopes and fears."

18 Dommerques, Pierre. "La Négritude Américaine." <u>Les Langues Modernes</u>, 60 (May/June), 94-98.
    Points out that at the center of the American black problem lies a concept of fundamental inequality promoted by whites. This is the real "tragedy," for this concept of inequality permeates the economic, social, and political life of blacks. There has been a new Negro movement in the United States in which such names and titles are prominent: James Forman, Roy Wilkins, Martin Luther King, Jr., CORE, SNCC, NAACP, Freedom Democratic Party, etc. In the area of literature, LeRoi Jones has become a well-known figure; he was instrumental in establishing the Black Arts Repertory Theatre. Ellison has presented the black American as an "invisible man" seeking to approach "western man." Considering all aspects, the problem has several side-by-side positions (for blacks): "to assume a rough, agitated stance on behalf of the Negro (Jones)"; "to uncover the dignity of blacks (Baldwin)"; and "to transcend one's identity (Ellison)."

19 Donadio, Stephen. "Looking for the Man." <u>PR</u>, 33 (Winter), 137-38.
    Reviews <u>Going to Meet</u> in relation to <u>The Fire</u>, which exemplified Baldwin's ability to "isolate and probe the inflamed regions of his consciousness." Now he is faced with two alternatives: to become a Negro representative; or to run the "risk of self-exposure to the point at which he might be considered a special case" (thus diminishing his political impact). He appears to have chosen the first despite that he is not now and never was an "ideology"; he is a writer, and this choice has had "effects not . . . suited to his temperament." The stories in <u>Going to Meet</u> add nothing to his stature, nor do they diminish it. At best, "they are composed in a prose oddly balanced between sheer banality and rhetoric as thick as jam." The balance is very precarious, and one step in the wrong direction could be "fatal."

20 Doughtery, Jim. "Who's Afraid of Nigger Jim." <u>Edge</u>, 5 (Fall), 116-20.

1966

Describes Blues and LeRoi Jones's Dutchman as revolutionary works in the tradition of the "classic American radicalism of Thoreau and Whitman." Neither is a playwright; thus
talent for language does not readily lend itself to writing
dialogue; speeches tend to become "narrative or oratory."
Blues "assumes and depicts a greater intellectual freedom";
it is a larger drama in size and scope, and Baldwin has
"more dramaturgic skill" than Jones. Blues cuts below the
stratum of race to "an idea of manhood"; it reveals how
much hurt there is in freedom, and it dares one to try it.

21 Eckman, Fern Marja. The Furious Passage of James Baldwin. New
   York: M. Evans, 254 pp.
   Describes Baldwin as the "dark man" who has rubbed salt
   in the "wounds of the nation's conscience," and as having
   "an accusing finger thrust in the face of white America."
   He is one of "the nation's greatest creative artists" who
   "embodies the paradoxes and the potentials of the integration battle in the United States." The extensive personal
   accounts, based on taped interviews, reveal in depth the
   man who is a kind of "distillation of the nation's experience as well as his own." He speaks continually of whites
   and Negroes; writing about the country's cultural "duality,"
   he assimilates both parts. He jabs at the "masochism latent
   in white Americans." He says defiantly that he is a writer,
   but his postscript concludes that there is no way to escape his role in the civil rights "revolution." Inevitably,
   he is castigated by white Americans as an "extremist" and
   "flailed by more radical Negroes as a moderate." He views
   himself as "a figure of Dostoevskian tragedy"; his "chasms
   of sorrow are fathomless," his "peaks of joy" are lofty.
   Some have argued that he "was inimical not only to white
   middle-class liberals but also to blacks." Whoever is his
   audience, he always asserts that to be a Negro artist in
   the United States remains a "very frightening assignment."
   Baldwin seems to detect a "conspiracy in adversity and
   feels himself a stranger everywhere, not least of all within himself." This work is the most important single source
   of autobiographical and biographical data, revealing dimensions and facets of the author's thought and personality
   not otherwise available.

22 Fiedler, Leslie A. "Caliban or Hamlet: An American Paradox."
   Encounter, 26 (April), 23-27.
   Declares that the Caliban-Hamlet paradox "resides at the
   heart of American literature" and is intricately bound up
   in the core of European-American cultural relations. The
   question, then, is: "How . . . to deal with one world

1966

without betraying the other, or with both without falsifying both." Fiedler uses a "literary anthropolitical" approach to satisfy the conditions of this paradox. The
Caliban-Hamlet paradox is found in novels, plays, and poems
of American writers in the "deep images that lie at their
hearts." These writers are turning away from "sophisticated literary cosmopolitanism" and are returning to a "willing suspension of intelligence" to the "crassest kind of
nationalism, nativism, and primitivism"--back to Caliban.
There is a movement toward "re-inventing" oneself in terms
of the "experiences and values, the attitudes and idioms"
of various ethnic and cultural groups. Yet, there are
those who still cling to the American Hamlet, brooding and
melancholy, who represents some type of Christ figure as
well as Oedipal image. Thus Caliban resembles the "earlier
European portraits of the indigenous American," and confusion arises when the American, who is sure he is Hamlet,
confronts the European who is convinced he is Caliban. Another confusion emerges from those "American Hamlets" who
are trying to persuade themselves that they are Calibans;
this is the case of Baldwin who wrote Go Tell It, Notes,
and Giovanni's Room with "delicate and scrupulous examination of conscience" and has "been impelled to move on
towards the brutal histrionics" of Another Country and
Blues.

23 Friedman, Neil. "James Baldwin and Psychotherapy." Psycho-
    therapy, 3 (November), 177-83.
        Sees that the Negro still remains "an invisible man" in
    formal psychotherapy literature. The scarcity of case
    studies of Negroes in therapy evokes at least two popular
    responses to this matter: make the person fit the frame of
    reference; or "stretch the frame of reference to fit the
    person." A third possible response is to throw away the
    theories and go to the "creative documents" to understand
    certain themes of persons' life histories. Thus, Baldwin's
    writings not only reveal "the life out of which they come,"
    they also provide an understanding of "the role played by
    the stereotypes (the fabled attributes) of the Negro in his
    own and other Negroes' non-identification with their race."
    It would be "generally good practice for therapists to
    make more extensive use of creative documents of the sub-
    cultures from which their clients come."

24 Gould, Jean. "Edward Albee and the Current Scene." In her
    Modern American Playwrights. New York: Dodd, Mead and
    Company, 187-88.

1966

Combines limited biographical data with brief notices of
his drama; notes Blues as a powerful propaganda piece com-
pleted after the death of Baldwin's friend, Medgar Evers.

25 Hernton, Calvin C. "Blood of the Lamb." In his White Papers
    for White Americans. New York: Doubleday, pp. 105-21.
        Argues that the "romance" of the times is the one "cur-
    rently going on between white Americans and a highly photo-
    genic Negro"--James Baldwin. He is admired by whites, is
    popular with the press, and has appeared in almost every
    worthwhile publication in America. Many Negroes express
    ambivalence toward him; quite a few envy him or "put him
    down" for no real reason. Yet, he has "enchanted and out-
    raged" people with his "great, eloquent syntax," his seem-
    ingly "boundless honesty and with his terrible but well-
    disciplined anger." There is a "phantom, an enigma" that
    seems to haunt most of Baldwin's writing--his father. Go
    Tell It, Giovanni's Room, Notes, The Fire, all have father
    figures who have "something to do with the hero's predica-
    ment." This father enigma goes further than his natural
    father; it projects itself to other powerful men in his
    life, e.g., Richard Wright and Elijah Muhammad. His so-
    journ in Europe helped him to master "the contradictory
    powers within himself"; he had come of age. His return to
    America came at a "ripe" time when the Negro upheaval gave
    whites no alternative but "to accept and put on display a
    man such as Baldwin who speaks of love, torture, agony and
    forgiveness." But is he satisfied? Has he achieved his
    ambition of becoming a "good writer? He is in the class
    with Camus, Sartre." He writes about "the blood of the
    lamb, sin, and redemption. He is . . . the categorical
    head of the newly emerging young . . . Existential Negroes."

26 Hernton, Calvin C. "A Fiery Baptism." In his White Papers
    for White Americans. New York: Doubleday, pp. 122-47.
        Affirms that "Baldwin's writing would undergo a fiery
    baptism." Blues was "brutal, crude, violent, and bold,"
    and because of its "straightforward, realistic and secular"
    treatment, whites found it "difficult to face what they
    have been hiding and gliding over for centuries." Blacks
    seemed enthralled by the "delight and moral vindication to
    see for the first time the true nature of their lives and
    their plight played back to them with dignity . . . Not
    only did whites recoil from the play, but the press took a
    critical approach and said that the play failed as a civil
    rights play." This drama represents a change in Baldwin
    as a writer and as a Negro. He is no longer "addressing a

123

predominantly white audience"; he no longer deals exclusively with the "subjective or moral coefficients of the white
world's inhumanity toward the Negro"; rather he deals with
the "raw, brutal, objective facts of the white man's bar-
barity toward black people." He has become a true "spokesman not just for the middle class but for the masses of his
people." He has become not only an "existential Negro" but
a "religious existentialist" as well. He has met the race
problem with aspects such as "hate, anguish, guilt, conscience, internal torture, sin, and iniquity." He has performed his new task excellently.

27 Hyman, Stanley Edgar. "Blacks, Whites and Grays." In his
    Standards: A Chronicle of Books for Our Time. New York:
    Horizon, pp. 22-27.
        Reprint of 1961.12.

28 Jones, B. F. "James Baldwin: The Struggle for Identity."
    British Journal of Sociology, 17 (June), 107-21.
        Questions "Who is James Baldwin?" His own personal ex-
    periences and "literary freedom" provide insight and even
    some answers to this question, especially from a sociologi-
    cal perspective. Hence the "Negro problem" for him is not
    a Negro one but a white one. Whites have created the "con-
    ditions which make being a Negro problematic." The great
    "white crime," in a Freudian sense, is that whites do not
    know what they do (in most cases), thus the "innocent" syn-
    drome, which causes confusion and tension. This situation
    is compounded when the tension, especially in whites, is
    actually released through aggression. What causes this?
    Baldwin sees a difference between the origin and persis-
    tence: economic gain was the origin--deprive Negroes of
    all power. But the persistence comes from the concept of
    sexual gain--Blues suggests that white men find Negro women
    more satisfying. If this is so, then it follows that white
    women feel the same way about Negro men--hence the myth of
    the male Negro's superior sexuality and the fear of it.
    Another factor for the persistence of exploitation and de-
    privation is "status-insecurity." The major way for oppor-
    tunity is education; and for the Negro child, available
    education is meaningless. Thus, the basic myth of white
    society--the worthlessness and inferiority of the Negro--
    is perpetuated. How, then, does the Negro respond? Bald-
    win offers two main ways: tragically to accept the myth; or
    angrily to fight against the myth. This approach has
    several weaknesses: 1) exaggerates the extent and inten-
    sity of white prejudice; 2) minimizes the responsibility of
    Negroes for their own situation; 3) attributes the evils of

"exploitation and oppression" to Christianity and whiteness rather than to social conditions. Whatever the flaws, the work is relevant and useful to the social sciences.

29 Jones, LeRoi. "Brief Reflections on Two Hot Shots." In his
    Home: Social Essays. New York: William Morrow, pp.
    116-20.
        Contends that Baldwin and Peter Abrahams, the South African writer, deny their blackness and hence their responsibility in the "racial struggle" by wanting to live free as "individuals" from its ugliness; "they will not even open their mouths to say anything but that they are well dressed, educated, and have feelings that are easily hurt."

30 Langer, Lawrence. "To Make Freedom Real: James Baldwin and
    the Conscience of America." Americana-Austriaca, 58,
    pp. 217-28.
        Recognizes Baldwin as an important figure in the contemporary American scene because "he speaks with a public as well as a private voice." At times, he possesses the "same kind of visionary impulse" that inspired Emerson and Whitman, the earnest regard for one's country in spite of its numerous "unflattering features." Notes, The Fire, Nobody Knows, Go Tell It, Another Country, and Amen Corner stress both the "dilemma of the American Negro in a white man's world," and the "dilemma of the white man in America." One of Baldwin's "firmest virtues" (until Blues) is his ability "to maintain the carefully cultivated perspective . . . of an American writing about Americans."

31 Littlejohn, David. Black on White: A Critical Survey of
    Writing by American Negroes. New York: Grossman, pp. 72-
    74, 110-37.
        Describes Baldwin's writing as having "been written out of some personal necessity, . . . a necessity . . . to transcend." From no other contemporary writer is there such a "sensation of writing as life"; it is all "so open and desperate and acute." His absolute honesty, his "latest variety," is evident especially in his best essays-- "the truth, no pretenses, no fictions, no metaphors." Each of Baldwin's three novels has been a stage--experiences lived, "transformed into words, then exorcised and transcended." Go Tell It was the first stage, "Baldwin's baptism of fire." He comes to terms with his boyhood experiences by defining and transcending them. Giovanni's Room, the second stage, manifested Baldwin's personal uncertainties, not just those of a racial, religious, or familial nature. It was "one of the most subtle novels of the

homosexual world," but the truth seemed "too fictionalized."
The third stage saw the publication of Another Country,
whose style of "screaming, no-holds-barred verbal violence,"
carried the book. The "race-war combats" are transmuted
into "sex combats"--which illustrates "Baldwin's theory of
the fundamentally sexual character of racism."

32 Macauley, Robie. "The Pre-empted Domain." Sat R, 49 (4 June),
   pp. 20-21.
      Provides a brief historical perspective for the "thirty-
   fourth Congress of International P.E.N." and its topic,
   "Literature and the Social Sciences on the Nature of Contemporary Man." The big question confronting the congress
   is: "Is it true that literature is becoming a secondary
   source--that writers themselves are taking their ideas of
   man from the newer disciplines?" If this is true, have
   writers surrendered their independent spirits? Of course,
   many writers seem quite unaware of the extent to "which
   they have been dispossessed," and this may account for the
   "prevalence of secondary source drama and fiction." For
   instance, Baldwin's talent manifests itself best in autobiographical essays; "whereas the same material goes lame
   in his fiction."

33 Materassi, Mario. "James Baldwin, Un Profeta del Nostro Tempo
   (Con un Breve Inedito)." Il Ponte, 22 (31 March), 359-60.
      Presents a brief biographical sketch and then discusses
   Baldwin as a writer and "prophet of our time." The movement that has been associated with the struggle of the
   American Negro is an important movement, for it speaks to
   the issue of individual liberty. Through his writings,
   Baldwin has carried issues to the public. Blues attempts
   to portray the "real" issues of the Negro problems; The
   Fire gives a prophetic picture of the consequences of ne-
   glect. Notes and Nobody Knows emphasize the struggles involved in the Negro's quest for identity--"to be a human
   specimen." Go Tell It is profoundly autobiographical rely-
   ing upon religious themes, and Going to Meet demonstrates
   Baldwin's desire to unify spiritual and cultural experiences. Another Country depicts the significance of human relationships, in all diverse manner.

34 Murray, Albert. "Something Different, Something More." In
   Anger and Beyond: The Negro Writer in the United States.
   Edited by Herbert Hill. New York: Harper and Row, pp.
   112-37.
      Refers to Baldwin's essay, "Everybody's Protest Novel,"
   which seems to reject "social protest in fiction as bad

art, a mirror of confusion . . . as sentimental fantasy con-
necting nowhere with reality." Although the case was overstated, many serious students of American literature were
impressed by what they all thought this "implied about his
own ambitions as a writer." He went on to describe the
hero of Wright's Native Son as "Uncle Tom's descendant" who
betrayed life. Four years earlier Ellison had written an
article about Wright's Black Boy, which was "generous almost to a fault." Ellison was very much aware of Wright's
political affiliations (i.e., a Marxist thinker), but he
recognized the broader literary significance. Baldwin
wrote "Many Thousands Gone" six years later and made no
mention of Black Boy or Ellison's commentary; he did say
that as a writer he had modeled himself on black musicians,
especially the blues singers. Yet his play, Blues, has
very little to do with the blues. Rather, it "fills the
stage with a highly stylized group of . . . militant self-
righteous Negroes hollering and screaming." Baldwin's
criticism of Native Son was valid to a point; the people,
the action, the situations, and the motivations were oversimplified. "They were exaggerated by an overemphasis on
protest," and these oversimplifications led inevitably to
"a false position based on false assumptions about human
nature itself." Thus, at the time, Baldwin's grounds for
rejecting Wright's work seemed solid; he did promise not
only something different but something more. "So far he
has not fulfilled that promise"; the only real difference
is his "special interest in themes related to the so-called
sexual revolution." Aside from this, Wright is still the
author Baldwin resembles most.

*35 Neal, Lawrence F. "The Black Writers' Role: James Baldwin."
     Liberator (April), pp. 10-11, 18.
        Cited in O'Daniel, 1977.39.

 36 Newman, Charles. "The Lesson of the Master: Henry James and
     James Baldwin." Yale Review, 56 (October), 45-59.
        Traces Baldwin's "literary antecedents" to Henry James,
     who had the Atlantic Ocean to separate his mind just as
     the "gulf of color cleaves Baldwin." Such oppositions can
     "prove disastrous in fiction" if they oversimplify charac-
     ter and conflict, but Baldwin's characters suffer no more
     from their color than James's suffer from their money. The
     problem for both is more universal--Baldwin's quest for
     identity, the "reflective burden of Western Man." He uses
     the Negro to show the white man what he is, a technique am-
     bitiously developed in Another Country, which is the result
     of a "long and certainly uplifting process." Go Tell It

1966

counters the "urbane elegance of his Jamesian style" with
the "jagged Negro folk poetry and religious rhetoric."
Giovanni's Room uses the "ambiguities of sexual desire as
the proof-text for a larger rebellion." In Notes and Nobody Knows, Baldwin discovers himself with a brilliance of
language precisely focused. His experiences are unique in
that "his artistic achievements mesh so precisely with his
historical circumstances." He is an artist speaking for a
"genuinely visible revolution."

37 Plessner, Monica. "James Baldwin und das Land der Verheissung:
    Zwischen Farboymbolik und Farbindifferenz," Merkur, 20:
    515-33.
        Argues that Baldwin cannot represent the "second Ameri-
    can Revolution" of freedom rides and sit-ins because the
    solution to the black problem is love, not justice. As a
    disillusioned Christian, he understands love purely emo-
    tionally, relinquishing it to the "natural" nature of man;
    hence he robs it of the ability to become a measure of the
    processes of social development. He is always more in-
    terested in individual suffering than in the general situa-
    tion for Negroes. Baldwin descended from and grew up in a
    "revival atmosphere," where Negroes had decided that if
    they were the "sons of Ham," then whites were "the sons of
    Cain." His works must be understood as "Ham's son exhort-
    ing the sons of Cain" not to kill Abel, the black American.
    Go Tell It attempts to demolish the loaded black-is-bad,
    white-is-good "color symbolism" that predominates in "Cal-
    vinistic America." The Fire indicates that no solution has
    been found showing that the Black Muslims' conceptions of a
    black god and a black promised land are as inadequate as
    the revival preachings in the storefront churches of his
    youth. Baldwin's sojourn in Europe taught him "color in-
    difference," which is preferable to the "color symbolism"
    of any group. He is a "religious romantic" who "emotion-
    alizes charity"; his secularized love ethic mingles "Agape,
    eros, sexus and caritas."

38 Redding, J. Saunders. "Since Richard Wright." African Forum,
    1 (Spring), 21-23.
        Presents the plaguing question: With Richard Wright's
    death, what American Negro writer can assume his place?
    Baldwin is the first to come to mind, but except for Go
    Tell It (his first and best novel), he has avoided some
    very special truths about the reality in which Negroes
    live. Other aspects that have been "equally damaging" to
    him are that he appears to subscribe to: 1) "the white
    man's view of the Negro reality"; 2) the "belief that the

Negro problem is nearly inaccessible"; 3) the "supposition
that there is something intrinsically more valid and valuable in 'white' experience . . . than in Negro, and the
Negro writer who deals with white people . . . with popular
success is . . . a better writer." Both Giovanni's Room
and Another Country "particularize" the white world even to
establishing a "referent" in the lives of his Negro characters. As an essayist, he has real "integrity." The Fire,
despite some "overwrought emotional and intellectual shame,"
is an "honest and urgent" work. Because Baldwin can arti-
culate so well the Negroes' tensions, he is an important
American writer.

39 Salem, James M. "James Baldwin." In American Drama from
    O'Neill to Albee, part I, A Guide to Critical Review. New
    York: Scarecrow Press, pp. 22-23.
       Gives selected reviews about Blues and Amen Corner.

40 Schroth, Raymond A. "Going to Meet the Man." America, 114
    (15 January), 92-93.
       States that Baldwin is the "first Negro artist to turn
    the language of Shakespeare and the Old Testament prophets
    into a psychological-literary weapon in the racial con-
    flict." The "savage beauty of his prose" and the basic
    rightness of his cause have promoted the wide acceptance of
    his work. Blues has a concentrated theme of "genital de-
    terminism"; Another Country portrays the brash, hip quali-
    ties of a potent young black man who defies whites. His
    best work, Go Tell It, sweeps the reader with "passages of
    great descriptive force."

41 Sontag, Susan. "Going to Theater, Etc." In her Against
    Interpretation and Other Essays. New York: Farrar, Straus
    and Giroux, pp. 150-57.
       Reprint of 1964.70.

42 Standley, Fred L. "James Baldwin: The Crucial Situation."
    SAQ, 65 (Summer), 371-81.
       Sees Baldwin as a continuous "subject of controversy
    both as a writer and as a man." Yet, he has become "firmly
    entrenched as a writer of significance" dedicated to his
    commitment of being a "good writer." To do this, he at-
    tests to certain critical attributes: 1) he must examine
    attributes, go beneath the surface, gain an adequate per-
    spective of man; 2) he must write of his own experience,
    "recreate out of the disorder of life, that order which is
    art"; 3) he must realize that being a writer is a "special
    vocation"; 4) he must assume personal and social

responsibility as a "special function" of his writing.
Thus, Baldwin's own vision provides the basis for his examination of the impact of urban life and society on the indi-
vidual--the "suppressed reaction against the imbalance of
power in the social-economic-political structure of society." He confronts the "crucial situations in the lives
of people"--the inescapable situations in which one must
"take an attitude and make a decision because existence
itself is confronted with a threat." Such situations require decisiveness and involve "the affirmation or denial
of the significance of life"--birth and death, love and
marriage, vocation, doubt, guilt, anxiety. One of the
principal forms in which the crucial situation is expressed
"consists of the search for identity." In his work, the
quest for identity always involves "the discovery and eli-
mination of illusion and delusion about oneself"; it always
involves another person(s) for "there can be no self-per-
ception apart from or outside the context of interpersonal
relationship." The lack of interpersonal relations is explicitly related to "the breakdown of communication between
persons" especially between the sexes, and the breakdown
produces misconceptions of people about each other. Only
love can bridge the gap of communication, for it can force
individuals "to see themselves as they are, to cease fleeing from reality and to begin to change it."

43 Strong, Augusta. "More Baldwin at His Best." Freedomways, 6
    (Winter), 63.
        Praises Going to Meet for its craftsmanship and revela-
    tion. "The Rockpile" and "The Outing" show the familiar
    Baldwin "fervent saints" who suffer to test their strength
    before future glory. He also uses the expatriate in "This
    Morning, This Evening, So Soon" and the artist in "Previous
    Condition." "Come Out the Wilderness" gives the woman as a
    counterpart to the lonely, tormented man. The title story
    reveals the mental pathology of a bigot and a lynching with
    the elements of sex and violence compounded.

44 Turner, Darwin T. "The Negro Novel in America: In Rebuttal."
    CLAJ, 10 (December), 122-34.
        Cautions readers of The Negro Novel in America (Bone,
    1965) that there are shortcomings, fallacies, and biases,
    which "vitiate Mr. Bone's commendable effort to evaluate
    Negro writers' novels according to literary criteria." He
    has not been content to confine himself to the role of
    "critic and historian," but he has "presumed to serve as
    psychiatrist, philosopher, and teacher not only for all
    Negro writers, but for all Negroes." The work is structured

in six parts: 1) The Novel of the Rising Middle Class: 1890-1920; 2) The Discovery of the Folk: 1920-1930; 3) The Search for a Tradition: 1930-1940; 4) The Revolt Against Protest; 5) Postscript--an Essay on Baldwin; 6) Epilogue-- Advice to Negro Writers. Parts 4 and 5 reveal the best work because Ellison and Baldwin "lend themselves to mythic and symbolic interpretations"; Bone can "propound" provocative explications even "if they do not always reflect the artists' intentions."

1967

1 ANON. "The Amen Corner." <u>Kirkus</u>, 35 (1 May), 582.
   Presents <u>Amen Corner</u> as a better play than the author's <u>Blues</u> because of the central character, the storefront evangelist, Sister Margaret, "a figure of real yearnings and consequence" rarely found on the Broadway stage, as well as the gospel singing atmosphere, the idiomatic speeches, and genuine sentiments.

2 ANON. "Baldwin." <u>PMLA</u>, 82 (June), 200.
   Presents annual secondary bibliography for 1966.

3 ANON. "Pick of the Paperbacks." <u>Sat R</u>, 50 (21 January), 40.
   Says that the best stories of <u>Going to Meet</u>, a collection dating from 1948 to the present, offer "an immediacy of experience felt and shared," viz. "The Outing" and "Sonny's Blues."

4 Bigsby, C. W. E. "The Committed Writer: James Baldwin as Dramatist." <u>Twentieth Century Literature</u>, 13 (April), 39-48.
   Assesses Baldwin's dilemma as essentially that of the artist "who is also, consciously or not, committed to a specific social problem." As an artist, he sees the need to view humanity as a whole and to escape the narrow vision of social limitations to the racial situation. The "continuing battle" that he has waged with "the spirit of Richard Wright" stems from reactions to the dehumanization operating in Wright's work--"literature and sociology are not one and the same." It is Baldwin's ability to maintain this distinction in his novels that raises his work "above the naive absolutism" of other writers. This does not mean that he "abandons faith in the validity of his own experience," but that this "experience is seen in the broader context of the human condition." <u>Another Country</u> subordinates the fact of miscegenation to the more fundamental problem

of "isolation and the desperate failure of human communication." The Fire points out the need for renewal in life,
the need to "confront with passion the conundrum of life."
Blues takes place in Plaguetown, U.S.A.; the "plague is
race" and the "concept of Christianity," which seems to
have the "power to destroy every human relationship." But
Blues is still a kind of 1930s "sociological play which
contains the right information and the right accusatory
attitudes toward poor whites and Southern justice but lacks
insights into prejudice and ability to create characters
beyond stereotypes." Baldwin's failure to accomplish the
high level of artistic responsibility in his drama present
in his essays and novels is indicative of the greater discipline demanded by drama and of his own increasing personal commitment to the civil rights struggle.

5 Burgess, Anthony. "American Themes." In his The Novel Now:
A Guide to Contemporary Fiction. New York: W. W. Norton
and Company, pp. 198-99.
Calls Baldwin "the most spectacular of the Negro novelists." Go Tell It presents "two opposed Negro attitudes
to the white community which persecutes him": the older,
traditional one, which "preaches acceptance of injustice as
an unalterable part of the Negro condition (and, by impli-
cation, of the human condition generally)"; and the new
one, "which holds that injustice must be fought against and
that the Negro must never rest until he has overcome it."
That Baldwin is "not wholly preoccupied with the Negro condition, but with the condition of all whom a monolithic
white society" exploits or rejects, is clear from Giovanni's
Room.

6 Butcher, Phillip. "James Baldwin." In Encyclopedia of World
Literature in the 20th Century, vol. 1. New York: Frederick Ungar Publishing Company, pp. 91-92.
Places Baldwin in the position of "a notable American,
not merely a gifted author." His personal confessions form
the "racial manifesto" that is "the heart of most of his
writing." Notes, Nobody Knows, and The Fire include "repor-
torial and autobiographical pieces, literary criticism and
angry, perceptive analyses of the race problem"; Go Tell It
is a "poetic" treatment of Negro life, and Giovanni's Room,
a sensitive narrative about white homosexuals in Paris, is
probably "his best long work of fiction to date." Another
Country, set mainly in New York, depicts whites and Negroes
in a "world of degradation, violence, and perversion."

7 Clarke, John Henrik. "The Origin and Growth of Afro-American
Literature." Negro Digest, 17 (December), 54-67.

1967

Argues that among black writers, "the period of the
1960s was the period of James Baldwin" who, more than any
other writer of the times, "has succeeded in restoring the
personal essay to its place as a form of creative literature." The Fire and other essays reveal his personal grie-
vance; but in the "alarmist" tradition of being concerned
with the improvement of human conditions, he "calls national
attention to things in the society that need to be corrected
and things that need to be celebrated."

8 Ethridge, James and Barbara Kopala. "James Baldwin." In
their Contemporary Authors, vol. I. Detroit: Gale Research
Company, pp. 43-45.
    Contains biographical sketch, comments about individual
works, quotations from reviews, and selected secondary
bibliography.

9 Farrell, James T. "Literary Note." American Book Collector,
17 (May), 6.
    Contends that the "writers who are in the public eye are
most affected . . . They seek to be zany or to create zany
characters." They are leftist and egocentric, like Mailer;
they are "literary confectioners," like Styron; they "dis-
infect" reality, like Updike; or they simply do not know
how to write a novel, like Baldwin. There is plenty of
talent in these writers, but they "lag behind their repu-
tations and press notices." They need to dedicate themselves to growth, development, and maturity.

10 Gayle, Addison, Jr. "A Defense of James Baldwin." CLAJ, 10
(March) 201-208.
    Observes that in Notes, Baldwin commented that someday
the dissatisfaction Negroes have with Wright may happen to
him. This is what has happened; American critics are beginning "to look behind . . . the brilliance" of his language
and are making special efforts "to attend the argument."
Critics, black and white, find it "uncomfortable" to confront the argument of Negro novelists, so they zero in on
some "non-literary trait of the Negro writer" (e.g., he
hates white people), and from this "evolves a literary
theory." In the book, The Negro Novel in America, author
Robert Bone has an "ax to grind," and Baldwin "becomes his
grinding stone," perhaps because he has inflicted such
"damaging blows upon the northern-liberal construction"
called the "American Creed." Bone fails to give both the
extrinsic and intrinsic approaches to Baldwin's works, just
as Cleaver did in his essay, "Notes on a Native Son," which
is more intent in defending Negro manhood than avenging
Richard Wright.

1967

11 Gayle, Addison, Jr. "The Dialectic of <u>The Fire Next Time</u>."
    <u>The Negro History Bulletin</u>, 20 (April), 15-16.
        Examines <u>The Fire</u> and shows that the two essays repre-
    sent two poles of a dialectic--"the ideal as opposed to the
    real; and . . . the second essay viciously satirizes the
    first." Baldwin demolishes the "idyllic vision" that the
    Negro is a Christ figure. There are no gods, black or
    white, and society can only be redeemed by conscious acts
    by people. Thus the "fate of society rests upon people,"
    and they have always been "pretty shaky resting places."
    The Negro is an American and to think of him as a Christ
    figure "is absurd"; he cannot transform America nor absolve
    her of her sins. The American dilemma "cannot be solved
    by postulating a black redeemer, who . . . will probably
    turn out . . . as helpless . . . as the white one."

12 Harper, Howard M., Jr. "James Baldwin--Art or Propaganda."
    In his <u>Desperate Faith: A Study of Bellow, Salinger, Mail-
    er, Baldwin, and Updike</u>. Chapel Hill, N.C.: University of
    North Carolina Press, pp. 137-61.
        Calls Baldwin "the best known Negro writer in America
    today." He is a popular success as well as a "serious
    artist," and the two roles are not mutually exclusive al-
    though they have forced him "to become a dual personality;
    both a fiery prophet of the racial apocalypse and a sensi-
    tive explorer of man's inmost nature." In the role of
    Negro spokesman "he has been forced into an activism" to
    which he is not totally committed, and in his role as ar-
    tist he is concerned with more basic problems than civil
    rights. Baldwin's essays represent a "fairly well defined
    criticism of American life"; he argues again and again that
    "man's only hope for discovery of truth lies in the relent-
    less examination of his own inner nature." <u>Notes</u>, <u>Nobody
    Knows</u>, and <u>The Fire</u> have "power and insight" and are sensi-
    tive to the falsity of national values in conflict with
    the American Negro. While the idea of "rebellion against
    injustice" is dominant in the essays, the idea of "accep-
    tance of the ultimate existential fact is there too."
    These views of the human condition are further illuminated
    in the fiction. <u>Go Tell It</u> is a "powerful account of the
    bleak physical environment and the lacerating emotional
    tensions of Negroes in the Harlem ghetto"; it is a "remark-
    able first novel and a considerable achievement." <u>Giovan-
    ni's Room</u> "tried too hard for universality"; it is re-
    strained, and what "it gains as a formal argument, it loses
    as a novel." <u>Another Country</u> is the most complex and "most
    sensational" novel; it is a "monument to the inarticulate
    desires of its characters." The trend toward "journalism

and propaganda" is confirmed by <u>Blues</u>, whose "shrill honesty
is . . . the cheapest sentimentality; it is not drama, but
melodrama masked as social criticism."

13 Lumley, Frederick. "U.S.A." In his <u>New Trends in 20th Century</u>
    <u>Drama: A Survey Since Ibsen and Shaw</u>. New York: Oxford
    University Press, pp. 338-39.
        States that "it was Elia Kazan who suggested to . . .
    Baldwin that he should write for the theatre." He has now
    written <u>Blues</u> and <u>Amen Corner</u>; "neither merits a reputation
    as a dramatist." In <u>Blues</u>, he shows his apprentice's hand
    in construction--cardboard characters, artificial action.
    <u>Amen Corner</u>'s dramatic treatment is still "wrong." He is
    an "outstanding polemical writer," and this is "what he
    should stick to."

14 Markholt, Ottilie. "Blues for Mr. Charlie Reconsidered:
    White Critic, Black Playwright: Water and Fire." <u>Negro</u>
    <u>Digest</u>, 16 (April), 54-60.
        Compares <u>Blues</u> with Duberman's <u>In White America</u>, the
    former closing after an unsuccessful run of five months,
    the latter playing over a year. Many critics condemned
    Baldwin "for preaching hate" and praised Duberman "for
    evoking compassion." Some critics charged Baldwin with
    "showering rhetorical spleen on the white man"; they
    appeared to be frightened by the sympathetic response of
    Negroes in the audience. Duberman says he hoped to evoke
    compassion for the Negro by "calling forth the binding
    emotions of pity and sympathy." In <u>Blues</u>, Baldwin shows
    that white people can be free only by rejecting their cul-
    ture of superiority; his Negroes do not hate whites; "hate
    is for equals." They "despise whites, hold them in con-
    tempt, pity them--but they do not need to hate."

15 Mitchell, Lofton. "The Nineteen Sixties: Broadway Recon-
    sidered." In his <u>Black Drama: The Story of the American</u>
    <u>Negro in the Theatre</u>. New York: Hawthorne Books, pp. 184-
    85, 200-201, 206-207.
        Cites Baldwin's statement that "the theatre is perishing
    for lack of vitality"; and this vitality has only one
    source: life. <u>Blues</u> seems more like a "brilliant series
    of essays than a play," but it is very "theatrically alive
    and flaming."

16 Palmer, Helen H. and Jane Anne Dyson. "James Baldwin." In
    their <u>American Drama Criticism</u>. Hamden, Conn.: Shoe
    String Press, pp. 22-23.
        Presents selected secondary sources on <u>Blues</u> and <u>Amen</u>
    <u>Corner</u>.

1967

17 Petersen, Fred. "James Baldwin and Eduardo Mallea: Two Essay-
     ists' Search for Identity." Discourse, 10 (Winter), 97-107.
          Draws a comparison between Baldwin and Eduardo Mallea,
     an Argentine writer whose work, The Personal Record of a
     Spiritual Suffering for Argentine, is a spiritual autobio-
     graphy focusing upon societal ills. He was an intellectual
     who centered his fiction around a hero figure who was either
     the "artistic projection of an ideal" or the "reflection of
     one aspect of the soul of man." Like Baldwin, Mallea had
     gone to Europe to "put into proper perspective and into de-
     finitive terms his feelings and intuitions about the funda-
     mental differences between the Old World and America."
     There are basically two differences plus an "admonition" at
     the end of the book, all of which form a "triangle" of con-
     cepts: 1) the spirit of liberty, which as a force in Ameri-
     can society distinguishes it from that of Europe; 2) the
     selfless spirit of giving in a religious sense frees man
     into "being"; 3) the severe exaltation of life calls for
     the focusing of all of one's energies on life. Baldwin is
     the "new man" in this literary expression; that is, he
     comes closest to the tradition in which Mallea was writing
     almost thirty years ago. It is interesting that critics
     are unable to describe his (Baldwin's) involvement in "the
     circumstances of the crisis" of the time; they cannot ac-
     cept him, cannot see him as the ultimate protagonist of
     his own work, or fail to understand that he is actually
     "living the revolution" that he describes in his essays.
     His book, Nobody Knows, stands as the "cornerstone" of his
     art; it represents his "search for himself--not only his
     personal self, but himself as a social being within the web
     of American life." Like Mallea, Baldwin is searching for
     "his authentic and complete identification." Behind all of
     this, however, there is the "artistic expression of both
     these men and intense humanism that has its origin in the
     individual." Their works are primarily personal; neither
     remains just at the personal level of expression.

18 Ploski, Harry A. and Roscoe C. Brown. "James Baldwin." In
     their The Negro Almanac. New York: Bellwether Co., pp.
     677-78.
          Presents a brief biographical account.

19 Scott, Nathan A., Jr. "Judgment Marked by a Cellar: The
     American Negro Writer and the Dialectic of Despair." The
     Denver Quarterly, 2, no. 2 (Summer), 5-35.
          Argues that a common cultural identity belongs to blacks
     and whites, especially evident in the bitter and nascently
     triumphant drama of the American experiment. Negro

literature, like jazz, spirituals, sorrow songs, pulpit and
secular oratory, is inseparably a part of American culture.
Go Tell It, with the world of the storefront church, compares favorably with Weldon Johnson's earlier dramatic ly-
ric. Both use a religious tradition but are a great distance from a genuinely Christian writer like T. S. Eliot.
Instead they reveal "a detritus of sentiment and rhetoric
which is the last residuum of pieties effective now only
in the degree to which they provide a sophisticated artist
with a sort of framework for his romance." "Everybody's
Protest Novel" marked Baldwin's entrance into literary life
with the artistic purpose of revealing "the disquieting
complexity of ourselves." Baldwin's dissatisfaction with
Wright resulted not from the element of "protest" but from
the "incorrigible commitment to a violent and narrow naturalism." This "acute discomfort" with the aesthetics of
naturalistic fiction was the result of Baldwin's internal-
ized Christianity, which, though repudiated, still pre-
vailed in his rejection of the "reductionist formulae" of
life. Go Tell It is "a passionate gesture of identification with his people" in the tradition of bildungsroman,
employing "Biblical idiom and imagery." But rather than
"being conceived Christianly" as in the work of Greene or
Bernaños or Updike, the spiritual landscape is desocialized,
"a world in which the traditions of Christian belief and
experience" are uninvolved "in the pressing existential
reality of human endeavor." Notes and Nobody Knows probe
deeply the meaning of Negro experience in America with the
author acting the role of "chief barrister for the black
multitudes at the bar of the American conscience." The "I"
of his early work becomes "the Negro in extremis, a virtu-
oso of ethnic suffering, defiance and aspiration" with a
mounting militancy in The Fire, Another Country, and Blues.

20 Wortis, Irving. "The Amen Corner." LJ, 92 (15 June), 2428.
    Focuses on Amen Corner as revealing "a religion of beau-
tiful desperation, a seeking out of a heavenly life to jus-
tify an earthly death" in the person of Margaret Alexander,
pastor of a Christian church.

21 Zeitlow, Edward R. "Wright to Hansberry: The Evolution of
    Outlook in Four Negro Writers." Ph.D. dissertation, Uni-
    versity of Washington.
    Asserts that Negro writing since the Civil War has been
oriented by the "outlook" toward racial situations in all
periods, e.g., optimism and affirmation; protest and anger;
etc. In the past three decades, two outlooks are evident:
Wright and Ellison represent the literature of "absurdity"--

the absurd man cut off from the God of tradition--and social commentary revealing the pathological personality in a
society uncertain of its metaphysical bases; 2) Baldwin
and Hansberry, in contrast, treat "affirmative engagements"
and the problems of individual beings rather than representative figures in an absurd social scene. Another Country
presents themes of love and maturity through characters who
achieve some success in understanding and shaping their
lives.

1968

1 Alexander, Charlotte. "The 'Stink' of Reality: Mothers and
Whores in James Baldwin's Fiction." Literature and Psychology, 18, no. 1: 9-26.
     Speculates that in Baldwin's fiction, physical intimacy
is a means to "emotional fulfillment," but this experience
brings risk and the "stink" of reality. In Giovanni's Room,
David wants a "clean yet satisfying emotional attachment"
without the "inevitable real obstacles" of such a relationship, mainly the "stink of meaningful physical intimacy."
This is an experience, then, of unreality, "remote from the
external world." Baldwin's characters always "seem groping
from an immense loneliness," in search of love. This quest
for love is the theme of Another Country, which opens with
"do you love me?" wailing from a saxophone. For the experience of love to be meaningful, one must face the reality
of intimacy, which results in a loss of innocence. Paradoxically, there is the revulsion of intimacy that his male
characters display, "rooted perhaps in early experiences
with mothers or mother-figures, . . . fixed . . . to the
psychic fact behind their tendency to hold themselves 'vir-
ginal,'" or to spoil "make-believe" images resulting in
"prostituting themselves for their own sex." In either
case these male characters avoid commitment to "legitimate"
heterosexual relationships. This theme is further expanded
in the notion that there are only "mothers or whores (the
ideal or the shattered ideal)."

2 Algren, Nelson. "Sashaying Around." Critic, 27 (October/
November), 86-87.
     Reviews Tell Me, which tells what happens to "white
people who make it," but it fails to tell "what happens to
black people who make it." Baldwin has previously written
prose with a voice of eloquent "black anguish"; it is perplexing that the same voice rings so "hollowly" in this
novel. All he seems to be doing is "shashaying around."

3 Alves, Helio O. "James Baldwin: O Calabouco Impossivel."
   Vertice, 28 (September), 657-63.
       Explores through a number of the author's essays the
   thesis that there can be no question of freedom for the
   Negro as long as the white is not free from the bondage of
   fear; thus both are caught in an impossible situation of
   imprisonment. A context for the civil rights movement in
   the U.S. is given with reference to Martin Luther King,
   Jr., Malcolm X, Rosa Parks, the Kerner Commission. Among
   the essays used are The Fire, "Nobody Knows My Name," and
   "Stranger in the Village."

4 Anderson, Jervis. "Race, Rage and Eldridge Cleaver." Commentary, 46 (December), 63-69.
       Points out that "until two or three years ago, not many
   people knew who Eldridge Cleaver was." Today, he is "na-
   tionally known"; he is the author of Soul on Ice, minister
   of information for the Black Panther Party, candidate for
   President on the Peace and Freedom party ticket, and a
   "literary idol of the black nationalists." He has come a
   long way since 1954--when ". . . Baldwin was still serving
   a hard apprenticeship in Paris, when mainstream American
   politics had nothing more radical to fear than . . . liberal Democrats." Also in 1954, Cleaver began serving a
   sentence for possession of marijuana. While in jail, he
   "read as much literature as his jailers would make available to him"; in this way he learned about Baldwin, Mailer,
   Wright, and Ellison. Today, as a "writer-activist," Cleaver has a close relation to "the style and tradition of
   Negro writing"; and in another tradition, he is "the essential stylist of the new black generation." His style as
   social advocate and writer "illuminates both the sense of
   itself which the militant generation now has and the ways
   in which Cleaver differs from the majority of Negro writers
   who preceded him." Despite some obvious differences, all
   Negro writers have had to wrestle with the "subtle embargo"
   that the white outlook places on their own sense of reality
   and their style of expressing it. Baldwin once said: "I
   was in effect prohibited from examining my own experience
   too closely by the tremendous demands and the very real danger of my social situation." Yet Ellison and Baldwin succeeded in breaking through these prohibitions and at the
   same time restrained their impulses to agitation and propaganda "within a sense of their vocation as artists." It is
   at this point that Cleaver departs from the "main tradition
   of Negro writing." Cleaver's attack on Baldwin was masked
   as a means to "avenge Baldwin's treatment of Wright," but
   it really was Cleaver's "way of demolishing Baldwin . . .
   to announce his own arrival upon the scene."

1968

5 ANON. "Baldwin." PMLA, 83 (June), 733.
       Presents annual secondary bibliography for 1967.

6 ANON. "Fat Cat on the Mat." TLS (4 July), p. 697.
       Questions why an "author, whose life is in the public
   domain, produces thinly disguised autobiography as fiction?"
   The answer lies somewhere in the "art" of writing, which
   makes "such subterfuge unquestionable." Better the novel,
   Tell Me, were called "Portrait of the Artist as a Fat Cat,"
   because it is itself "too fat, too catty and inartistic."
   There are some redeeming features that help to "salvage"
   the novel; Baldwin's "peculiar candor" regarding his return
   to Harlem gives the novel an existential "core." Here
   alone do the human relationships "sound true."

7 ANON. "Milk Run." Time, 7 June, p. 104.
       Sees two Baldwins: the "racial rhetorician, the politi-
   cal pamphleteer, the literate prophet"; and the "questioning novelist, the private man" with his personal problems
   that "he must defeat or be defeated by." Go Tell It was a
   "marvelous" work; Giovanni's Room rendered the homosexual
   experience with candor and courage; Another Country was a
   "deeply disappointing novel"; and now Tell Me is "further
   evidence that as a fictioneer Baldwin is in great danger of
   becoming deeply irrelevant." The latest work "rambles like
   a milk train over the same run . . . covered in Another
   Country."

8 Bannon, Barbara. "Tell Me How Long the Train's Been Gone."
       Publishers Weekly, 193 (1 April), 33.
       States that Baldwin's view in Tell Me is "bleak, imply-
   ing that it's too late for anything but tragedy and more
   tragedy." There are several stories being told: Leo's re-
   living of his past through flashbacks; the story of Leo's
   career; Leo's relationship with his brother; the bisexual
   private life of Leo.

9 Baxter, Katherine. The Black Experience and the School Curri-
       culum. Teaching Materials for Grades K-12: An Annotated
       Bibliography. Philadelphia: Wellsprings Ecumenical Cen-
       ter, p. 32.
       Includes Blues for high school students in spite of its
   "earthy" language because of its focus on the injustice of
   a white supremacist society and the murder of a black youth
   by a white man.

10 Bigsby, C.W.E. "James Baldwin." In his Confrontation and
       Commitment: A Study of Contemporary American Drama, 1959-

140

1966. Columbia, Missouri: University of Missouri Press,
pp. 126-37.
    Reprint of 1967.4.

11 Britt, David. "The Image of the White Man in the Fiction of
    Langston Hughes, Richard Wright, James Baldwin, and Ralph
    Ellison." Ph.D. dissertation, Emory University.
        Contends that several constants emerge from the study:
    the image of the white correlates directly to the self-image
    of a black protagonist; whites appear in a willfully de-
    structive opposition to Negro characters in various forms
    of exploitation. Baldwin and Wright are in the protest
    tradition with the former exploring the subtle and in-
    ternalized results of racism on whites and blacks, and the
    latter attacking the overt evidences of injustice. Hughes
    and Ellison treat more consciously the values within the
    Negro community that the artist can celebrate, especially
    the vision of dignity and humanity.

12 Brown, Sterling. "A Century of Negro Portraiture in American
    Literature." In Black Voices. Edited by Abraham Chapman.
    New York: New American Library, pp. 564-89.
        Reprint of 1966.13.

13 Clarke, John Henrik. "The Origin and Growth of Afro-American
    Literature." In Black Voices. Edited by Abraham Chapman.
    New York: New American Library, pp. 632-45.
        Reprint of 1967.7.

14 Cleaver, Eldridge. "Notes on a Native Son." In his Soul on
    Ice. New York: McGraw-Hill, Inc., pp. 97-111.
        Reprint of 1966.15.

*15 Coleman, J. "Tell Me How Long the Train's Been Gone." Obser-
    ver (23 June), p. 24.
        Cited in Book Review Index. 1968 Cumulation.

16 Davenport, Guy. "If These Wings Should Fail Me, Lord!"
    National Review, 20 (16 July), 701.
        Points out that Tell Me as a "topical novel takes its
    chances." Rage and dismay are "highly perishable emotions
    . . . from which to issue novels," and in this, the "weak-
    est" of Baldwin's novels, seems "scotch-taped together."

17 Dodson, Owen. "Playwrights in Dark Glasses." Negro Digest,
    17 (April), 31-36.
        Declares that the key to unlocking "the magic and wonder
    of artistic creation" is universality. Although each

1968

creation has a "local habitation," it must also be universal. <u>Blues</u> is a "confused and eloquent play," which sometimes "goes in the direction of the great Greek drama."

18 Elliott, George. "Destroyers, Defilers, and Confusers of Men."
    <u>Atlantic Monthly</u> (December), pp. 74-80.
        Argues that American writers have quite a "tradition of
    ignoring the State, both in literature and in life." Wri-
    ters have narrowed "politics" into some "mean" or "nasty"
    abstraction. Currently, there are some writers who are not
    content to ignore or generalize politics, society, or the
    state; they are claimed as part of the "modernist movement"
    by some, and by others as "nihilists." There are three
    main types of nihilistic writers: destroyers, defilers,
    confusers. The destroyers are the "most congenial," for
    they rage against injustice, social evil. Thus, their
    writings can be "purgative for one who shares the emotion."
    Baldwin is a "destroyer" sometimes, as in <u>The Fire</u>. The
    rage is generated by societal evils, and only "wholesale
    destruction of the evil" will satisfy justice. The defilers
    use "unconventional modes of expression" to denigrate, and
    they are probably better off than destroyers since they are
    "not aiming so much to effect social action as to affect
    the reader's state of mind." A confuser is not set upon
    immediate annihilation; he will settle for producing con-
    fusion in his readers' minds. Barth's <u>Giles Boat-Boy</u> moves
    in confusion, and Albee's <u>Tiny Alice</u> offers "insoluble con-
    tradictions" to its internal confusion. There was a time
    when "nihilistic exhortation made a kind of sense," but
    there are such things as the state, as social order, as
    society, and "literature is inextricably connected" with
    them, "for good or for ill." A new world is emerging, and
    "who is to dream its shape better than writers."

19 Emanuel, James A. and Theodore L. Gross. "James Baldwin,
    1924-." In <u>Dark Symphony: Negro Literature in America</u>.
    New York: Free Press, pp. 296-300, 588-89.
        Combines salient biographical features with brief over-
    view of works to date emphasizing Baldwin's moral urgency
    and lucid vision, his attempt to eliminate inherited super-
    stitions and religious attitudes as well as self-created
    illusions, and his effort to speak the simple but painful
    truth. In fiction, Baldwin's central problem is the con-
    flict between naturalistic and transcendental elements; his
    essays offer "a permanent and unique contribution to Ameri-
    can literature by broadening the scope of racial issues to
    political and social levels in human, personal terms."

20 Fagg, Martin. "Confrontations." Books and Bookmen, 13
    (August), 18-19, 38.
        Describes Tell Me as having "great power and eloquence"
    but traveling over "much of the same territory that he has
    already explored in depth": problems of the artist, quest
    for identity, difficulties of adjustment, etc. The book
    begins on a note of intensity that is neither strident nor
    self-indulgent because "it is so perfectly controlled by
    the lucid, supple grace" of Baldwin's prose. Tell Me is a
    "resonant and affecting book," which breaks no new ground
    but does consolidate "an already potent reputation."

21 Fremont-Smith, Eliot. "Books of the Times: Another Track."
    The New York Times (31 May), p. 27.
        Argues that Tell Me is "a disaster in virtually every
    particular--theme, characterization, plot, rhetoric." It
    is the "disorganized, flash-backing, life outline" of Leo
    Proudhammer, a famous Negro actor; it is a "sad book" of a
    talented and powerful author "puffing up an old, unused and
    now very private track."

22 Gayle, Addison, Jr. "Perhaps Not So Soon One Morning." Phy-
    lon, 29, no. 4 (Winter), 396-402.
        Denies the thesis of Herbert Hill's Soon One Morning
    "that the Negro writer is finally being assimilated into
    the American literary community" by showing that Ellison
    and Baldwin, who are used to support Hill's claim, are
    still judged by racial rather than aesthetic criteria and
    that their major themes are alienation and estrangement not
    assimilation.

23 Gilman, Richard. "News from the Novel." New Republic (17
    August), pp. 27-36.
        Contends that the novel is not dying; it will "obey its
    own urgencies and lead its unpredictable life." Novels go
    on being written, and occasionally some "renew and continue
    the art of fiction." The present "cultural times" make it
    possible for a writer like Baldwin "to produce a work of
    fiction whose spirit, method . . . and policy are entirely
    retrograde by an alert criterion of the contemporary."
    This new novel, Tell Me, has a number of themes, "none of
    which is realized, nor brought to any conclusion in the
    imagination." He has invented a complex life in which he
    has been unable to find a principle of coherence for its
    parts.

24 Green, Martin. "The Need for a New Liberalism." Month, 226
    (September), 141-47.

1968

Reviews Fern Marja Eckman's <u>The Furious Passage of James Baldwin</u>.

25 Hall, Stuart. "You a Fat Cat Now." <u>New Statesman</u>, 75 (28 June), 871.
       Points out that the whole mood of black militancy has "revolutionized the inner experience of being." The "world is divided [now] between Ellison and Baldwin," and it is the latter's force, his "currents of feeling," his "total exposure," which give him power to recreate that "American territory of the mind located somewhere between Harlem and Washington Square." Baldwin is an "authentic master of the language," and <u>Tell Me</u> comes out of the "same bag" as <u>Another Country</u>; both have a loose, narrative structure.

26 Hicks, Granville. "From Harlem with Hatred." <u>Sat R</u>, 51 (1 June), 23-24.
       Calls <u>The Fire</u> an "extraordinary polemic," and <u>Tell Me</u> a "flat and commonplace" novel. In the latter, "there is scarcely a sentence . . . that couldn't have been written by any moderately competent hack." Like <u>Another Country</u>, it "raises some perplexing questions" about Baldwin's novels. <u>Tell Me</u> is rather "shadowy and dim," and only Caleb, one of the Harlem characters, is convincing.

27 Hildick, Wallace. "Bait." <u>Listener</u>, 79 (27 June), 843.
       Points out that most "good novelists" have always tried to blend the thrilling and psychological exploration to arouse the readers' curiosity and enlist their sympathies. Baldwin's <u>Tell Me</u> uses the "groundbait" of the "backstage success story" to capture his readers. The problem of color is basic, yet he writes so well of one's "wish fulfillment urge to succeed, that the larger theme of race is blurred" and "consequently ineffectual."

28 Howard, Maureen. "Through the Looking Glass." <u>PR</u>, 35 (Fall), 612-19.
       Characterizes <u>Tell Me</u> as an example of Baldwin's "artless dodging of the issues"--"he's fudging all the way."

29 Howe, Irving. "James Baldwin: At East in Apocalypse." <u>Harper's</u>, 237 (September), 94-100.
       Recounts that only "two or three American novelists have thus far managed to write novels in which Negro men and women come through as credible figures." Faulkner, a Southerner, is the best example of a white person, and Wright and Ellison are two Negro writers. Baldwin is one of the emerging Negro writers who has not yet reached fulfillment.

1968

Notes is a collection of "brilliant, nervous essays--ges-
tures of repudiation, glimmers of intention." Go Tell It
is a "delicate narrative, blending memoir and fiction," but
his major talent is as an essayist. Another Country came
at the time "when the Negro revolt was beginning to gather
strength," and Baldwin could not avoid voicing the "imperatives of protest" even though it would be "damaging to [his]
literary achievement." Tell Me is a "remarkably bad novel,
signaling the collapse of a writer of some distinction."
He seems to have lost that "controlled exactness of diction"; there appears to be deceit "through rhetorical in-
flation and hysteria, whipping himself into postures of
militancy and declarations of racial metaphysics which
. . . seem utterly inauthentic." One of the signs of this
"trouble" is his "compulsive use of obscenities"; they come
as emotionally affecting as punctuation. Also, he seems
"to have lost respect for the novel as a form" and readily
slips into the "clichés of soap opera."

30 Jackson, Katherine G. "Books in Brief." Harper's, 237
      (July), 104.
         Sees Tell Me as containing "many, many stories," endur-
      ing commitments, human certainties and uncertainties,
      heart-breaking relationships, family struggles.

31 Kapp, Isa. "In Perspective and Anger." New Leader, 51
      (3 June), 18-20.
         Believes that a "new kind of invisibility has entered
      Negro-white relations: the block to emotional vision im-
      posed by statistics, sociologizing and the albatross image
      of the Negro as a Problem." Tell Me is uneven in quality,
      but Baldwin forces his readers to return to scenes of "in-
      dividual incidents of prejudice, to linger over the indig-
      nities" set upon persons who smolder with outrage. The
      novel gives an account of an "unsentimental re-education in
      what it means to be a bright, expectant, sensitive Negro in
      America." Somewhere in the middle of the book, Baldwin's
      language changes "with a vengeance and . . . by cascades of
      four letter words; he seems to lose some of the controlled
      writing and eloquent rhetoric that launched his distin-
      guished essays." Despite this, he is not at the mercy of
      his rhetoric or his rage; there is considerable "tender-
      ness, physical pleasure, and charm."

*32 Langer, Johannes. "James Baldwin." Ry Højskoles Julehilsen
      1968, pp. 25-31.
         Cited in O'Daniel, 1977.39.

1968

33 Llorens, David. "Books Noted: <u>Tell Me How Long the Train's Been Gone</u>." <u>Negro Digest</u>, 17 (August), 51-52, 85-86.
    Describes Baldwin as the "voice of an unusually civilized mind in this primitive land," who could "indeed be our greatest writer." <u>Tell Me</u> may be "the most important novel of this crucial decade in American history." In an era of lovelessness, he has written a "rejoicingly beautiful novel" emphasizing his message: "that one can only face in others that which one faces in one's self."

34 Long, Robert E. "From Elegant to Hip." <u>Nation</u>, 206 (10 June), 769-70.
    Contends that <u>Notes</u> and <u>Nobody Knows</u> are "works of rare distinction in contemporary American writing." In these works, Baldwin's intelligence "functions brilliantly, cooly, preserving always a sense of proportion." <u>Tell Me</u> reveals "little aesthetic control" with poorly created characters and an awkward flashback-within-flashback technique. His once "polished prose now seems lusterless, and his diction fluctuates incongruously from the elegant to the obscene."

35 McNamara, E. "Book Review." <u>America</u>, 118 (29 June), 817.
    Describes reading <u>Tell Me</u> as a "definite letdown." The book is a "tired excuse for a novel"; the characters are the "sheerest stale stereotypes, cloaked in purple rhetoric."

36 Madden, David. "The Fallacy of the Subject-Dominated Novel." <u>English Record</u>, 18 (April), 11-19.
    Contends that an artist can become so involved in raw material that he neglects "the mysterious dictates of art," and writes a "subject-dominated novel." The most obviously subject-dominated works are the "thesis or propaganda," the "exposé or protest" works. Baldwin's <u>Blues</u> and Jones's <u>The Dutchman</u> concentrate solely on the "new trend in Negro subject matter" and are "rather crude, artless, and preachy, full of violence and sex."

37 Maloff, Saul. "Proudhammer's Progress." <u>Newsweek</u>, 3 June, p. 94.
    Believes that the trouble with <u>Tell Me</u> lies in the "first-person narration," a method that can be "treacherous or liberating." Proudhammer, the main character, is "unbelievable," and the prose style is entirely too "fussy, inflated, operatic, and mannered fine." There are some good passages that remind the reader that "Baldwin is, after all, still a writer to be reckoned with."

38 Margolies, Edward. "The Negro Church: James Baldwin and the
    Christian Vision." In his <u>Native Sons: A Critical Study
    of Twentieth-Century Negro American Authors</u>. New York:
    J. B. Lippincott, pp. 102-26.
        Cites the Negro church in the South as one of the few
    cultural institutions that had some success in being trans-
    planted to the North. Initially, the church was to "serve
    the spiritual needs of the community," but as time went on
    the church "came to function as a kind of community news-
    paper linking the new migrants to their Southern past."
    The migration to the Northern cities "constituted the most
    abrupt break in the Negro cultural experience since the
    days of the African slave trade." It produced anxieties as
    people moved from a rural to an urban way of life, and the
    ill-defined mores, prejudices, and barriers of the North
    kept the Negro on "ever-shifting grounds whose pitfalls
    were at once invisible and treacherous." For the Southern
    Negro migrant, the emotional stresses were intolerable. It
    was precisely in this area that the Negro church functioned
    so effectively as an integrative force. It connected the
    Negro with his former life in the South and "gave him a
    socially acceptable outlet for his rage, his terror, and
    his frustrations." The church also functioned as "a poli-
    tical force, drawing together persons of diverse . . . ori-
    gin and directing them toward goals." This "transfer of
    religious energies" to political and social causes is ap-
    parent in the works of Baldwin. Even when the religious
    context is not specific, it becomes inherent in such ex-
    periences as sexual relations--hetero- and homosexual;
    ritualistic qualities--music, jazz, blues; identity crises
    --alienation, self-destruction; and social outrages--injus-
    tices, prejudices, racism.

39 Miller, Adam David. "It's a Long Way to St. Louis: Notes on
    the Audience for Black Drama." <u>The Drama Review</u>, 12
    (Summer), 147-50.
        Examines one of the playwright's important questions:
    "For whom am I creating?" The audience is the biggest ques-
    tion facing the Negro playwright, for the predominantly
    white audience is ignorant of the black experience and has
    "hard-to-change preconceptions" about these experiences.
    Langston Hughes and Lorraine Hansberry were integrationists
    who felt that "society could be changed so that whites and
    Negroes could live side by side in harmony." Baldwin's
    <u>Blues</u> poses questions for whites even though he attempted
    to address himself to "an American audience . . . the body
    politic of the country." Also, the comic playwrights "fall

1968

into the trap of either catering to the good will of a
white audience, or of making statements irrelevant to Negroes." Ossie Davis' Purlie Victorious and Douglas Turner
Ward's Day of Absence speak to the white audience to point
out that "while folks need Negroes." But there are a few
who address their work to Negro audiences, e.g., Bullins'
How Do You Do and Clara's Ole Man, and Marvin X's Take
Care of Business.

40 Moon, Eric. "The Book Review: Fiction." LJ, 93 (1 June),
    2256.
        Contends that Leo Proudhammer's name in Tell Me is
    "ludicrous symbolism," and points to the obvious "cracks
    that appear to be opening up in the author's talent."

41 Morse, J. Mitchell. "Masters and Innocents." Hud R, 21
    (Autumn), 529-31.
        Believes that writing "good fiction" takes a special
    talent, and if a writer does not have it, no degree of in-
    tellectual clarity and acuity will make up for it. Bald-
    win and others (Mary McCarthy, Edmund Wilson, C.P. Snow,
    John Hersey, etc.) write "excellent expository prose but
    fall to pieces when they write fiction." Tell Me is a
    "long fictionalized popularization" of the title essay in
    Notes; the novel is "as cheap as the essay is brilliant."
    He seems so much concerned with the message "that he ne-
    glects the medium"; not that he lacks talent for the med-
    ium, but in this work, he "trips up on elementary matters
    of fact."

42 Murray, John J. "Tell Me How Long the Train's Been Gone."
    Best Sellers, 28 (1 July), 38.
        Points out sarcastically that "Little Jimmy Baldwin . . .
    has decided that he is the one and only spokesman for his
    race." He has become, therefore, "a cross between a socio-
    logist, evangelistic journalist, and artist." It becomes
    increasingly evident that his reputation as a writer is not
    enhanced by this "most recent foray."

43 Noble, David. "The Present: Norman Mailer, James Baldwin,
    Saul Bellow." In his The Eternal Adam and the New World
    Garden. New York: George Braziller, pp. 195-224.
        Argues that the works of Mailer and Baldwin have "left
    the civilized world of middle class consensus to explore a
    dark and untamed foreign continent." Their writings are
    filled with "the grotesque, the perverse, the criminal and
    even the insane." Like James Cozzens, they see that it is
    impossible "to restore the agrarian simplicity of George

Bancroft." The gigantic industrialism is contaminating the "American Garden" and suffocating the "native Adam"; the very "citadel of the American dream is being undermined by the growth of a social monster." Mailer's Naked and the Dead used an army platoon representing a cross section of America; each member was "found spiritually and morally wanting . . . each sought a scapegoat for his own selfishness and fears." The novels of Baldwin make "spiritual capital" out of Mailer's thesis that "Negroes remain an uncorrupted band of saints within the general corruption of white society." Another Country offers hope only to those "solitary saints who have the strength to reject the eternal temptation of the sinners who will always dominate society." Go Tell It depicts the "earthly hell" of the Negro in white America with poverty, spiritual and physical, being the "gift of the white man to the black." Giovanni's Room presents a "slashing analysis of the impotence of white America." The implications of these earlier works of Baldwin are that the "primitive Negro who could accept suffering and deny guilt could save white America . . . from the burden of guilt imposed by the inhibitions of civilization." But this "romantic primitivism" is so extreme that it contradicts his "framework of social salvation." He cannot posit a reality beyond a particular character for this would constitute an abstraction that, ultimately, would be artificial. Bellow's novels, like those of Henry James, are concerned with "the American apocalyptic imagination," and they all begin with a "destructive criticism and gradually work toward a constructive goal."

44 Phillips, Louis. "The Novelist as Playwright: Baldwin, Mc-
    Cullers, and Bellow." In Modern American Drama: Essays in
    Criticism. Edited by William E. Taylor. Deland, Florida:
    Everett/Edwards, pp. 145–62.
        Cites three contemporary novelists who have turned
    their talents to the theater: Baldwin, Carson McCullers,
    and Saul Bellow. They "have all felt the need to use the
    dramatic form to express, develop, and amplify the themes
    that have formed the basis of their many novels." Baldwin
    is the one who seems "least entranced by the American thea-
    tre." His plays include Amen Corner, an adaptation of Gio-
    vanni's Room, and Blues. In this last work, he displays
    amazing "ability to see the white community of a small
    southern town through its own eyes and . . . to portray the
    wider issues in a racial murder."

45 Puzo, Mario. "His Cardboard Lovers." New York Times Book
    Review (23 June), p. 5.

1968

Points out that "tragedy calls out for a great artist,
revolution for a true prophet." Baldwin predicted the
"black revolution" that is now changing society, and his
new novel, Tell Me, is "an attempt to recreate, as an artist this time, the tragic condition of the Negro in America." Unfortunately, he has not been successful; the novel
is "simpleminded" and "one dimensional" with "mostly cardboard characters." It has a "polemical" rather than "narrative tone" with a "poor selection of incident." The construction of the novel is "theatrical, tidily nailed into a
predictable form," and the characters make the book sound
like a "soap opera." Perhaps it is time for Baldwin to
"forget the black revolution and start worrying about himself as an artist who is the ultimate revolution."

46 Redding, J. Saunders. "The Negro Writer and His Relationship
     to His Roots." In Black Voices. Edited by Abraham Chap-
     man. New York: New American Library, pp. 612-18.
         Reprint of 1960.6.

47 Richardson, Jack. "The Black Arts." New York Review of
     Books, 11 (19 December), 10-12.
         Includes Tell Me among several books reviewed and sees
     it as a work about blackness written "with all the zest of
     a penance performed for the sake of party discipline"
     about a world made of "sociological constructions." Bald-
     win speaks of blackness as a condition of his own existence
     but is not comfortable with it as a subject for fiction;
     the personal life of his essays is complex and courageous,
     diluted in Leo Proudhammer. Thus, his novel mirrors what
     is happening in new black literature: instead of analyzing
     the lunacy and madness behind the slogans of the racial
     struggle, the literature has begun to embody both.

*48 Sander, Hans Jochen. Das Menschenbild im Schaffen von James
      Baldwin. Ph.D. dissertation, Jena.
          Cited in Bruck, 1975.6.

49 Sheed, Wilfrid. "Novel-time for Mr. Baldwin." Book World,
     2 (2 June), 4.
         Suggests that Tell Me is an opportunistic and "careless
     book" by Baldwin, after a silent period of six years. Al-
     though the book is compelling with its real concern for the
     family of Leo Proudhammer, the author "seems to lose his
     own identity; the authority leaves his voice; the mind-
     clearing arrogance fails him."

50 Shrapnel, Norman. "Sermon of Protest." <u>Manchester Guardian</u>
    <u>Weekly</u>, (4 July), p. 11.
        Contends that <u>Tell Me</u> as a protest novel goes for the
    "broad impact" but leaves the reader "unsatisfied, with a
    passionately mournful sermon," containing at least "one
    bold stroke of originality"--making the underdog, Leo Proud-
    hammer, start at the top.

51 Standley, Fred L. "James Baldwin: A Checklist, 1963-67." <u>BB</u>,
    25 (May/August), 135-37, 160.
        Lists both primary and secondary sources for the period
    as well as some earlier items.

52 Strout, Cushing. "<u>Uncle Tom's Cabin</u> and the Portent of Mil-
    lennium." <u>Yale Review</u>, 57 (Spring), 375-85.
        Refers to Baldwin's 1949 essay, "Everybody's Protest
    Novel," which condemns <u>Uncle Tom's Cabin</u> as being an "hys-
    terically moralistic melodrama." There is no doubt that
    Mrs. Stowe "was hot about the crime of slavery" just as
    Baldwin "is hot and fearful . . . about the race problem,"
    but her novel deliberately "aimed to undercut self-righteous
    moralizing." Baldwin seems to have read Mrs. Stowe out of
    context missing her "sense of the great horror of slavery."
    He is appalled by her sentimentality, but he loses sight of
    the sources of it. Much of the cruelty, violence, and sen-
    timentality in her novel has an "extremely realistic basis";
    much in <u>Uncle Tom's Cabin</u>, Mrs. Stowe felt and experienced.
    However, Baldwin has misread the story as social propaganda
    reducing its "theological meaning" to a "medieval terror of
    witches"; he fails to see that her novel was in "large part
    a protest against the Calvinist doctrine of human inability
    to merit salvation." Instead, Baldwin describes protest
    novels as a mirror of "individuals' confusion, dishonesty,
    panic, trapped and immobilized in the sunlit prison of the
    American dream." To misread <u>Uncle Tom's Cabin</u> is "not to
    commit an aesthetic crime, but it is to suffer a major fail-
    ure of historical comprehension."

53 Thompson, John. "Baldwin: The Prophet as Artist." <u>Commen-</u>
    <u>tary</u>, 45 (June), pp. 67-69.
        Describes <u>Tell Me</u> as a "beautifully formed" novel arriv-
    ing at "a crucial moment" with an "expert testimony" on the
    relations of black Americans and white Americans. The ma-
    terial of the novel "is not sensational in itself"; violence
    permeates the work, but there is "no relishing of it, no
    gory details." Instead, the essence of the work is the pre-
    sent social crisis: "those who rule America do not

1968

understand themselves" or those they rule. <u>Tell Me</u> is "a
masterpiece by one of the best living writers in America";
its language is "precise, well-ordered, very sophisticated,"
and a "strong intelligence holds each of the elements in
place."

54 Toynbee, Philip. "Don't Go Tell It on the Mountain." <u>Atlan-
tic Monthly</u>, 222 (July), 91-92.
Argues that <u>Tell Me</u> is a "remarkably bad" novel. Baldwin has shown that he has talent to write; he has the understanding of the situations that he shares with all American
Negroes. There is no lack of material for <u>Tell Me</u> and no
lack of "driving emotions about violent public events,"
yet this is a book "which lacks . . . everything else. It
is a wan stereotype, mournfully plodding from one hack convention to the next." Perhaps Baldwin's "raw skinned pil-
grimage" through racist America has been too painful, and
he has retreated into "the most effective of all unreali-
ties, the unreality of the ham novel."

55 Trout, Lawana. "The Teaching of Protest and Propaganda Literature." <u>NALF</u>, 2 (Fall), 46-52.
Describes a teaching unit that focuses upon propaganda
and protest literature. <u>Go Tell It</u> and <u>The Fire</u> are two of
the materials used. Students read portions of them and
role play scenes from the contexts. Other works also used
are: <u>To Kill a Mockingbird</u>, <u>In White America</u>, <u>Huck Finn</u>,
<u>Nigger</u>, <u>Malcolm X</u>, etc.

56 Williams, David. "New Novels." <u>Punch</u>, 255 (3 July), 34.
Contends that "a strong creative talent and an unquench-
able anger are both hard at work" in Baldwin's <u>Tell Me</u>.
The book is "fluent" with "scenes of great power" so that
the reader believes in the world created by Baldwin and in
the "justice of his anger."

1969

1 Abramson, Doris. "Negro Playwrights in America." <u>Columbia
Forum</u>, 12 (Spring), 11-17.
Recalls that in 1929, the Kregwa Players of Harlem declared that "plays about Negro life must be written by Negro authors who understand from birth and continual association just what it means to be a Negro today." Years later,
Langston Hughes reiterated the same thesis. There appear
to be two categories of Negro playwrights: 1925-1959--
Negro dramatic art reflecting the desire for cultural

assimilation (e.g., Garland Anderson's Appearances, Lorraine Hansberry's A Raisin in the Sun); and 1960 on--a revolutionary change in stance dramatically and socially (e.g., LeRoi Jones's The Toilet and Dutchman, Douglas Turner Ward's Day of Absence and Happy Ending, Baldwin's Blues). The demands of Negro and white theater audiences have always played a significant part in the way in which "Negro playwrights have presented their reality in the theatre." It was apparent by 1959 that "Negro playwrights were about to be assimilated artistically," but out of "the turmoil of the sixties, out of insurrections and marches," there emerged a new type of Negro drama that sought to translate into a "kind of Living Newspaper" what is happening in the streets. Still, Negro playwrights are in the same position today that they were in yesterday; they must find patronage. Some have done so through "compromise or easy message" as Purlie Victorious by Ossie Davis and Amen Corner by Baldwin. Others have taken the opposite stance by presenting a "brutal attack that reaches the conscience of whites only through a sado-masochistic exchange" as in Baldwin's Blues.

2 Abramson, Doris. Negro Playwrights in the American Theatre, 1925-1959. New York and London: Columbia University Press, pp. 146-47, 274-75.
     Contends that Amen Corner is "not a bad play so much as a sentimental, old-fashioned one." It did develop the theme of "religious disillusion," which paved the way for Baldwin's outright rejection of the religious in favor of physical force in Blues.

3 ANON. "The Amen Corner." Choice, 6 (May), 382.
     Views Amen Corner as "personalizing in the service of the universal" and having an autobiographical framework that reveals "a man/artist's agony" as well as "an equal portion of bitterness and love."

4 ANON. "Baldwin." PMLA, 84 (June), 896.
     Presents annual secondary bibliography for 1968.

5 ANON. "Novelist Directs Play." Tallahassee Democrat (14 November), p. 7.
     Notes briefly that Baldwin has "embarked on a new career --directing plays." He has chosen John Herbert's Fortune and Men's Eyes to be performed in Istanbul, the city that Baldwin is now calling "home."

6 ANON. "Tell Me How Long the Train's Been Gone." Publishers Weekly, 195 (26 May), 57.

1969

Comments that <u>Tell Me</u> has scenes of poignancy but is un-
successful as a whole work. Leo Proudhammer is presented
hovering between life and death after a heart attack; he reviews his past including a love affair with a white actress,
and his hopeless, homosexual, incestuous love for his
brother.

7 Banta, Thomas J. "James Baldwin's Discovery of Identity."
   <u>Mawazo</u>, 2, no. 1 (June), 33-41.
       Presents three "main contexts" in which Baldwin's con-
   tributions must be studied: 1) historical, emphasizing the
   political and legal conditions in America during his life-
   time; 2) personal, emphasizing the relevant and dramatic
   psychological aspects of his relation to his family, church,
   and whites; 3) social, looking at his relationship with
   Wright and Cleaver. If the Negro revolution in America is
   to be understood, it is important to understand Baldwin,
   the man and his writing, for his work has paralleled the
   development of the revolution. A careful reading of his
   work reveals that he has "certainly not written the same
   book over and over." Although his writing is intensely personal, there is "something about all people and about all
   time." It is true that the Negro problem of identity has
   "special aspects," but the "common problem . . . is finding
   out who one is, where one fits into the . . . scheme of
   things." A new era in American history is fast approaching,
   an era when every man on earth "will realize his own identity" and when all will appreciate the "diversity of the
   human species."

8 Bergman, Peter. <u>The Chronological History of the Negro in
   America</u>. New York: Harper & Row Publishers, pp. 411-12.
       Presents a brief biographical sketch with a few comments
   about Baldwin's major works. <u>Notes</u> "established Baldwin as
   a major contemporary American voice." He is probably "one
   of the best essayists in American letters today."

9 Bluefarb, Sam. "James Baldwin's 'Previous Condition': A
   Problem of Identification." <u>NALF</u>, 3 (Spring), 26-29.
       Examines Baldwin's story, "Previous Condition" (1948) as
   the author's attempt to "find a form of identification in
   the white world" but who, ironically, "also fails to find
   even a place for himself in the black world." This story
   of the "alienated and invisible man in miniature" predates
   Ellison's novel, <u>Invisible Man</u>, by some four years. Baldwin portrays the "hero's sensitivity and intellectuality
   that form the ingredients of his invisibility"; he reveals
   the plight of the "black artist-intellectual" in both the
   white and black world.

10 Cade, Toni. "Black Theater." In <u>Black Expression</u>. Edited by
      Addison Gayle. New York: Weybright and Talley, pp. 134-43.
            Advocates that "the theater of Black People" of the six-
      ties began with the stage production of <u>Blues</u> as a distinct
      voice from the "muted voice of Negro drama of the fifties."

11 Clarke, John Henrik. "The Alienation of James Baldwin." In
      <u>Black Expression</u>. Edited by Addison Gayle. New York:
      Weybright and Talley, pp. 350-53.
            Reprint of 1964.22.

12 Cleaver, Eldridge. "Notes on a Native Son." In <u>Black Expres-</u>
      <u>sion</u>. Edited by Addison Gayle. New York: Weybright and
      Talley, pp. 339-49.
            Reprint of 1966.15.

13 Corona, Mario. "La Saggistica di James Baldwin." <u>Studi Ameri-</u>
      <u>cani</u>, 15:433-37, 450-51, 462-63.
            Discusses the essays of Baldwin, which are seen to be of
      more credit to him than his novels. <u>Notes</u> is a major work
      of profound importance, and has received favorable reviews
      by outstanding critics, e.g., Bone, Kazin, Gorlier. Bald-
      win has mastered a "taut and incisive style," and in writ-
      ing about what it means to be a Negro, he has transcended
      the specificity of the issue and has given meaning to what
      it means to be a man. Because of his intellect, brilliance,
      honesty, and courage, he has become a spokesman not only
      for his people but for the need for positive black-white
      relations.

14 Fuller, Hoyt W. "Contemporary Negro Fiction." In <u>The Black</u>
      <u>American Writer</u>. Edited by C.W.E. Bigsby. Vol. I: <u>Fic-</u>
      <u>tion</u>. Deland, Florida: Everett/Edwards, pp. 229-43.
            Reprint of 1965.33.

15 Gayle, Addison, Jr. "Perhaps Not So Soon One Morning." In
      his <u>Black Expression</u>. New York: Weybright and Talley,
      pp. 280-88.
            Reprint of 1968.22.

16 Geller, Allen. "An Interview with Ralph Ellison." In <u>The</u>
      <u>Black American Writer</u>. Edited by C.W.E. Bigsby. Vol. I:
      <u>Fiction</u>. Deland, Florida: Everett/Edwards, pp. 153-68.
            Reprint of 1963.32.

17 Gibson, Donald B. "Wright's Invisible Native Son." <u>American</u>
      <u>Quarterly</u>, 21, no. 4 (Winter), 728-38.
            Contends that most critics who write about Wright's
      <u>Native Son</u> "do not see Bigger Thomas"; they see only an

outer person, and the inner essential person is invisible.
Baldwin's views are "patently false," and he is "too simple"
in his pronouncements about Bigger. Probably "the critic
most responsible for the perception of Bigger Thomas as a
social entity" has been Baldwin, who also conceived of some
arguments about the limitations of the protest novel. Yet,
with all his persuasiveness of language, he failed to see
Bigger the person.

18 Gross, Theodore L. "The Idealism of Negro Literature in
    America." Phylon, 30 (Spring), 5-10.
       Points out that any description of the contributions by
    Negroes to American literature "must inevitably account for
    the recurrent violence that is found" in so many of the
    works, e.g., brooding sexuality in Jean Toomer's Cane, bru-
    tal murder in Wright's Native Son, race riot in Ellison's
    Invisible Man, and vengeance and suicide in Baldwin's Ano-
    ther Country. Violence is "purgative" in these and other
    books by modern Negro writers; "it releases hostility and
    announces the existence of black men in a convulsive, un-
    predictable manner"; it "tears aside the historical cur-
    tain" and presents the "private drama of lives" that were
    scarcely imagined because "they were reflected only in the
    fiction of white authors." These Negro writers have "shed
    the mythologies that have been thrust upon them." Violence
    is a "natural and expected" feature of these writings, for
    in the "absence of a coherent and useable literary tradi-
    tion," the Negro writer has remained very close to fact;
    the really first "significant artistic achievement" has
    been in the form of autobiography. Although inspiration
    varies, the accomplished art is characterized by a "perva-
    sive idealism," which seems paradoxical in terms of the
    violence presented and the frustration out of which it emer-
    ges. Like the early Transcendentalists, Negro writers have
    derived much of their ideological attitudes and moods from
    the church; and even though some have tried hard to de-
    nounce the theology of their parents, they have retained
    "techniques of diction and tone and musical phraseology
    that shape their secular idealism." The most obvious of
    these is Baldwin, "whose work gains much of its strength
    from the oratory and ritual of the church . . . he learned
    as a child." In addition, writers like Baldwin and Ellison
    are "forever scrutinizing themselves as Americans"; they
    are "as self-conscious about their social and literary role
    in this country as Emerson was of America's position in the
    tradition of European culture." They also are "equally
    self-conscious of Negro life and art"; they too are
    "defensive."

19 Haslam, Gerald W. "Two Traditions in Afro-American Litera-
      ture." Research Studies, 37 (September), 183–93.
          Quotes Ellison's response to a question regarding cul-
      tural dualism in black Americans: the traditional oral
      modes of their African forefathers; and the various written
      genres of European Americans. The "highest plateaus of
      literary excellence" emerge when the two interface. Today,
      in the black arts movement, two schools of writing have
      evolved: the black revolutionary group and the black ex-
      perience writers. The outstanding member of the former is
      LeRoi Jones; the latter boasts of Wright, Ellison, Brooks,
      and Baldwin. Go Tell It is a "high point" in Baldwin's
      literary career because it uses black traditions and topics;
      Nobody Knows stands as an "eloquent, important statement
      from an American intellectual."

20 Henderson, David. "The Man Who Cried I Am: A Critique." In
      Black Expression. Edited by Addison Gayle. New York:
      Weybright and Talley, pp. 365–71.
          Identifies characters in the work as real–life writers:
      Harry Ames (Richard Wright) and Marion Dawes (James
      Baldwin).

21 Iden, Peter. "Konflikt als Theater oder Konflikttheater:
      James Baldwin's Blues für Mister Charlie in Mannheim und
      Weisbaden." Theater Heute: Zeitschrift für Schauspiel,
      Oper Ballett, 10 (February), 12–13.
          Describes the theme of Blues as both a pleading for the
      cause of the oppressed Negro in America's racial battle and
      an attempt to muster something akin to an understanding of
      the conduct of the white oppressor. The "passion of parti-
      sanship" and a "distance of observation" are thus bound to-
      gether, often in pathos. Baldwin's final thesis is that
      mediation is not possible and that the "antimonies" are in-
      dissoluble. The severity of the oppositions in the politi-
      cal reality of America leads to the author's often plain-
      tive words for its analysis. The play is also a "requiem
      for the figure, Parnell, a white editor, whom Baldwin cre-
      ates for his premise of Compassion-Distance." In this
      play, one dimension of the confrontation of blacks and
      whites is "potency," understood throughout as the sexual
      superiority of the black, which stands over against impo-
      tence and thus subverts the political condition of power
      and powerlessness.

22 Leahy, James. "James Baldwin." In his Twentieth Century
      Writing: A Reader's Guide to Contemporary Literature.
      New York and London: Newness Books, pp. 41–43.

1969

Calls Baldwin "the most widely known Negro writer" and "potentially one of the most important novelists now writing in English." At his best, he achieves what Conrad defined as the "novelist's task, to make the reader hear, feel, see." Baldwin's writings have been substantial. Go Tell It, Giovanni's Room, Another Country, and The Fire exemplify his "prophetic mission: prophecy (the advocacy of one particular mission to the problems of life) involving a denial of diversity, a narrowing down . . . of the complexity of human experience, the individuality of individual existence."

23 Lee, Brian. "James Baldwin: Caliban to Prospero." In The Black American Writer. Edited by C.W.E. Bigsby. Vol. I: Fiction. Deland, Florida: Everett/Edwards, pp. 169-79.
      Contends that although Baldwin is praised as "one of America's greatest essayists," he obviously wants "to be recognized first as a novelist." The very social conditions that he diagnoses in his essays are the same ones that make the "creation of a fictional world" almost impossible for a Negro novelist--the "ambiguities and ironies" of life lived on two levels: "that of the Negro, and that of the man." The possible modes of existence for one "seeking refuge from a society which refused to acknowledge one's humanity are necessarily limited," but Baldwin has explored with some thoroughness the "various emotional and spiritual alternatives available." Go Tell It explores the psychology of religious experience, and Giovanni's Room and Another Country present the "micro-cosmic world of sexual love." His latest novel, Tell Me, has the hero "use his art to transform his sorrows into life"; but the autobiographical elements are not very well concealed. Like the hero, Baldwin is a "fat cat," and this novel is his "Big Deal"; however, in some ways the work is "not as good as those he wrote previously"--it lacks "the intensity of much of his earlier writing."

24 Long, Robert E. "Love and Wrath in the Fiction of James Baldwin." The English Record, 19 (February), 50-57.
      Calls Go Tell It Baldwin's "best novel"; it is "impressive partly because it is not a conventional protest novel." The novel attempts and achieves presentation and understanding of a "particular reality of American life." The basic theme in Go Tell It is that "the church is an escape from self-knowledge and a painful confrontation" with the meaning of one's "blackness in a white world," and "all of his subsequent writing" is an expansion of this theme. Notes elucidates the meaning of the confrontation,

describing that the biblical curse upon Ham underlies the
division between the Negro and the white man. Hence, the
"white man is condemned to perpetual innocence" fleeing
from a confrontation with his black brother; and the Negro,
a victim of oppression must "live with a self-destroying
hatred for the white man." Giovanni's Room grows out of
Baldwin's analysis of race in Notes; all of the characters
are white, but Giovanni "may be interpreted as a Negro."
David avoids a confrontation with Giovanni and destroys
him and himself. In his early period (1950s) Baldwin wrote
as "a brilliant critic of American life"; he saw the "larger dimensions of the issue of race." His third novel,
Another Country, shattered this earlier composure and objectivity. Yet beneath the "apparent formlessness" of this
novel, there is a serious theme of the fear of the self and
the failure of love. Two "disfranchised minorities," the
Negro and the homosexual, become the two heroes of culture
and the possibility of social regeneration, but the rigidity of American moralism will not allow love between two
males to be "totally pure." Thus, the collapse of Baldwin's affirmation of love in Another Country "leaves him
with nowhere to go" except to "darkness and then to violent
rage" either at himself or against the white world. Tell
Me, his "crowning disaster" as a novelist, continues this
theme of the "bleeding heart whom no one will love," which
leads finally to rage. "Once the apostle of love, Baldwin
now seems merely a prophet of despair."

25 Long, Robert E. "The Vogue of Gatsby's Guest List." Fitz-
    gerald-Hemingway Annual. Edited by Matthew J. Bruccoli.
    pp. 23-25.
        Shows the affinity between Baldwin's use of "the guest
    list device" in Tell Me and Fitzgerald's use in The Great
    Gatsby, including method of introduction, language, and
    purpose.

26 Meserve, Walter. "James Baldwin's 'Agony Way.'" In The Black
    American Writer. Edited by C.W.E. Bigsby. Vol. II:
    Poetry and Drama. Deland, Florida: Everett/Edwards, pp.
    171-86.
        Sees that Baldwin's writing has become one means for
    self-satisfaction as well as a "consolation for a sensitive
    and imaginative person." He has written mainly about him-
    self, and today he is still seen as one "who sees both his
    life and his work as 'the agony way.'" Notes carried his
    message that he wanted to be an "honest man and a good wri-
    ter," but he also indicated that nobody cared, which re-
    vealed his "sense of betrayal and the absence of love which

1969

were his 'agony way.'" <u>Nobody Knows</u> became his "<u>cri de</u>
<u>coeur</u>," while <u>Go Tell It</u> and <u>Amen Corner</u> "parlayed a youth-
ful agony into a philosophic view of life." <u>Tell Me</u> reveals Baldwin's great sensitivity to this search; he believes that through love he will find an identity. Unfortunately, "such a simplistic approach to life does not always bring him the response that he himself needs in contemporary life." And, because he wants to be honest, he
"feels that he must also say unpleasant things"; hence
<u>Blues</u> was written to "shock people and upset them." The
ambivalence found in Baldwin's writing serves two purposes:
an effective artistic device; and a "logical retreat for an
insecure person." His fusion of race and sex, "both
treated . . . with considerable violence," illustrates that
ambivalence. The Negro is presented "ambivalently in both
race and sex." Some critics have called his characters
"stereotypes," but Baldwin insists that his "people are important"; their problems are "embedded in their agonizing
souls." In the "agonizing life" he sees, "each hero presents an aspect of his own past"; even the careers "that
each covets--preacher, pianist, writer, actor--show his own
passion for artistry that is personally creative." Certainly Baldwin's "instincts are with man, and if his life
is 'the agony way,' he best illustrates his most repeated
idea by travelling the same road he advocates for all
others."

27 Mitra, B. K. "The Wright-Baldwin Controversy." <u>Indian Jour-</u>
    <u>nal of American Studies</u>, 1:101-105.
        Traces the background of the "quarrel between a grown up
    son, Baldwin, and his spiritual father, Wright," which de-
    veloped with the publication of Baldwin's essay, "Every-
    body's Protest Novel." His quarrel with Wright centered on
    the larger issues of intention, aim, and values of the wri-
    ter. Although both felt rage at being a Negro, their ways
    of dealing with rage have been radically different. Wright
    made fiction convey "the rage itself, brutal, pure, violent
    and unconstrained"; while Baldwin has tried "to penetrate
    and analyze the rage and convert it into a recognizable hu-
    man emotion." Baldwin saw Wright's character, Bigger Tho-
    mas, "as a failure" because "he is presented as a monster,
    a being deprived of all the attributes of human experi-
    ences." Wright never examines the causes of this violence
    in Bigger's soul; thus he remains subhuman and a monster.
    What this means is that a "necessary dimension of life" is
    cut away, the dimension of human relationship, shared ex-
    periences. This is a "limitation of all protest novels;
    the larger reality is never presented."

28 Nower, Joyce. "The Traditions of Negro Literature in the
      United States." NALF, 3 (Spring), 5-12.
          Believes that "American literature by black writers has
      gone largely unnoticed in the classroom." That which has
      appeared has consisted mainly of folklore and dialect poems.
      Yet there is a body of Negro literature "which does what
      literature has always done--namely, it reflects the unique
      experience of writers within their own culture," and it
      also "transcends that . . . experience and partakes of the
      universal situation of man." Between 1854 and 1967, more
      than 200 full-length novels have been written by black
      Americans ranging in themes from the protest against sla-
      very to "an indictment of American society, black and
      white, for its dullness and stagnancy." The ignorance of
      white critics, regarding the "black experience in white
      America," has left "vast areas" of analysis untapped. Bald-
      win is one of those authors who has contributed to the de-
      velopment of a "Negro literary tradition."

29 Petersen, Clarence. "Equivocal Quotes." Book World, 3
      (17 August), 13.
          States that in Tell Me Baldwin's "visions are lucid, his
      characters real, and his insights expert and moving."

30 Silvera, Frank. "Towards a Theater of Understanding." Negro
      Digest, 18 (April), 33-35.
          Makes an assessment of Amen Corner as a play that addres-
      ses compassion, "that ability to see and feel the human pre-
      dicament from another's point of view." Baldwin wrote the
      play "in a flush of inspiration which drove him past con-
      ventional forms of dramaturgy." His work "images the Negro
      as he sees himself--not consuming his genius, protesting
      against invisibility." His characters are seen "emerging--
      digging themselves out--achieving their realization of
      self." He presents the Negro in his total humanity.

31 Thelwell, Mike. "Another Country: Baldwin's New York Novel."
      In The Black American Writer. Edited by C.W.E. Bigsby.
      Vol. I: Fiction. Deland, Florida: Everett/Edwards, pp.
      181-98.
          Contends that the "New York literary establishment"
      greeted Another Country with "fatuous, inept, . . . dis-
      honest criticism." Some critics went so far as to lose
      their "tenuous grip" on their craft; they even gave vent to
      "parochial, ill-tempered, irrelevant, and distasteful at-
      tacks on Baldwin's personal life and character." Another
      characteristic of some of the critics was "an ill-disguised
      tone of patronage," and others made the "error of doing

1969

battle with the vision of experience." In fact, this latter group's hysterical outcry delegated "urbane and sophisticated New York" to the role of "another country," one of
"repressive, white, middle-class babbitry." In the middle
of all this "strident middle-class chauvinism and moral
rigidity" stood the "intelligent and sensitive review" of
Granville Hicks. He saw the flaws as insignificant beside
the "illuminating energy and passionate interpretation of
experience and social and emotional reality." In terms of
literary culture, Another Country "takes on monumental proportions as it represents a direct assault, not only on a
few sterile sexual and social taboos, but on the cultural
hegemony, the dictatorship of perception and definition, of
the Anglo-Saxon vision as it operates through the literature onto the society." It presents an assertive black
consciousness that refutes and demolishes certain cherished
notions about the "quality of life" in society, a "relentless vision of white society and white characters as they
are registered in a black consciousness." Finally, although the book has faults, "its accomplishments and its
importance far outweigh them." Whether or not one agrees
with the "vision of the meaning of contemporary experience
presented," no one denies that "the book is an accurate,
perceptive, and truthful expression of the texture, feeling,
and consistency of that experience." This is the major responsibility of the novelist, and Baldwin has been "com-
pelled to write more for truth and relevance" in this book
than for art. The "revolution of consciousness" that he
has evoked is as much a "social reality" as a literary one;
he has broken through a "dead-end of platitudes, sociological clichés, complacent white assumptions, . . . which
have, since the thirties, just about lost their usefulness."

32 Tischler, Nancy M. "Typical Patterns." In her Black Masks:
    Negro Characters in Modern Southern Fiction. University
    Park, Pa.: Pennsylvania State University Press, pp. 180,
    189-90.
        Asserts that the implied thesis of Go Tell It is that
    the religious zeal and emotionally charged religious ser-
    vices of the black church are an escape for Negroes "who
    anticipate no happiness or success in this world."

33 Tuttleton, James W. "The Negro Writer as Spokesman." In The
    Black American Writer. Edited by C.W.E. Bigsby. Vol. I:
    Fiction. Deland, Florida: Everett/Edwards, pp. 245-59.
        Argues that the American Negro, "speaking for himself,
    has rarely been heard above the din and babble of white
    voices speaking for him." In 1965, Robert Penn Warren

published <u>Who Speaks for the Negro?</u>, which was an attempt
to record comments from a variety of black voices. What he
found was that "beyond the non-negotiable demand for respect and recognition, no single voice spoke for the Negro."
Individuals spoke for themselves; and there was no consensus as to what should be done, when, how--the same "dilemma
of the black writer." For the public seems to expect that,
in some sense, he should be a "spokesman for his race." In
addition, every black writer bears the dilemma of Richard
Wright, who set the example of the "literature of social
protest." Baldwin took Wright to task "for his naturalistic reduction of the complex Negro experience to that of
racial victim." <u>Invisible Man</u> is still the "best American
novel written by a Negro because of Ellison's great imaginative gifts and his . . . devotion to craft." It is a
"more powerful articulation of Negro protest than <u>Native
Son</u> and all of Baldwin's work" because of its richness of
language and the imaginative complexity of its social and
political references.

34 Weales, Gerald. "The Negro Revolution." In his <u>The Jumping-
    Off Place: American Drama in the 1960's</u>. London: Mac-
    millan, pp. 125-34.
        Indicates that the 1960s ushered in a new era in Negro
    drama. Baldwin's <u>Blues</u> and LeRoi Jones's <u>Dutchman</u> created
    a "stir far greater than the usual excitement about talen-
    ted new playwrights." They and their characters reflected
    "the new militancy in Negro circles." <u>Blues</u> reiterates the
    message of <u>The Fire</u>: "Negroes and whites are trapped by
    the way Negroes are treated in this country and the pre-
    conceptions that lie behind that treatment." Until whites
    give Negroes the "freedom to be what they want . . . neither
    race can escape a relationship based on abstraction and
    suffused with hate, which cripples the country as a whole."
    But for Jones, Baldwin is "an establishment writer, . . .
    interested in his own sensitivity." He pleads for love;
    Jones's work is more "concerned with the care and /feeding
    of hate." It is only because <u>Dutchman</u> and <u>Blues</u> appeared
    almost within a month of each other that the two play-
    wrights have been "bracketed together."

                            1970

1 Adelsen, C. E. "Love Affair: James Baldwin and Istanbul."
   <u>Ebony</u>, 25 (March), 40-46.
       Describes the opening performance of John Herbert's play,
   <u>Fortune and Men's Eyes</u>, directed by Baldwin in Istanbul,

1970

Turkey. Although the play is a "bitter protest," Baldwin
"turns the topical into the timeless." Out of a "regional
complaint, he fashions a poem of universal complaint, a
statement of outrage at the human animal's unremitting
cruelty to its kind."

2 Alexander, Jean A. "Black Literature for the 'Culturally Deprived' Curriculum." NALF, 4 (Fall), 96-103.
      Argues that schools "must provide educational programs
   that will enable students to develop democratic and realistic attitudes for living in today's world." Many educators
   have failed to explore ways to solve the "American Dilemma"
   of hostility between whites and nonwhites. Racial harmony
   cannot be attained without a "nationwide acceptance and ap-
   preciation for cultural differences." The cultural appre-
   ciation is an evolutionary process stimulated by a "well-
   rounded educational system." The impact of literature as
   an influential force leading to cultural understanding cannot be denied; hence the introduction of black literature
   into school curricula is essential. Some of the recommend-
   ed works include: Margaret Walker's Jubilee, Frederick
   Douglass' Narrative of the Life of Frederick Douglass, an
   American Slave, Wright's Black Boy, Baldwin's The Fire, etc.

3 ANON. "Baldwin." PMLA. 1969 International Bibliography. I:
   139.
      Presents annual secondary bibliography for 1969.

4 ANON. "Black Anti-Semitism." Choice, 7 (October), 1096.
      Notes that the nine essays of uneven quality by both
   Jews and blacks (including Baldwin) in Black Anti-Semitism
   and Jewish Racism were stimulated by the 1968 New York City
   school strike, but several go beyond it to the broader area
   of Jewish-black relations.

5 ANON. "The Fire Next Time." Booklist, 66 (15 July), 1384.
      Lists The Fire as a new edition of "two essays written
   in the 1960's that express eloquently the feelings of a
   Negro American."

*6 ANON. "Tell Me How Long the Train's Geen Gone." Observer
   (1 March), p. 30.
      Cited in Book Review Index. 1970 Cumulation. Edited by
   Gary C. Tarbert. Detroit: Gale Research Company, p. 27.

7 Ayer, Gertrude Elise. "Notes and My Native Sons--Education in
   Harlem." In Harlem: A Community in Transition. Edited by
   John Henrik Clarke. New York: Citadel Press, pp. 143-44.

164

Recalls briefly in a section called "Remembering James
Baldwin," his early school days at P.S. 24.

8 Bakewell, Dennis, comp. The Black Experience in the United
   States. Northridge, Calif.: San Fernando Valley State
   College Foundation, pp. 21, 123.
        Lists primary bibliographic sources held at San Fernando
   Valley State College.

9 Bell, Bernard W. "The Afroamerican Novel and Its Tradition."
   Ph.D. dissertation, University of Massachusetts.
        Explores major novels by seven authors to reveal how
   their use of idiom, symbols, myths, rituals, and music have
   spoken to the condition of being black and marginal in a
   racist white society: Charles W. Chesnutt, Paul L. Dunbar,
   James W. Johnson, Jean Toomer, Richard Wright, Ralph Ellison, and Baldwin. One difference in perspective between
   white and black authors is that the former uses "the lore
   of the oppressor"--property, productivity, commercialism,
   industrialism, and imperialism--while the latter uses the
   "lore of the victims of oppression"--personal freedom, importance of human spirit, tragic-comic vision of life, zest
   for life, redemptive power of suffering and patience, cosmic view of humanity, etc.

10 Bone, Robert. "The Novels of James Baldwin." In The Black
    Novelist. Edited by Robert Hemenway. Columbus, Ohio:
    Charles E. Merrill Publishing Company, pp. 111-33.
         Reprint of 1965.17.

11 Cartey, Wilfred. "The Realities of Four Negro Writers."
    Roots, I, no. 1:145-59.
         Reprint of 1966.14.

12 Cleaver, Eldridge. "Notes on a Native Son." In The Black
    Novelist. Edited by Robert Hemenway. Columbus, Ohio:
    Charles E. Merrill Publishing Company, pp. 231-42.
         Reprint of 1966.15.

13 Corrigan, Robert A. "Afro-American Fiction: A Checklist
    1853-1970." Midcontinent American Studies Journal, 11:
    114-35.
         Identifies "all works of fiction published by Afro-
    American writers in book form" for the period 1853-1970
    (includes Baldwin).

14 Fabre, Michel. "Pères et Fils dans Go Tell It on the Mountain
    de James Baldwin." Etudes Anglaises, 23, no. 1:47-61.

1970

Points out that the basic function of the "story," <u>Go
Tell It</u>, is the fulfillment of the prophecy that the black
adolescent, John, would grow up to be a preacher just like
his father. But there is a "quasi-Faulknerian unveiling"
of John's relationship to his father, if Gabriel really is
his father, and the justification of the "latter's scornful
hardness towards the boy." John finds himself "stripped of
his rights as the elder son" in preference for Roy, the
younger of the boys. The family relationships are further
complicated by the inability of the father and sons to communicate. "Reciprocal love is prevented," it appears, as
much by "psychological inevitability--holiness standing
opposed to happiness"--as by "divine ordinance, the saint
being in reality a sinner." The novel plays with a "whole
constellation" of father figures--unknown father, mythical
or real/legitimate father, putative father--which corres-
ponds to a "whole constellation" of sons--natural, born of
adultery, adopted, prodigal, etc. This novel is "a barely
fictionalized account of James Baldwin's own life." The
writing of <u>Go Tell It</u> represents his attempt "to free himself," and at the same time his need to prove himself as a
writer "worthy before Wright."

15 Fleming, Robert E. "Contemporary Themes in Johnson's <u>Auto-
biography of an Ex-Coloured Man</u>." <u>NALF</u>, 4 (Winter), 120-24.
Justifies the reading of the <u>Autobiography of an Ex-
Coloured Man</u> by James Weldon Johnson. The "lasting significance" of this work can be found in the many themes that
appear later in black fiction--namelessness, racial self-
hatred, the black mother's ambiguous role, and the characterization of the white patron/white liberal. Black authors
have continued to employ the theme of namelessness, e.g.,
Baldwin's <u>Nobody Knows</u>, Ellison's <u>Invisible Man</u>. Black
self-hatred is seen in <u>Invisible Man</u>, William Demby's
<u>Beetlecreek</u>, and Baldwin's <u>Go Tell It</u>. The role of the
black mother has two sides: the loving and sacrificing
qualities, as well as the destructive "harpy" qualities,
and are manifested in Wright's <u>Black Boy</u> and <u>Native Son</u>,
and Ann Petry's <u>The Street</u>. The theme of the ineffectual
white liberal is seen in <u>Native Son</u>, John Williams' <u>The Man
Who Cried I Am</u>, and Baldwin's <u>Another Country</u>.

16 Fox, Elton E. "Ruby Dee." In his <u>Contemporary Black Leaders</u>.
New York: Dodd, Mead and Company, p. 233.
Tells of the formation of Association of Artists for
Freedom in New York, which included Baldwin, John Killens,
Ruby Dee, Ossie Davis, etc.

17 Gerstenberger, Donna and George Hendrick. "James Baldwin."
    In their The American Novel, a Checklist of Twentieth Cen-
    tury Criticism and Novels Written Since 1789, vol. III of
    Criticism Since 1960-1968. Chicago: Swallow Press, pp.
    14-17.
        Presents selected secondary sources on specific novels
    and of a general nature on Baldwin.

18 Gibson, Donald B. "Introduction." In his Five Black Writers:
    Essays on Wright, Ellison, Baldwin, Hughes, and Leroi Jones.
    New York: New York University Press, pp. 11-28.
        Asserts candidly the political, moral, and social dif-
    ferences among the writers, but expresses how they agree on
    "the condition of the black man in America." Gibson advo-
    cates that Baldwin is a better essayist than a novelist,
    but traces in the fiction from Go Tell It to Tell Me a move-
    ment "from the purely individual and private toward the
    social"; he also thinks that the fiction and essays are
    converging in terms of political and moral content; per-
    sonal acceptance of responsibility, social concern, a defi-
    nition of American society, and the nature of the human
    condition.

19 Hare, Nathan. "Prejudice." Sat R, 53 (24 January), 34.
        Includes Black Anti-Semitism and Jewish Racism among
    the comments on several works treating cultural, political,
    and religious prejudice, and emphasizes Baldwin's conten-
    tion that "it is not the Jew who controls the American
    drama; it is the Christian."

20 Hernton, Calvin C. "Blood of the Lamb: The Ordeal of James
    Baldwin." In Amistad I: Writings on Black History and
    Culture. Edited by John A. Williams and Charles F. Harris.
    New York: Vintage Books, pp. 183-99.
        Reprint of 1966.25.

21 Hernton, Calvin C. "A Fiery Baptism: Postscript," in Amistad
    I: Writings on Black History and Culture. Edited by John
    A. Williams and Charles F. Harris. New York: Vintage
    Books, pp. 200-25.
        Reprint of 1966.26.

22 Hicks, Granville. "Another Country." In his Literary Hori-
    zons: A Quarter Century of American Fiction. New York:
    New York University Press, pp. 84-105.
        Reprint of Hicks: 1953.15; 1956,13; 1961.10; 1962.37;
    1964.42; 1968.26.

1970

23 Howe, Irving. "Black Boys and Native Sons." In his A World
    More Attractive: A View of Modern Literature and Politics.
    Freeport, N.Y.: Books for Libraries Press, pp. 98-122.
      Reprint of 1963.44.

24 Kapenstein, H. M. "Black Anti-Semitism and Jewish Racism."
    LJ, 95 (15 February), 676.
      Points out that the work possesses an intemperate title
    that does not reflect the need for understanding the troub-
    led democratic commitment expressed by the authors of the
    essays (including Baldwin), especially on the question of
    changing the traditional coalitions.

25 Keller, Joseph. "Black Writing and the White Critic." NALF,
    3 (Winter), 103-10.
      Questions the assumption that the literary critic is
    "sensitive and educated" and on his "own say-so, the best
    reader." There is "an arrogance" in this assumption since
    many critics err in their assessment of "the nuances of
    core words in their network of associations." An example
    of this "insensitivity" is Edward Margolies' view that
    Lyle in Blues is portrayed "sympathetically" when in real-
    ity Baldwin has made Lyle venomous by the structure of
    language in the work. The big question is: "Can a white
    critic understand black literature?" Darwin Turner thinks
    "probably not," because a white critic "has never faced the
    critical need to understand Negro attitudes." Thus, the
    critic must be content to be "carefully analytical, avoid-
    ing as much as possible the limitations of judgment."

26 Leary, Lewis. "James Baldwin." In his Articles on American
    Literature 1950-1967. Durham, N.C.: Duke University
    Press, pp. 21-23.
      Presents selected bibliographic sources, primary and
    secondary, on Baldwin.

27 May, John R., S.J. "Images of Apocalpyse in the Black Novel."
    Renascence, 23 (Autumn), 31-45.
      Contends that "there has been a strong apocalpytic
    strain in . . . the best literature of the American tradi-
    tion." Apocalypse is a form of eschatology, "which deals
    with the ultimate fate of man and the world." This apoca-
    lyptic tradition has had a significant influence on the
    "literary imagination found in the best of recent black
    literature." The works considered are: Ellison's Invisible
    Man, Baldwin's Go Tell It, LeRoi Jones's The System of
    Dante's Hell, and Wright's Native Son. Baldwin's novel has
    a specifically religious setting, and the "last judgment is

either the author's revelation of the specific 'sin' of man
that has triggered . . . catastrophe or the very presence
of hell on earth," and "new creation" becomes "the sense of
accomplishment and personal dignity that violence alone can
achieve." Reference is made to Irving Howe's "James Baldwin at Ease in Apocalypse," which presents Baldwin's intention as a writer of fiction: "to dissolve the stereotype
of the Negro as 'a social phantom of hatred-and-condescen-
sion' and to provide instead a variety of personalities, in
all of their individuality and complexity."

28 Morsberger, Robert E. "Segregated Surveys: American Litera-
    ture." NALF, 4 (March), 3-8.
       Observes that literary works by Negroes have been omit-
    ted from "standard textbooks." These anthologies, many
    having widespread usage, are either void of selections by
    Negroes, contain "superficial" historical slants, or have
    only scant selections, e.g., a poem of Dunbar, an excerpt
    from Booker T. Washington, an essay by Baldwin. "Name-
    dropping of Negro writers" in these textbooks is not enough;
    students need broad exposure to some of the truly "fine
    Afro-American writers."

29 Murray, Albert. "James Baldwin, Protest Fiction, and the
    Blues Tradition." In his The Omni-Americans: New Perspec-
    tives on Black Experience and American Culture. New York:
    Outerbridge and Dienstfrey, pp. 142-70.
       Reprints sections I and II of 1966.34, and revises III
    with stress on the argument that in spite of assertions to
    the contrary, Baldwin as novelist, playwright, and spokes-
    man resembles Richard Wright more than any other author.
    Except for his special interest in the sexual revolution,
    Baldwin has not fulfilled his promise of "something dif-
    ferent, something more." Unlike Ellison, who draws heavily
    from the blues tradition--"the product of the most compli-
    cated culture, and therefore the most complicated sensi-
    bility in the modern world"--Baldwin and Wright seem to
    have missed the literary possibilities in the blues idiom
    that, in terms of cultural assimilation, is "Omni-American
    precisely because it sounds as if it knows the truth about
    all the other music in the world and is looking for some-
    thing better."

30 Nower, Joyce. "Cleaver's Vision of America and the New White
    Radical: A Legacy of Malcolm X." NALF, 4 (March), 12-21.
       Describes Cleaver's Soul on Ice as "a collection of
    essays that conveys a world perspective on oppression and
    its sources." He addresses his work to black and white

youth who "are free in a way that Americans have never been
before." The "growing deviation from the middle class
code" by white youth is eliciting a response from society
previously experienced only by blacks. Two antecedents of
Soul on Ice are Ernest Gaines's Of Love and Dust and Baldwin's Go Tell It, both of which deal with escape towards
freedom. The freedom is depicted as "small, desperate physical acts between stretches of spiritual suffocation."
Concepts of manhood and freedom are intertwined; so are
they both "bound up with the idea of self-defense." The
right of self-defense is the "antithesis of submission"
because "it keeps alive the sense of self." In some ways,
Soul on Ice is the "logical extension and consolidation of
the ideas of Malcolm X," who "denounced all forms of racism
and advocated black self-determination" in separate black
communities.

31 Palmer, Helen and Jane Anne Dyson. "James Baldwin." In their
American Drama Criticism, supplement I. Hamden, Conn.:
Shoestring Press, p. 11.
    Presents selected secondary sources on Blues.

32 Palosaari, Ronald G. "The Image of the Black Minister in the
Black Novel from Dunbar to Baldwin." Ph.D. dissertation,
University of Minnesota.
    Traces the image of the black minister in novels by
black authors from about 1900 to the 1950s and praises
Baldwin as creating the finest literary portrait of a
minister. Although the ministry offered some advantages as
a career, in general, the novelists reject the ministry as
another form of a distasteful racial role the black man is
forced into by white society.

33 Podhoretz, Norman. "In Defense of James Baldwin." In Five
Black Writers. Edited by Donald B. Gibson. New York: New
York University Press, pp. 143-47.
    Reprint of 1962.51.

34 Polner, Murray. "Black Anti-Semitism and Jewish Racism."
Commonweal, 92 (17 April), 120.
    Sees Black Anti-Semitism and Jewish Racism (including
Baldwin's essay of the same title) as insisting that racial
and religious groups must meet as equals; that Jews are not
the enemy of blacks because the country's real power is not
in their hands; and that Jews need to reach for authenti-
city and blacks for recognition.

35 Raich, W.A.D. "'Telling It Like It Is': An Examination of
    Black Theatre as Rhetoric." <u>Quarterly Journal of Speech</u>,
    56 (April), 179-86.
        Believes that "theatre can be an excellent yardstick
    with which to gauge the depth and sincerity of a movement."
    Just as Irish nationalism was greatly assisted by the Irish
    theater, so too could black activism in the U.S. be assis-
    ted. Various plays are cited as revealing "the movement of
    which they are an expression and what the Black political
    movement is saying rhetorically to America through the
    Black Theatre." Some of the plays presented are: LeRoi
    Jones's <u>Dutchman</u>, Ben Caldwell's <u>The Militant Preacher</u>,
    Sonia Sanchez's <u>The Bronx Is Next</u>, Marvin X's <u>Take Care of</u>
    <u>Business</u>, Hansberry's <u>A Raisin in the Sun</u>, Baldwin's <u>Blues</u>,
    etc.

36 Reilly, John M. "'Sonny's Blues': James Baldwin's Image of
    Black Community." <u>NALF</u>, 4 (July), 56-60.
        Argues that Baldwin's leading theme--the discovery of
    identity--"is nowhere presented more successfully than in
    the short story, 'Sonny's Blues.'" It states dramatically
    the motive for his "polemics in the cause of Black freedom,"
    and it also "provides an esthetic linking his work in all
    literary genres, with the cultures of the Black ghetto."
    The basis of the story and its relationship to the purpose
    of his writing in general lie in the use of the "blues as a
    key metaphor." The essential quality of the blues "is its
    combination of personal and social significance in a lyric
    encounter with history."

37 Rupp, Richard H. "James Baldwin: The Search for Celebration."
    In his <u>Celebration in Postwar American Fiction: 1945-1967</u>.
    Coral Gables, Florida: University of Miami Press, pp.
    133-49.
        Contrasts Baldwin and Ellison: Baldwin is "anguished,
    solemn, sublimely idealistic . . ."; Ellison is "Rabelai-
    sian, funny, tough-minded, and awkward." Clearly, Baldwin
    is the "Paleface," and Ellison is the "Redskin" (to use
    Philip Rahv's distinction). But the biggest difference is
    their attitude toward celebration. "Festivity present in
    Baldwin's early works declines into hopelessness as his
    fiction develops; whereas, Ellison, using a variety of
    tricks, styles, and modes, embraces the world with jokes
    and riotous laughter." In his essays, Baldwin hopes for an
    "ideal American society, transcending guilt, race, and vio-
    lence"; but his fiction projects an "increasingly violent

and incoherent world, incapable of celebration." Experiences of life drive one away from community and celebration; no real celebration exists in Go Tell It, Another Country, and Nobody Knows. Even in The Fire, which "places primacy on the spirit of celebration," the wish awaits fulfillment. Celebration requires "corporate existence," but since personal identity is a pervasive concern for Baldwin, he has no time for a corporate identity. Many of his works reveal a search for a type of "secular equivalent" to "religious celebration," but he has difficulty in finding a social context that will give "form and meaning" to the celebration. This context is impossible in Giovanni's Room and Another Country; a gap exists between "the self and society," destroying the "ability of the characters to relate to each other." Baldwin is ever searching "for a spiritual connection between the self and society, between black and white." He "wishes to force Americans to a confrontation of their own experience." Only when Americans face themselves can "there be cause for real celebration."

38 Scott, Robert. "Rhetoric, Black Power, and Baldwin's Another Country." Journal of Black Studies, 1 (September), 21-34.
    Defines rhetoric as "pointing to the special relationship that humans have to one another; . . . they seek continually to elicit varying modes of cooperation; men are persuading and persuaded animals." Baldwin's novel, Another Country, shows the sharpening of "a special language and ideology from which the thrust for black power has developed." His insight into "the dynamics of the white-black relationship in America may aid our understanding of the motivation of the rhetoric of black power."

39 Solotaroff, Theodore. "Irving Howe and the Socialist Imagination." In his The Red Hot Vacuum and Other Pieces on the Writing of the Sixties. New York: Atheneum, pp. 133-41.
    Suggests that Baldwin's early works embodied a "meliorist ideology of the Fifties" stressing uniformity rather than the "plight and protest" experience of Negroes.

40 Standley, Fred L. "James Baldwin: The Artist as Incorrigible Disturber of the Peace." Southern Humanities Review, 4 (Winter), 18-30.
    Reflects on the "widespread opinion which until recently tended to denigrate Baldwin as an author and to emphasize his role as a leader in the Negro struggle for civil rights." These views have never been accurate in evaluating him and fail to "consider his own conception of himself." This is not to deny that he has been an outspoken

activist in the "struggle for social, economic and political justice for the black minority," but it reveals his sense of "communal responsibility" as being consonant with his view of himself as a man of letters. Baldwin attempts to show that "the public life and the private life are an indivisible whole"; the role of the artist "is to present the existential knowledge of experience to man." Only when he discovers it can there be "an adequate perspective of man"; thus Baldwin seeks "to go beneath the surface" and define man in light of his artistic "openness to and awareness of experience." He writes out of his own experience, creating out of the "disorder in life that order which is art." Hence, his conception of art and of himself as a literary artist involves both "personal and social responsibility." His task as a writer is "pervaded by an ethical vision and historical orientation that includes concern for his own generation and his descendants"; he describes the artist as "an incorrigible disturber of the peace" with whom "all societies have battled." But for Baldwin, the novel "must be more than a sociological treatise . . . or a black polemic." What is most significant is "the artist's vision of mankind, in all of its baffling and enigmatic complexity." The quest for identity is indispensable in his novels; this quest "involves the discovery and the rejection of illusion and delusion about oneself." Love is the motivating force for "overcoming the existential abyss between oneself and another person." This love embodies the only redemptive power capable of aiding man in defining his humanness. Also, man's responsibility for fashioning his own destiny is all-important; this view is a forthright "attack upon the philosophy of naturalistic determinism."

41 Turner, Darwin T. "James Baldwin," in his Afro-American
    Writers. New York: Appleton-Century-Crofts, pp. 37-40.
        Presents selected bibliography of Baldwin, mostly of a
    secondary nature in the series of "Goldentree Bibliographies in Language and Literature."

42 Utley, Francis Lee. "The Morality of Rhetoric." The CEA
    Critic, 32 (March), 11-14.
        Contends that "rhetoric is an art and not a science,"
    and reviews the historical tradition of rhetoric from Plato
    through the Middle Ages up to "its recent revival as one of
    the viable arts." Rhetoric can be controlled by "objectivity," but the real question is "whether rhetoric can be
    kept from the malicious user." One of the tests of the
    "morality" of rhetoric is that it transcends the barriers
    of time. Twentieth-century rhetoric has sought its moral

1970

basis in social purposes. Baldwin had to activate his own conscience so that his rhetoric could "persuade others."

43 Williams, John A. "Harlem Night club." In Harlem: A Community in Transition. Edited by John Henrik Clarke. New York: Citadel Press, pp. 170-71.
Reports on a publication-day party for Another Country at Big Wilt's Smalls Paradise or the Club.

1971

1 Adams, George R. "Black Militant Drama." American Image, 28 (Summer), 107-28.
Points out that American plays dealing with the "Black Power Revolt" are comprised of "a complex of reaction components." One of these components is the personal one, which "depends upon one's previous life-history." The social component is another one closely linked to the personal one; it may take the "form of defensive rejection of statements in the play dealing with the nature of the 'good society.'" The esthetic component is the result of "innate sensitivity and intelligence"; it stems from a specific type of training or a fusion of "personal and learned responses." The psychological component is primarily unconscious; "it is a response to aspects of the play which analogically recapitulate the mental growth of the viewer or imitate his mental structure." The critical article deals with the "psycho-esthetic" component of black militant drama. This type of response is "triggered by heightened anxieties on the levels of the other reaction components." The viewer is thus sensitized to the major patterns of the play "which duplicate the unconscious patterns in his psyche." Blues is a "superego play" with the black community "functioning as the conscience of a society." Baldwin also presents the conflict between the "self-preservation efforts of the ego and the violent, erotic, threatening demands of the id" using the symbolical superego (Meridian) to link the two. Thus, the play "recapitulates the growth of a superego whose authority and energy come from societal values," which Baldwin "takes to be genuine (Black) American values: love, honesty, friendship, courage, moral responsibility, social justice." Hence the play arouses anxiety by developing the superego.

2 Adams, Phoebe. "Short Reviews: Books." Atlantic Monthly, 227 (June), 103-104.

Includes brief view of <u>Rap on Race</u> as a transcript of
taped conversations considering the causes and manifesta-
tions of racial prejudice--"blunt, peppery and spontaneous."

3 ANON. "Baldwin." <u>PMLA</u>. <u>1970 International Bibliography</u>, I:
   122.
       Presents annual secondary bibliography for 1970.

4 ANON. "Black Talks to White." <u>TLS</u> (20 August), p. 1000.
       Justifies the transcribing of Mead and Baldwin's discus-
   sions on the basis of their "moral and intellectual characters." <u>Rap on Race</u> offers "no solutions, no comfort, no
   ending to the sufferings of what men experience in race relations in America."

5 ANON. "Briefly Noted." <u>New Yorker</u>, 47 (12 June), 116.
       Notes that the dialogue becomes an argument in <u>Rap on</u>
   <u>Race</u> between Margaret Mead, stubbornly rational, and James
   Baldwin, passionately assertive.

6 Bannon, Barbara. "How James Baldwin and Margaret Mead Got Together for <u>A Rap on Race</u>." <u>Publishers Weekly</u>, 199 (31 May),
   104-105.
       Presents the story behind the taped recording of dia-
   logue sessions between Baldwin and Mead that became the
   text of their book.

7 Bennett, Stephen B. and William W. Nichols. "Violence in
   Afro-American Fiction: An Hypothesis." <u>Modern Fiction</u>
   <u>Studies</u>, 17 (Summer), 221-28.
       Starts with a comment from Fanon's <u>Black Skin, White</u>
   <u>Masks</u>, pointing out the "paradoxical condition in which a
   kind of revolutionary rebirth can result from the life-in-
   death of total oppression." Many plays in the contemporary
   black theater "set out to map a zone of nonbeing" leading
   to revolution. Much of American popular culture has roman-
   ticized violence and emphasized its horror; there has also
   been a tendency to "identify violence with chaos." Afro-
   American fiction neither identifies violence with chaos nor
   glorifies violence in the popular sense. Instead, the
   "finest black fiction" searches for "meaning in the violence . . . a search that leads in . . . two directions:
   toward self-destruction and toward the creative violence of
   self-discovery." Both <u>Go Tell It</u> and <u>Another Country</u> have
   characters whose "willful acts of self-destruction become
   affirmations."

1971

8　Brown, Lloyd W.　"The West Indian as an Ethnic Stereotype in
Black American Literature."　NALF, 5 (Spring), 8-14.
　　Suggests that "West Indians . . . have not been popular
with Afro-American leaders and writers." These "foreigners"
from the West Indies have been called "monkey chasers," and
their experiences seem irrelevant to the American experience. Even Baldwin takes up the West Indian stereotype in
his latest novel, Tell Me. The "West Indian's notorious
arrogance" comes under attack in the person of Leo Proudhammer's father, "a Barbadian immigrant to Harlem."

9　Broyard, Anatole.　"Poet and the Anthropologist."　The New
York Times (21 May), p. 37.
　　Contends that it is the "black man's rhetoric . . . that
makes it difficult for well-meaning whites to talk to him
today." Rap on Race is important because it "gives one
white a chance to speak for all those who may be baffled, a
chance to get inside the black rhetoric with James Baldwin,
the most publicized black writer of our time." Margaret
Mead, his partner in this discussion, is an excellent
.choice, for no one can accuse her of being a "racist or a
bleeding heart." The book may not be rich in "tangibles"
but it is in "perspectives."

10　Cohn, Ruby.　"James Baldwin."　In her Dialogue in American
Drama. Bloomington, Ind.: Indiana University Press, pp.
188-92.
　　Argues that in analyzing plays by America's best-known
playwrights, one can readily focus on the dialogue, but in
looking at plays by American novelists and poets, there are
many variables to focus upon, e.g., time elapses, characterization, setting, media, etc. Many of the dramatizations
contribute nothing new to the "dialogue of drama," and the
plays are "diminished versions of the fiction." Despite
this, "several significant novelists have made sporadic
efforts at direct dramatic impact." Baldwin is one such
writer who published his first novel, Go Tell It, and followed it with his first play, Amen Corner, which ironically
emerged "as a diminishing version of Go Tell It." Instead
of the "complexity and compassion" of the novel, he writes
a "thin play," which has as the main plot, a "sub-plot" of
Go Tell It. The play's characters lack density and their
dialogue lacks the "richness of speech" found in Baldwin's
novel. His second play, Blues, also portrays flat characters; the white portraits are "incredible," and the black
portraits are "insulting." Baldwin's novels capture what
he "claims he tried to put into the play--something ironic
and violent and perpetually understated in Negro speech."

But the dialogue of his plays "too often sinks to the merely saccharine, the temper tantrum, and the overstated in both Negro and white speech."

11 Conlin, J. J. "Margaret Mead and James Baldwin." Best Seller, 31 (15 May), 94.
    Points out that in Rap on Race both Mead and Baldwin claim to be freer of bias than the average black or white person; that they discuss childhood, education, work against a background of race; that they "resolve nothing and perhaps clarify nothing."

12 Davis, Arthur P. and J. Saunders Redding. "James Baldwin." In their Cavalcade: Negro American Writing from 1760 to the Present. Boston: Houghton Mifflin, pp. 571-86.
    Gives brief introductions, of a biographical and bibliographic nature, to excerpts from Go Tell It and The Fire.

13 Davis, Charles T. "The Heavenly Voice of the Black American." In Anagogic Qualities of Literature. Edited by Joseph P. Strelka. University Park, Pa.: Pennsylvania State University Press, pp. 107-19.
    Reviews the depiction of the Negro in relation to religious phenomena, from the "black Sambo" stereotype to the Negro "peculiarly receptive to divine influence." It is the spiritual that is usually cited as "supporting the black man's possession of the 'heavenly voice.'" The "folk sermon" was closely linked to the spiritual and was an "efficient" means for conveying "a sense of communication with God." In Baldwin's Go Tell It, the sermon has a definite "art form" with a rhythmical pattern that "transcends words in importance." The congregation makes an additional contribution to the "art form"; it gives the sermon a "sense of continuity"--the "reaction to the preacher's rhetoric." Baldwin realized this in the depiction of the congregation in Go Tell It; this sensitivity to the reaction of the congregation is "most brilliant" in the third and last part, "The Threshing-Floor," which records John's experience of conversion. "No writer of fiction" has presented the "heavenly voice" of God "more skillfully than Baldwin has." He reproduces the "art form" of the folk sermon and explores its effect; he is "both preacher and congregation."

14 Diamond, Stanley. "Tape's Last Krapp." New York Review of Books, 17 (2 December), 30-31.
    Contends that Margaret Mead had nothing to lose, and Baldwin had nothing to gain in their seven and a half hour

discussion, which really was a "mock engagement." The book, Rap on Race, is interesting not for what they think, but rather for the way they reveal themselves--"she inadvertently; he with the theatrical skill of the psychic stripper that he is."

15 Dickstein, Morris. "The Black Aesthetic in White America." PR, 38 (Winter), 376-96.
      Points out that "in the general hubbub of voices loosed by the sixties," the voice of black people is the "most compelling." In the midst of the plethora of written black expression, there is the inevitable question regarding the nature of "criticism." Some critics say that whites should stand off and not make judgments about the depiction of the "black experience"; others urge black people to "develop indigenous cultural institutions," such as theaters, periodicals, etc., with white participation or support. Wright's Native Son and Black Boy changed American culture forever, and their "social theme, the condition of the black man," helped his successors "to find their own directions." Wright's books embody "a fundamental pattern of black writing," that of Bildungsroman, or how he got his consciousness raised. Ellison's Invisible Man "transposed the bildungsroman into a freewheeling, episodic, surreal mode," whose hero could arouse diverse kinds of consciousness. Baldwin has his "spiritual style rooted in the Negro church," and his essays reveal this far more than his novels, which "helps account for their superiority." His problem as a novelist is not just "his difficulty in fully imaging other people," but his "false notion of the novel," which has caused him to create "an aimless assortment of characters." Yet, Baldwin has captured the "brilliance" of personal introspection and has nurtured a prose style that presents the psychological complexity of man's quest for an identity. The continuing "relevance of Baldwin's books, then, especially the three volumes of essays, lies not in their eloquence, which no other black writer has achieved, but in their vigorous dissent from a cultural mood that excessively devalues inwardness."

16 Dickstein, Morris. "Wright, Baldwin, Cleaver." New Letters, 38, no. 2 (Winter), 117-24.
      Reiterates a previous statement that Wright's Native Son changed American culture forever and discusses the work in detail. His books enunciate a "fundamental pattern of black writing, that of bildungsroman," or how one gets his consciousness raised. Ellison's Invisible Man "transposed the bildungsroman into a freewheeling, episodic . . .

form" whose hero could arouse diverse kinds of consciousness. Baldwin's spiritual consciousness is "rooted in the
Negro church," but his essays follow the pattern far more
than his novels do, and this may account for "their superiority." His problem as a novelist has been his "difficulty
in fully imagining other people" so that they do not appear
as "an aimless assortment of characters." In Another Country, the feelings of the characters are "vigorous and
sharp," but in the last novel, Tell Me, a "long, dismal
failure," Baldwin "seems to have lost all ability to command belief."

17 Donald, David. "A Fascinating Book." Virginia Quarterly
Review, 47 (Autumn), 619-22.
        Contends that Rap on Race does not contribute much to
our understanding of race, or to racial understanding, and
that both Mead and Baldwin mouth truths and truisms. It is
a fascinating book because "it offers self-drawn character
portraits." Both recognize race and the pressing problem
of the time and that the present problems are rooted in the
past; yet, while Baldwin insists on the guilt of white
Americans for past injustice, Mead refuses to accept for
anyone but herself.

18 Elam, Julia C. "The Afro-American Short Story: From Accommodation to Protest." Ph.D. dissertation, Carnegie Mellon
University.
        Introduces an anthology of short stories that records
the black experience and illustrates the story as an art
form in thematic units: survival, flight, selfhood, militancy, and soul. Critical commentary and notes emphasize
the need for a classroom course in the subject, the role of
sociological and formalistic criticism, and the universality
of black literature.

19 Ellison, Curtis W. "Black Adam: The Adamic Assertion and the
Afro-American Novelist." Ph.D. dissertation, University of
Minnesota.
        Studies the persistent effort by novelists to define
the possibility for achieving the "American Dream" of individual freedom by showing an isolated black protagonist
bearing the burden of the dream in major works by William
Wells Brown, James Weldon Johnson, Jean Toomer, Richard
Wright, James Baldwin, and LeRoi Jones. Wright and Baldwin
represent in their work the integrationist impulse of the
civil rights movement between 1950 and 1964. Resolution of
the protagonist's fictional role involves a triple function
for the author: 1) psychologically by means of "black rage"

against social conditions; 2) intellectually by articulat-
ing a "way out" of racist bondage showing the author's
place in the scale of integration--black nationalism;
3) symbolically by contributing to the continuing definition of the American dream.

20 Elman, Richard. "A Rap on Race." New York Times Book Review
    (27 June), p. 5.
        Insists that anyone can talk about the race problem and
    not listen, always avoid expressing true feelings openly,
    refer to other cultures and pseudo-historical truths, in-
    terrupt whenever possible, call oneself a prophet or a poet,
    and contend that one is being sincere and objective. Then
    all this can be transcribed, and anyone can call it a book.
    But for the book to be a success, one must "either be a
    world-famous white-liberal anthropologist [Mead], or a
    brilliant black writer [Baldwin], or else there isn't much
    of an audience."

21 Fabre, Michel. "Fathers and Sons in James Baldwin's Go Tell
    It on the Mountain." In Modern Black Novelists: A Collec-
    tion of Critical Essays. Edited by M. G. Cooke. Engle-
    wood Cliffs, N.J.: Prentice-Hall, pp. 88-104.
        Reprint in English of 1970.14.

22 Ford, Nick Aaron. "Introduction." In his Black Insights:
    Significant Literature by Black Americans--1760 to the
    Present. Waltham, Mass.: Ginn and Company, pp. 192-219,
    300-301.
        Presents an anthology of primary sources in four divi-
    sions: Pathfinders, Torchbearers, Alienated, and Revolu-
    tionists. Baldwin's selections in "Alienated" ("The Dis-
    covery" and "Gabriel's Prayer") are introduced by a bio-
    graphical sketch and general comments. Ford credits Bald-
    win with an ability to give life and breath to characters,
    to create suspense, and to express love, hate, anger, and
    sorrow passionately. Unlike the black revolutionists,
    Baldwin respects the Uncle Toms of the past: "their in-
    telligence and their spiritual force and their beauty"; and
    their swallowing of pride to do what the whites wanted "in
    order to acquire a new roof for the schoolhouse, new books."

23 Foster, David E. "Cause My House Fell Down: The Theme of the
    Fall in Baldwin's Novels." Critique, 13, no. 2:50-62.
        Recalls that the "theme of man's fall from innocence--
    his loss of Eden--forms a significant part" of each of
    Baldwin's first three novels: Go Tell It, Giovanni's Room,
    and Another Country. Surprisingly, this theme does not

1971

appear significantly in his recent novel, Tell Me. "Generally, to be 'fallen' in these novels is either to be a
black man in a white world, or a homosexual in a straight
world; in each novel, Baldwin strives for a fusion of traditional motif and contemporary interpretation." A careful
analysis of this theme of man's fall in his three novels
reveals Baldwin's changing vision and suggests that "the
successively poorer quality of these novels results as much
from the stress of this change as from a failure in imagination." Go Tell It is his best novel; Giovanni's Room has
"flawed characterization and weaknesses in its plot"; and
Another Country has "strained diction and strident tone."
Baldwin's "God-centered vision" gave brilliance to Go Tell
It, but his disillusionment with the "Christian redemptive
theme" is evidenced in the two succeeding novels. He
"fails" in these works, "because to describe a world as
'fallen' and redeemed by a carnal grace, or not redeemed at
all, is to contradict the inherently Christian nature of
the metaphor itself."

24 Freese, Peter. "James Baldwin und das Syndrom des Identitäts-
verlustes: 'Previous Condition' im Lichte des Gesamt-
werkes." Literatur in Wissenschaft un Unterricht, 4
(September), 73-98.
    Argues that "Previous Condition" is a "seminal" work.
An analysis of it in connection with Baldwin's other writings, with his life experiences, and with other Negro authors can reveal the essential content and form of his
works. The phrase, "Going to Meet the Man," stands for
the adventure of the meeting between blacks and whites that
leads to anxiety and hatred; liberation from this threat
is seldom possible for the black. "Previous Condition" refers to the personal history of the hero and to the earlier
state of Negroes in general, which gives a representative
meaning to the events in the story. This work and others
by Baldwin say that if self-development is hindered by poverty and discrimination, then the black must develop forms of
behavior that may enable him to face the contradictions of
his environment. These forms represent the outer aspect of
the "syndrome of alienation and loss of identity." In
Baldwin's works, the "syndrome" of "running, acting, hiding,
and waiting" on the one hand and "being afraid, hating,
wishing to kill, and screaming" on the other conjures up
the danger of insanity. Peter's odyssey through the world
in "Previous Condition" is a circular journey back to Harlem and thus back to the previous condition of his individual past and that of his race. Caught between the white
world and the black, he is indeed "homeless."

1971

25 Fuller, Hoyt W. "Contemporary Negro Fiction." In <u>The Black</u>
       <u>American Writer</u>. Edited by C.W.E. Bigsby. Vol. I: <u>Fiction</u>.
       Baltimore, Md.: Penguin Books, pp. 229-43.
           Reprint of 1965.33.

26 Gayle, Addison, Jr. "The Function of Black Literature at the
       Present Time." In his <u>The Black Aesthetic</u>. New York:
       Doubleday, pp. 383-400.
           Analyzes <u>Go Tell It</u> and Ellison's <u>Invisible Man</u> as fic-
       tion embodying the concept of cultural assimilation; the
       former's John Grimes fuses the black and white cultures
       "even at the risk of destroying the black."

27 George, Felice. "Black Woman, Black Man." <u>Harvard Journal of</u>
       <u>Afro-American Affairs</u>, 2, no. 2: 1-17.
           Includes a discussion of Baldwin and other black authors
       on the general subject of the black female's relationship
       with the black male.

28 Gerard, Albert. "The Sons of Ham." <u>Studies in the Novel</u>, 3
       (Summer), 148-64.
           Categorizes the "predicament of the black hero in the
       Negro novel" as being determined by a "twofold alienation,
       of which the fate of . . . Ellison's invisible man was a
       perfect illustration": his "obsessive determination to
       assert himself before the white society which rejected
       him"; and his rejection of "the black society in which his
       being had its roots." Thus, it seems that a Negro "must
       first recognize and accept himself as a Negro before assert-
       ing himself as a man." In fact, it is this principle one
       finds in the conclusion of <u>Invisible Man</u>, and the beginning
       of Baldwin's <u>Go Tell It</u>. In this latter work, the focus is
       on the "choice that each man must make at the moment when
       he arrives at personal responsibility for his ideas and his
       acts." "Integration" becomes the distinct theme of the
       novel. First, there is the "inner integration of person-
       ality"; the characters "do not suffer from the dissociation
       of self with which the white man is afflicted." Second,
       there is the "integration of the transcendental experience";
       although the characters have "moral problems which torture
       them, they are immune to metaphysical anguish." Finally,
       there is the "integration of community," which is best de-
       picted by the revelation of love, certainty, and sublime
       joy through the conversion experience physically assisted
       by the congregation. The church is not a collection of ab-
       stractions, but a "living whole" giving solidarity to its
       people.

29 Gibson, Donald B. "The Politics of Ellison and Baldwin." In
    The Politics of Twentieth-Century Writers. Edited by George
    Panichas. New York: Hawthorne Publishing Company, pp.
    307-20.
        Refers to a 1968 poll of forty black writers to deter-
    mine who was considered by them as the most important black
    American writer of all time. The results showed Wright to
    be first, Langston Hughes second, Baldwin third, and Elli-
    son fourth. If the poll had been taken twenty years earli-
    er, the results might have included Phyllis Wheatley, Paul
    Laurence Dunbar, or Countee Cullen, more politically con-
    servative writers. Yet, Ellison and Baldwin have indicated
    that they have intentionally chosen to be "nonpolitical in
    their writing," which may well constitute "a political ges-
    ture." On the surface, Baldwin is "nonpolitical in that
    his perspective is consistently moral rather than politi-
    cal"; he is far more concerned than Ellison with themes sup-
    porting the necessity of love and responsibility. Baldwin's
    plots, situations, and incidents are "far more aligned with
    the traditional novel" than are those of Invisible Man.
    Another Country reveals far more "social consciousness than
    either Go Tell It or Giovanni's Room"; thus, his stance is
    moral rather than political. He is no more nor less sympa-
    thetic toward, nor critical of, the black characters than
    the white. Even though neither Ellison nor Baldwin be-
    lieves himself to be a polemicist in his fiction, the na-
    ture of his work reveals ideas and attitudes that either
    directly or indirectly support political positions and re-
    ject others. This means that it is the critic's responsi-
    bility to point out where the writer stands politically,
    even when persons like Baldwin and Ellison may not know.

30 Gross, Theodore L. "The Major Authors: Richard Wright, Ralph
    Ellison, James Baldwin." In his The Heroic Ideal in Ameri-
    can Literature. New York: The Free Press, pp. 148-80.
        Contends that of the three authors under discussion,
    "Wright is least sophisticated and more direct." Ellison
    is the "most self-conscious and literary"; his writings
    have "increasingly tended toward the idealistic," a type of
    "Emerson of American Negro writing." Baldwin "penetrates
    into all aspects" of Negro life and controls his views of
    violence "by a fundamentally idealistic view of the indi-
    vidual." The central theme in much of his work is the
    "possibility of caritas between whites and blacks in Ameri-
    ca." He has analyzed the "stereotypes of Negro life" that
    have "constricted the American imagination and rendered
    both whites and blacks impoverished through the denial of

human complexity." But Baldwin has moved beyond the revelation stage, beyond exposing black and white myths; "he has created a mythology of his own in which whites and blacks have been liberated from old stereotypes only to be imprisoned in new ones"--blacks are beautiful; whites occupy a house that Negroes may never want to enter; whites are pale, effete, and inadequate, etc. The central problem to Baldwin as an artist lies in the use of his realistic essays to describe "Negroes as victims and then as men" and then to move to creating "preternatural heroes who are always black." Within the "realistic forms of the essay," he was drawn to the "apocalyptic sermon and romantic fable," which polarized characters into types or symbols. Later, he presented his political and social ideas with increasing militancy so that his words became "weapons as they once were with Richard Wright."

31 Hart, Jeffrey. "Baldwin's Comeback Bid." Tallahassee Democrat (17 January), p. 2B.
    Refers to Baldwin's "An Open Letter to My Sister, Angela Davis" in The New York Times of January 7, 1971, as "posturing humanitarianism" that fails to deal with the legal charges against her and ignores the dead judge and others in the case. Also, this is seen as Baldwin's comeback bid after several years of "more wrathful figures" in center stage.

32 Ickstadt, Heinz. "Gesichter Babylons: Zum Bild der Großstadt im Modernen Amerikanischen Roman." Jahrbuch für Amerikastudien (Heidelburg), 16:60-76.
    Argues that for authors like Bellow, Ellison, and Baldwin, the modern city figures merely as a social milieu for the characters, not as the symbol of "apocalypse and cultural renewal" as it was for authors like Emerson and Hart Crane. Nor is it linked to a "larger criticism of urban civilization" as it was by Dreiser, Fitzgerald, and Dos Passos.

33 Kattan, Naim. "L'éclatement du Mythe." Quinzaine Littéraire. 126 (October), 12.
    Sees that the American novel has become more realistic and regional in the past ten to fifteen years. The hero or antihero, be he Jew, Catholic, or black, is involved in the "Quest of Who He Is." Malamud, Bellow, Updike, Baldwin candidly deal with their characters and present their actions in clear and coherent prose styles. Malamud and Bellow write about the Jew's struggle to be a "person"; Updike shows the struggle "to be" by the WASP, the White

1971

Protestant; Baldwin depicts the black man as always struggling to escape his "invisibility" to attain self-awareness.

34 Kazin, Alfred. "Brothers Crying Out for More Access to Life."
    Sat R, 54 (2 October), 33-35.
        Comments on ten recent books by black writers, including
    Rap on Race by Baldwin and Margaret Mead in which the lat-
    ter practices "a friendly but obstinate questioning of his
    emotional position" of oratory and exhortation that focuses
    on "the sudden concreteness of his suffering."

35 Lee, Brian. "James Baldwin: Caliban to Prospero." In The
    Black American Writer. Edited by C.W.E. Bigsby. Vol. I:
    Fiction. Baltimore, Md.: Penguin Books, pp. 169-79.
        Reprint of 1969.23.

36 Lee, Robert A. "James Baldwin and Matthew Arnold: Thoughts
    on 'Relevance.'" CLAJ, 14 (March), 324-30.
        Argues that there has been a "rapid decline in James
    Baldwin's stature as the major Negro writer in America."
    Tell Me has been "marked" as the work heralding his "col-
    lapse," or in not so harsh terms, "the decline" of his
    talent. This latest work is by "almost unanimous account,
    a disaster." Critics have long debated as to whether Bald-
    win is a better essayist or novelist; Stephen Spender sug-
    gests that his "impatience" makes him a better essayist
    (which is the "common judgment"). Despite the criticisms,
    there is "tacit recognition" that whatever he may be saying
    it is as a "member of the literary intelligentsia."

37 McGlashan, Colin. "Mismatched." New Statesman, 82 (6 August),
    181.
        Wishes that Baldwin had "had the decency to bury the
    disaster" that resulted from his encounter with Margaret
    Mead. In Rap on Race, one sees "two brilliant and articu-
    late people . . . journeying through banality, boredom, and
    occasional incoherence, relieved from time to time by an
    odd nugget of information or experience."

38 McPherson, James A., et al. "Blacks in American Culture, 1900-
    1970." In their Blacks in America: Bibliographical Essays.
    Garden City, N.Y.: Doubleday, pp. 257-59, 281-82, 285-86.
        Includes selected primary and secondary bibliographic
    items.

39 McWhirter, William A. "After Years of Futility Baldwin Ex-
    plodes Again." Life, 30 July, p. 63.

1971

Presents biographical data, statements of ideas and
opinions on several subjects, especially on Baldwin's role
as a writer.

40 Mayfield, Julian. "And Then Came Baldwin." In Harlem, U.S.A.,
    rev. ed. Edited by John Henrik Clarke. New York: Collier
    Books, pp. 155-70.
       Reprint of 1963.57.

41 Mead, Margaret. "A Rap on Race: How James Baldwin and I
    Talked a Book." Redbook, 137 (September), 70-75.
       Points out that the first idea for Rap on Race came out
    of a conversation with Art Aveilhe, a young black editor
    from Lippincott. Mead agreed that her experiences in New
    Guinea gave her different viewpoints of "caste" than most
    Americans. She had lived and worked with the people in
    their own villages, where she had gotten to know them "as
    people--as individuals--with pride, dignity, and a sense
    of their own identity." Mead had never met Baldwin, but
    she had admired his writing; the two were interested in the
    project. After only five minutes at the first meeting, the
    two knew they "would be able to talk about things that mat-
    tered in a way that mattered." They had "three long bouts
    of talking" in the course of one weekend always "trying to
    reach a point at which understanding came clear." At the
    end, Baldwin returned to France to finish a book, and Mead
    "plunged back" into her work at the American Museum of
    Natural History. Like any real conversation, this book
    "stopped at a point in time, but it also continues because
    it is read and there is much more to say."

42 Meaddough, R. J. "Ideas Whose Time Has Passed." Freedomways
    (Third Quarter), p. 307.
       Describes Margaret Mead as "Saint Paul" and Baldwin as
    "Joan of Arc" in Rap on Race. Mead presents "the most
    rational approach to race relations that theory can pro-
    vide," and Baldwin champions the cause of the oppressed and
    flings "the bloody residue into the jaws of the oppressors."
    The book "rings with honesty," but one feels like he is
    watching a "Louis and Marciano fight to a draw" with Muham-
    mad Ali waiting in the wings.

43 Mellard, James M. "Racism, Formula, and Popular Fiction."
    Journal of Popular Culture, 5 (Summer), 10-37.
       Points out that "the history of racism in American lite-
    rature lies primarily in popular literature and principally
    in popular fiction." This is so because popular fiction is
    a "manifestation of popular culture--its ideologies,

attitudes, biases, prejudices." The characterization of black people in popular fiction has generally been limited to a "few types, stereotypes, or formula roles." The "formula" approach is more evident especially in the "familiar topos" of the sexual fantasies of Americans (black and white, male and female). Baldwin's Going to Meet employs the sexual topos ironically, to portray that the "black man is sacrificed for the sexual release of the white."

44 Miller, Albert H. "A Rap on Race." Critic, 30 (September), 72.
Reveals clearly in Rap on Race "the tragic and potentially explosive gulf that still divides too many black and white Americans on the issue of race discrimination." Mead and Baldwin touch upon many subjects: integration as denial of blacks; black power; ignorance and insensitivity of Americans to the seriousness of social problems; destructive racial conflict, etc.

45 Miller, Ruth. "James Baldwin." In her Blackamerican Literature: 1760–Present. Beverly Hills, Calif.: Glencoe Press, pp. 510–45.
Gives a brief introduction to a longish excerpt from Go Tell It that stresses the history of a family and of being born black in white America.

46 Minudri, Regina. "Rap on Race." LJ, 96 (July), 2379.
Focuses, in the dialogue between Margaret Mead and Baldwin in Rap on Race, on various concepts of race and their individual reactions to them in a "highly personal yet somehow universal way."

47 Moore, John R. "An Embarrassment of Riches: Baldwin's Going to Meet the Man." In The Sounder Few: Essays from The Hollins Critic. Edited by R.H.W. Dillard, George Garrett, and John R. Moore. Athens, Ga.: University of Georgia Press, pp. 121–36.
Reprint of 1965.57.

48 Ognibene, Elaine R. "Black Literature Revisited: 'Sonny's Blues.'" EJ, 60 (January), 36–37.
Presents as themes the question of prejudice and stereotypes, the generation gap, the search for self-identity. The principal focus of the story is the narrator--"the respectable schoolteacher, the 'white' Negro, Sonny's big brother"--who, in contact with Sonny and his music, undergoes a gradual enlightenment by making the blues his own.

1971

49 Patterson, Lindsay. "Introduction." In his Black Theater: A
   20th Century Collection of the Work of Its Best Playwrights.
   New York: New American Library, pp. ix-xi.
      Praises The Fire as continuing to exert moral force on a
   social problem and Amen Corner as a moving and indepth
   treatment of "an urban spiritual experience and its con-
   comitant contradictions."

50 Ploski, Harry, et al. "Black Writers, Scholars and Poets."
   In their Reference Library of Black America, Book III. New
   York: Bellwether Publishing Company, pp. 2-3.
      Describes Baldwin as "the most widely quoted Negro wri-
   ter of the past decade," gives biographical sketch, comments briefly about main books, and quotes Cleaver that the
   author's work is flawed by "total hatred of the blacks."

51 Podhoretz, Norman. "In Defense of a Maltreated Best Seller."
   In Contemporary Literature. Edited by Richard Kostelanetz.
   New York: Books for Libraries Press, pp. 232-37.
      Reprint of 1962.51.

52 Schrero, Elliot M. "Another Country and the Sense of Self."
   Black Academy Review, 2 (Spring/Summer), 91-100.
      Uses Faulkner's Absalom, Absalom as a "touchstone" in
   examining the characters' quest for identity in Baldwin's
   Another Country. Both of these novels raise the question
   of "racial identity by dealing with sexual pairings across
   the color line." The action of Absalom, Absalom is
   "straightforward and distinct"; the action in Another
   Country has four distinct aspects involving "pairs of
   lovers variously doomed or damned." In the former, all
   personal relationships "belong to a march of generations"
   and "take their place in a process" with a past and a
   future; the latter's relationships are also a part of a
   social process, but the process is contemporary, "cut off
   from the past that produced it and lacking an intelligible
   future." The different "social sicknesses" in both novels
   manifest themselves in the "failings" of the individuals
   whose lives are depicted in the novels--the failure of
   honor, pride, and pity in Faulkner's work; the emptiness
   of life, the bleakness of black people, the hatred of self
   in Baldwin's work.

53 Sheed, Wilfrid. "James Baldwin: Tell Me How Long the Train's
   Been Gone." In his The Morning After: Selected Essays and
   Reviews. New York: Farrar, Straus and Giroux, pp. 76-78.
      Reprint of 1968.49.

54 Singh, Raman K. "The Black Novel and Its Tradition." <u>Colo-</u>
   <u>rado Quarterly</u>, 20 (Summer), 23-29.
   Suggests that "a theory of the novel is helpful" in
   "approaching the subject" of the novel. In studying the
   novel, the <u>meaning</u> is of greater interest than the <u>source</u>
   of the work; thus too much focus on race could lead to
   hastily formed conclusions about causal relationships between the novel and the race of the novelist. At the same
   time it is essential to recognize that white authors' depiction of the "Identity Quest" generally incorporates the
   quester withdrawing into himself or dropping out; the reader
   is left more with a "sense of loss of identity than the
   discovery of one." The Afro-American novelist gives an
   opposite view; the characters withdraw only to emerge re-
   newed. Baldwin's <u>Go Tell It</u> has the protagonist trying to
   free himself from God, and yet at the end, he "finds it in
   his heart to feel a measure of warmth for his undeserving
   father."

55 Starke, Catherine Juanita. <u>Black Portraiture in American</u>
   <u>Fiction</u>. New York and London: Basic Books, pp. 204-207,
   222-25.
   Observes that in <u>Go Tell It</u>, Baldwin has his teenaged
   hero break with "traditional stock and archetypal images
   of blacks in fiction." He has the hero, John Grimes, reach
   out to find his "separate and particular identity in proper relatedness with other people." John is confronted
   with obstacles that channel him in "culturally prescribed
   ways." In <u>Tell Me</u>, the hero succeeds in "surmounting the
   frustrations of life in the slums" and finds in the end
   that he "has conquered the city only to find that the city
   is stricken with the plague."

56 Stephens, Martha. "Richard Wright's Fiction: A Reassessment."
   <u>Georgia Review</u>, 25 (Winter), 450-70.
   Quotes Ellison and Baldwin who insisted that "Wright
   could not write about <u>real</u> Negroes." Ellison pointed out
   that Wright could not find "among his own people evidence
   of the tenderness, nobility, and devotion to family."
   Some critics have stressed that "in his best work, Wright
   attains an emotional power that neither Ellison nor Baldwin
   has achieved." Perhaps one should not "make a wholly persuasive case" for or against Wright on the basis of Ellison's and Baldwin's assessment of him. Their views on the
   race issue, formed as they were in a different period, seem
   "on the whole more balanced than Wright's, at times even
   more intelligent"; but their strategy as novelists, though
   different, "is not necessarily superior."

1971

57 Thelwell, Mike. "Another Country: Baldwin's New York Novel."
    In The Black American Writer. Edited by C.W.E. Bigsby.
    Vol. I: Fiction. Baltimore, Md.: Penguin Books, pp.
    181-98.
        Reprint of 1969.31.

58 Turner, Darwin T. "Afro-American Literary Critics." In The
    Black Aesthetic. Edited by Addison Gaylr, Jr. New York:
    Doubleday, pp. 57-74.
        Praises Baldwin and Ellison as "the two best-known
    writers-critics" who come close to being "the professional
    critics among black writers."

*59 Welsch, E.K. "A Rap on Race." LJ, 96 (15 September), 2484.
        Cited in Book Review Digest, 1971.

60 Wolff, Geoffrey. "Muffled Voice." Newsweek, 24 May, p. 48.
        Reports on Rap on Race, the recorded dialogue between
    Baldwin and Margaret Mead, as characterized by "ungruding
    respect, warm affection, intellectual intimacy and raw con-
    frontation." They share "a moral and intellectual vocabu-
    lary," and they both want and despise the same things;
    especially they agree that America has reached a critical
    point of either mending its intolerance and hypocrisy or
    going under.

61 Zahorski, Kenneth. "Margaret Mead and James Baldwin: A Rap
    On Race." CLAJ, 14 (June), 470-73.
        Recalls that for "centuries readers have received great
    pleasure, and considerable mental stimulation from the re-
    corded conversations of the knowledgeable, articulate, and
    witty," e.g., Boswell's biography of Johnson has many de-
    lightful "verbal pyrotechnics." Although the recorded dia-
    logue between Margaret Mead and Baldwin in Rap on Race
    does not display the "polish and urbane wit" of the John-
    sonian exchanges, it does possess "dynamism, clarity, in-
    cisiveness, and a considerable number of memorable lines."
    The title is misleading because the book consists of a rap
    on more than race--it is an exchange of ideas upon a wide
    variety of vital and volatile social issues, e.g., marriage,
    injustice of the judicial system, influence of Christianity,
    impact of nuclear power, etc. Rap on Race is a "truly re-
    markable and significant social document"; it is also a
    "fascinating human drama."

1972

1 Adelman, Irving and Rita Dworkin. "James Baldwin." In their
The Contemporary Novel: A Checklist of Critical Literature
on the British and American Novel Since 1945. Metuchen,
N.J.: Scarecrow Press, pp. 29-34.
Presents selected secondary bibliography both of a gene-
ral nature and on specific works by Baldwin.

2 Aldridge, John W. "Celebrity and Boredom." In his The Devil
in the Fire: Retrospective Essays on American Literature
and Culture, 1951-1971. New York: Harper and Row, pp.
155-68.
Reprint of 1966.1.

3 ANON. "Baldwin." PMLA. 1971 International Bibliography.
I:142.
Presents annual secondary bibliography for 1971.

4 ANON. "Black Leader." TLS (17 November), p. 1390.
Points out that although Baldwin had a sincere admiration of Malcolm X, he disliked the "Black Muslims and their
dogma of racial superiority." One Day has two distinct
tones: the first part dealing with Malcolm's early days in
Harlem is "sharp, funny, and precise"; the second half,
after Malcolm's conversion, is "slow-moving and suffused
with a sentimentality almost comparable to that of a Vic-
torian religious tract."

5 ANON. "March Winds: One Day When I Was Lost." National Review, 24 (22 December), 1415.
Announces that One Day is a "screenplay" about Malcolm X.

6 ANON. "Misconnexions." TLS (28 April), p. 469.
Contends that No Name "is not an easy book to read," nor
was it "an easy book to write." One reason for the difficulty in reading is that there is a "lack of articulation
between the two halves, which often do not seem to have
much to do with one another." There is an apparent "de-
sertion of formal design" and in some places even of syntax.

7 ANON. "No Name in the Street." Booklist, 68 (15 July), 953.
Explains that No Name in its anguish and outrage fuses
personal history with the period of the 1960s in tone poems
on the Harlem ghetto, visits to the South, etc., which depict "the devastating effect of the failure of the private
life on U.S. public conduct."

1972

8   ANON. "No Name in the Street." Choice, 9 (November), 1209.
        Suggests that No Name is a "restless chronicle and bit-
    ter polemic concerning the last few years" by "an estab-
    lished writer who has tried to go home again" through seek-
    ing to identify himself with the current black militant
    mood. Baldwin recounts friendships with black martyrs--
    Evers, King, Malcolm X--but "the book strikes one as self-
    serving and pompous."

9   ANON. "No Name in the Street." Kirkus, 40 (15 March), 356.
        Claims that No Name is a "touchy and self-regarding sur-
    vey" of the awful events of the 1960s--deaths of Martin
    Luther King and Malcolm X, etc.--and through verve and bib-
    lical raciness, it never comes to grips with history or the
    self, but is replete with "psychological and ideological
    disingenuousness."

10 ANON. "No Name in the Street." New York Times Book Review
        (4 June), p. 20.
        Describes No Name as a memoir, chronicle of and commen-
    tary on the abortive civil rights movement through vivid
    characterizations of the personalities behind the events of
    the sixties.

11 ANON. "No Name in the Street." New York Times Book Review
        (3 December), p. 72.
        Reprint of 1972.10.

*12 ANON. "No Name in the Street." Observer (16 April), p. 32.
        Cited in Book Review Index. 1972 Cumulation. Edited
    by Robert C. Thomas. Detroit: Gale Research Company,
    p. 23.

13 ANON. "No Name in the Street." Publishers Weekly, 201
        (13 March), 63.
        Argues that Baldwin communicates in No Name as poet,
    craftsman, and thinker in these autobiographical sketches
    with a racial theme: childhood memories, escape to Paris,
    fame as writer, King's funeral, etc.

14 ANON. "Nowhere Man." The Economist, 243 (22 April), 76.
        Sees Baldwin as writing No Name as an exile--as an out-
    sider in the black world of Harlem, the white world of
    Europe, and the African world of Algiers--a book with two
    themes: the assassination of Martin Luther King, Jr., and
    the effort to free Tony Naynard from prison. Though filled
    with poignancy, the book has characters who do not come
    alive.

15 ANON. "Random Notes." <u>National Review</u>, 24 (14 April), 411.
      Announces the May publication of <u>No Name</u>, "Baldwin's
    latest nonfiction effort."

16 Bailey, Anthony. "Black and White." <u>New Statesman</u>, 84
      (3 November), 643-44.
      Describes reading <u>One Day</u> as "eating cold toast without
    butter or marmalade: a dry, crumbly sensation." Also, the
    life and death of Malcolm X "do not furnish the best vehi-
    cle by which an immensely talented writer can express in
    cinematic terms the problems of race in America today."
    Finally, one wonders if Baldwin really was "inspirited" to
    do this "job"; he seems to have "plenty of heart . . . but
    not enough soul."

17 Baker, Houston A., Jr. <u>Long Black Song: Essays in Black
      American Literature and Culture</u>. Charlottesville, Va.:
    University Press of Virginia, pp. 40, 54-55, 81-83.
      Refers to Baldwin's works in several places. <u>The Fire</u>
    associates the black man's conception of the fateful apo-
    calypse with the acquisition of freedom; Baldwin places the
    responsibility for mankind's salvation in the hands of "the
    sensitive intellectual"--artists, writers, thinkers--who
    functions to bring about "the freedom of the black American
    with the threat (rather than the actual instigation) of an
    apocalyptic event." <u>Go Tell It</u> and Ellison's <u>Invisible Man</u>
    exhibit definite affinities of style and sensibility with
    Douglass' <u>Narrative of the Life of Frederick Douglass, an
    American Slave</u>, especially in: the autobiographical im-
    pulse, the use of irony, and the movement from bondage to-
    ward freedom. <u>Go Tell It</u>, <u>Native Son</u>, and <u>Invisible Man</u>
    are lauded for their use of the "norm of the black man of
    culture" established for this century by W.E.B. DuBois; the
    authors of these works use a detached point of view, the
    standard literary prose, and characteristic Western lite-
    rary forms.

18 Barksdale, Richard and Keneth Kinnamon. "James Baldwin." In
      their <u>Black Writers of America: A Comprehensive Anthology</u>.
    New York: Macmillan, pp. 722-25.
      Presents an introductory view of Baldwin in terms of
    biography and literary themes, with a selected secondary
    bibliography, as prefatory to "Everybody's Protest Novel"
    and "Sonny's Blues."

19 Bell, Pearl K. "Writers and Writing: Horseman of the Apoca-
      lypse." <u>New Leader</u>, 55 (12 June), 14-15.

Contends that The Fire was prophetic regarding America's
future if it refused to confront severe racial problems in
a "radically new way." Now in No Name, Baldwin has used
the suffering in the Old Testament Book of Job to depict
his rage and despondency about racist America--its trials,
assassinations, funerals, and despair. The book is a "bitter dirge for the civil rights movement of the 1960's."
But his "misguided propensity for sinister sweeping char-
ges" against white Americans leads him to "short-circuit
his strong intelligence." He frequently indulges in self-
conscious arrogance about his "celebrity status in the
world he claims to despise and reject." While his "apocalyptic rhetoric" seems to serve as an "effective kind of
moral warning," it is not an authentic reflection of the
reality Baldwin tries to make of it.

20 Braithwaite, Edward. "Race and the Divided Self: Rap on
Race." Black World, 21 (July), 54-68.
Comments on and interprets the significance of Margaret
Mead and Baldwin's Rap on Race with special focus on the
implications of three central experiences of the American
hemisphere: destruction of the Indians, domination of
Europe, and the institution of slavery. The book reveals
"the terrible complexity of the problem of human differences based on race in the United States and in the modern
mercantilist world." The dialogue of the book shows the
"uncontrollable (because sub-conscious) psycho-intellectual
forces that exist within a racially plural society" with
Baldwin and Mead becoming the personae or the media by
which the forces speak--the black liberal and white liberal,
respectively. Baldwin exhibits a radical disinclination to
"go back" and accept the value of his African, alternative
ancestral heritage until late in the "rap" and prefers the
integrating concept of being American. Ultimately, Baldwin's acceptance of himself as "surrealist integument of
the collective experience of an historical group" becomes
a painful and eloquent statement of the subdominant black
minority.

21 Breaux, Elwyn E. "Comic Elements in Selected Prose Works by
James Baldwin, Ralph Ellison, and Langston Hughes." Ph.D.
dissertation, Oklahoma State University.
Contends that these three authors use many comic devices
and elements as well as comic structure in selected prose
works. They especially use irony and satire to portray the
black man as both a practitioner and a victim of religion
and religious rituals. The analysis of Baldwin focuses on
Go Tell It and Tell Me.

22 Breed, Paul F. and Florence Sniderman. "James Baldwin." In
     their Dramatic Criticism Index. Detroit, Mich.: Gale Re-
     search Company, pp. 63-74.
          Presents selected secondary sources on Blues and Amen
     Corner.

23 Brudnoy, David. "Blues for Mr. Baldwin." National Review, 24
     (7 July), 750-51.
          Praises passages of No Name as bespeaking reality (Ameri-
     can racism) but condemns the book as a whole because of its
     "bold hate"--of the white race, Western civilization, and
     America--and its tendency to "blame everything unhappy for
     his [Baldwin's] group here, his race--on others." It is
     "a cry of despair" mingled with "a savage shriek of apoca-
     lyptic fury" with "loathings transcending analysis and verg-
     ing on hysteria."

24 Burke, William M. "Modern Black Fiction and the Literature of
     Oppression." Ph.D. dissertation, University of Oregon.
          Examines representative works of leading black American
     fiction writers of the past thirty years to reveal the
     myths and symbols of the "literature of oppression" reflect-
     ing the unique experiences of black America: Ellison,
     Wright, Baldwin, John A. Williams. Three kinds of white
     men are explored: the good man who understands oppression
     and is committed to action; the bad man or lyncher moti-
     vated by hate; and the blind and naïve man who is misguided
     or apathetic. The black man pursues identity and dignity.
     Baldwin's Go Tell It reflects the futility of escape into
     religion; and "This Morning, This Evening, So Soon" ex-
     plores exile as a response to racism.

25 Caute, David. "Pigs and Pigmentation." Listener, 87 (18 May),
     659.
          Sees two types of writers: those who put themselves "at
     the service of their books"--slaves of literature; and
     those who put their books "at the service of themselves"--
     slaves of heroism. Baldwin has "crossed the Rubicon," and
     has gradually "changed his skin." When the "historical
     barometer climbs beyond a certain point of tension, fiction
     withers and dies." Black fiction, especially flourished
     during those years when the Negro represented both to him-
     self and to whites a problem of "irrational injustice on
     the smooth skin of a fundamentally healthy and hopeful or-
     ganism--America." But, when the confrontation between
     blacks and whites became violent and revolutionary, the
     "fact spoke more strongly than fiction." In No Name,
     Baldwin has become preoccupied with "convincing his

1972

readers" that there is a problem; he fails to stretch himself imaginatively and intellectually and loses that "magic"
that he had displayed so eloquently in the past.

26 Collier, Eugenia W. "Thematic Patterns in Baldwin's Essays:
A Study in Chaos." Black World, 21 (June), 28-34.
    Asserts that a basic assumption unifies all of Baldwin's
essays from Notes to The Fire: that life, both personal
and political, is "a wild chaos of paradox, hidden meanings,
and dilemmas" because of men's inability to face the truth
about their own nature and, thus, their desire to "erect an
elaborate facade of myth, tradition, and ritual behind
which crouch, invisible, their true selves," sometimes in
the form of vicious racism. Baldwin is especially in-
terested in pointing out the dualities and paradoxes of
America and its elaborate structure of myths embodied in
the "American dream"--"success is possible for anyone who
really tries"; social mobility; individuality; the Protestant ethic, etc. Baldwin's envisioned solutions for the
chaos and complexities include a personal philosophy rooted
in 1) "the acceptance, totally without rancor, of life as
it is, and men as they are: in the light of this idea, it
goes without saying that injustice is commonplace"; and
2) "that one must never, in one's own life accept these injustices as commonplace" but must fight them with all of
one's strengths (Notes).

27 Cowan, Kathryn Osburn. "Black/White Stereotypes in the Fiction of Richard Wright, James Baldwin, and Ralph Ellison."
Ph.D. dissertation, St. Louis University.
    Shows that both white and black writers have used racial
stereotypes of characters in their fiction, especially in
the fiction of social protest, and draws heavily on Gordon
Allport's The Nature of Prejudice for defining and illus-
trating those stereotypes.

28 Deemer, Charles. "James Baldwin's Baptism." Progressive, 36
(August), 37-38.
    Points out that Baldwin "has long been a champion of the
Person over the People." His fight against racial and
other injustices began with Notes through Nobody Knows and
The Fire; now with No Name there is a "disappointment." In
this latter work he "fits much of his commentary into an
ideological framework . . . one in which the devil is more
recognizable than the savior." The dramatic center, hold-
ing the book together, "is not there."

29 DeMott, Benjamin. "James Baldwin on the Sixties: Acts and
Revelations." Sat R, 55 (27 May), 63-66.

1972

Calls <u>No Name</u> "a reconstruction of James Baldwin's activities and states of mind during the Sixties" and sees it
as another expression of the author having "in the last decade to function as the public voice of rage or frustration
or denunciation or grief" in <u>The Fire</u>, <u>Notes</u>, etc. This
book is a collection of fragments--reports, comments,
glimpses--unified by ruminations of a discursive and historical nature on the meaning of black-white relationships.
In spite of its limitations--bitterness, emotional intensity, etc.--the book suggests a possible coherent view of
recent times. By this and other books, Baldwin "retains a
place in an extremely select group: that composed of the
few genuinely indispensable American writers."

30 Freedman, Janet. "No Name in the Street." <u>LJ</u>, 97 (15 April),
    1453.
        Views <u>No Name</u> as "another bitter autobiographical po-
    lemic" by an elder statesman separated from the rising
    generation of black leaders, yet Baldwin retains his
    "strength and vision."

31 Gale, George. "Disconnecting James Baldwin." <u>Spectator</u>, 228
    (22 April), 621-22.
        Points out that Baldwin has "turned to the Bible's
    greatest poet, Job, for the text and title of . . . his
    long-awaited personal statement on what happened in and to
    America through the political and social agonies of her re-
    cent history." Fortunately, the work is not about what
    happened to America, but rather about "what happened in
    and to James Baldwin." It is an "acutely self-conscious"
    piece of work, with autobiographical fragments told with
    "successful candour." Occasionally, he makes "mountains
    of verbiage" out of small "molehills of experience." It is
    evident that Baldwin has been able to "disconnect" himself
    from his childhood, family, and early poverty; now there is
    only much "solitariness" in his life since he has torn him-
    self away from his "roots."

32 Gitlin, Todd. "Yet Will I Maintain Mine Own Ways Before Him."
    <u>Nation</u>, 214 (10 April), 469-70.
        Contends that Baldwin "is one of the few moralists now
    writing who writes with grace." <u>No Name</u> continues his
    "odyssey" for self identity; and the failure of this book
    to "stand as a unity" is not totally his fault, for the
    times prevent "a transcendence either in word or deed."
    The writing is "characteristically beautiful," almost "too
    beautiful," for there are times when the eloquence of his
    writing "brushes away difficult matters."

1972

33 Goodman, George. "The End of a Drought." St. Petersburg
    Times (28 June), 8-D.
        Describes the publication of No Name as "the end of a
    drought" for Baldwin, a drought that involved both a period
    of extended illness and "an emotional writing block." He
    also has scheduled for publication a new novel, Beale
    Street, and is under contract to write and direct a film
    in Germany entitled "The Inheritance."

34 Gross, Barry. "The 'Uninhabitable Darkness' of Baldwin's
    Another Country: Image and Theme." NALF, 6 (Winter),
    113-21.
        Examines Another Country from the perspective that
    "black is not black, and white is not white, that dark is
    not dark, and light is not light." Baldwin means to mea-
    sure the "individual success of his characters" by how
    close they come to this realization. There are no simple
    solutions to man's desperate attempt to "escape his private
    dark dungeon" into the light of the world. Before he can
    do this, he must come face to face with his "personal and
    collective guilts," he must "pay his dues." Baldwin
    vividly demonstrates that without the struggle to expose
    the secrets of one's own "dungeon," the entire world would
    be an uninhabitable darkness.

35 Haney, Robert W. "James Baldwin in Search of Self." Chris-
    tian Science Monitor, 64 (21 June), 11.
        Suggests that No Name is "no book for the timid nor for
    the reader offended by the language of the pavement and
    exorcisms of all things white." Baldwin explores the re-
    lations between whites and blacks with the "energy . . . of
    a populist muckraker exposing the operations of a slaughter-
    house." He writes with "controlled informality" vividly
    depicting the sights, sounds, and feelings of his experi-
    ences of being black in white America. He comes very close
    to defining himself "solely in terms of his blackness"; a
    person who chooses to define himself so narrowly "cannot be
    expected to be objective, or even sympathetic to people as
    people."

36 Harrison, Paul Carter. "Nommo and the Black Messiah." In his
    The Drama of Nommo. New York: Grove Press, pp. 83-84.
        Contends that while theater, as a secular institution,
    has the function of providing the proper focus required for
    the survival of blacks, the black church has had the role
    of edification, wherein "ceremony reflects the collective
    memory, communal spirit" and clarity of vision. The reli-
    gious ceremony focusing the power of the spirit invests

the community with the strength to aid preservation. <u>Go
Tell It</u> amply reveals "the staggering force of the spirit."

37 Holbert, Cornelia. "No Name in the Street." <u>Best Sellers</u>,
    32 (1 June), 111.
        Points out that in "a few thousand words" in <u>Go Tell It</u>,
Baldwin has told a story that "vital statistics by good and
great men" could never accomplish. Now in <u>No Name</u>, he presents all his deep hurt in a "profile of love and sorrow."

38 Horwitz, Cary. "For the Future <u>LJ</u> Takes Notice Of." <u>LJ</u>, 97
    (1 April), 1354.
        Describes <u>No Name</u> as essays relating events of the past
decade in terms of Baldwin's experiences and reactions:
exile in Europe, the Algerian rebels, civil rights movement, political consciousness and activism, the assassinations, black leaders, the South, and the future of a white-
dominated society.

39 Inge, M. Thomas. "James Baldwin's Blues." <u>Notes on Contempo-
    rary Literature</u>, 2, no. 4 (September), 8-11.
        Examines the "narrator" of Baldwin's "Sonny's Blues,"
who appears as a "well-educated, sophisticated black who
feels that he has successfully escaped the sordid environment inhabited by most of his race." It is this attitude
that prevents him from understanding and appreciating Sonny.
The "controlling metaphor" of the work is music, and for
Sonny the music offers "salvation." In the end, it is
music that promises to "save Sonny's life and future."

40 Jordan, Jennifer. "Cleaver vs. Baldwin: Icing the White
    Negro." <u>Black Books Bulletin</u>, 1 (Winter), 13-15.
        Quotes from Cleaver's <u>Soul on Ice</u> those statements
attacking Baldwin for his criticism of Wright's <u>Native Son</u>
and his exposé of Mailer's "racist trash that it really
was." Baldwin very astutely recognizes all of Mailer's
"verbal masturbation" and Cleaver's uninformed submission
to Mailer's "seduction." Cleaver is "so flattered by the
fact that Mailer wants to become a 'white Negro' that he is
oblivious to the racism that is obvious to Baldwin."

41 Kempton, Murray. "What a Problem!" <u>New York Review of Books</u>,
    18 (29 June), 3-4.
        Reviews three books on racism and anti-Semitism, includ-
ing <u>No Name</u>, an account of Baldwin's experiences since <u>The
Fire</u> in 1968. The book is "informed with the wit of despair," substituting "his own not-often-enough-requited love
for all Mankind."

1972

42 Kent, George E. "Baldwin and the Problem of Being." In his
   Blackness and the Adventure of Western Culture. Chicago:
   Third World Press, pp. 139-51.
      Reprint of 1964.46.

43 Kent, George E. "Struggle for the Image: Selected Books by
   Or about Blacks during 1971." Phylon, 33 (Winter), 304-23.
      Sets the criteria for selecting books in the survey:
   "recovering an image insufficiently explored in the past,
   consolidating or intensifying an image for greater understanding," pioneering in new directions. Books are classified into the following categories: history and autobiography, fiction, anthologies and poetry, criticism, and
   the ideological situation. Baldwin's Nobody Knows is
   listed in the history and autobiography section, and Rap On
   Race is entered in the section on ideological situation,
   with a reference that it reveals the "pressures of feeling
   . . . more clearly than Tell Me and No Name." It is felt
   that there have been "strong gains in all categories," but
   much more needs to be done "if the literature is to impose
   the illusion of fully confronting the density, complexity,
   and variety of black realities."

44 Long, Richard and Eugenia W. Collier. "James Baldwin." In
   their Afro-American Writing: An Anthology of Prose and
   Poetry, vol. II. New York: New York University Press,
   pp. 619-23.
      Introduces Baldwin as "a brilliant essayist and inspired
   writer of fiction and drama" who verbalized the experiences
   and attitudes of black America from the Wright-Ellison
   generation to the revolutionary 1960s; praises his essays
   for their use "of rhetorical devices, firm and decisive
   imagery, precision in wording, and effective use of irony."

45 Lumley, Frederick. "The State of the Drama: U.S.A." In his
   New Trends in 20th Century Drama. A Survey Since Ibsen and
   Shaw. New York: Oxford University Press, pp. 348-49.
      Insists that neither Blues nor Amen Corner "merit a re-
   putation as a dramatist" for Baldwin. Throughout Blues
   there is evidence of "the apprentice's hand in construction"; his "cardboard characters" offend the viewers' sen-
   sitivities. Amen Corner is a "slight improvement"; he has
   a good plot, but again "the dramatic treatment is wrong."
   Baldwin's "cause" can be "championed," but his claims as a
   dramatist cannot.

46 McGlashan, Colin. "Staging-Post." New Statesman, 83
   (21 April), 531.

Argues that Baldwin has "been proudly adopted as an ornament to the society he so eloquently condemned." He led his "brave and brilliant truce parties" in the sixties, and now with his first major statement in four years, "he has lost his way." No Name, written, it seems, "into a void in expectation of a silence," may be a "staging-post" on Baldwin's "journey towards redefining himself and his role."

47 Matlaw, Myron. "James Baldwin." In his Modern World Drama. An Encyclopedia. New York: E.P. Dutton, p. 56.
Gives abbreviated biographical sketch and overview of Baldwin's literary career as essayist, novelist, and playwright with emphasis on "his searing portrayals of the deepseated sense" of anguish over "the history of slavery and oppression in a predominantly white society."

48 May, John R. "Ellison, Baldwin, and Wright: Vestiges of Christian Apocalypse." In his Toward a New Earth: Apocalypse in the American Novel. Notre Dame, Ind.: University of Notre Dame Press, pp. 145-71.
Presents virtually a reprint of 1970.27.

49 Mowe, Gregory and W. Scott Nobles. "James Baldwin's Message for White America." Quarterly Journal of Speech, 58 (April), 142-51.
Quotes from Baldwin's "The Dangerous Road Before Martin Luther King," written a decade ago, and shows how prophetic his words were. In 1961, he was an acclaimed novelist and essayist; in 1971, he resides in Istanbul and Paris, "a frustrated self-exile from the struggle." But the rhetoric of Baldwin has already "contributed significantly to the understanding if not solution of the racial problem in America." Not only have his rhetorical themes been addressed to white Americans, he has been writing and speaking to black Americans and has had an impact on the black community. The extensive and varied reflections on the race problem have at least four persistent themes: 1) the root of the "Negro Problem" is the refusal of whites "to make the psychological adjustments necessary to acknowledge the humanity of the black"; 2) present solutions for and attitudes toward the race problem "are doomed to failure because they do not address themselves to the deeper issue of identity"; 3) "America will be called to account for her sins"; 4) "the promise of redemption if Americans will honestly reassess their past and reinterpret their reality and the reality of the black man." Setting up categories is helpful for purposes of analysis, but there is a danger of assuming that Baldwin's themes are static and clearly

defined; such is not the case. The impact of "an artist-
Negro's ambivalence and increased black militance" has left
definite impressions on him: the increased personal rage
and the need to control it so it won't destroy him; the increased militancy and the need to establish "communion with
his audience" to communicate his vital message. Any analysis of his persuasiveness must look at both the "unconscious persuasion of Baldwin, the introspective thinker,"
and "the conscious persuasion of Baldwin the writer and
propagandist."

50 Muggeridge, Malcolm. "Books." Esquire, 77 (May), 55.
      Says little about No Name except that it is Baldwin's
effort at "working his passage back" to the status he en-
joyed before the Black Power boom.

51 Prescott, Peter S. "The Train's Long Gone." Newsweek,
      29 May, pp. 84-86.
      Contends that No Name is Baldwin's "angriest book, his
most sclerotic." He moves from a "thickening of thought"
to a "coarsening of argument" to finally a "deterioration
of language" until it becomes all "very embarrassing" to
anyone who admires his early work. Perhaps this "ramble
toward digressions, self-pitying asides and truculent bel-
ligerence" will become embarrassing to Baldwin. He "duti-
fully" goes through the motions: the white man is a conscious liar, his civilization is built on hypocrisy, Black
Panthers can't get a fair trial, etc. He has been absorbed
by white America in previous books, but now he is apparently
"paying his dues to Eldridge Cleaver" who accused him of
shameful love of the whites.

52 Ray, Robert. "James Baldwin's Insecurities." Books and Book-
      men (September), p. 61.
      Recounts a series of historical events that affected
Baldwin's life, e.g., Dorothy Counts entering a North
Carolina school, slaying of Bobby Hutton and Martin Luther
King, Jr., etc. There are two "fatal flaws" regarding his
proclamations: he has a tendency to dress up his hatred
into a "highly erudite, literary exercise"; and he does not
provide the slightest hint "as to how he wants to change
the system." No Name offers some insight into the talented
writer "spinning out his self doubts and insecurity."

53 Reid, Kenneth R. "James Baldwin's Fiction: Literary Artistry
      in Special Pleading." Ph.D. dissertation, Kansas State
      University.

1972

Traces the progress of Baldwin as a writer and assesses
his literary achievement in relation to the author's view
of himself as primarily a novelist but who considers all
fictional forms as his métier. His interest in the affective potential of literature is central; he has addressed
the consciences of contemporaries with a literature characterized by personal intensity and emotive language that reveals areas of spiritual darkness and self-delusion in the
society. Go Tell It has thematic richness and structural
simplicity; Giovanni's Room shows a transition in the author's focus of attention, style, and structure; Another
Country is diffused because of its numerous theses and mul-
tiple purposes; and Tell Me shows an accommodation with the
concept of self that previously had exhibited unrelieved
spiritual discontent.

54 Rowell, Charles H. "Afro-American Literary Bibliographies:
    An Annotated List of Bibliographical Guides for the Study
    of Afro-American Literature, Folklore and Related Areas."
    Ph.D. dissertation, Ohio State University.
        Provides those interested in Black Studies with a de-
    scriptive list of bibliographic tools for research in
    literature, folklore and music, journalism, and background
    sources.

55 Rude, Donald. "'My Dungeon Shook': A Study Guide." In his
    Alienation: Minority Groups. New York: John Wiley, pp.
    43-48.
        Reprints Baldwin's essay, "My Dungeon Shook," followed
    by a series of study questions and suggested projects for
    further study on a comparative basis with the essay.

56 Scheller, Bernhard. "Die Gestalt des Farbigen bei Williams,
    Albee, und Baldwin und ihre Szenische Realisieurung in
    DDR-Auffübrungen." Zeitschrift für Anglistik und Amerikan-
    istik, 20:137-57.
        Includes Blues as an important social drama among seve-
    ral plays that have had an impact within the German Demo-
    cratic Republic upon the perception of the condition of
    blacks in the realistic settings of stage productions,
    along with Williams' Orpheus Descending and Albee's The
    Death of Bessie Smith.

57 Sheppard, R. Z. "Ashes." Time, 29 May, p. 84.
        Reveals Baldwin's personal position as a "middleman be-
    tween black rights activists and white liberals" and shows
    No Name to be a "collection of reminiscences raked from his

private disasters and public disappointment." A constant
emphasis on guilt and his own "unreasonable sense of inadequacy" is coupled with his sense of the inability as an
artist to change the world; he appears crushed by the
"truth that the struggle for political freedom is decided
by raw power."

58 Smith, Sidonia A. "Patterns of Slavery and Freedom in Black
American Autobiography." Ph.D. dissertation, Case-Western
Reserve University.
    Explains how autobiography, originating in the slave nar-
rative, reflects the self-discovery and self-expression,
and racial and personal history of black experience characterized by forms of social imprisonment. Two patterns are
still prevalent in the autobiographical works today: a
break into a community that allows self-expression and fulfillment in a social role; and a break away from an en-
slaving community that forbids self-expression and condemns
the individual to an oppressive social identity.

59 Standley, Fred L. "*Another Country*, Another Time." *Studies
in the Novel*, 4 (Fall), 504-12.
    Briefly reviews some of the reactions to *Another Country*
from being called a "failure on a grand scale" to a portrayal of a "vision of life" with "remorseless insistence
on a truth." The plot can be classified on the basis of
"four principal narrative strands involving two main characters": 1) Rufus and Leona (black man, white woman); 2) Ida
and Vivaldo (black woman, white man); 3) Richard and Cass
(white couple); and 4) Eric and Yves (white homosexuals).
These narrative strands converge and intertwine at various
points in a "kind of phantasmagoria of interracial . . .
and intersexual . . . relations." The novel is symbolically
rich in its setting (urban environment) and title. The
former is a kind of wasteland where the characters struggle
to live and to relate to one another in an attempt to jus-
tify their own existence. The latter is "strongly reminiscent of Hemingway's short story, "In Another Country,"
which looks at the interrelations of persons "maimed--
physically and psychologically--and alone." In addition,
the title can be analyzed from several other perspectives:
1) geographically--New York, another country in America;
2) ethically--values of the dominant white population lead
to spiritual destruction; 3) psychologically--the mystery
embodied in the sexual experience; and 4) thematically--
variety of subjects modulated in other works as well as
this one. Baldwin has analyzed and presented thoroughly
the "intricacies and complexities of motivation, attitude,
and feeling in *Another Country*."

60 Stone, Edward. "The Two Faces of America." Ohio Review, 13,
      no. 2:5-11.
          Contends that "more movingly than any other fiction
      writer of the post-World War I years, Sherwood Anderson
      showed the repressive force at work" in American society.
      Then in 1963, another writer appeared, James Baldwin, whose
      utterances ushered in a new authenticity in literature.
      Although his "balance sheet" of two colors is a new one,
      one can readily substitute the two faces set down by Haw-
      thorne: for "white American, read Puritans; for suspicion
      and lack of respect, even terror, at the joy of the very
      force of life, read superstition."

*61 Turner, Darwin. "Afro-American Authors: A Full House."
      College English, 34 (January), 15-19.
          Cited in Rush, 1975.24; however, Professor Turner re-
      ports he has never written such an essay.

62 Wade, Melvin and Margaret Wade. "The Black Aesthetic in the
      Black Novel." Journal of Black Studies, 2 (June), 391-408.
          Points out that "fundamental to the development of a
      conceptual picture of a people is the relationship which
      exists between the culture and the artist." Both culture
      and artist "function to express the collective personality
      of the people"; thus, it is imperative that the artist par-
      ticipate in the interchange with activities and events of
      the culture. This produces two types of artist: "those
      influenced by abstracted formal elements of the culture and
      those influenced by the abstracted content of the culture."
      The question of relation between artist and culture is
      closely tied to debate over the nature of the "Black Aes-
      thetic," viz., repudiation of a peculiarly distinct Afro-
      American aesthetic (J. Saunders Redding) vs. advocacy of
      the inherent existence of the "black aesthetic" (Lawrence
      P. Neal). In Afro-American segments of society, an oral-
      aural basis "has shaped the process of perception" and af-
      fected the form of culture; this is especially evident in
      the prevalence of black music as incorporated into the meta-
      physical structure of the novel, and particularly so with
      jazz (William Attaway, Blood on the Forge; Ellison, Invis-
      ible Man) and blues (Langston Hughes, Simple Speaks His
      Mind). A second major source of formal models incorporated
      into the metaphysical structure of the novel has been oral
      folklore (e.g., the ghettorization leading to naturalism
      in Wright's Native Son; biological determinism in Baldwin's
      Go Tell It, with man perceived as evil by nature; or Ish-
      mael Reed's The Freelance Pallbearers, showing black humor
      in the madmen inhabiting the universe). Another type of
      novel showing the evil of man is the psychoanalytic novel:

1972

Chester Himes's The Primitive; Arna Bontemps' Black
Thunder; Jean Toomer's Cane.

63 Walker, Jim. "No Name in the Street." Black Creation, 3,
    no. 4 (Summer), 51-53.
        Points out that No Name "touches upon a multitude of
    themes, from the most personal and intimate"--Baldwin's
    family, loves, travels--to the "most universal and public."
    The language reveals a mature writer reflecting on his life
    and his world and "attempting to make a statement of what
    he has seen and known and, most important, felt." The work
    is divided into two sections: "Take Me to the Water," and
    "To Be Baptized." The first section is punctuated by pas-
    sages of universality, and a command of English that could
    come only from the most mature of writers. In Section II,
    Baldwin becomes "absolutely immersed in the experience of
    trying to make real and vivid . . . the moral failure of
    America." In addition, he examines Malcolm X, the Black
    Panthers, Huey Newton, Eldridge Cleaver, and the funeral
    of Martin Luther King. Although No Name may be slightly
    redundant, it transcends the limitations of structure and
    repetition; it is "certainly worthwhile reading."

64 Watkins, Mel. "The Fire Next Time This Time." New York Times
    Book Review (28 May), pp. 17-18.
        Recalls that "when Baldwin emerged as an essayist in
    1955, the civil rights movement was barely ambulatory."
    His "passions, honesty and persuasiveness" did much to
    "free the impasse in racial discourse," and his essay style
    set a literary precedent that would later develop into the
    "New Journalism" as expressed in No Name, "a memoir, a
    chronicle of and commentary" on the civil rights movement.

65 Weatherby, W.J. "Jimmy Come Home." Manchester Guardian
    Weekly (6 May), p. 22.
        Praises Baldwin as "a crafty raiser of a reader's con-
    sciousness"; says that "no writer since Dostoevsky has a
    more direct relationship with the reader." No Name is a
    personal history of the civil rights movement of the six-
    ties employing shorthand references to explain why it ended
    as it did. The book shows Baldwin as the only one of the
    "older writers who can deal with the superbly cool
    generation."

66 Weeks, Edward. "The Peripatetic Reviewer." Atlantic Monthly,
    229 (June), 108.
        Contends that in No Name Baldwin "is more eloquent" than
    DuBois, "more penetrating" than Wright, and is "the arch-

accuser of white civilization and of the United States."
He writes as an outraged and frightened man who shows the
conflict "between [his] life as a writer and [his] life
as--not spokesman exactly, but as public witness to the
situation of black people."

67 Williams, Shirley Anne. "The Black Musician: The Black Hero
as Light Bearer." In her Give Birth to Brightness. New
York: Dial Press, pp. 145-66.
Points out that the music in Baldwin's work is more than
a metaphor. The musician becomes an "archetypal figure
whose referent is black lives, black experience and black
death." He is a kind of hope for "making it in America"
and the bitter mockery of never making it well enough to
escape the danger of being black, "the living symbol of
alienation from the past and hence from self and the rhyth-
mical link with the mysterious ancestral past." Music,
then, is the "medium" through which the musician "achieves
enough understanding and strength to deal with the past and
present hurt." "Sonny's Blues" depicts the relationship
one has with his "personal and group history." Sonny's
music and his life become fused with the musical group, and
this sustains him. Even in Another Country, Rufus, a drum-
mer, defines the novel in terms of the other characters'
relationship to him. In Blues, the black experience is
vividly portrayed, accented throughout by the black chorus,
echoing the need to free the "yoke of oppression whose
reins are held by whitetown."

1973

1 Acharya, Gayatri. "Some Uses of Autobiography in Afro-American
Literature: A Preliminary Approach." Current Bibliography
on African Affairs, 6 (January), 360-66.
Includes No Name as one of the important autobiographical statements; sees the author's earlier works as "marked
by a disturbing ambiguity in offering resolutions to the
problem posed"; and views No Name as his prosocialism
document.

2 ANON. "Baldwin." PMLA. 1972 International Bibliography. I:
153.
Presents annual secondary bibliography for 1972.

3 ANON. "The Black Arts." Ebony Pictorial History of Black
America. Vol. IV: The 1973 Year Book. Chicago: Johnson
Publishing Company, pp. 102-10.

1973

Describes the "uncertain seventies" as a period of "soul-searching" for black artists and thinkers. The sixties had produced a "cathartic explosion of creative activity," and the civil rights movement had generated "passionate intensity and guarded hope." But with the white establishment's move toward "neo-conservatism," the black artist has found the seventies to be a time "to create a common consciousness based on a proven humanism." One of the results of this thrust was the establishment of some new journals and literary magazines directed toward providing a forum for scholarship in a black context, e.g., Black Scholar, Black Creation, Renaissance II. This movement toward autonomy was also enhanced by the appearance of black-owned publishing houses such as Dudley Randall's Broadside Press, and the emergence of black intellectual/artistic groups such as the Black Academy of Arts and Letters. Novels, analytical studies, anthologies, essays by blacks have reached print despite the national trend "to cool the enthusiasm of white publishers for black subjects." Baldwin's No Name appeared and gave a "sort of retrospective view of his involvements during the turbulent sixties."

4   ANON. "Books for Young Adults." LJ, 98 (15 December), 3692.
    Describes A Dialogue as an exchange of opinions by "two distinguished black authors a generation apart."

5   ANON. "Briefly Noted: Non-fiction." Book World, 34 (25 August), 15.
    States that A Dialogue was transcribed from a television dialogue on the "Soul" program of NET. The "conversation" ranges "widely and deeply" on topics related to the black experience in America.

6   ANON. "A Dialogue." Kirkus, 41 (1 July), 719.
    States that the transcript of a television tape (1971) shows "black solidarity" triumphant over "tough honesty" in A Dialogue between Baldwin and Nikki Giovanni, with the former stressing the black man's machismo masking as self-respect and raging at the emasculating "black mamma," and the latter emphasizing revolutionary impatience for change and rage at "the jiving black hustler."

7   ANON. "A Dialogue." LJ, 98 (1 March), 771.
    Views A Dialogue as the transcript of a meeting between Baldwin and Nikki Giovanni discussing blacks and whites in America and the world dramatized in the confrontation between man and woman, established and new writer, and two generations of black experience.

208

8 ANON. "A Dialogue." Publishers Weekly, 203 (18 June), 68.
   Describes the transcript of A Dialogue between Baldwin
   and Nikki Giovanni as intense and candid in its groping con-
   fessional-vernacular prose. She demands that black men no
   longer run out on their responsibilities to black women and
   their children.

9 ANON. "One Day When I Was Lost." Booklist, 69 (1 February),
   505.
   Sees Baldwin's screenplay, One Day, as an anthem on the
   life of Malcolm X containing "religious amens, dirges, im-
   provisations on youth and violence," and a final hallelujah,
   plus the words and thoughts of the slain black leader.

10 ANON. "One Day When I Was Lost." Booklist, 69 (1 June), 942.
   Sees One Day as an "effective kaleidoscopic screenplay"
   with more impact than the original autobiography.

11 ANON. "Playboy Interview: Huey Newton." Playboy, 20 (May),
   84.
   Discusses Newton's view of Eldridge Cleaver's attack on
   Baldwin in Soul on Ice; a meeting of Newton and Cleaver
   with Baldwin, involving a long kiss on the mouth between
   the latter two.

12 Baskin, Wade and Richard Runes. "James Baldwin." In their
   Dictionary of Black Culture. New York: Philosophical
   Library, Inc., p. 34.
   Presents a brief biographical sketch of Baldwin.

13 Beitz, Ursula. "Amerikanische Protestdramen." Weimarer Mei-
   trage, 19, no. 7:153-60.
   Cited in O'Daniel, 1977.40, but does not treat Baldwin.

14 Boyd, George N. and Lois Boyd. "James Baldwin." In their
   Religion in Contemporary Fiction: Criticism from 1945 to
   the Present. San Antonio, Texas: Trinity University
   Press, pp. 9, 24-25.
   Presents secondary sources on a special subject in
   Baldwin's works.

15 Chapman, Abraham. "Concepts of the Black Aesthetic." In The
   Black Writer in Africa and the Americas. Edited by Lloyd
   W. Brown. Los Angeles: Hennessey and Ingalls, pp. 26-27.
   Aligns Baldwin with Wright as proponents of a black aesthetic based on their feeling of "the rejection and humili-
   ation of the black man by the West" and "the alienation and
   estrangement of the black artist in the West" compared to

1973

Ellison's "sense of complete synthesis with Western culture," his feeling of "belonging undividedly in American
literature," and "his disavowal of African origins in his
form of expression."

16 Cook, Bruce. "One Day When I Was Lost." Commonweal, 99
    (12 October), 47.
        Recounts that The Autobiography of Malcolm X was written
    with black journalist, Alex Haley. Baldwin did a screen-
    play adaptation of the book, which has now been published
    as One Day and is "no substitute for the original." In
    fact, "it is not much worth reading at all, except for
    those who have a special interest in Baldwin."

17 Cosgrove, William. "Modern Black Writers: The Divided Self."
    NALF, 7 (Winter), 120-22.
        Argues that "most modern black works can be placed along
    a continuum defined by the titles of two major black novels:
    Native Son and Invisible Man." Along the "invisible man"
    continuum are the "revolutionary writings" of LeRoi Jones,
    Ellison, Baldwin, Cleaver, Malcolm X, and the earlier wri-
    ters such as DuBois and Claude McKay. These writers pic-
    ture the black as not being an integral part of America.
    At the opposite end of the continuum, "native son," are
    some of the same writers, only this time they are insisting
    upon the "Americanness of native blacks." They contend
    that the only identity available to a black is as an Ameri-
    can. Baldwin, Ellison, Cleaver, and Malcolm X suggest that
    the "invisible black man in America can become the native
    son of America without the total destruction of America."
    All of these writers try to provide answers to the same
    question: "What is the place of the black writer, and
    black man, in American society?"

18 Fabre, Michel. The Unfinished Quest of Richard Wright. Trans.
    by Isabel Barzun. New York: William Morrow, pp. 290, 355,
    357-58, 362, 382, 422, 456, 475, 479, 518.
        Presents biographical data involving Baldwin in relation
    to Wright.

19 Hay, Samuel. "African-American Drama, 1950-1970." The Negro
    History Bulletin, 36 (January), 5-8.
        Quotes Alain Locke's 1926 charge that "Negro dramatic
    art must . . . have the courage to be original, to break
    with established dramatic convention . . . and have the
    courage to develop its own idiom." The plays by blacks for
    the period 1950 to 1970 share some common traits and can be
    grouped into three basic categories: drama of accusation,

drama of self-celebration, and cultural nationalist drama.
"Protest" is the term used to describe the drama of accusation, and generally these plays accuse the following: the
white power structure, specific kinds of whites, Afro-
Americans themselves. Examples of this type of drama are:
William Branch's A Medal for Willie, Baldwin's Blues,
Jones's Dutchman. Sometimes referred to as "folk," the
drama of self-celebration "feeds from the life experience
and style of African Americans." The earliest types were
musicals--the fusion of a sketchy plot, song, and dance.
Examples of self-celebration drama are: Ed Bullins'
Clara's Ole Man, Hughes's Tambourines to Glory, Hansberry's
A Raisin in the Sun. Cultural nationalist drama attempts
"to build a cultural nation" organized around a basic idea,
which the incidents in the play illustrate. The characters
usually represent human drives and prejudices: the white
devils, the Negro assimilationists-victims, the black libe-
rator. Examples of cultural nationalist drama are: Ben
Caldwell's The Militant Preacher, Baldwin's Blues, Jones's
Dutchman.

20 Holbert, Cornelia. "A Dialogue." Best Sellers, 33 (1 Septem-
    ber), 247-48.
       Depicts A Dialogue as the expression on the "sorrow of
    the black man and the black woman, and in a smaller way on
    the sorrow all men and women experience"--the difficulty of
    understanding the viewpoint of the opposite sex.

21 Jackson, Jocelyn E.W. "The Problem of Identity in the Essays
    and Selected Novels of James Baldwin." Ph.D. dissertation,
    Emory University.
       Studies the quest for identity in the essays and novels
    of Baldwin. The major concept of the study deals with a
    "four-part identity-crisis event": recognition, under-
    standing or perception, acceptance, and identification of
    oneself (including Baldwin himself). His "pilgrimage
    toward self-actualization assumes a threefold dimension":
    artistic, personal, and national. Existentialism presents
    a "possible norm of evaluation for the problem of identity
    in Baldwin's writing."

22 Kazin, Alfred. "The Imagination of Fact: Capote to Mailer."
    In his Bright Book of Life: American Novelists and Story-
    tellers from Hemingway to Mailer. Boston: Little, Brown
    and Company, pp. 207-42.
       Uses Capote's label of his book, In Cold Blood, as a
    "nonfiction novel" to illustrate the meticulous treatment
    involved in "fact writing." There are now many "public

events, matters of record, horrors taking place in the well-publicized arena that are the domain of reality." Baldwin is one person who has been able to "turn every recital of his own life" into a literary work of "distinction." In Notes he described himself as a young man alienated from his father. In Tell Me, he transferred his father-son quarrel to a quarrel with a brother, and in Giovanni's Room he "made everybody white just to show that he could." In Notes, Nobody Knows, and The Fire, Baldwin is more professionally enraged than the actual James Baldwin. Perhaps the "new art-journalism, journalism as a private form," has already had its day in the sixties, and it no longer astonishes its readers. The world of common experiences is one that journalists have felt comfortable to set down; it is their confidence that allows them to do this, but the writer of fiction finds the world "so hard to get hold of."

23 Kent, George E. "Outstanding Works in Black Literature During 1972." Phylon, 34 (December), 307-29.
    Analyzes books in black literature that "represent certain main lines of development in autobiography, fiction, poetry, and criticism." Baldwin's autobiographical statements "have always been a tool for discovering dimensions of public American realities and for arriving at coherent political statements." No Name differs slightly from Notes, Nobody Knows, and The Fire in that No Name recognizes the failure of "a new consciousness" to emerge and the appearance of more sinister forms of oppression. His autobiographical writings are a "fusion of the frank and highly composed confessional with public events."

24 Koehmstadt, Carol L. "James Baldwin." In her Plot Summary Index. Metuchen, N.J.: Scarecrow Press, p. 184.
    Lists selected sources for learning plot summaries of The Fire, Go Tell It, and Nobody Knows.

25 Larry 5X. "Baldwin 'Baptised' in Fire This Time." Muhammad Speaks (23 February), p. 25.
    Contends that No Name represents a shift in thought about America from Baldwin's earlier view in the sixties of the need and possibility for accommodation and reconciliation between blacks and whites to a new motif of "the apprehension of betrayal" symbolized in the death of Martin Luther King, Jr. Baldwin now clearly confronts the treachery of his beloved republic and recognizes both that the U.S. "does not know what to do with its black population now that blacks are no longer a source of wealth" and that "the Western nations have been caught in a lie, the lie of their pretended humanism."

26 Lenz, Günther H.   "James Baldwin."   In <u>Amerikanische Literature der Gegenwart</u>. Edited by Martin Christadler. Stuttgart: Alfred Kroner, pp. 155-89.

Argues that Baldwin's tone has over the years become radicalized, witnessed especially in his 1971 letter to Angela Davis. Although he has clearly departed from his early emphasis upon cooperation with the American white majority, his social and political assessments still remain indefinite. His political opinions, as well as his conception of literature, are enclosed by boundaries of experiences and thoughts that have been determined by the problematics of identity. Baldwin's greatness lies in the fact that he acknowledges these boundaries with determined openness and is thus able to transcend them.

27 Macebuh, Stanley. <u>James Baldwin: A Critical Study</u>. New York: Joseph Okpaku, 194 pp.

Includes a detailed analysis of the works, especially the novels, an attempt to place Baldwin within a tradition in black literature, and a select bibliography, using the presuppositions of a necessary link between politics and literature, cultural rather than practical criticism, and the black aesthetic as relevant to the author. Chapter II, "The Amen Corner," reveals Baldwin's dual heritage of "fear" and veiled anger, his view of man "as a theological rather than as a political animal," his struggle with theological terror and apocalyptic dread as an individual, his movement toward a more public voice, and "a chronological spiral of rage" in his works. "Baldwin's Quarrel with God" (chapter III) explores his refutation of the church and theological terror of his family and youth in order to "claim for himself that freedom of imagination" so essential for a serious artist--freedom from a medieval sense of dread and sin and terror by pursuing various forms of love in <u>Go Tell It</u>: erotic, homosexual, familial, and social, especially in the latter the failure of human relationships. "The Pain Examined" (chapter IV) analyzes <u>Giovanni's Room</u> as a novel treating "the implications of homosexuality in a cosmology that is buttressed on a terrified vision of the relationship between man and God" and asserts that it is one of the few novels in America to treat homosexuality "with some measure of creative seriousness." "Baldwin's Blueprint for a New World" (chapter V) shows <u>Another Country</u> as an attempt "to encompass and to more fully examine the roots of America's social malaise" with love as a serious social issue; he moves from a view of <u>Homo Theologicus</u> that insists on spiritual realities and apocryphal dreads to a concern with "the socio-political ambience of man's life." "The Agony of Blackness" (chapter VI) presents

1973

a brief historical survey of the development of black
literature in America; a comparison of the views of Marcus Garvey and Baldwin with emphasis on the agony of being
black; and the sexual sensibility expressed in Baldwin's
art, i.e., the move from a sexual "heroism" of male characters in the early novels stressing "an intensely individ-
ualistic search for personal identity" to Tell Me in which
sexual heroism becomes "a powerful symbol of the kind of
'love' upon which committed political action can be based."
"From Allegory to Realism" (chapter VII) suggests that from
Another Country to Tell Me, Baldwin moved from a vision of
life "as a matter of private myth-making to one in which
public action had become all important"--a move from allegory and myth to reality and contemporary history. The
conclusion asserts that Baldwin finally fashioned out of
his private history and the turbulent social and political
affairs of his time a public voice both dignified and terrifying that has expressed "his moral disgust and passionate fury" in an era of moral ambiguity, thereby attaining
"a place in the history of American letters that few so far
can claim in this century."

28 Maginnis, Ruth. "A Dialogue." LJ, 98 (15 November), 3476.
    Advocates that A Dialogue between Baldwin and Nikki Gio-
    vanni treats the special situation of the black writer in
    America, sex, race, humanity, power, and the freedom to
    think and write.

29 Mapp, Edward. "One Day When I Was Lost." LJ, 98 (1 February),
    432.
    Concludes that One Day, based on Alex Haley's The Auto-
    biography of Malcolm X, is a hybrid showing the outlines
    of Malcolm X's career but lacking the strength, wisdom, and
    charisma of the real person.

30 Pownall, David. "James Baldwin." In his Articles on Twen-
    tieth Century Literature: An Annotated Bibliography, 1954-
    1970. New York: Kraus-Thomson Organization Ltd., pp.
    133-40.
    Presents annotated secondary bibliographic entries.

31 Prescott, Peter and Walter Clemons. "Readout: The Year in
    Books." Newsweek, 1 January, p. 53.
    Contends that some "good writers presented readers with
    their worst books," including Baldwin's No Name, "an angry,
    sclerotic memoir that degenerates into surprisingly ill-
    written and old-fashioned harangue against white Americans."

32 Schatt, Stanley. "You Must Go Home Again: Today's Afro-
     American Expatriate Writers." NALF, 7 (Summer), 80-82.
          Looks at the twenties when "American expatriate writers
     lived a bohemian life in Paris while they searched for a
     new prose form." Fifty years later, Paris is literally
     swarming with Afro-American writers who are grappling with
     "something far more complex than anything Hemingway or Fitz-
     gerald ever needed to ponder: the historical, cultural,
     and mythic strands of their Afro-American identity." Un-
     able to find acceptance in the emerging African nations and
     reluctant to go home to a second-class citizenship, they
     are accused of having lost touch with their roots. Bald-
     win's Go Tell It won "ecstatic reviews," but when he pub-
     lished Giovanni's Room, he was criticized for writing a
     novel about two homosexuals living in France, "a subject he
     obviously knew nothing about." It is no surprise that in
     Going to Meet, he reflects the concern of the black man's
     exile and identity. In his attempt to explore his "place
     in America's hegemony," Baldwin has returned home; this re-
     turn has become a "public verification of [his] courage and
     manhood."

33 Schraufnagel, Noel. From Apology to Protest: The Black Ameri-
     can Novel. Deland, Florida: Everett/Edwards, pp. 30-31,
     70, 87-90, 103-104, 151-53, 185-87.
          Refers to Baldwin's criticism of Bigger (Wright's Native
     Son) as a "subhuman who is not representative of a way of
     life that can be comprehended by most white people." There
     is little of the realities of Negro life revealed in the
     novel, and Wright has created a "social symbol" concen-
     trating on the "fantastic adventures of Bigger." This con-
     cern with social propaganda is reflected in his characters.
     Ellison, on the other hand, has emphasized Negro history in
     his novel and is "able to show the effects of racism with-
     out concentrating on it to the exclusion of themes that are
     more universal in nature." Baldwin continues the trend of
     presenting the black experience in Go Tell It and uses the
     "framework of the protest novel." In Giovanni's Room, he
     abandons racial themes entirely and exposes the "puritani-
     cal corruptness of America that makes the expression of
     love impossible"; the novel is therefore "more propagandis-
     tic than Go Tell It." In Another Country, Baldwin stresses
     "the desire for revenge against the white world that blacks
     experience." In this novel, he attacks white society not
     only on racial grounds but for its sexual mores as well,
     but the "emphasis on propaganda causes him to contrive the
     plot to such an extent that his artistic integrity is ques-
     tionable." In his fourth novel, Tell Me, he concentrates

on the problems associated with existence in a racist
society. Although this novel is an "overtly propagandistic
novel," it is Baldwin's best since Go Tell It, and he mana-
ges to remain in control of his material as he reveals his
own search for security as the narrative progresses.

34 Seyersted, Per. "A Survey of Trends and Figures in Afro-
    American Fiction." American Studies in Scandinavia, 6:67-
    85.
        Begins with a reference to J. Saunders Redding's state-
    ment that the Negro writer has always known who he is; his
    identity has been locked into the white man's fantasy con-
    struct of the slave, and emancipation did not free him.
    For 200 years, most black writers portrayed their fellow
    blacks largely the way the whites wanted to see them. Some
    Afro-American writers refused to follow this trend and in-
    sisted on an "open-eyed exploration of the true black ex-
    perience," e.g., W.E.B. DuBois and Sutton Griggs. Jean
    Toomer's Cane was the first fictional work by an Afro-
    American that is artistically satisfying and Wright's Na-
    tive Son became one of the most important works in black
    American fiction, along with Ellison's Invisible Man and
    Baldwin's Go Tell It. Baldwin has become more productive
    than other black writers, but "he had to go abroad to get
    started," to know his American roots: "that knowledge is a
    prerequisite for self acceptance." The Fire, No Name, Tell
    Me, Another Country, and Go Tell It focus upon the relation-
    ship of honesty and violence in the process of "change in
    the black man's image of himself"; Baldwin suggests that
    love can provide a solution to the problems of black and
    white men. Lastly, Ernest Gaines's Miss Jane Pittman mer-
    ges the black protest of Wright with the "detachment and
    the universality of the Greeks and the great Russian wri-
    ters"; this novel "combines something of the best of
    Toomer, Wright, Baldwin, and Ellison."

35 Shockley, Ann Allen and Sue P. Chandler. "James Baldwin." In
    their Living Black American Authors: A Biographical Dic-
    tionary. New York: R. R. Bowker Company, p. 9.
        Presents brief biographical data about Baldwin as well
    as an incomplete primary bibliography of his books.

36 Shucard, Alan. "A Dialogue." LJ, 98 (1 June), 1835.
        Sees A Dialogue as Baldwin and Giovanni reaching out for
    each other across differences of age and sex in an effort
    to redefine the world in their own terms.

37 Walker, Warren S. "James Baldwin." In his <u>Twentieth Century Short Story Explication</u>, Supplement. Hamden, Conn.: Shoe String Press, pp. 6-7.
    Presents selected secondary sources on two of Baldwin's stories, "Previous Condition" and "Sonny's Blues."

38 Whitlow, Roger. "1940-1960: Urban Realism and Beyond." In his <u>Black American Literature: A Critical History</u>. Chicago: Nelson Hall, pp. 127-30.
    Praises Baldwin as "one of the two or three most gifted contemporary American essayists," weaves a brief biographical account with short comments on the literary works, stresses the influence of religion and the church on his work. The book contains "1,520-title-bibliography of works written by and about black Americans."

1974

1 Ackroyd, Peter. "A Little Black Magic." <u>Spectator</u>, 233 (6 July), 22.
    Argues that "Baldwin is a professional fugitive" who is always "on the run"--from color in <u>Giovanni's Room</u>, from class in <u>Tell Me</u>, and now from his own sex in <u>Beale Street</u>. He always stays "close" to his material; the narrative literally "breathes with Baldwin's own life." There is always that "same, impassioned prose" with a "relic of the evangelical past," and he constructs the language as if it were "the hallowed container of sacred meanings." That is why he has never "aspired to a casual Yankee mimeticism," and his "black allegories" fall closer to D.H. Lawrence than his "mentor," Richard Wright.

2 Aldridge, John W. "The Fire Next Time?" <u>Sat R/W</u> (15 June), pp. 20, 24-25.
    Argues that it is "now possible for a white critic to judge James Baldwin on his merits as a novelist without inciting all the liberal pieties to riot, and without . . . minimizing the importance of the very great deal he has taught us about the black experience in America." In the last twenty years he has become the most distinguished black writer and "monitor of conscience" and "remaker of consciousness." He has repeatedly tried to convince his readers that he writes of the dilemmas of all people, not just blacks. He has gone beyond racial themes and focuses upon varied aspects of sexual love; it is this thematic extension that serves as a "kind of universal anodyne for the disease of racial separatism." Yet, his new novel, <u>Beale</u>

Street, has an atmosphere that is "pretentious and cloying with goodwill and loving kindness and humble fortitude and generalized honorableness." He has produced a fantasy in which the black characters "living in Harlem are . . . so noble and courageous that one is constrained to wonder how . . . the conditions in the black urban ghetto are anything other than idyllic."

3 Alexander, Charlotte. "The 'Stink' of Reality: Mothers and Whores in James Baldwin's Fiction." In Kinnamon, James Baldwin, 1974.49, pp. 77-95.
   Reprint of 1968.1.

4 ANON. "Baldwin." PMLA. 1973 International Bibliography, I: 155.
   Presents annual secondary bibliography for 1973.

5 ANON. "Blacks and Blues." TLS (21 June), p. 656.
   Recalls that Love Story, the "all WASP fest of sodden hankies," was never a very strong book, but Baldwin's Beale Street presents a strong story of "pent-up hostility of love frustrated and perverted by a history of injustice." The book is not just another "angry and embittered novel," nor is it an oversimplified "heart-warming vignette of an embattled ethnic minority who have a monopoly of very wonderful human values." One thing is for sure, just as it "took a regressive fantasist to shed a tear over Love Story," so it will take one to remain unaffected by Beale Street.

6 ANON. "Briefly Noted." Book World (26 May), p. 14.
   Announces publication of Beale Street.

7 ANON. "Briefly Noted: Fiction." New Yorker, 50 (8 July), 79-80.
   Points out that "all the terrible things that happen to the people in this very disappointing book [Beale Street] are entirely credible, but little else about it is."

8 ANON. "A Dialogue." Choice, 10 (February), 1851.
   Finds A Dialogue, involving two black writers a generation apart, a stimulating exchange covering a host of topics: the influence of whites on black lives and literature; blacks' views of themselves in a hostile white society; blacks' ignorance of their literary past; the dangers of power; the lack of freedom for blacks and whites. It contains enticing fragments, unexplained comments, and provocative ideas.

9 ANON. "If Beale Street Could Talk." Booklist, 70 (1 July),
       1179.
          Interprets Tish and Fonny in Beale Street as both await-
       ing release--from pregnancy and imprisonment respectively--
       and sees the author as using black humor, anger, and anxiety
       to question whether the birth of a child "may or may not
       signify a light in darkening despair."

10 ANON. "If Beale Street Could Talk." Kirkus, 42 (15 March),
       317.
          Suggests that Beale Street's "Raisin in the Sun whole-
       someness" makes it anomalous for the 1970s. Though some-
       times saccharine, it has "a genuinely sweet and free spirit"
       that makes an affirmation of the humanity of black people,
       especially in the showdown between the two black families.

*11 ANON. "If Beale Street Could Talk." Observer (16 June),
       p. 33.
          Cited in Book Review Index. 1974 Cumulation. Edited
       by Gary C. Tarbert. Detroit: Gale Research Company,
       p. 25.

12 ANON. "If Beale Street Could Talk." New York Times Book Re-
       view (1 December), p. 70.
          Says that Baldwin risks writing about real life from the
       point of view of a young woman in the 1950s and wins a good
       book in Beale Street.

13 ANON. "A Selected Vacation Reading List: Fiction." New
       York Times Book Review (2 June), p. 34.
          States that in Beale Street, Baldwin "risks writing from
       the point of view of a young woman."

14 Bannon, Barbara. "If Beale Street Could Talk." Publishers
       Weekly, 205 (25 March), 49.
          Discusses Beale Street as a "bittersweet love story" be-
       tween Tish and Fonny and a revelation of the deep family
       love of the Rivers' home in the face of adversity.

15 Bell, George E. "The Dilemma of Love in Go Tell It on the
       Mountain and Giovanni's Room." CLAJ, 17 (March), 397-406.
          Analyzes Baldwin's pervasive theme of the possibility of
       love in Go Tell It and Giovanni's Room. Yet from a theolo-
       gical and/or psychological context of a "morality based on
       fear, guilt, and corruption," the possibility of love cut-
       ting across racial barriers is slight indeed. This is not
       to say that Baldwin's novels "fail to provide answers," for
       love is an attainable goal if one is "willing to live

1974

existentially and abandon the puritan mythology of man's corruption." Although "lasting love" is never achieved in Go Tell It, there is "inherent optimism" in the work, and in spite of the overt pessimism, Giovanni's Room explores the theme of the search for love in greater depth.

16 Bell, Pearl K. "Blacks and the Blues." New Leader, 57 (27 May), 3-5.
Refers to Baldwin's early essay, "Everybody's Protest Novel," and his contention that the "protest novel must never be confused with art." The "pigeonholes of protest" impose a false concept of order on the creative artist by debasing and misrepresenting the "intricately perplexing individual nature of black experience." The real business of the novelist, according to Baldwin, was not the "inflammatory manipulation of social responsibility and reform, but the far more difficult and courageous revelation of man's complexity." While he has been correct about the objectives of fiction for the artist, his own novels "have been on the whole uninteresting and fatally strained." Indeed, he has never really been "at home in the novel"; his real power as a writer is to be found in his essays, especially the autobiographical ones. The latest novel, Beale Street, is his "shallowest work of fiction," and ironically, he commits those very "atrocities of distortion and stereotyping" that he deplored in Wright's Native Son. In Beale Street, he tries to capture the "manner of the blues ballad," but instead he comes out with an "ethnic soap opera--complete with cardboard characters shoved through pseudotragic charades of doom and catastrophe."

17 Bennett, Joanne S. "James Baldwin: A Contemporary Novelist of Manner." Ph.D. dissertation, Indiana University.
Points out that Baldwin has "achieved distinction" as an American novelist and essayist of manners. He has included in his writing analyses of "the basic moral assumptions of an era, often an era in transition." He places his characters who represent the primary "manners of the time" in situations that illustrate the conflicts inherent in society. Go Tell It depicts the society of Harlem in the 1940s; Giovanni's Room portrays an "anatomy" of Parisian homosexual social milieu in which a white American seeks escape from the brutality of his homeland; Another Country attempts to capture the social life of the New York Baldwin knows, and Tell Me views the changing society of the 1960s.

18 Bigsby, C.W.E. "Faith in the Power of Love." Manchester Guardian Weekly (29 June), p. 22.

Sees <u>Beale Street</u> as another literary example of Baldwin's persistent thematic emphases—a conviction about the
power of love that lapses into "a painful and disabling sentimentality" on one side and as "the only force which could
sustain him against the insistent logic of racial history"
on the other. <u>Beale Street</u> embodies faith in "the redemptive power of love balanced by an equal and opposite insistence on white culpability."

19 Bone, Robert A. "James Baldwin." In Kinnamon, <u>James Baldwin</u>,
      1974.49, pp. 28-51.
         Reprint of 1965.17.

20 Brignano, Russell C. <u>Black Americans in Autobiography</u>. Dur-
      ham, N.C.: Duke University Press, pp. 64-65.
         Includes a listing of and brief comments on <u>Notes</u>, <u>No-
      body Knows</u>, <u>The Fire</u>, <u>Rap on Race</u>, and <u>No Name</u>.

21 Broyard, Anatole. "No Color Line in Clichés." <u>The New York
      Times</u> (17 May), p. 37.
         Argues that Baldwin has "picked the bone clean" when be-
      ing critical of America, especially white America. When he
      consistently presents scenes of garbage in the streets of
      Harlem, he needs to be reminded that "the City Health Code
      stipulates that garbage must be put out in proper contain-
      ers." <u>Beale Street</u> is a "vehemently sentimental love
      story"; and Baldwin appears so dated in this novel that
      even Wright is "more contemporary."

22 Butterfield, Stephen. "James Baldwin: The Growth of a New
      Radicalism." In his <u>Black Autobiography in America</u>. Am-
      herst, Mass.: University of Massachusetts Press, pp. 183-
      200.
         Contends that 1961 was a "dividing line in American his-
      tory, a time when all the race issues left unsettled by Re-
      construction were coming back to the surface." Autobiogra-
      phies written after <u>Nobody Knows</u> (1961) belong to a new era
      of "reawakened political commitment." The black masses
      were taking the initiative, "forcing the middle class to
      respond to their militance one way or the other." Baldwin
      deserves close attention as one of the important writers
      who was making a "transition in his writing." Although he
      has always followed his own independent path, he was be-
      coming "radicalized himself through seeing what happens to
      black people who attempt to carry out their vision of
      change within American society as it is." The impact of
      the black revolution has influenced Baldwin's tone and mes-
      sage, especially in his essays; in <u>Notes</u> (1955) and even

1974

Nobody Knows (1961), his values were still Christian, and
his language revealed the "moral assumptions of Christianity and political liberalism"; in "An Open Letter to My
Sister Angela Davis" (1971), he was more revolutionary
"though still marked by occasional sermon echoes and a
certain quality of gentleness"; and in No Name (1972), he
declared openly that there was "no hope for peace as long
as capitalism exists." The scope of his work illustrates
the "long, tortuous, self-examining, reluctant process by
which black writing . . . has concluded that America has
no intentions of voluntarily redressing the wrongs of slavery and discrimination; . . . henceforth, blacks must be
prepared to undertake massive, organized resistance against
efforts to suppress them."

23 Cleaver, Eldridge. "Notes on a Native Son." In Kinnamon,
    James Baldwin, 1974.49, pp. 66-76.
        Reprint of 1966.15.

24 Clemons, Walter. "Black and Blue." Newsweek, 27 May, p. 82.
        Contends that in Beale Street, Baldwin "means to tell a
    story that will move [one] like . . . the great old blues
    songs--a lyric cry of pain." But the music in the novel is
    not "authentic blues"; instead, it is like the phony music
    "piped into elevators." There are some scenes that may
    give the reader hope, but as a novel, "it is an almost to-
    tal disaster."

25 Cosgrave, Mary Silva. "Outlook Tower." Horn Book, 50
    (October), 158.
        Argues that Beale Street is a novel of love that sus-
    tains Tish and Fonny in their struggles against racial op-
    pression and civil and human inequity amid "ecstatic mo-
    ments of lovemaking, warm feelings of family unity, flashes
    of laughter, and bits of sharp ridicule."

26 Curley, Arthur. "The Book Review: Fiction." LJ, 99
    (1 April), 1957.
        Describes the characters of Beale Street as "stereotypi-
    cal but affirms that this tale of black survival in an un-
    just and brutal society is emotional dynamite." The bal-
    ance of "bitterness and love" that has been associated with
    Baldwin's other writings seems to have shifted toward the
    latter.

27 Dance, Daryl C. "You Can't Go Home Again: James Baldwin and
    the South." CLAJ, 18 (September), 81-90.

Argues that Baldwin, like many other black artists, has
found that in his efforts to express the plight of the
"black man in America, he has been forced to deal . . .
with that inescapable dilemma of the Black American--the
lack of a sense of a positive self-identity." In one's
search for roots, the American Negro has looked to Africa,
yet he finds himself too removed from this strange country.
Baldwin has noted several times that there is a "distance
between the Black African experience and the Black American
experience." Yet he has quested for his identity abroad--
specifically in France--and ultimately he has arrived at
the realization that "he, like all of his characters who go
abroad, must return to America." His return to America,
mainly New York, was incomplete, for he still had to make
his "odyssey to the South"--there, not Africa, was where it
all began for him. Only after he made his trip to the
South was he able to "appreciate the positive results of
these beginnings." The trip to the South was emotionally
taxing to Baldwin, and when he returned to New York, he was
suffering from "severe neurotic disorders." He says that
in "going home," he was faced with the threat of the real
loss of his manhood. Thus, having found his home in the
South, he realized that "he cannot go home again," for it
may mean extinction.

28 Davis, Arthur P. "Integrationists and Transitional Writers:
    James Baldwin." In his From the Dark Tower: Afro-American
    Writers, 1900-1960. Washington, D.C.: Howard University
    Press, pp. 216-26.
       Sees that Baldwin "has served as a kind of measuring rod
    for the nation's social conscience." He is a kind of "pub-
    lic witness" who has reported through his essays "the ra-
    cial sickness which America has." He has the ability to
    put into "brilliant prose" the frustrations of Negroes and
    because of his "excellence as a writer," he has appealed to
    large numbers of whites. His first major publication, Go
    Tell It, is a realistic and revealing novel about Harlem
    ghetto life; many critics consider this work Baldwin's best
    novel. His second novel, Giovanni's Room, treats openly
    and with dignity the homosexual theme; it is a plea for
    honesty in sexual matters. Another Country deals with
    black-white relationships, homo- versus heterosexual re-
    lationships, and marital versus extramarital relationships,
    "each of them crossing and recrossing the paths of the
    other two." The novel seems to make a plea for "a deeper
    and more unbiased understanding of human failures and vir-
    tues, as they are influenced by racial, class, and sexual

considerations." His last novel, <u>Tell Me</u>, is his weakest,
for Baldwin does not know the world of the theater as he
does the world of the ghetto. His essays are found in four
collections: <u>Notes</u> presents Baldwin's avowed integrationist stance; <u>Nobody Knows</u> deals largely with the identity
problems faced by most American Negroes; <u>The Fire</u> is a warning to America to come to its senses; and <u>No Name</u> shows
signs of his weariness and disgust with the American racial
situation. If there is one theme that runs through most of
Baldwin's work, it is this: "America's great trouble is
that it refuses to look objectively at its history and its
essential nature." It is blinded by a system of racial and
other myths that have no relationship to reality; thus the
nation "stumbles forward, headed for inevitable disaster."

29 Davis, Arthur P. "James Baldwin." In his <u>From the Dark Tower:</u>
<u>Afro-American Writers, 1900-1960</u>. Washington, D.C.:
Howard University Press, pp. 286-89.
   Presents a selective bibliography of primary and secon-
dary sources for Baldwin.

30 DeMott, Benjamin. "James Baldwin on the Sixties: Acts and
Revelations." In Kinnamon, <u>James Baldwin</u>, 1974.49, pp.
155-62.
   Reprint of 1972.29.

31 Detweiler, Robert. "Blues Lament." <u>Christian Century</u>, 91
(31 July), 752.
   Recalls that Beale Street in Memphis "was a home of
blues composition," and the novel <u>Beale Street</u> "is written
as a blues lament," which explains the two sections of the
book: the "long lyric-evocative celebration of suffering"
("Troubled About My Soul") and the second section ("Zion")
with its "fade away." The lack of plot resolution mirrors
the lack of resolution in the black families' efforts to
free Fonny, the "hero" of the novel. Images of "separation"
and of "attempted reunion pervade the book." Although Baldwin presents depth of feeling, he has "not transcended the
clichés of language, theme and place. The novel moves one
but does not convince."

32 Donlan, Dan. "Cleaver on Baldwin and Wright." <u>Clearing</u>
<u>House</u>, 48 (April), 508-509.
   Quotes from Cleaver's <u>Soul on Ice</u> regarding Baldwin's
criticism of Wright. These statements from Cleaver reflect
a conflict in the point of view he and Baldwin have regarding the black man's experience. Basically, Baldwin's
criticism of Wright's <u>Native Son</u> emanates from different

philosophical positions: "Baldwin is a humanist; Wright a
naturalist." Cleaver is "unable to assimilate Baldwin's
view" because like Wright, Cleaver also feels that "man is
a product of society." Cleaver is "alienated by Baldwin's
humanistic, rather than deterministic, orientation." Also,
Cleaver views social involvement, i.e., the black man's
struggle against the social forces, as a "sign of virility,
and . . . it is Wright's virility that Cleaver most admires." Cleaver lashes out against Baldwin's homosexuality
as well as his humanism, which seems to him (Cleaver) to
minimize the importance of the black power struggle.

33 Duffy, Martha. "All in the Family." Time, 10 June, pp. 94-96.
    Classifies the novel, Beale Street, as "a deadline
drama." As a novel, it is "not a success, being too sentimental and predictable."

34 Dupee, F.W. "James Baldwin and the 'Man.'" In Kinnamon,
    James Baldwin, 1974.49, pp. 11-15.
    Reprint of 1963.24.

35 Edwards, Thomas. "Can You Go Home Again." New York Review of
    Books, 21 (13 June), 37.
    Sees the irony in Baldwin's title, Beale Street, but
contends that the novel "does not succeed in telling a convincing story" about "black lovers in the repressive hands
of white justice." The novel "goes wrong" because Baldwin
does not take the "trouble to get things right." One cannot read the novel as "social drama" since he has written
it so "flatly and schematically" that he drives one "to
imagining ways in which the story might be more believable."
So one must read the novel allegorically, a kind of Romeo
and Juliet story.

36 Fabre, Genevieve. "A Checklist of Original Plays, Pageants,
    Rituals and Musicals by Afro-American Authors Performed in
    the United States from 1960-1973." Black World, 23 (April),
    81-97.
    Lists Blues and Amen Corner and places of first
production.

37 Fabre, Michel. "Fathers and Sons in James Baldwin's Go Tell
    It on the Mountain." In Kinnamon, James Baldwin,1974.49,
    pp. 120-38.
    Reprint of 1970.14.

38 Freese, Peter. "James Baldwin." In his Die Amerikanische
    Kurzgeschichte nach 1945: Salinger, Malamud, Baldwin,
    Purdy, Barth. Frankfurt: Athenäum Verlag, pp. 246-320.

1974

Summarizes Baldwin's life and work, then focuses upon
his short stories. Baldwin has repudiated his conciliatory
position with regard to whites and has changed over to the
radical camp; nevertheless, he still believes that humans
can improve. One central theme in his short stories is
the complicated relationship between sexuality and racism.
The stories are over-shadowed by his novels, drama, and
essays, but a dozen stories published since 1948 present
many problems of importance for modern Afro-American lite-
rature--the insurmountable difficulties of the search for
identity in an unfriendly white world, for one. The possibility of escape is explored but rejected; in exile the
black remains in a "no man's land" between blacks and
whites; all possibilities of flight are illusions. The
stories stand between art and propaganda, between the depiction of individual problems and an "enraged accusation
against the social discrimination of blacks in America."

39 Giles, James R. "Religious Alienation and 'Homosexual Consciousness' in City of the Night and Go Tell It on the
Mountain." College English, 36 (November), 369-80.
    Analyzes John Rechy's City of the Night and Baldwin's Go
Tell It regarding religious and homosexual motifs. Each
belongs to a "minority group"--Recy is gay and Chicano;
Baldwin is gay and black. In Go Tell It, there is the constant reference to "the natural man" who is a part of "human nature that is inherently sinful and which consequently
must be repressed." Sex is labeled evil except in marriage;
so the church forces many of its parishioners to "go under-
ground with their sexual desires." Both novels attempt to
"wed the theme of homosexuality to the theme of an oppressive religion which attacks and even tries to deny human
love and sexuality." These two works end with a denial of
religion and "a yearning for meaningful human contact";
both are clearly autobiographical. Perhaps the reason that
Baldwin has "played down the homosexual content" of Go Tell
It is that he has "never been as comfortable with his homosexuality as Rechy."

40 Goldman, Suzy B. "James Baldwin's 'Sonny's Blues': A Message
in Music." NALF, 8, pp. 231-33.
    Describes theme, form, and image in "Sonny's Blues" as a
"blend" of perfect harmony rising "to a thundering cres-
cendo." In the story, Baldwin creates four time sequences
in four movements: 1) narrator learns of Sonny's arrest
and must confront his own past; 2) narrator writes to Sonny
in prison and communication begins; 3) narrator recalls
events that fuse past, present, and future; 4) narrator and

Sonny begin a new relationship. The finale brings out two
themes of "interpersonal communication and music together."

41 Gounard, Jean-François. "La Carrière Singulière de James Bald-
     win: 1924-1970." Revue de L'Université d'Ottawa, 44:
     507-18.
          Presents a detailed biographical account of Baldwin and
     states that Go Tell It is a "profound autobiographical
     novel" incorporating numerous significant events of his
     early life. The career of Baldwin, as evidenced by his
     writings, is closely related to specific experiences in
     his life: from his young preaching days in a Harlem church
     to his stay in the Swiss Alps to his residence in Paris.
     Another Country, Giovanni's Room, The Fire, Nobody Knows,
     Amen Corner, Blues, Tell Me, Rap on Race reflect three
     classes of writing: 1) a "dressing down" in which Baldwin
     writes about the great "travails" producing the civil
     rights movement; 2) a concern and interest in the many
     problems of man in general and his own in particular;
     3) an emphasis on the prophetic nature of the artist's
     work.

42 Hernton, Calvin C. "A Fiery Baptism." In Kinnamon, James
     Baldwin, 1974.49, pp. 109-19.
          Reprint of 1970.21.

43 Hill, William B. "The Best in Books: A Fall Survey--Fiction."
     America, 131 (16 November), 302.
          Calls Beale Street a "story of star-crossed lovers" that
     manifests Baldwin's "eloquence."

44 Howe, Irving. "James Baldwin: At Ease in Apocalypse." In
     Kinnamon, James Baldwin, 1974.49, pp. 96-108.
          Reprint of 1968.29.

45 Hughes, Langston. "From Harlem to Paris." In Kinnamon,
     James Baldwin, 1974.49, pp. 9-10.
          Reprint of 1956.14.

46 Jordan, June. "If Beale Street Could Talk." Village Voice,
     20 June, pp. 33-35.
          Concludes that Beale Street is a "flat, thin story that
     takes place at no particular time, and that spins ahead,
     wobbly, without a particular voice, until it stops with a
     strained and tacky conclusion." The narrator is not a be-
     lievable woman, but resembles a fatuous man with woman-
     hating ideas.

1974

47 Kent, George E. "James Baldwin and the Problem of Being." In
      Kinnamon, James Baldwin, 1974.49, pp. 16-27.
         Reprint of 1964.46.

48 Kim, Kichung. "Wright, the Protest Novel, and Baldwin's
      Faith." CLAJ, 17 (March), 387-96.
         Quotes Wright's statement that "all literature is pro-
      test," and Baldwin's reply that "all literature might be
      protest but all protest was not literature." He found
      Wright's Native Son unreal; Bigger was a "straw-figure
      fabricated out of white America's fantasy about her black
      countrymen." However, to many black Americans, Bigger is
      only too real; there seems nothing "mythic about Bigger."
      Therefore, they find no difficulty in accepting "Wright's
      testimony that Bigger's mono-maniacal character accurately
      reflects what happens to the urban black in America whose
      life is overwhelmed by the obsessive fear, anger, and
      frustration caused by the daily oppression he suffers."
      How then does one reconcile the reality many black Ameri-
      cans see in Bigger with Baldwin's description of him "as a
      character . . . who exists only within the diseased fantasy
      of the white American?" There is a need to understand that
      Baldwin's description seems "to be an expression of his
      hope and homage to what man might be." In his later works,
      there is less hope; his loss of faith in America represents
      "an end to another naive dream of an innocent idealist."

49 Kinnamon, Keneth, ed. James Baldwin: A Collection of Criti-
      cal Essays. Englewood Cliffs, N.J.: Prentice-Hall,
      169 pp.
         Anthologizes a collection of previously published essays
      by several authors, preceded by an introduction and fol-
      lowed by "A Chronology of Important Dates" and a selected
      bibliography: Alexander, 1974.3; Bone, 1974.19; Cleaver,
      1974.23; DeMott, 1974.30; Dupee, 1974.34; Fabre, 1974.37;
      Hernton, 1974.42; Howe, 1974.44; Hughes, 1974.45; Kent,
      1974.47; Newman, 1974.53; Reilly, 1974.57; Williams,
      1974.63. The introduction argues that "a proper under-
      standing of Baldwin and his work must take into account a
      complicated amalgam of psychological and social elements
      sometimes thought to be antithetical"; it includes bio-
      graphical data, a summary of recurring themes--quest for
      love, confrontation with reality, the writer's need to save
      the world, concern with intimate areas of experience; and
      comments on the diversity of opinions about Baldwin's work.

50 McClusky, John. "Books Noted." Black World, 24 (December),
      51-52, 88-91.

Reevaluates more than a decade of Baldwin's work--from "admiration of the arrogance of the early essays to rejection of the Old Testament predictability of the later fiction." Beale Street has a synthesis of many of Baldwin's literary concerns: the "brooding cat reared in Harlem"; his "struggle toward some sense of clarity and achievement in his art and life"; the "forces" compelling him "toward some form of destruction"; the attack on "the use of religion to shut off . . . the horror and mystery within one's experience"; and the presence of fathers bent upon the destruction of their sons. In Beale Street, there is love and pain and truth, and "the sense of family and of hope survives the ordeal."

51 Major, Clarence. "James Baldwin: A Fire in the Mind." In his The Dark and Feeling: Black American Writers and Their Work. New York: Joseph Okpaku, pp. 73-83.
     Contends that Baldwin has become "what many people the world over consider the greatest American essayist since Ralph Waldo Emerson." His writing career has earned him international recognition as a writer, and his writing has "wide meaning beyond itself when looked at along with aspects of his personal life." Baldwin's early writings reflect much of his self-consciousness and confusion, and his later writing reveals his deep concern with racial justice and the civil rights movement. Over the years, he has become a "famous writer," but in a way, he has "also become a preacher--his original ambition." He has struck "a fire in the mind of the nation."

52 Mitchell, Louis D. "If Beale Street Could Talk." Best Sellers, 34 (1 June), 106-107.
     Sees Beale Street as presenting two views of Baldwin: the battle between bitterness and love is won by the latter; the recognition that to show an outcome totally incongruous with expectation is to enter into the realm of irony. He shows the many possibilities of Negro life in America couched in a "bitter-sweet love story." His style is "straight, simple, powerful, and never dull," focusing upon the struggle of black people in a "restrictive and unjust society."

53 Newman, Charles. "The Lesson of the Master: Henry James and James Baldwin." In Kinnamon, James Baldwin, 1974.49, pp. 52-64.
     Reprint of 1966.36.

1974

54 Oates, Joyce Carol. "A Quite Moving and Very Traditional
   Celebration of Love: If Beale Street Could Talk." New
   York Times Book Review (26 May), pp. 1-2.
      Contends that although these are "turbulent" times forc-
   ing many writers to be "a propagandist" or paradoxically
   "an indifferent esthete," it is also "the best possible
   time for most writers--the sheer variety of stances available to the serious writer, is amazing." Baldwin's career
   has not been an "even one," and his works have been both
   praised and denounced. Beale Street is his latest novel,
   and "it might have been written . . . in the 1950's." Its
   suffering, confused people trapped in the "garbage dump of
   New York City" give no evidence of having benefited, even
   psychologically, from the "Black Power and other radical
   movements to sustain them." Yet the book is a moving celebration of love not only between a man and a woman but between members of a family.

55 Prasad, Thakur Duru. "Another Country: The Tensions of Dream
   and Nightmare in the American Psyche." In Indian Studies
   of American Fiction. Edited by M.K. Naik, S.K. Desai,
   S. Mokashi-Punekar. Dharwar: Karnatak University; Delhi:
   Macmillan India, pp. 296-310.
      Sees Another Country within the mainstream of American
   fiction and Baldwin as a "typical heir to a peculiarly
   American line of the family of Western Man"--a Negro. His
   realization of being both disinherited and despised in the
   only land where he belongs creates a crisis of identity, a
   devastating rage, a blend of aspiration and frustration,
   and, thus, a tension between "the American dream and the
   American nightmare." The novel articulates the "brutality,
   hate and ignorance that are meted out everywhere in the
   sacred name of racial superiority."

56 Randall, Dudley. "James Baldwin." Black World, 24 (December), 91-92.
      Reviews Keneth Kinnamon's edition, James Baldwin, of
   thirteen critical essays by diverse hands as giving Baldwin's work "academic weight." The various pieces treat not
   only specific novels, such as Go Tell It and Another Country, but some essays deal more generally with the writer.
   The critics suggest that Baldwin "is best as an essayist,
   and that his novels are flawed when he becomes an essayist
   and rhetorician."

57 Reilly, John M. "'Sonny's Blues': James Baldwin's Image of
   Black Community." In Kinnamon, James Baldwin, 1974.49,
   pp. 139-46.
      Reprint of 1970.36.

58 Rosenblatt, Roger. "Lord of the Rings" and "White Outside."
    In his Black Fiction. Cambridge, Mass.: Harvard Univer-
    sity Press, pp. 36-54, 151-58.
        Introduces the study with a series of important ques-
    tions regarding literary criticism of black fiction:
    1) Should black writers address themselves just to the con-
    ditions of black life, or to a more universal range of sub-
    jects? 2) Is a black or white critic better able to judge
    the quality of black fiction? 3) Is "social protest" the
    only goal and theme of black writers? 4) Is black fiction
    a special genre? 5) Is black fiction separable from modern
    American fiction as a whole? The first black novels written
    in America were concerned with "proving that black people
    were as good as the whites, as honorable, intelligent, and
    decent." But by 1920, Walter White was leading his "flight"
    back to the ghetto and away from the "white world," and
    Wright's Bigger Thomas was "taking on the white world with
    murder" in his heart. And by 1960, Kelley and Baldwin were
    again having their "heroes and heroines . . . surviving be-
    cause they have become just as good as whites with whom
    they deal, just as self-seeking, treacherous, and
    dishonorable."
        In Go Tell It, Baldwin depicts a "cyclical damnation
    drawing heavily on Christian doctrine." Everybody in the
    novel wants to change, because everyone wants to be saved--
    change means salvation--but there is no change. In the end,
    everything is "upside down"--hate destroys the hater and
    love destroys the lover. In Another Country, Baldwin drops
    the biblical style, although some allusions remain, and
    "the sense of organization changes--from focusing on indi-
    vidual characters, one by one, to a wide angle view of an
    entire people." The novel is designed as a modern Inferno
    with lovers throwing themselves at each other in "lust and
    violence." Baldwin sees "the white characters as the prime,
    though not the sole, movers in all this evil." The struc-
    ture of the novel consists of Book I, which "focuses on the
    low and hopeless life" primarily of Rufus; and Books II and
    III, which represent a "redemptive movement"--redemption is
    achieved by freedom in life's experiences.

59 Smith, Barbara. "Banked Fires on Beale Street." National
    Observer, 13 (20 July), 21.
        Compliments Baldwin the writer whose style, when he
    "gets it together . . . makes breath taking rhythm that the
    true Baldwinian can identify as easily as a jeweler spots
    the real thing in a handful of glass." But this style is
    "too often stilted in Beale Street." Stilted "rhetoric
    creeps in" so that the characters do not emerge as real.
    Although there are a few glowing embers in the novel, the

1974

"fire of Baldwin's earlier writing has been temporarily
banked."

60 Straub, Peter. "Happy Ends." New Statesman, 87 (28 June),
930.
Describes Baldwin's earlier writings as revealing "the
most elegant, precise and conscious prose styles ever be-
stowed on any modern writer." The present novel, Beale
Street, has a "central problem with its voice"; it contains
much "affected writing," which is the "very emblem of the
engaged, lazy imagination."

61 Thomas, David. "Too Black, Too White." Listener, 92
(25 July), 125.
Sees the "holy rollers" in Beale Street "less sympathe-
tically drawn" than the "Negro gospel fever" of Go Tell It.
Beale Street is a sort of "fable" about the "Negro's quest
for cultural freedom in the alien environment of present
day New York." However, the black images seem to exist in
"opposition to everything white"; surely there must be some
"other shades."

62 Webster, Ivan. "If Beale Street Could Talk." New Republic,
197 (15 June), 25-26.
Calls Beale Street a "major work of black American fiction," perhaps Baldwin's "best novel yet." It is a "first
person suspense narrative with a New York street love story"
told through the eyes of a young woman. In fact, the women
"carry the book"; all of them are "extraordinary."

63 Williams, Shirley Anne. "The Black Musician: The Black Hero
as Light Bearer." In Kinnamon, James Baldwin, 1974.49,
pp. 147-54.
Reprint of 1972.67.

64 Wills, Antony A. "The Use of Coincidence in 'Notes of a Native Son.'" NALF, 8, no. 3 (Fall), 234-35.
Points out that the "task of the non-fiction writer is
to transmit truth, whereas that of the novelist or short
story writer is to create the illusion of truth." To attain this result, the writer may use similar techniques,
but the nonfiction writer may have greater difficulty since
he is often limited to facts. The novelist has many liber-
ties in his writing, e.g., compressing time, fusing characters, using symbols, etc. The biographer, however, can use
these devices only if they are true; he must be aware of
connections in the events of one's life. One connection is
"concidence," which goes beyond mere cause and effect

relations, and Baldwin uses coincidence extensively in
Notes. He links events (e.g., father's death, sister's
birth, father's funeral, Harlem race riot) by using coincidence, yet he juxtaposes the events so that they have a
further connection than mere coincidence. The connection
becomes "more explicit as symbols of the death of the old,
hating Baldwin, and the birth of a new determination."

1975

1 Allen, Shirley S. "Religious Symbolism and Psychic Reality in
   Baldwin's Go Tell It on the Mountain." CLAJ, 19 (December),
   173-99.
       Argues that Go Tell It "deserves a higher place in cri-
   tical esteem than it has generally been accorded." It is
   an important interpretation of the "black experience" comparable to Invisible Man and Native Son. Baldwin weaves
   the black vs. white conflict in his novel as well as the
   more universal problem of a "youth achieving maturity, with
   literary parallels in David Copperfield, Great Expectations,
   The Brothers Karamazov." The theme of the work is the
   "ritual symbolization" of a youth's initiation into manhood
   --the "psychological step from dependence to a sense of
   self." There is extensive use of biblical allusion and
   Christian ritual for symbolic expression of the "psychic
   realities he wishes the reader to experience." Each of the
   parts of the book has a title and two epigraphs referring
   to the Bible or Christian hymns, and throughout there are
   passages from the King James Bible. The major characters
   are identified with their "favorite texts of scripture."
   But all this religious "apparatus" serves not only as "psychological and social milieu for the action," but also
   gives "symbolic expression and archetypal meaning" to the
   characters and events. The effect of the religious symbolism keeps the reader aware of the "universal elements"
   in the work and through such symbolic identification, Baldwin lifts the problem of being a "victim of persecution out
   of a particular racial situation in twentieth-century United States and places it in a larger historical and religious context." Also, by means of biblical allusion, he
   substitutes "Hebrew archetypes for the Freudian Greek myth
   in interpreting the father-son confrontation." Thus, the
   main action of Go Tell It is linked with universal human
   experience through the use of the religious symbolism and
   the Freudian psychic realities.

1975

2   ANON. "Baldwin." <u>PMLA</u>. <u>1974 International Bibliography</u>,
        I:167.
            Presents annual secondary bibliography for 1974.

3   ANON. "Best Young Books for Young Adults, 1974." <u>Booklist</u>,
        71 (15 March), 747.
            Includes <u>Beale Street</u>, the story of a young black couple,
        separated by his unjust imprisonment, who are supported by
        their love for each other and the determination of her lo-
        yal family.

4   ANON. "If Beale Street Could Talk." <u>Publishers Weekly</u>, 207
        (21 April), 49.
            Calls <u>Beale Street</u> a bittersweet love story of Tish and
        Fonny told in a gentle vein.

5   ANON. "Parents Protest School Texts Use to Officials."
        <u>Florida Times-Union</u> (19 November), p. B4.
            Includes Baldwin among a list of authors that are objec-
        tionable because of "an overabundance of obscene language,
        sex and leftist political leanings."

6   Bruck, Peter. <u>Von der "Store-front Church" zum "American
        Dream": James Baldwin und der Amerikanische Rassenkon-
        flikt</u>. Amsterdam: Verlag B.R. Grünner, 147 pp.
            Recognizes that the discussion of Afro-American litera-
        ture has become increasingly "politicised" in the past de-
        cade, usually alternating between the extremes of assimila-
        tionism or a black aesthetic; reveals the book's methodo-
        logy of discussing relevant possibilities for action in
        Baldwin's protagonists and of interpreting classic American
        myths and motifs with a definition of their intended audi-
        ence and the author's self-chosen role as artist. Part I
        treats Baldwin's essays in contrast to the works of Wright,
        LeRoi Jones, and Eldridge Cleaver with the purpose of spe-
        cifying his stand in the politics of the race conflict,
        with stress on a love ethic, and his desire to continue
        "the wedding of the two races." Baldwin does not write for
        a black audience but wishes to correct the racial ignorance
        of the white readership. Part II traces Baldwin's develop-
        ment as a writer in his fiction, with focus on the novels
        as presenting heroes who suffer from their racial plight
        and are unable to determine their own lives. <u>Go Tell It</u>
        shows the father-son conflict between Gabriel and John
        Grimes, the black church as oppressive, and the need to
        accept one's own origin as prerequisite for self-determina-
        tion and freedom. <u>Giovanni's Room</u> initiates the central
        theme of the homosexual as a marginal character who becomes

a "symbolic black"; and the failure between David and Giovanni reveals the white American's lack of understanding
and emotional commitment emanating from a Puritan heritage
and an inability to love. Another Country explores interracial relations in two black/white couples: Rufus and
Leona, and Vivaldo and Ida. Love fails for the former
couple, with Rufus commiting suicide as a retreat from
racism; love also fails for the latter after black Ida becomes a kind of helpful teacher to Vivaldo, showing him
the true living conditions of the black. The only viable
alternative is the white Negro--the homosexual--presented
in Eric's life-style. The book has no main protagonist or
central plot. Blues presents the futility of black self-
determination with the murder of Richard and implies the
need for a retreat from society. Tell Me portrays Leo
Proudhammer, Baldwin's "first non-victimized hero" who
pursues interracial love with white Barbara in a kind of
"ideally harmonious affair." Leo represents a kind of
existential modification of changed attitude toward the
world, with no effort to change the world--only a love ethic can transform the situation. Thus, Tell Me is a dead
end for Baldwin as a novelist; he is not a black writer but
one who writes for the ruling class as "a universal minority writer."

7 Bryant, Jerry H. "John A. Williams: The Political Use of the
      Novel." Critique, 16, no. 3:81-100.
         Compares Baldwin's Go Tell It to the technique used by
      Williams in Sissie; especially stresses the political and
      sociological concerns in fictional form.

8 Cunliffe, Marcus. "Angela Doesn't Feel Free." Manchester
      Guardian Weekly (7 June), p. 14.
         Reviews A Dialogue and Angela Davis: An Autobiography
      and prefers the latter to "this self-regarding miscellany"
      or "rambling rap" in which Baldwin and Nikki Giovanni offer
      "literary rhetoric" but do not seem to be listening to each
      other.

9 Doherty, Gail and Paul Doherty. "Paperback Harvest: Litera-
      ture." America, 133 (18 October), 236.
         States that Beale Street escapes the "trap" of forcing
      the charcters into political postures. Baldwin "gives his
      characters the full range of joys, rages, affections, and
      delusions that are the human lot."

10 Edwards, David and Ian H. Birnie. James Baldwin and North
      America. London: SCM Press Ltd, pp. 1-25.

Looks at the "lives of great Christian heroes" and aims
at pupils in the ten to thirteen age group. The aim of the
series of books is "to identify some of the most difficult
problems facing the world today and then to examine the contributions of Christians toward solving them." This publication focuses on Harlem and the deep South, with special
emphasis upon the racial highlights: civil rights movement, Martin Luther King, Jr., and James Baldwin, whose
life is treated extensively. In 1954, Go Tell It appeared,
and, since then, Baldwin has written more books, "each of
which has helped people to understand more clearly the
feelings of the American Negro as he has struggled for
freedom and justice." Even though he writes about men's
cruelty to one another, Baldwin "has a hope . . . that one
day race prejudice will be overcome."

11 Fleischauer, John F. "James Baldwin's Style: A Prospectus
for the Classroom." CCC, 26 (May), 141-48.
Explores Baldwin's nonfiction prose style in the essay
"Notes of a Native Son" in order "to help make students
more aware of the significant elements of his and their own
prose." The study points out that the author's paragraphs
average a little over seven sentences each, that he uses
three subordinate clauses for every four sentences he
writes, that most sentences contain at least two main clauses, that 64 percent of his verbs are active, that about
10 percent of the sentences begin with some major subordi-
nation, etc. His artistic techniques are models for student writing: use of variety, tendency to use repetition
and parallel structure rather than conjunctions or logical
indicators, development of generalizations by amplification
or division through series, etc. Most of his writing focuses on the question of identity in a prose that is insistent and direct, but his allusions and images are biblical and their forms are classical. Because he seeks "a
universal tradition through which to speak of universal
man," and the tradition he is a part of has excluded him,
he writes from estrangement and exile about the inevita-
bility of accepting American culture.

12 Grossman, Henry. "An Album of Famous People Simply Being
Themselves." People Weekly, 20 December/6 January, p. 67.
Presents a portrait of Baldwin pausing "for a weary look
at the world around him."

13 Jackson, Edward Merica. "Fathers and Sons: An Analysis of
the Writings of James Baldwin." Ph.D. dissertation, Syra-
cuse University.

Describes certain motifs or patterns that appear consistently in Baldwin's works: the father-son conflict,
graphic portrayal of sexual experiences, and racial conflicts. There are others, but these three seem to dominate
his work. In the father-son conflict, a <u>Bildungsroman</u>
theme emerged--the search for the father, the revolt of the
son from the values of the father. Baldwin's characters
search for a father in three ways: 1) religion serves as a
surrogate father as in <u>Go Tell It</u> and <u>Amen Corner</u>; 2) art
serves as a father as the son turning to music in <u>Amen Cor-
ner</u> or drama in <u>Another Country</u>; 3) rebellion against the
sexual traditions of the father as in <u>Another Country</u> and
<u>Blues</u>; some of the sons even turn to other men. Finally,
Baldwin uses the father-son archetype to discuss race relations; America is the father, but the black sons are
bastards, therefore, "America cannot bring itself to love
the bastard children."

14 Küster, Dieter. "James Baldwin: Tell Me How Long the Train's
    Been Gone." In <u>Amerikanische Erzählliteratur 1950-1970</u>.
    Edited by Frieder Busch and Renate Schmidt-von Bardelehen.
    Munich: Fink, pp. 142-54.
       Argues that Leo Proudhammer's life depicts the following
    thematic circle: "the prejudice of whites against blacks;
    diverse reactions of blacks to a life of oppression and de-
    pendence; the meaning of these reactions for the condition
    of the black American in general; and the reciprocal inter-
    weaving of the destinies of blacks and whites." The inner
    unity of the episodic plot adheres to the depiction through-
    out of the relations between blacks and whites in contempo-
    rary America. The conformity of a sick society offers "a
    Leo" no possibility to overcome the problems of the race
    question or to assist the black American to achieve justice.
    The train to understanding has departed. Whites must learn
    that their power will be answered by black retaliation; the
    Black Power movement is a reality.

15 Manna, Tony and Jan Yoder. "Bicentennial Browsing: Focus on
    Black Literature." <u>EJ</u>, 64 (December), 79.
       Begins with an interview with Darwin Turner about the
    "selection and use of Afro-American literature," including
    a bibliography. Baldwin's <u>Beale Street</u> is listed under the
    bibliographic heading, "Going Through Human Experience."

16 Materassi, Mario. "La Concilizaione Degli Opposti in 'Notes
    of a Native Son' di James Baldwin." <u>Paragone</u>, 302 (April),
    15-18.

1975

Analyzes the structural organization of Notes and shows
how Baldwin presents a series of opposites: father-son,
death-life, white-black, man-society, etc. Two paradigms
are set up for discussing the opposites: contrasting the
opposites and reconciling the opposites. Notes stresses
that to some extent the black man is a kind of "Everyman"--
an individual trying to find his own identity and his place
in society.

17 Moller, Karin. The Theme of Identity in the Essays of James
     Baldwin: An Interpretation. Göteborg, Sweden: Acta Uni-
     versitatis Göthoburgensis, pp. 1-189.
     Advocates that the Baldwin essays published in book form
     express the fundamental perspective and interests of the
     author and that the theme of identity is the most consis-
     tent and pervasive one in his work, involving five major
     issues: race, nationality, sexuality, art, and morality.
     On pursuing the theme of identity, Baldwin uses both a
     "dialectic quality" and a "lyrical affirmation" to estab-
     lish "the existence of polarities and incompatibilities of
     all kinds" in order to discover the synthesis that he calls
     "identity": struggle/inevitability, good/evil, innocence/
     experience, death/life, etc. Obviously the Bible has pro-
     vided many of the ideas and symbols relative to the theme
     of identity: tree of knowledge, new Jerusalem, myth of the
     Fall, the new Adam, doctrine of creation, etc. Devoting a
     critical chapter each to Notes, Nobody Knows, The Fire,
     Nothing Personal, and No Name, Moller concludes with a sum-
     mary of major points germane to the volumes of essays:
     racial identity as Afro-American identity; imprisonment as
     the enacting of enforced and debasing roles; acceptance of
     black experience as a form of "bluesy celebration of ex-
     perience"; national identity and heritage of America as
     hinging on racial history; "the vision of America as a
     place of promise-laden chaos"; sexual identity as being in-
     timately related to morality; the role of the artist-writer
     as a public "witness" in the effort to create a better
     world through personal responsibility and commitment; the
     recognition of moral and metaphysical forces operating in
     human life; the concept of time involving the metaphors of
     life as a "journey," "passage," or "voyage" implying both
     beginning and ending as well as the need for acceptance and
     affirmation as a source of significance. Baldwin's quest
     of identity has been an effort to dramatize his personal
     situation as an Afro-American and "to render it universally
     intelligible by infusing physical reality and concrete
     facts with myth and metaphysics." The book also contains
     selected primary and secondary bibliographies.

18 Moss, Robert F. "The Arts in Black America." Sat R, 2 (November), 12-19.
     Points out that the coup in Nigeria brought the "demise" of the Second World and Black Festival of Arts and Culture. Still this minor setback cannot stop the "steady growth" in black creative effort. Contemporary gifted black figures are "embodying in their own life and work the potential integration of black America through peaceful means." Unfortunately, this line of development was "seriously retarded by the riots of the Sixties, so accurately predicted by Baldwin in The Fire." Out of the "wreckage" has come a new breed of black artists, led by Imanu Baraka (LeRoi Jones) and Ellison, Baldwin, etc., "who have allied themselves with a rising black middle class." Much of the black creative efforts retain a defiantly political tone-- waging battles against racial stereotypes, job discrimination, Jim Crow laws, etc. The overriding theme of most black-American art remains the "denial of the black man's humanity by white America."

19 Peden, William. "The Black Explosion." In his The American Short Story: Continuity and Change 1940-1975. Boston: Houghton Mifflin, pp. 134-47.
     Asserts that Going to Meet is "the most important single short story collection" after the generation of Hughes, Wright, and Himes, that the title story is "the most powerful story of a recent American black writer, and that the volume surpasses telecasts and news stories in showing what it means to be black in a white man's world." The work also shows a resemblance to another piece by Baldwin, "Come Out the Wilderness," and to James Alan McPherson's Hue and Cry.

20 Plumpp, Sterling. "If Beale Street Could Talk." Black Books Bulletin, 3 (Fall), 42-43.
     Argues that Beale Street is good but not great because in it the author intensely fights the demons of religion and skin color until they have dissipated the impact of the plot, and because Tish's point of view is ambitious but not convincing. Nevertheless, the novel reveals how the light-skinned fail to challenge the inhumanity of society and how Baldwin has "dipped his pen in the survival pulse of black America."

21 Pratt, Louis Hill. "The Mystery of the Human Being: A Critical Study of the Writings of James Baldwin." Ph.D. dissertation, Florida State University.

1975

Focuses on developing a "clearer definition of James
Baldwin's legacy and a more thorough assessment of the impact which his literary artistry has had on our culture."
The study involves a critical analysis of his short stories,
novels, drama, and essays, as well as a discussion of his
literary philosophy based on four hypothesis: 1) the theo-
retical foundations on which his art rest; 2) the wide
range of critical reactions to Baldwin's writings; 3) the
patterns of criticism substituting social for literary criticism; 4) the contribution of his work to the modern
American literary tradition.

22 Przemecka, Irena. "Search for Identity in the American Negro
    Novel." Kwartalnik Neofilologiczny, 22, pp. 185-90.
        Affirms that the question of "What is an American?" must
    also include "Who am I?" Baldwin left America because he
    was seeking answers to these questions and wanted to save
    himself from becoming "merely a Negro" or "merely a Negro
    writer." He learned in Europe "What It Means to Be an
    American" and that the search for identity is complicated
    for the American Negro, but the search must not end by con-
    forming to the preconceptions of whites.

23 Ro, Sigmund. "The Black Musician as Literary Hero: Baldwin's
    'Sonny's Blues' and Kelley's 'Cry for Me.'" American
    Studies in Scandinavia, 7, no. 1:17-48.
        Presents "two case studies of the intellectual and ideo-
    logical sources" of the black hero in Afro-American fiction:
    Baldwin's "Sonny's Blues" and Kelley's "Cry for Me." Black
    postwar fiction illustrates an interdependence between so-
    ciety and art. "Sonny's Blues" possesses a "modern Euro-
    American intellectual stance" in which Sonny is conceived
    in "the image of Kierkegaard-Sartre-Camus and provided with
    an authentic black exterior"; simultaneously, the dimen-
    sions of "Negritude or soul" gradually become a focal
    point, spelling the end of the esthetic upon which Bald-
    win's Sonny was predicated. These stories illustrate
    vividly what happens when fiction is subjected to the pres-
    sures of ideological change. Sonny's music is conditioned
    by racial factors, the despair of the black ghetto, the
    fear of victimization, the testimonies of "frenziedly pious
    church sisters." As Sonny realizes the real meaning of
    what he is playing, his music acquires the significance it
    has in Go Tell It and in Baldwin's essays: "that of put-
    ting himself and his audience in touch with their ancestral
    past." Racial heritage is thus a prominent feature. Sonny
    is also endowed with "peculiar charisma and insight" into
    the nature of human existence; he comes as close to being

"Absurd Man" as any literary hero of the 1950s. Such concepts as "Dread (Angst), nausea, alienation, and absurd
freedom" characterize his isolated stance as a "vision of
human life." What Sonny is conveying in words and imagery--
"chaos, disorder, and nothingness"--is ultimately Kierke-
gaard's "sickness unto death," Sartre's "nausea," and
Camus' "experience of absurdity and unreality." The qualities intended to prove Sonny's universal humanity ("his
equality with the white man") were what made him "most of-
fensive in the eyes of the next generation of black
writers."

24 Rush, Theressa Gunnels et al. "James Baldwin." In their
Black American Writers: A Biographical and Bibliographical
Dictionary, vol. 1. Metuchen, N.J.: Scarecrow Press, pp.
44-48.
    Presents a selected bibliography of primary and secon-
dary sources on Baldwin and his works.

25 Smith, Cynthia Janis. "Escape and Quest in the Literature of
Black Americans." Ph.D. dissertation, Yale University.
    Illustrates clearly how the Bible provided the literary
metaphor for slave narratives by comparing the experience
of flight with the Hebrew exodus and the New Testament
quest of salvation through Christ. Ironically, however,
Christianity gave comfort to the slave and to the slave-
master, thus showing an inconsistency between what was professed and what was practiced, and thereby revealing a conflict between biblical imagery and religious experience.
This conflict between religious language and experience continues to be both a central issue in the works as well as a
source of artistic inspiration to Jean Toomer, Richard
Wright, James Baldwin, and LeRoi Jones.

26 Tedesco, John L. "Blues for Mister Charlie: The Rhetorical
Dimension." Players, 50 (Fall/Winter), 20-23.
    Points out that Blues reflects the changes in the
"American racial condition which developed not long before
the play's production in 1964." During the period, the
"first blush of success" seemed to be emerging as a result
of the civil rights movement. Blues presents a vision of
race relations that "reveals the potential danger of violent white backlash" and "illustrates the need for a re-
newed sensitivity to black demands on the part of white institutions." Although there are "certain confusions in
structure," the play is a "significant and compelling
social drama" worthy of serious consideration.

1975

27 Turner, Darwin T. "Visions of Love and Manliness in a
       Blackening World: Dramas of Black Life from 1953-1970."
       Iowa Review, 6, no. 2 (Spring), 82-99.
          Sees two types of drama by black playwrights of the
       period: "Black Arts drama, including Black Revolutionary,
       Ritual, and Black Experience"; and "Traditional," meaning
       "emulating styles of American drama rather than seeking
       styles identifiable with black culture." He examines the
       works of eight dramatists in relation to three questions:
       "What is the 'good life'? What is love? and What is man-
       hood or manliness?" and concludes that "they say that the
       contemporary black community lacks manliness and love."
       Blues is described as a traditional drama, stressing the
       similarities between blacks and whites, examining the dilem-
       ma of middle-class blacks, and using black characters who
       challenge whites verbally but passively reject physical
       confrontation. Amen Corner is viewed as "Black Arts drama"
       ignoring the relationship between blacks and whites, stres-
       sing the need for human love in the black family and com-
       munity, and rejecting the church that embodies only a god
       of wrath.

28 Vandyke, Patricia. "Choosing One's Side with Care: The
       Liberating Repartee." Perspectives on Contemporary Litera-
       ture, 1, no. 1 (May), 105-17.
          Examines the concept of "repartee" from a Freudian per-
       spective in selected "ethnic and minority short fiction."
       Repartee consists of "liberating the victim of hostile ra-
       cial and ethnic joking" by "turning the tables on the
       aggressor." For it to operate, certain conditions must be
       met: There must be an aggressor, a victim, and a sympathe-
       tic listener. Malamud uses this technique in presenting
       the Jew and his Jewishness. Baldwin uses it in a different
       way; he uses it in Going to Meet "to liberate, ironically,
       the white sheriff and to liberate, symbolically, the black
       man from the white racist's peculiar dependence." By focus-
       ing on the white man's point of view, Baldwin exploits the
       "pernicious dependency" of whites on the black man's sex-
       uality. In a "comic coup," he forces the "unexpected unity
       between attack and counterattack" that is repartee.

                                1976

1 Ackroyd, Peter. "Wide-eyed." Spectator, 237 (11 September),
       26.
          Describes the American cinema as "at its worst . . . an
       elaborate and colourful repository of social codes and

                                242

beliefs." Therefore, it is only natural for Baldwin, in
The Devil, to turn to it in his own "endless process of
self identification." He sees films as "both insidious and
malicious in themselves," and "subtly corrupting to those
who watch them." This book is more for those who read Baldwin than for those who go to the cinema.

2 Anderson, Jervis. "Blurred Reflections on Hollywood." New
   Leader, 59 (24 May), 18.
        Cites Baldwin's use of a quote from T. S. Eliot, "who ob-
   served that the people cannot bear very much reality."
   Baldwin then goes on to say that although this may be true,
   people can bear more reality than one might wish. This position may seem to contradict his charge that white Americans have refused to confront reality. He has consistently
   pointed out that "most whites shun things as they are, especially relating to blacks, by taking refuge behind safe
   and comfortable illusions and by falsifying whatever they
   are not quite able to sidestep." Hollywood is the great
   falsifier of life and the world. The Devil is Baldwin's
   attempt to set forth his argument against the film indus-
   try, but the book lacks "the natural and sustained fluency
   that marks his better efforts."

3 Anderson, Mary Louise. "Black Matriarchy: Portrayal of Women
   in Three Plays." NALF, 10, no. 3 (Fall), 93-95.
        Treats three dramas that embody common tendencies of the
   stereotypical black matriarch: Hansberry's A Raisin in the
   Sun; Baldwin's Amen Corner; and Alice Childress' Wine in
   the Wilderness. Amen Corner portrays how Sister Margaret
   copes with the common characteristics of the matriarch who
   regards the male as undependable; helps to emasculate him;
   thinks of mothering as most important; shields her children
   from and tries to prepare them for the white world's prejudices; and is very religious.

4 ANON. "Baldwin." PMLA. 1975 International Bibliography,
   I:160.
        Presents annual secondary bibliography for 1975.

5 ANON. "Books Briefly." Progressive, 40 (August), 44.
        Shares Baldwin's view that "the movies tell us a great
   deal about ourselves." Baldwin is a "consummate writer,
   and his ruminations on the films . . . are illuminating."
   His "blackness is the glue" of The Devil, and he has a
   clear and important view of the films.

1976

6 ANON. "Comparison/Contrast: Native Son and Go Tell It on the
   Mountain." In Writing about Black Literature. Edited by
   Chester Fontenot. Lincoln, Neb.: Nebraska Curriculum Development Center, pp. 43-45.
        Compares in a student essay how the hero of each novel
   fails and speculates on the extent to which the failure is
   due to personal choice and to forces beyond his control.

7 ANON. "Criticism of Religion in Go Tell It on the Mountain."
   In Writing about Black Literature. Edited by Chester
   Fontenot. Lincoln, Neb.: Nebraska Curriculum Development
   Center, pp. 61-66.
        Presents in a student essay the criticism of religion,
   and those who profess to be devoted believers, by a series
   of contradictions and spoofs on everything that is supposed
   to be holy--names, sermons, behavior.

8 ANON. "The Devil Finds Work." Booklist, 72 (1 April), 1082.
        Describes The Devil as "autobiographical musings" of the
   author about movies, emphasizing what blacks perceive in
   white-produced films, in an "eloquence tinged with religious fervor."

9 ANON. "The Devil Finds Work." Book World (5 December), p. H5.
        Describes The Devil as "one of America's most graceful
   and penetrating essays" on Hollywood. Baldwin writes "mov-
   ingly" of the impact of movies and "rips the hypocrisy" especially of "black movies of recent years."

10 ANON. "The devil finds work." Choice, 13 (Spring), 804.
        Praises The Devil as a book appealing to the moral imag-
   ination by examining the hidden assumptions of movies, especially those exploring "the terror of the experience of
   growing up black in America," and revealing "the victim-
   victimizer relationships" of films as they play "with the
   harsh, complex realities of human degradation." He sees
   this as a game individuals seem unaware that they play in
   order to maintain "the myths that preserve that
   degradation."

11 ANON. "The Devil Finds Work." Kirkus, 44 (1 March), 282.
        Concludes that The Devil shows the only truth that Bald-
   win recognizes in American films to be "in those rare moments when rage, terror, and pain" are shown; finds that
   most films are "testaments to falsehood, self-serving images of blacks conjured up out of the need to reassure or
   exonerate white audiences," e.g., The Defiant Ones, star-
   ring Sidney Poitier and Tony Curtis.

*12 ANON. "The Devil Finds Work." Observer (19 September), p. 27.
        Cited in Book Review Index. 1976 Cumulation. Edited by
    Gary Tarbert. Detroit: Gale Research Company, p. 22.

13 ANON. "The Devil Finds Work." Publishers Weekly, 209
        (8 March), 64.
        Expresses in The Devil the author's feelings and thoughts
    about white-black relationships and attitudes as expressed
    in Hollywood films with the conclusion that "white people
    have no principles whatever."

14 ANON. "It Appears Johnny's Teacher Can't Read." Tallahassee
    Democrat (7 June), p. 4.
        Bemoans the fact that American parents "have been fuss-
    ing for years over the fact that Johnny can't read." Now
    it appears that perhaps the reason he can't read is because
    his teacher can't read. After all, colleges are no longer
    requiring prospective teachers to read Shakespeare or Hem-
    ingway, instead they are reading such "mediocrity" as Play-
    boy and Beale Street.

15 ANON. "Random Notes: October Titles." National Review, 28
        (15 October), 1132.
        Announces the publication of Little Man by Baldwin. "It
    makes good reading for adults and for little kids growing
    up in Scarsdale."

16 ANON. "Religious Reading: Importance in Understanding." In
    Writing about Black Literature. Edited by Chester Fontenot.
    Lincoln, Neb.: Nebraska Curriculum Development Center,
    pp. 56-60.
        Interprets in a student essay the meaning of Go Tell It
    as a novel in which John Grimes finds it difficult to ac-
    cept religion as valid because of the nature of his rela-
    tionship with Gabriel, the stepfather who hates him.

17 Ayd, Joseph D. "The Devil Finds Work." Best Sellers, 36
        (August), 172-73.
        Explains that by using films and fragments of various
    autobiographical data as his "take-off point," Baldwin has
    written a "wide-ranging essay about what it means to grow
    up black in the United States." Although he reveals au-
    thentic feelings and attitudes, the book is "somewhat ar-
    cane" in that he holds that only he, a black man, can under-
    stand a black. Also, he writes like one who has been in-
    fluenced by "a French view of films"; he takes movies too
    seriously and demands more from them than the original
    "mogul who made them ever intended."

1976

18 Bontemps, Arna. "The Black Contribution to American Letters:
    Part I." In The Black American Reference Book. Edited by
    Mabel M. Smythe. Englewood Cliffs, N.J.: Prentice-Hall,
    p. 765.
       Summarizes that Baldwin's personal essays--Notes, Nobody
    Knows, The Fire--and their favorable conjunction with the
    black protest movement suggest that he might revive "an old
    and possibly outdated literary form."

19 Brossell, Gordon. "A Lamb among Wolves: Letter to Editor."
    Tallahassee Democrat (20 May), p. 4.
       Responds to several "brainless" comments in the paper
    regarding Baldwin's Beale Street. American society has
    come a long way from its "Howdy Doody" existence; now wri-
    ters like Baldwin have an opportunity to publish their
    works. They can portray life as it really is; after all,
    for Baldwin the "ghetto is the ghetto, not Disney World."

20 Bryant, Jerry H. "American Dream Language." Nation, 223
    (3 July), 25-27.
       Describes Baldwin's thesis in The Devil as an exposure
    of the white American filmmakers' attempt to falsify the
    American racial experience in a most obvious and destruc-
    tive way. He uses the movies as a "pot for mixing" a num-
    ber of his own ideas, principally his own "spiritual and
    intellectual evolution and white America's assiduous cling-
    ing to its self-delusory dreams of reality." Something has
    happened to Baldwin's style in this work; his sentences are
    "jerky, convoluted . . .; his discussions seem to be going
    somewhere, then terminate in a dead end." His prose and
    his ideas seem to "struggle."

21 Bryant, Jerry H. "Wright, Ellison, Baldwin--Exorcising the
    Demon." Phylon, 37 (June), 174-88.
       Contends that one of the most active debates of the
    "hyperactive Sixties" was over the use of political and
    social concerns as criteria for judging literary works.
    Wright, Ellison, and Baldwin have been praised and damned;
    many good and bad judgments were expressed, but the tenden-
    cy to use political and social criteria has been healthy:
    "It connected literature with life." Fiction became for
    Wright "a way of confirming his own subjective independence
    . . . in defiance of both the black and the white habit of
    hiding feelings." Ellison and Baldwin both show a "height-
    ened understanding of their art." Ellison is "symbolic and
    allegorical"; Baldwin is "impressionistic and metaphorical."
    Beneath them both there is emerging a greater self-aware-
    ness, and a "more intense determination to embrace their

blackness as a high value and as a means for changing the face of America." All three writers start from the same place--the complaint that blacks "are cordoned off from their truest and most basic emotions and the expressions of them." Wright is the contemporary black freedom movement's "prophet"; Ellison is its "philosopher"; and Baldwin is its "poet." Sadly enough, his poetic powers appear to be declining since Go Tell It. Giovanni's Room, Another Country, Tell Me, and Beale Street all deal increasingly with his struggle of blackness and homosexuality, and "his fiction diminishes in quality accordingly."

22 Burks, Mary Fair. "James Baldwin's Protest Novel: If Beale Street Could Talk." NALF, 10, no. 3 (Fall), 83-87, 95.
Sees Beale Street as presaging a new trend in black writing "toward moderation and away from complete nihilism of the Black Revolution" whereby reality replaces pathological escapism and ethnocentricity is based not in black superiority and purity but in self-worth and cultural heritage. Beale Street is Baldwin twenty years ago repeating his protest in the use of specific stereotypes and themes: the plantation tradition of mulattoes as superior to black field niggers; the racist white cop; the white man's lust for black women; latent homosexuality; the liberal Jewish lawyer. Nevertheless, Baldwin creates "moments of moving, unforgettable beauty": he transforms the stigma of moral laxity between Tish and Fonny to a kind of "idealized love, innocently seeking fulfillment"; he employs a new stereotype of the Puerto Rican rape victim unacceptable to WASPs and unaccepting of blacks; he uses the Rivers family as embodying "goodness and purity, symbolic of black mythopoeia used as a psychic safety valve"; and he uses the relationship of Tish and Fonny to signal both the crucifixion and the coming of the Messiah--"the symbolism of the unborn child bears the full weight of the novel's protest . . . the will of the black man to survive as a race."

23 Carey, Gary. "The Devil Finds Work." LJ, 101 (15 April), 1044.
Presents The Devil as a "badly blended mix" of film criticism, social history, and autobiography that oscillates between the banal and incomprehensible because it is garbled in thought, punctuation, and sentence structure, and selects a small group of films for discussion.

24 Carlsen, G. Robert, Tony Manna, and Jan Yoder. "1975 Books for Young Adults Poll: Love Stories." EJ, 65 (January), 98.

1976

> Describes the "beautiful love experiences" between Tish
> and Fonny as "poetically constructed," revealing "passion,
> joy, commitment, and pain."

25 Collier, Eugenia W. "Steps Toward a Black Aesthetic: A Study
   of Black American Literary Criticism." Ph.D. dissertation,
   University of Maryland.
   Establishes the background, context, and milieu for
   black American literary criticism with primary focus on
   1910 to 1930 and a summary of critical trends from 1930 to
   1970. The study treats black Americans as a colonized peo-
   ple--"a race of people dominated by another race"--and it
   argues that the literary criticism by blacks reflected a
   common pattern of response to colonization in earlier
   times, i.e., accommodation, but has moved toward independ-
   ence in the last four decades.

26 Combs, Orde. "The Devil Finds Work." New York Times Book Review (2 May), pp. 6-7.
   Says that Baldwin's "17th book bearing his name" does
   not call for rejoicing. In fact, "it brings forth . . .
   pain, for this work teems with a passion that is all re-
   flex, and an anger that is unfocused and almost cynical."

27 Dahlin, R. "Blacks and the Movies and the Theme of James
   Baldwin's New Dial Book." Publishers Weekly, 209
   (19 January), 58.
   Points out that The Devil contains "Baldwin's coolly
   reasoned analysis of the effects that Hollywood's dream
   factories had on black men and women of his generation."
   The idea for this book came from Esquire magazine, which
   commissioned Baldwin to write an article on black movies,
   and "he started out with the idea of fulfilling his jour-
   nalistic assignment." In his analysis, Baldwin sees that
   "nothing has changed with black characters in films"; the
   same stock characters who have been around for years are
   still here today. There are other failings, which he
   points out, and he is most certain about "one thing: the
   total misrepresentation of the black experience."

28 Daniels, Mark R. "Estrangement, Betrayal and Atonement: The
   Political Theory of James Baldwin." Studies in Black
   Literature, 7, no. 3 (Autumn), 10-13.
   Disputes Cleaver's contention that Baldwin's work is
   void of a political perspective. His political theory can
   be inferred from the essays (Nobody Knows, Notes) and rests
   upon "one of the most enduring themes in political theory"
   --the concept of estrangement, especially focusing upon the

separation of blacks and whites as symbolic of a universal
phenomenon--dehumanization, a betrayal of man's "true
nature through construction of pernicious structures."
Atonement is possible by accepting the responsibility for
"making a rendezvous with history and reorganizing society."

29 Eddleman, Floyd E. "James Baldwin." In his American Drama
    Criticism, supplement 2. Hamden, Conn.: Shoe String
    Press, pp. 15-16.
        Presents selected sources on Baldwin's drama.

30 Emanuel, James A. "James Baldwin." In Contemporary Novelists.
    Edited by James Vinson. London: St. James Press; New
    York: St. Martin's Press, pp. 82-86.
        Gives selected biographical data, lists books published
    by Baldwin, and interprets briefly the fiction. Go Tell It
    is considered his best novel and focuses on John Grimes's
    "anguished choice between church and jail," which "meta-
    phorically opposes the demands of those institutions as the
    forces that have long constricted but spiritualized black
    people." Giovanni's Room explores love as defined by homo-
    sexuality and stresses that love can inspire magnanimity
    and charity and that morality begins in honesty about one-
    self. Another Country "dramatizes the racist destruction
    of interracial affections" and focuses on the effort "to
    try to be better than the world." Tell Me is Baldwin's
    "least impressive work" and emphasizes Leo Proudhammer's
    view of religion as useless in the racial struggle, and vio-
    lence as an inadequate substitute. Beale Street reveals
    the lack of love or mercy in the black church, truth and
    justice in American law, and "neither hope nor sanctuary in
    anything but familial and personal love." Going to Meet
    contains stories dealing with the father-son relationship,
    black identity, and psychopathic race hatred.

31 Gaither, Edmund B. "Afro-American Art." In The Black Ameri-
    can Reference Book. Edited by Mabel M. Smythe. Englewood
    Cliffs, N.J.: Prentice-Hall, p. 841.
        Says that the decade of the sixties brought growth,
    development, and consolidation for the Afro-American artist,
    but as the old civil rights movement, with its prointegra-
    tion stance, lost energy, a new nationalism and pragmatic
    political realism appeared among blacks. New artists saw
    in Baldwin "that one could be an artist, militant, and
    black."

32 Harris, Jessica. "Book Reviews." Essence, 7 (August), 39.
        Sees The Devil as the author's detection of the movies
    as symptoms of the social ills of the society because they

1976

influence the way people see themselves--as a country and
as individuals, especially in the image of the black man on
the screen.

33 Holloway, Clayton Glenn. "James Baldwin As a Writer of Short
    Fiction: An Evaluation." Ph.D. dissertation, Bowling
    Green State University.
        Analyzes his short fiction with concentration on charac-
    ter, theme, and technique, and some attention to biographi-
    cal parallels. Chapter 1 gives a biographical sketch and
    places each story in relation to the novels, plays, and es-
    says. Chapter 2 summarizes Baldwin's theory of fiction and
    presents his image of the creative writer. Chapter 3 tries
    to establish his reputation as a literary artist by survey-
    ing critical opinions about him. Chapters 4 through 6 pre-
    sent a thematic analysis of the short stories. The last
    chapter applies Baldwin's aesthetic principles to his short
    fiction and shows his sympathetic characters, realistic
    events, fidelity to black folk expression, and reflection
    of the psyche of oppressed people. His aesthetic inten-
    tions as expressed in interviews and essays are clearly
    illustrated by his short fiction.

34 Hughes, Langston. "Black Influences in the American Theater,
    Part I." In The Black American Reference Book. Edited by
    Mabel M. Smythe. Englewood Cliffs, N.J.: Prentice-Hall,
    pp. 692, 703.
        Points out that in the theater about "90 percent of the
    plays about blacks drop their final curtain on defeat--
    usually death." A serious drama about blacks seemingly
    cannot end happily, from Uncle Tom's Cabin to Blues; hence
    the stereotype of black drama has become "the unhappy end-
    ing--spiritually and physically defeated, lynched, dead."

35 Johnson, Helen Armstead. "Black Influences in the American
    Theater, Part II, 1960 and After." In The Black American
    Reference Book. Edited by Mabel M. Smythe. Englewood
    Cliffs, N.J.: Prentice-Hall, p. 709.
        Says that Blues is structurally unclear but that Juan-
    ita's speech after Richard Henry's death exemplifies that
    black playwrights as well as white ones treat not only the
    intervention of God in human affairs, but also His failure
    to intervene.

36 Lee, A. Robert. "A Critical Review: James Baldwin: The
    Devil Finds Work." NALF, 10, no. 3 (Fall), 84-85.
        Deals with the most recent work, The Devil, and makes
    mention of two forms used by Baldwin: "colloquy"--Rap on

Race and A Dialogue; "confessional"--No Name and One Day.
These "looser forms" have not served Baldwin especially
well, for these later works seem to "meander," or merely
"rap." The Devil does have centrality of focus which
serves two purposes: a critique of film and an essay in
"racial-cultural clarification." He explores the often
"flatly contradictory tensions between processed, movie-
screen images of racial truth and the truth he . . . has
been obliged to feel on the pulse." He uses his own movie-
going as a kind of "time-reel" and explores the screen
language of race. It is obvious in the work that Baldwin's
eye, "inner or outer, hasn't dimmed."

37 Lehmann-Haupt, Christopher. "Books of the Times." The New
York Times (4 June), p. 37.
Argues that except for Baldwin's "testifying honestly to
his own experience at the movies" in The Devil, the book
offers nothing new in its basic thesis that Hollywood's
films reflect American racial biases and stereotypes.

38 Mauro, Walter. Baldwin. Florence: La Nuova Italia, p. 147.
Combines biographical sketch, primary and secondary
bibliography (including a very helpful list of items by
Italian critics in the sixties and seventies) with an interpretive perspective of Baldwin that emphasizes the revolutionary dimension of his work as a man of letters because of his effort to show the interrelationship between
the prophetic quality and function and the practice of
literary life.

*39 Miura, Mitsuyo. "Fonny's Inner Change." Kyushu American
Literature (Fukuoka, Japan), 17:25-28.
Cited in Anon., 1976.4.

40 Moore, Rose B. "Book Is Like Friend: Letter to Editor."
Tallahassee Democrat (29 June), p. 6.
Replies in a letter to the editor that Beale Street is
loaded with dirty words and has a plot that degrades
blacks.

41 Moss, Robert F. "The Devil Finds Work." Sat R, 3 (29 May),
38.
Asserts that The Devil as film criticism treats movies,
social history, and autobiography in a sometimes provocative manner--white film stars on black temperament, inter-
rogation by the FBI, effects of racial inequality on a
white cab driver. But Baldwin recycles history for his own
polemical use and oversimplifies all forms of evil--

1976

        materialism, fascism, cruelty--"as viruses of a 'sick' white culture" whose antidotes are black goodness and resilience.

42 Nilsen, Allen Pace, Karen B. Tyler and Linda Kozarek. "Books for Young Adults." EJ, 65 (May), 91.
      Places Beale Street in the category called "Reluctantly Yours, Books to Tempt the Hesitant."

43 Nordell, Roderick. "The Devil Finds Work." Christian Science Monitor, 68 (21 July), 19.
      Concludes that the reader would find difficulty seeing the films in the same way after going through The Devil, though the book grinds the faces of white Americans "into the racial ignorance, sin, and insensitivity that obsess him" in its use of obscenities, crotchety syntax, and sweeping generalizations.

44 O'Connor, Bronwen. "Loins and Shadows." New Statesman, 92 (5 November), 646.
      Calls Little Man "a child's story for adults" with "no plot," some blood, lots of skipping and jumping and fighting up and down the New York streets.

45 Ostendorf, Bernhard. "James Baldwin, 'Sonny's Blues.'" In Die Amerikanische Short Story der Gegenwart: Interpretationen. Edited by Peter Freese. Berlin: Schmidt, pp. 194-204.
      Argues that although Baldwin in "Sonny's Blues" turns away from the church to jazz and blues, he does not succeed in substituting them for religion's mask of self-hatred." From his own experiences Baldwin recognizes the therapeutic function of the blues, but he fails to invest his fictional world of "blues people" with the "openness, ambivalence, and antagonism to ideology" that they demonstrate in real life. They are, like Baldwin himself, "estranged saints." Religion is demythologized in the story, but the profane world of blues and jazz is unfortunately made sacred. No trace of irony can be found in the story to justify these distortions of the blues; Baldwin seems incapable of perceiving the secular aspects of the black world except through "religious glasses."

46 Peel, Marie. "Through a child's eyes." Books and Bookmen, 22 (November), 76.
      Contends that Little Man, told through "four-year-old" TJ's consciousness, will be read by adults and children, white and black. The reality achieved by means of rendering

the living thread of Harlem speech and by the drawings and
watercolors of Yoran Cazac enhance the impact on the reader.

47 Ploski, Harry A. and Warren Marr, II. "James Baldwin." In
    their The Negro Almanac: A Reference Work on the Afro-
    American. New York: Bellwether Company, pp. 714, 813, 559.
        Presents brief biographical sketch; gives data on open-
    ings of Blues and Amen Corner; and tells of the film, The
    Negro and the American Promise, in which Martin Luther King,
    Jr., Malcolm X, Kenneth Clark, and Baldwin discuss for Indi-
    ana University their motivations, doctrines, methods, goals,
    and place in the American Negro's movement for social and
    racial equality.

48 Pratt, Louis Hill. "James Baldwin and 'the Literary Ghetto.'"
    CLAJ, 20 (December), 262-72.
        Affirms the position that there has been a trend in
    "white criticism" of black writing to label black writers,
    a process that limits "severely the expansion of the tal-
    ents of Negro writers" and confines them to a "literary
    ghetto." The grouping of black artists appears to be "re-
    presentative of a subtly masked form of racism," for exam-
    ple, Baldwin being labeled a "protest writer" and spokes-
    man for the black community. Hence, this categorization
    serves as a "substitution of social for artistic criticism";
    his aesthetic achievements in literature are minimized or
    denied, and his aesthetic perspective is ignored.

49 Redden, Dorothy S. "Wright and Native Son: Not Guilty."
    NALF, 10, no. 4 (Winter), 111-15.
        Refutes appraisals of the novel made by D. Cohn, J. Bald-
    win, I. Howe, and R. Bone, who claim Wright was "the wit-
    less instrument of wild and overpowering feelings over
    which he had no control." Baldwin commented on the "mur-
    derous bitterness" and violence in his essay, "Alas, Poor
    Richard" (Nobody Knows). Howe saw the necessity of the
    Negro to release his rage in order to "assert his humanity."
    Bone stated that Native Son presented a "guilt of the na-
    tion thesis"; and Cohn saw it as an "advocacy of hate" and
    an "incitement to violence." The novel, however, is not
    choked with uncontrollable rage, hatred, or vengefulness
    but is "taut with emotion" that is both "contained and
    transcended."

50 Reed, Claude. "The Devil Finds Work." Unique, 1 (Premier
    Issue), 32.
        Advocates that The Devil is a book conveying "genuine
    insights" with a "disturbing urgency" in its charting of

1976

the progression, retrogression, and stagnation of American
films from the 1930s through the 1970s, especially in their
superficial view of reality and their manipulation of the
public mind, e.g., in the projection of a mythical image of
blacks.

51 Rhode, Eric. "Book Reviews: Personal Views: Explorations in
Film." Sight and Sound, 45 (Autumn), 260.
        Portrays Baldwin's The Devil as a "commentary on the
movies as visionary, and unusual, as D.H. Lawrence's
Studies in Classical American Literature." The theme focuses in on the "power to possess" that movies may have as
well as the instances of "how falsity may creep into" a
Hollywood production.

52 Robinson, Kathryn. "Adult Books for Young Adults: Nonfiction." School Library Journal, 23 (September), 144.
        Reviews Baldwin's critical discussion in The Devil re-
garding "movies past and present and what he considers is
their effect on society."

53 Rosa, Alfred F. and Paul A. Eschholz, eds. "James Baldwin
(1924-), American." In their Contemporary Fiction in
America and England, 1950-1970. A Guide to Information
Services. Detroit: Gale Research Company, pp. 47-52.
        Presents a selective bibliographic listing of primary
and secondary sources for Baldwin.

54 Sader, Marion. "James Baldwin." In Comprehensive Index to
English Language Little Magazines 1890-1970. Vol. I: A
to Butler. Edited by Marion Sader. Millwood, N.Y.:
Kraus-Thomson Organization Ltd., pp. 202-203.
        Presents a selective bibliographic listing, both primary
and secondary, on Baldwin.

55 Saito, Tadatoshi. "Ralph Ellison and James Baldwin in the
1950's." In American Literature in the 1950's. Annual
Report. Tokyo: American Literature Society of Japan,
pp. 32-40.
        Briefly analyzes Baldwin's Go Tell It and Ellison's In-
visible Man within the context of the historical milieu of
the 1950s (e.g., 1954 Supreme Court decision) and as heirs
to Richard Wright's Native Son with emphasis on the American Negro's lack of identity. Ellison argues that the
Negro must discard false names imposed upon him by white
America, recognize his namelessness, and yet hope that the
invisible man has a socially responsible role to play.
Baldwin's title and chief character, John Grimes, indicate

that this regenerate son of America will lift the curse of Ham from the American Negro, transform his shame and suffering, and symbolize the eve of his salvation and his liberation as a human being.

56 Sarotte, Georges Michel. Comme un Frère, Comme un Amant, l' Homosexualité Masculin dan le Roman et le Théâtre Americain de Herman Melville á James Baldwin. Paris: Flammarion, pp. 7-9, 13-15, 33-36, 116-24.
See Sarotte, 1978.13.

57 Schwank, Klaus. "James Baldwin: Blues for Mister Charlie." In Das Amerikanische Drama der Gegenwart. Edited by Herbert Grabes. Kronberg: Athenäum Verlag, pp. 169-84.
Presents a brief biographical sketch, a selected secondary bibliography, and interprets the play as reflecting the dual influences of the social drama of the past thirty years as well as the psychological drama of O'Neill, Miller, and Williams. The chief weakness of Blues can be found not only in the "not-always-successful" combination of propagandistic and psychological drama but also in Baldwin's failure to follow dramatic conventions. The extensive use of the flashback technique is sometimes confusing because the audience cannot always follow the chronology of events. Nevertheless, it is an effective drama focusing on black and white social problems in America in the sixties.

58 Smith, Eliot F. "Making Book on a Cranky Spring." Village Voice, 29 March, p. 43.
Calls The Devil "a passionate attack on racial images" depicted and reinforced in both old and new movies.

59 Smith, Sally. "James Baldwin: The Expatriate Becomes Disillusioned." Atlanta Constitution (19 May), p. 21.
Emphasizes the inherent and expressed optimism of Baldwin that blacks will both survive and triumph in the United States.

60 Turner, Darwin T. "James Baldwin." Encyclopedia International, vol. II. New York: Grolier, pp. 328-29.
Contains brief biographical sketch with emphasis on his reputation as a distinguished essayist.

1977

1 Allen, Shirley. "The Ironic Voice in Baldwin's Go Tell It on the Mountain." In O'Daniel, James Baldwin, 1977.40, pp. 30-37.

1977

        Analyzes <u>Go Tell It</u> as a novel based on three different
kinds of irony: irony in the narrator's diction, irony of
statement and even in the action, and an ironic voice as a
character; argues that Baldwin suggests in the novel that
all irony is somewhat malicious, that human problems cannot
be solved either by "sophisticated detachment" or by "common sense reasonableness." Nevertheless, the final irony
of the story is the validation of the tenets of that Christian faith professed by the characters even when they mis-
interpret it.

2 ANON. "Baldwin." <u>PMLA</u>. <u>1976 International Bibliography</u>.
     I:179.
        Presents annual secondary bibliography for 1976.

3 ANON. "Ebony Book Shelf." <u>Ebony</u>, 32 (June), 30.
        Notes the publication of <u>Squaring Off: Mailer vs. Bald-
win</u> by W.J. Weatherby as a series of portraits of the two
authors as artists, friendly enemies, deadly friends, etc.,
and a record of their opinions on power, poverty, competi-
tion, conformity, blacks, and whites.

4 ANON. "Little man, little man." <u>Booklist</u>, 74 (15 September),
     158.
        Sees this "child's story for adults," told in black ver-
nacular, and reflecting the New York ghetto childhood of
"five-year-old" TJ, as a loosely strung series of incidents
and impressions. TJ's impressions are of days playing in
the street and "pondering the way of things."

5 ANON. "Little Man, Little Man." <u>Kirkus</u>, 45 (1 September),
     932.
        Calls <u>Little Man</u> "an empathic, resonantly muted glimpse
of TJ's world." The story is told through the eyes of this
"four-year-old" black child who seems older.

6 Baker, Houston A., Jr. "The Embattled Craftsman: An Essay on
     James Baldwin." <u>Journal of African-Afro-American Affairs</u>,
     1, no. 1:28-51.
        Points out that in the past two decades, Baldwin "has
received more attention from literary and social critics
than any other black American author." He has been seen as
an "implacable agent of reform ceaselessly hammering at the
American consciousness," and an "evangelist" urging America
"to repent" because it is later than one thinks. Yet today,
there are less enthusiastic reactions to him, and an increased effort has been made to view him in "the light cast
by his earlier works." An examination of his works reveals

that his "quest," or journey, has been "circular, beginning
and ending with the black urban masses," and his expression
is reflective, as that of "an 'engaged' black voice,"
though a voice with differing emphases in the various
works. Go Tell It reveals the author as an embattled
craftsman struggling for a sensibility whereby to present
a "black cultural tradition." Notes subsequently portrayed
the artist's credo and his journey abroad to implement it.
Nobody Knows fails both to overcome an inherent diffusion
and to present the "Ole Country" of the South adequately.
Another Country presents the artist's return from Europe as
a touchstone for showing the need to move "beyond the
strictly aesthetic demands" and obtain success in a racist
society. The Fire marks the end of a stage of development
by stressing the necessity for love that is "a commitment
to self-knowledge" and a refusal to embrace terror and loneliness. Tell Me employs a black and celebrated artist in
truce with a black revolutionary to challenge the white-
dominated society. No Name attempts to speak boldly
against the white West and for the Third World in a public
voice, but rejecting a black racism. Finally, Beale Street
presents and praises the familial concept and action inherent in "a genuine concern for one another" and males who
are positive figures. Thus, Baldwin, the black embattled
artist, portrays the tortuous but inexorable evolution
toward a new life.

7 Bannon, Barbara. "Little Man, Little Man." Publishers Weekly,
211 (21 March), 78.
Describes Little Man as "a child's story for adults"
narrated by a New York black boy in the patterns and rhythm
of black speech and expressing "black pride and sensitivity,
the warmth of human relationships and the ability to survive in the dehumanizing ghetto."

8 Berghahn, Marion. "The Transitional Phase--Time of Scepti-
cism." In his Images of Africa in Black American Literature. London: Macmillan, pp. 171-88.
Discusses two critical opinions regarding the changes
that have taken place in Afro-American literature: 1) white
patrons were the driving force of the Harlem Renaissance
and when they did not propel the movement, it collapsed;
2) Afro-American emphases were the origins of the Harlem
Renaissance, and the Great Depression created only a temporary recession in the literary activity. A "thematic shift
of emphasis" occurred between 1930 and 1960, which gave
Afro-American literature a "new quality." There was a dis-
appearance of "primitivism"; growing economic and social

crises had little room for "dreams of paradises." The
Zeitgeist of the post-Harlem Renaissance period can be
gauged from the writings of Wright, Ellison, and Baldwin,
"who dominated the literary scene." Wright's writing deals
with the Afro-American image of Africa primarily influenced
by Marxism. Ellison and his characters find their "identity only inside the United States"; Africa represents some
place foreign and alien. Compared with the attitudes of
Ellison and Wright, "Baldwin's relationship with Africa is
more direct and more personal," yet it is virtually impossible to define his "position vis-à-vis Africa." His attitude towards his African ancestry is connected with "his
views on sin"; Africa "embodies . . . the 'dark,' mysterious and 'sinful' past of the black." In his earlier writings, Baldwin even saw Africans as "simpler and more de-
vious, more directly erotic and at the same time more subtle and . . . proud." By 1960, he moved to a new position;
he saw the growing importance of the "new post-colonial
African states," and began to identify positively with
Africa. Although he has joined "the chorus of Black Nationalists," he still argues that "colour is unimportant."
He has been too "deeply influenced by the West and above
all by Christianity" to "cast off" its culture completely.
Unlike Wright, Baldwin does not fail to recognize just how
much he has been influenced by this Western culture, and
this recognition enables him "to transcend his Western
value system."

9 Bluefarb, Sam. "James Baldwin's 'Previous Condition': A
Problem of Identification." In O'Daniel, James Baldwin,
1977.40, pp. 151-55.
Reprint of 1969.9.

10 Brooks, A. Russell. "James Baldwin As Poet-Prophet." In
O'Daniel, James Baldwin, 1977.40, pp. 126-34.
Advocates that Baldwin's literary works show his self-
designated role as the "poet-prophet" whose fundamental
mission has been "uncompromisingly radical" and "disin-
terestedly probing for sources, causes and roots" in the
diagnosis of the race problem in America. By getting
Americans to see the complexities of history--past and
present--lies the hope to "change the Western assumptions,
and make it a larger civilization than it ever has been
before."

11 Brooks, A. Russell. "Power and Morality as Imperatives for
Nikki Giovanni and James Baldwin: A View of A Dialogue."
In O'Daniel, 1977.40, pp. 205-209.

Contends that A Dialogue reveals the transition in Nikki
Giovanni from a "supporter of the black revolution to har-
binger of black love" in her works--from Black Feeling,
Black Talk, Black Judgement (1970) to A Dialogue; but that
"the Baldwin of 1973 is, by and large, the Baldwin of 1953"
who "has never advocated power for blacks except as it
should lead to control of their own image and of their
future."

12 Coles, Robert. "James Baldwin Back Home." New York Times
Book Review (31 July), pp. 1, 22-24.
   Describes Baldwin as being "glad to be back home" because even while living abroad he was not able to extri-
cate himself from the events in the United States, e.g.,
the Patty Hearst case, the Weathermen, etc. Perhaps now
that he has finished Little Man and his long "apprenticeship" in France, he will "do justice to a subject that has
haunted him: his people's struggle, through the passion of
religious faith, for some understanding of what life means,
if anything."

13 Collier, Eugenia W. "The Phrase Unbearably Repeated." In
O'Daniel, James Baldwin, 1977.40, pp. 38-46.
   Reprint of 1964.26.

14 Collier, Eugenia W. "Thematic Patterns in Baldwin's Essays:
A Study in Chaos." In O'Daniel, James Baldwin, 1977.40,
pp. 135-42.
   Reprint of 1972.26.

15 Farrison, William Edward. "If Baldwin's Train Has Not Gone."
In O'Daniel, James Baldwin, 1977.40, pp. 69-81.
   Gives the background of the author's writing of Tell Me;
analyzes the narrative line, structure, coherence, and
technique; finds the characters--Leo Proudhammer and Barbara King--lacking in insight, resourcefulness, human and
wholesome vitality; and sees the novel as obstructed by
"phallus-consciousness" and a plethora of sexual acts.
Beale Street, though a simpler story and shorter, also has
flaws: no clear relation between the title and the narrative; no characters eliciting high regard from the reader;
and weakly motivated actions for several characters. If
Baldwin regains his devotion to the "art of fiction" as
exemplified in Go Tell It, he may still "reach the greatest heights of distinction."

16 Ferguson, Alfred R. "Black Men, White Cities: The Quest for
Humanity by Black Protagonists in James Baldwin's Another

1977

<u>Country</u> and Richard Wright's <u>The Outsider</u>." <u>Ball State</u>
<u>University Forum</u>, 18 (Spring), 51-58.
    Analyzes two black protagonists in Wright's <u>The Outsider</u>
and Baldwin's <u>Another Country</u> who "strive for and fail to
achieve their humanity," the full realization of the self.
Both characters (Rufus--<u>Another Country</u>; Cross--<u>The Out-</u>
<u>sider</u>) struggle for self-realization in the city, but the
differences in their responses to the city "constitute the
differing nature of their quest." The image of the city
reflects the theme of each novel: <u>Another Country</u>--the intense conflict between what Baldwin "assumes man historic-
ally is--or has been--but cannot be . . . because of the
malforming pressures of the city"; <u>The Outsider</u>--the potential for man to realize himself in a historical framework
is initially rejected so that he is alienated from the city,
which is "a metaphorical repository of accumulated human
history." Baldwin's city "prevents the complete extrusion
of the individual personality through a successful quest
for identity because it is an inhuman environment remote
from "life enhancing values." Wright's character does not
see the city as an enemy; to him it "exists as a historical
presence," and he dwells "outside of any context at all."

17 Fisher, Lester Allen. "The Uses and Effects of Violence in
    the Fiction and Drama of James Baldwin." Ph.D. disserta-
    tion, Brown University.
       Believes that Baldwin is "invariably honored for his
achievement as an essayist and is insufficiently honored as
a novelist, short story writer, and dramatist." Few critics have given his fiction and drama the "sensitive and
considered reading" his work deserves; there is a need for
a broader critical perspective of Baldwin's works. Violence and disorder prevail in his books, and his characters
live their lives negotiating relationships with others so
as "to cope with the inharmonious and destructive elements
of their world." In <u>Tell Me</u>, the characters use violence
to "respond to the effects of violence" for various reasons:
relationships to environment; method of initiation; method
of self-creation; mode of love; mode of self-transcendence;
mode of regeneration. In <u>Beale Street</u>, the effects of violence are mitigated by love, which helps the characters define themselves and affirm their sense of identity.

18 Ford, Nick Aaron. "The Evolution of James Baldwin as Essay-
    ist." In O'Daniel, <u>James Baldwin</u>, 1977.40, pp. 85-104.
       Contends that Baldwin is the most talented American
essayist since Emerson and that his other works are clearly
inferior in style and substance to the volumes of essays.

His best writing lies in "the general area of unstructured, instinctive, and emotional utterance often unsupported by rational safeguards." Like Emerson, his contributions are not made via "logic and rationality" but rather by "pragmatism and prophecy" whereby he provokes "humane thought" and announces "eternal truths" intended "to elevate the consciousness of the reader from animal passion to spiritual or philosophical contemplation." Analyses of the style, content, and method of Notes, Nobody Knows, The Fire, and No Name are presented. For example, Baldwin typically uses first-person narration, uninhibitedly exposes the "awful truth," consistently employs a vivid imagery to elicit emotional involvement, and frequently relates personal examples to illustrate or enhance general truths. His dominant theme is "what it means to be black in a nation and a world dominated by 'white' power in social, political, religious, artistic, and ethical matters." His best book thus far is The Fire: "a beautiful book, a challenging book, a powerful book, . . . a profoundly philosophical book."

19 Gibson, Donald B. "Individualism and Community in Black History and Fiction." BALF, 11, no. 4 (Winter), 123-29.
        Views Another Country as having a central character, Rufus Scott, whose problem is not "the failure of love" as Baldwin contends but rather the lack of a "support system" in the form of a "reliable community." Beale Street represents a change in Baldwin's concept of the problem of a character as a problem of consciousness to defining the problem in more communal terms with value inherent in group effort, especially the viable strength in the black family.

20 Gibson, Donald B. "James Baldwin: The Political Anatomy of Space." In O'Daniel, James Baldwin, 1977.40, pp. 3-18.
        Uses ideas and analyses of previous essays (Gibson, 1970.18 and 1971.29) as context and basis for amplifying his views of Go Tell It, Giovanni's Room, Another Country, and Tell Me. He concludes that Baldwin "comes closer to putting himself on the printed page than most contemporary novelists and than any contemporary essayist"; this "ability to express the innermost, deepest longings of his psyche" is simultaneously his greatest strength and weakness because of the fact "that his analysis of his own personal needs is indistinguishable in his mind from his analysis of the world and its society." Although an explicit change is discernible between his earlier emphasis on love and personal feeling for another, i.e., "inner space," to "consideration of the role of the 'public space' in

1977

determining the nature, character and quality of human experience," Baldwin nevertheless retains in both the fiction
and essays basic presuppositions that are "highly subjective reflections of personal need and desire." Thus, his
social analysis is limited in scope and ultimately conser-
vative, with no solution "in the framework of his politics";
while he confronts the system with a morally based rhetoric,
he does not question its basic operations; "perhaps further
questioning, about the uses of power in society for example,
would unsettle too many things that have been thus far set-
tled for him."

21 Gounard, Jean-François. "L'Avenir de James Baldwin." Europe,
no. 578/79 (June/July), pp. 186-97.
    Sees four essential points inherent in the writing of
Baldwin: 1) the particular role of sex in personal relationships, with special focus on homosexuality; 2) the need
to understand what it means to be black or white; 3) the
awareness of himself as a writer; 4) the acceptance of the
role of prophet for responding to the American racial problem. He comments on and interprets: Go Tell It, Giovanni's
Room, Another Country, Blues, and Tell Me.

22 Greene, J. Lee. "Black Literature and the American Literary
Mainstream." In Minority Language and Literature: Retrospective and Perspective. New York: Modern Language
Association of America, pp. 20-28.
    Argues that the generation of black writers who followed
the Harlem Renaissance molded "their literary representa-
tion and interpretation of the black experience in America"
around the cultural symbol of black aspirations focused on
"the mythic Promised Land of the North" as evidenced in
such works as Jean Toomer's Cane, Wright's Native Son,
Ellison's Invisible Man, and Baldwin's Go Tell It. The
biblical-cultural paradigm of Adam and Eve is also evidenced in black literature especially after 1940 in the
form of black men and white women respectively, with Eve
as the forbidden fruit and evil temptress who destroys the
black, as in Baldwin's Another Country.

23 Hagopian, John V. "James Baldwin: The Black and the Red-
White-and-Blue." In O'Daniel, James Baldwin, 1977.40,
pp. 156-62.
    Reprint of 1963.38.

24 Hajek, Friederike. "James Baldwin: Beale Street Blues."
Weimer Beiträge: Zeitschrift für Literaturwissenschaft,
Asthetik und Kulturtheoric, 23, no. 6:137-50.

Gives a brief introduction to the author's literary
works and emphasizes Beale Street.

25 Haskell, Ann S. "Baldwin: Harlem on His Mind." Book World
    (11 September), p. E6.
        Describes Little Man as "an exciting, perhaps, an impor-
    tant book," but it is flawed by a "skewed" concept of its
    audience--a children's book for adults, or an adult story
    for children? The work is "competently, sometimes exciting-
    ly" illustrated with pen and ink drawings and water colors
    by Yoran Cazac.

26 Hatch, James and Omanii Abdullah, eds. Black Playwrights,
    1823-1977: An Annotated Bibliography of Plays. New York
    and London: R. R. Bowker, p. 12.
        Gives annotations for Blues, Amen Corner, and One Day,
    including data about production and publication.

27 Hollowell, John. "Novelists and the Novel in a Time of Cri-
    sis." In his Fact and Fiction: The New Journalism and the
    Nonfiction Novel. Chapel Hill, N.C.: University of North
    Carolina Press, pp. 3-20.
        Describes Notes and The Fire as documentaries of "the
    harsh realities" of the American black.

28 Jarrett, Hobart. "From a Region in My Mind: The Essays of
    James Baldwin." In O'Daniel, James Baldwin, 1977.40,
    pp. 105-25.
        Proclaims Baldwin a "great writer" who "by choice, by
    talent, by calling" was directed to the essay, "the form
    that shows him at his excellence." Jarrett presents 1) an
    overview of Baldwin's conception of the writer performing
    a "special mission"; 2) mentions motifs that recur in the
    essays--hatred for his father; concern about religion,
    Christianity, the church; the significance of being black
    in a white-dominated world; 3) explores some of the tech-
    niques used and faults manifested by Baldwin--his "self
    projection which identifies the author with the reader and
    vice versa"; his insights; his frequent contradictions; his
    discovery of the South and what it symbolizes--terror, lack
    of class distinction, strength of black men.
        "Stranger in the Village" (Notes) is treated as remark-
    able, baffling, and excellent in showing "why it is that
    white people have found it so difficult, if not impossible
    to regard black people as human beings."
        In summary, some of Baldwin's essays are dated by virtue
    of being topical; many have also contributed significantly
    to the social changes that have occurred in America and re-
    main "major interpretations of our era." Others may,

1977

however, "possess timelessness. [People] are too close to
tell." But Baldwin does expose and interpret for his
readers "what [people's] minds and spirits need to know."
"Many Thousands Gone" may be his "most profound expression"
while "Alas Poor Richard" is his best and The Fire "should
be read by many more than those hordes who have already
read it."

29 Jones, Harry L. "Style, Form, and Content in the Short Fiction of James Baldwin." In O'Daniel, James Baldwin,
1977.40, pp. 143-50.
Advocates that the short fiction, largely found in Going
to Meet and written between 1948 and 1965, provides a basis
for some studies on Baldwin's development as a writer because these "short works seem to contain in microcosm the
universe that later manifests itself in Baldwin's major
works." The greatest strength of his short fiction is the
"creation of patterns of static reference, presenting de-
scriptions or affective states in his characters," or "producing a telling conative impact on his readers." His
stories lack "the kind of cyclical structures that make for
good narrative art," and he uses them "as a means of artistically imposing his ideological positions on the nature
and purposes of fiction." "Sonny's Blues" is his "most per-
fectly realized story" according to the criteria pertain-
ing to an aesthetic whole.

30 J.R. "For the Intermediate Library." Junior Bookshelf, 41
(April), 123.
Sees Little Man as defying categorization and being hard
to read by children but as a portrayal of childhood that
needs to be shared by all who remember what it is to be
"less than four feet high."

31 Kent, George E. "Baldwin and the Problem of Being." In
O'Daniel, James Baldwin, 1977.40, pp. 19-29.
Reprint of 1964.46.

32 Korzus, Margaret Gertrud Charlotte. "James Baldwin's Concept
of the Artist and the Rebel: An Interpretation Based on
Albert Camus and Otto Rank." Ph.D. dissertation, University of Denver.
Analyzes Baldwin's concept of the artist in his role as
rebel--rebel demonstrating artistic sensibility, rebel as
ordinary man or woman. This role represents the "proto- and
arche-types of all artists and all rebels": their personal
natures that bring them into conflict with the society
that nourishes them. Rebellion, creativity, defiance,

passion are necessary experiences for the artist so that he can counteract the "illusion of innocence," a dangerous and destructive force, which "denies the reality of pain, anguish, suffering, and death." Baldwin as rebel and artist shows an affinity to the French writer Camus and the German psychologist Rank; both have "intellectualized a concept of the artist and the rebel which finds dramatization in Baldwin's fiction."

33 Lash, John S. "Baldwin beside Himself: A Study in Modern Phallicism." In O'Daniel, James Baldwin, 1977.40, pp. 47-55. Reprint of 1964.49.

34 Lehman, Paul. "The Development of a Black Psyche: An Interview with John Oliver Killens." BALF, 11, no. 3 (Fall), 83-89.
Reports Killens' observation that Ellison and Baldwin were concerned with explaining blacks to "white folks" in contrast to his own artistic concern.

35 Lester, Julius. "Children's Books." New York Times Book Review (4 September), p. 22.
Quotes a description that called Little Man "a child's story for adults," but it does not compare to such works as Henry Roth's Call It Sleep or Harper Lee's To Kill a Mockingbird, which changed the perceptions of adult reality because "the presentation of children's reality was so intense." The overriding "virtue" of Baldwin's book is his masterful language, an effective blend of black English and children's talk. Although the book has been written by an honored author, it is only a "slight book" that lacks "intensity and focus."

36 Millican, Arthenia Bates. "Fire as the Symbol of a Leadening Existence in Going to Meet the Man." In O'Daniel, James Baldwin, 1977.40, pp. 170-80.
Analyzes "Going to Meet the Man," title story in Going to Meet, as employing fire "as a symbol of frustration, which Jesse, the protagonist, experiences as a boy of eight, as a young adult (no doubt in his twenties), and as a deputy sheriff forty-two years old" whose own frustrations have prevented him "from priming the depths of his own personality because he must do what his forefathers ordained for him." He cannot escape the burden of his heritage, viz., to perpetuate the Southern bureaucracy of white superiority. Fire is also used in a literal and symbolic sense in other works of fiction and nonfiction by Baldwin.

37 Molette, Carlton W. "James Baldwin as Playwright." In O'Dan-
    iel, James Baldwin, 1977.40, pp. 183-88.
        Views the dramas, Amen Corner and Blues, as a director
    and from the perspective of their appropriateness for pro-
    duction, not as literature. He sees Amen Corner as "built
    upon the rhythms of the Afro-American church" with rhythm
    as its dominant force and as the means of eliciting a sense
    of community or belonging; also, it is about love that
    transcends "the petty bickering, the jealousies, the family
    fights." The play's chief fault is its repetition in
    speeches in several two-character scenes. Blues is a com-
    plex play that "tries to explain whites to blacks and
    blacks to whites" and involves several paradoxes: Lyle
    Britten is not a "demonic redneck character" but a real man
    backed into the corner by a system; Richard Henry will
    destroy "Mr. Charlie" to save himself but will be destroyed
    by the system in doing so; the leader of the whites and
    the leader of the blacks talk about the progress they are
    making but know it is a lie. Also, the play uses multiple
    fluctuations among representational and soliloquy styles.
    Baldwin the artist as novelist has depended as a playwright
    upon many other artists and has achieved success upon the
    stage unlike many other novelists.

38 Murray, Donald C. "James Baldwin's 'Sonny's Blues': Compli-
    cated and Simple." Studies in Short Fiction, 14 (Fall),
    353-57.
        Contends that in the world of "Sonny's Blues" Baldwin
    deals with "man's need to find his identity in a hostile
    society" and in a "social situation which invites fatalis-
    tic compliance." Through an awareness of himself through
    artistic creation (music), a young boy grows into adult-
    hood. Sonny's brother, the narrator, is forced to face
    reality first by examining his own past and his present,
    and then recognizing Sonny as "both a creative individual
    and a brother." He realizes also that "love is what life
    should be about."

39 O'Daniel, Therman B. "James Baldwin: A Classified Biblio-
    graphy." In his James Baldwin, 1977.40, pp. 243-61.
        Contains the most complete listing of primary and second-
    ary sources to date.

40 O'Daniel, Therman B., ed. James Baldwin: A Critical Evalua-
    tion. Washington, D.C.: Howard University Press, 273 pp.
        Anthologizes a collection of secondary sources: Allen,
    1977.1; Bluefarb, 1977.9; Brooks, 1977.11; Collier,
    1977.13, 14; Farrison, 1977.15; Ford, 1977.18; Gibson,

1977.20; Hagopian, 1977.23; Jarrett, 1977.28; Jones,
1977.29; Kent, 1977.31; Lash, 1977.33; Millican, 1977.36;
Molette, 1977.37; Orsagh, 1977.41; Perry, 1977.42; Reilly,
1977.44; Turner, 1977.48; Turpin, 1977.49; Zahorski,
1977.52. Also, contains the most complete primary and
secondary sources to date, compiled by O'Daniel, 1977.39.

41 Orsagh, Jacqueline E. "Baldwin's Female Characters--A Step
Forward?" In O'Daniel, James Baldwin, 1977.40, pp. 56-68.
    Emphasizes that in contrast to the "well-accepted fact
that there have been very few, if any, well-developed and
believable women characters in English and American literature," the literature of Baldwin presents "female characters who are extraordinarily strong, dynamic, and, even
more importantly, interesting." A central feature of these
women characters that differentiates them "from other fic-
titious females" is that "they act and are not condemned
for doing so." Additionally, they are believable and without an aura of mystery because "they weep, they laugh, they
strike, they bleed"; and "they scrutinize life, come to
grips with it, and transcend their old existence in a beautiful but understandable way." Another Country illustrates
the careful and clear development of "three memorable, dynamic, and very different women": Leona, Cass, and Ida.
Tell Me presents Baldwin's "most extensive female portrait"
in Barbara, who comes closest to being a protagonist than
any other female character in his fiction, but she ultimately lacks credibility because "she has no flaws" and is
"a fantasy."

42 Perry, Patsy Brewington. "One Day When I Was Lost: Baldwin's
Unfulfilled Obligation." In O'Daniel, James Baldwin,
1977.40, pp. 213-27.
    Argues that Baldwin's scenario One Day fails to present
the complex nature and stature of Malcolm X as a man and
as a leader because of the author's single-minded, inordi-
nate emphasis on violence in America, because of his "transformations of important persons and events," and because of
his undercutting of the contributions, achievements, and potential for achievement by Malcolm. Thus, Baldwin does not
even begin "to encompass or even suggest the meaning of
Malcolm . . . a man of noble proportions."

43 Raphael, Frederick. "The Defiant One." New Statesman, 93
(25 February), 260-61.
    Describes Baldwin as not being idle. "The eloquence of
his prose, its feverish urgency, is informed with the force
of his whole remarkable personality, from which the gestures

1977

of the orator and of the preacher cannot be divorced." The
Devil is a "sermon with a celluloid text," with a few "fine
passages," but there are too many stretches of "pseudo-
academese that smack of make-weight."

44 Reilly, John M. "'Sonny's Blues': James Baldwin's Image of
Black Community." In O'Daniel, James Baldwin, 1977.40,
pp. 163-69.
    Reprint of 1970.36.

45 Sheed, Wilfrid. "Twin Urges of James Baldwin." Commonweal,
104 (24 June), 404-407.
    Begins with the evaluation that when Baldwin "goes
wrong . . . it usually seems less a failure of talent than
of policy." In his early days the "twin urges"--"an urge
to please and a mission to scold"--came together to make
"very good policy," i.e., white liberals accepted a spank-
ing that pleased and scolded. But after a while the
"liberal guilt gave out," and now the times seem to call
for something different. The Devil shows Baldwin "groping"
for a new subject--the movies. Since he is a preacher at
heart seeking a "genuine quasi religious vocation," the
movies do not afford him a sincere topic; thus the tone of
the work is false.

46 Thornton, Jerome Edward. "James Baldwin and the Christian
Tradition." Ph.D. dissertation, State University of New
York at Buffalo.
    Analyzes Baldwin's "Christian tradition," which is seen
in relation to his characters and as the basis for the tension between agnostic and religious "elements of his style."
He has used, to his advantage, the symbolism and imagery of
religion in order to "argue" his belief in agnosticism as an
intellectual counterpoise" to the anti-intellectual emo-
tionalism of the church.

47 Turner, Darwin T. "James Baldwin." In Contemporary Dramatist,
2nd. ed. Edited by James Vinson. New York: St. Martin's
Press, pp. 61-64.
    Gives biographical data, list of primary works, and
selected bibliographic sources; contends that Baldwin is
least known as a dramatist. His drama repeats the message
of other works, viz., "that people must love and understand other people if they wish to save the world from destruction." Sees the theme of Blues in the tragedy of two
characters, white journalist Parnell and black minister
Meridian Henry, "who see the destruction of their hope for
love between the races"; and the theme of Amen Corner as

the ultimate realization by a black female minister "that
love and compassion for human beings are more important
than a fanatically rigid enunciation of God's law."

48 Turner, Darwin T. "James Baldwin in the Dilemma of the Black
     Dramatist." In O'Daniel, James Baldwin, 1977.40, pp. 189-
     94.
         Describes the issue that distinguishes two groups of
     contemporary black playwrights from each other as being
     the decision "whether the black writer should direct him-
     self to a white audience--to entertain them, or to educate
     them about black people--or should direct himself to a
     black audience--to educate them to awareness of their
     needs." He argues that Blues was written for a white audi-
     ence and patterned on the protest tradition, while the
     earlier Amen Corner, artistically superior in both theme
     and characterization, "seems more clearly designed as a
     drama written about black experience for a black audience."
     The dominating theme of all of Baldwin's work is that "hu-
     man beings must learn to give themselves totally to other
     human beings if humankind is to survive."

49 Turpin, Waters E. "A Note on Blues for Mister Charlie." In
     O'Daniel, James Baldwin, 1977.40, pp. 195-98.
         Contends that Blues, though frequently tagged by re-
     viewers as "badly written," successfully combined the au-
     thenticity of a nightmare and the blues into "an expres-
     sionistic outcry that captures the distilled agony of
     this racially tormented, mid-twentieth-century America."

50 Weatherby, W. J. Squaring Off: Mailer vs. Baldwin. New
     York: Mason/Charter, 217 pp.; London: Robson Books,
     217 pp.
         Describes the author's personal experiences (interviews,
     discussions, dinner parties) with Norman Mailer and James
     Baldwin. He relates those experiences to their works and
     asserts that the two writers are "reverse sides of the same
     coin, representative figures of the sixties, when blacks
     and whites were struggling creatively to understand each
     other." He argues that both were involved "in a common
     quest in public even though in different directions and
     styles" as "frontline voyages for a lot of fellow Ameri-
     cans." Weatherby's book is indispensable for a realistic,
     reportorial perspective of both writers and a record of
     their escapades, adventures, and interrelations, and es-
     pecially, their opinions and views on power and poverty,
     blacks and whites, competition and conformity, artistry and
     social action, friends and acquaintances, etc. The author

1977

> relates events from 1959, the first time he met Baldwin,
> and 1961, his first acquaintance with Mailer, to 1976.

51 Weixlmann, Joe. "Staged Segregation: Baldwin's Blues for Mr.
   Charlie and O'Neill's All God's Chillun Got Wings." BALF,
   11, no. 1 (Spring), 35-36.
       Cites the fact that Blues has "more often been assailed
   than lauded," with much of the criticism focusing on the
   play's structure--the play reads well but stages poorly.
   Perhaps it is Baldwin's "imperfect sense of stage craft,
   not his rhetoric" that makes Blues "second-rate." There
   is the pervasive image of segregation in Blues, which is
   repeatedly reinforced just as it is in O'Neill's All God's
   Chillun Got Wings, but Baldwin tends to make points with
   words instead of actions, and O'Neill allows "physical
   effects to substitute for verbal ones."

52 Zahorski, Kenneth J. "James Baldwin: Portrait of a Black
   Exile." In O'Daniel, James Baldwin, 1977.40, pp. 199-204.
       Views Rap on Race as possessing "an abundance of thought-
   provoking ideas, illuminating insights, and memorable passages" but concentrates on exploring "the convictions,
   values, attitudes, hopes, fears, and biases" of Baldwin.
   Some of the issues covered by Baldwin include American
   materialism, democracy, violence, racism, and search for
   identity. Although "notes of optimism" are expressed occasionally, the book is pervaded by "an aura of frustration, bitterness, despair, and anguish" on Baldwin's part.
   Nevertheless, it is a valuable work in providing "a profoundly personal perspective on this renowned black writer."

1978 (Preliminary)

1 ANON. "Baldwin." PMLA. 1977 International Bibliography.
   I:1962.
       Presents annual secondary bibliography for 1977.

2 ANON. "Controversy over Robeson Play Continues in Forum on
   His Image." The New York Times (14 May), p. 49.
       Reports on a forum at Hunter College treating the con-
   troversy about a play entitled "Paul Robeson." Panelists on
   the subject of "Paul Robeson--The Play, the Protest, the
   Legacy and the Lessons" included Baldwin, Ossie Davis,
   Paul Robeson, Jr., and others. Baldwin argued that the
   play presented Robeson as a "misguided, tragic hero," which
   was "pernicious perversion of the essence of Paul Robeson,"
   and he contended that the American public wants its black

hero to be a "chocolate John Wayne." The playwright, Mr. Dean, objected to Baldwin's criticism on the grounds that Baldwin had not seen the work.

3 ANON. "Little Man, Little Man." Bulletin of the Center for Children's Books, 31 (January), 73-74.
Sees Little Man, a "vignette of a Harlem childhood," as too much of "a picture book format" for adults and "too mature in concept and sedate in pace" for children.

4 Dance, Daryl C. "James Baldwin." In Black American Writers: Bibliographical Essays. Edited by M. Thomas Inge et al. New York: St. Martin's Press, pp. 73-120.
The most significant, though selective, annotated bibliography of Baldwin to date because it includes both primary works (full length, short stories, essays, interviews and discussions, manuscripts, and letters) and secondary works (biography, criticism--individual works, general studies, personal criticism of Baldwin, and future needs).

*5 Daniels, Mark R. "Little Man, Little Man." Best Sellers, 37 (December), 292.
Cited in Current Book Review Citation, 3 (June), 5.

6 Davis, Arthur P. "Novels of the New Black Renaissance (1960-1977): A Thematic Survey." CLAJ, 21 (June), 457-63.
Places Baldwin as a transitional figure among the writers of the post-1960 era of "the New Black Renaissance." Baldwin's three later novels show him "traveling deeper and deeper into 'blackness'": Another Country illustrates the influence of the "Black Revolution of the 1960's" and portrays a new convention--the abused and mistreated white mistress; Tell Me uses a black nationalist, Christopher, and gives the author an opportunity to express the attitudes of the black arts movements; Beale Street treats the inner-city Negro life, is strongly anti-middle-class. But Baldwin's "black novels" are defective, and he remains a "writer 'wandering between two worlds.'"

7 Gaylin, Willard. "Being Touched, Being Hurt." Psychology Today, 12, no. 7 (December), 117-20, 138-39.
Develops the concept of "touching" and relates it to other areas of human expression, e.g., music, literature, etc. One "delightful aspect" of being touched is that "almost invariably, it carries with it an element of surprise," and this emotional element can "precipitate major changes in relationships and feelings." The birthday scene between mother and son in Baldwin's Go Tell It "starts with what

1978

might be called the feeling of being touched but then moves
into something too profound," too intense, for that "gentle
and delicate emotion." The spontaneous expression of love
and the element of surprise stimulate an "overwhelming
flood" of emotions that previously had been dormant and
unappreciated.

8 Geringer, Laura. "Little Man, Little Man." School Library
Journal, 24 (January), 84.
Summarizes the narrative line and stresses how TJ re-
alizes "the fragility of his childhood world."

9 Jackson, Blyden. "James Baldwin: A Critical Evaluation."
CLAJ, 21 (June), 571-72.
Reviews O'Daniel's volume of the same name (1977.40);
finds it "an orchestrated symposium" that sees Baldwin as
"an important American writer and a public figure" who is
"essentially a moralist."

10 Kurkjian, James W. and William Banks. "The Properties of Empathy Explored and Developed Through Literature." The
Personnel and Guidance Journal, 56, no. 10 (June), 634-36.
Summarizes counseling trends and focuses upon counselor
empathy as essential to all approaches. Counselor empathy
is "understanding a client's experience cognitively and
affectively." Imagination, another property of empathy,
can facilitate the entry of the counselor into the client's
world. It operates similarly in reader or audience empathy
for a novel or play; thus there is a basis for equating
the reading of a novel with a counseling session. If a
literary experience reflects a life experience, it is possible to gain "empathic understanding of a life experience
through literature." The situation of the white counselor
with a black client is common and demonstrates how literature can provide a white counselor with a cognitive and
affective understanding of the "black experience." Neil
Friedman's article "James Baldwin and Psychotherapy"
(1966.23) shows how Baldwin's fiction serves as a model for
understanding the experiences of a black client. Not only
does Baldwin's work increase empathic understanding, it can
also show the white counselor how he is perceived by the
black client. Thus, with a better understanding of the
client's world, the counselor will possess a clearer self-
understanding in terms of who he is perceived to be.

11 Lask, Thomas. "'Amen Corner' by Baldwin Staged by Arts Consortium." The New York Times (23 April), p. 54.

1978

Reviews the production of <u>Amen Corner</u> by the New York
Arts Consortium, "finds it "full of zest and brio" in spite
of excessive length and asserts that it is an exposition of
community life "full of pathos and caustic human, irritating superstituion, and shrewd folk wisdom."

12 Pratt, Louis Hill. <u>James Baldwin</u>. Boston: Twayne Publishers,
    157 pp.
        Explores Baldwin's literary art in order to delineate
    the broader concerns rather than "the provincial problems
    of white versus black," viz., "the universal concepts of
    freedom versus slavery, liberation versus oppression, real-
    ity versus illusion, identity versus darkness, confusion,
    and chaos." Chapter 1, "Common Experience, Uncommonly
    Probed," treats Baldwin's artistic philosophy as it per-
    tains to his conception of the "business" of a writer as
    well as some major recurrent themes. The second chapter,
    "The Fear and the Fury," examines the short stories in
    <u>Going to Meet</u> as they exemplify his interest in the psycho-
    logical states of characters with primary focus on aliena-
    tion. "Love Denied, Love Fulfilled," chapter 3, presents
    detailed analyses of the novels in terms of style, theme,
    and technique and as they illustrate the need for estab-
    lishing a personal social atmosphere in which love can "sur-
    vive and flourish." Chapter 4, "The Darkness Within," in-
    terprets the dramas within the context of Baldwin's aesthe-
    tic perspective and as embodying the common themes of illu-
    sion versus reality and the search for identity. "The Con-
    frontation of Experience," chapter 5, takes full cognizance
    of the sociological dimension of Baldwin's essays but also
    emphasizes their artistic achievement in his use of lang-
    uage, style, and technique in that form of expression that
    may be his "major contribution to American letters." The
    final chapter, "The Scheme of Things: New Worlds and Be-
    yond," surveys the critical opinions about Baldwin's sta-
    ture as writer and concludes that the critical assessments
    of the seventies have rejected "the narrow context of
    sociology" as the basis of judgment for his work, and have
    moved toward a more comprehensive evaluation that stresses
    "the consummate artistic skill which transcends the social
    value of his artistry." A selected bibliography includes a
    listing of primary sources and an annotated listing of se-
    lected secondary items.

13 Sarotte, Georges Michel. <u>Like a Brother, Like a Lover: Male
    Homosexuality in the American Novel and Theater from Herman
    Melville to James Baldwin</u>. Trans. by Richard Miller. New

273

1978

York: Anchor Press/Doubleday, pp. 27-29, 54-60, 96-103,
170-71.
Explores three varieties of homosexual desire--homo-
eroticism, homosexuality, and homogenitalism--as a perspective of the American novel and theater from Melville to
Baldwin. In Giovanni's Room, David, the protagonist,
attempts to conform to "the American virile ideal," thus
creating a schizophrenic mode of experience; the novel suggests that homosexuality cannot be viable in America until
sexual prejudices are overcome. Another Country presents a
"love story" in an atmosphere of "purity, peace and mystic
union" for Eric and Yves, with the author's purpose being
"to make their love acceptable to the reader, to make the
reader feel sympathy for this male couple by creating
situations that are traditionally associated with love between men and women"; it is a bisexual novel that ends on
"a note of homosexual hope." Go Tell It embodies symbolically the rite of passage for John by the male kiss from
Brother Elisha--"like a deflowering to mark the passage
from innocence to knowledge." In Baldwin's works "woman is
present, waiting--involuntarily--to come between boys who
are in love"; for him "the one who is loved must always re-
tain a certain degree of heterosexuality if he is to remain
the beloved." Baldwin's treatment of homosexuality and
heterosexuality involves interracial mixing; however, Tell
Me focuses on "intraracial homosexual initiation" in Leo
Proudhammer who discovers "true love with his own sex and
race in Christopher." Baldwin is incapable of identifying
with a white or black "who is only heterosexual, or with a
homosexual who is exclusively homosexual, unless he is an
adolescent."
Baldwin's novels vacillate between two polar extremes:
"his settling of accounts with the white race--since he
feels that they are what has forced him to hate himself--
and his homosexual love for the white man, with whom he
desperately tries to identify." Tell Me suggests that
Baldwin has worked through his "seeming self-hatred" and
his "hatred for blacks in general."

14 Standley, Fred L. "James Baldwin." In Dictionary of Literary
Biography: American Novelist since World War II. Edited
by Richard Layman. Detroit: Gale Research Company.
Gives selective bibliographic listing and combines biographical data and critical comment into an interpretive
overview of Baldwin's literary achievement that stresses
his conception of the artist, his thematic concerns, and
his techniques in several works. The primary emphasis is
that Baldwin prefigures in Go Tell It the themes and motifs
pursued further in subsequent works.

No Date

1 Ayman, S. E. "No Country of Young Men." Standards, pp. 78-82.
   Cited in 1972.1.

2 Forman, Enid G. Put Me In Print: A Story of James Baldwin.
   Washington: The Associated Publishers, 14 pp.
      Cited in 1977.39; and in National Union Catalog 1956-
   1967, vol. 37. Totowa, N.J.: Rowman and Littlefield,
   1970, p. 238.

3 Jones, Mary E. "CAAS Bibliography No. 5: James Baldwin."
   Mimeographed. Atlanta, Ga.: Atlanta University's Center
   for African and African-American Studies, pp. 1-20.
      Cited in 1977.39; and annotated in 1978.4.

Addenda

1957.5   Ellison, Ralph. "Society, Morality, and the Novel." In
         The Living Novel. Edited by Granville Hicks. New York:
         Macmillan, pp. 58-91.
              Cited in 1977.39; however, the essay does not mention
         or allude to Baldwin.

1964.75 Gordon, Caroline. "Letters to a Monk." Ramparts (Decem-
         ber), p. 4f.
              Cited in 1977.39; however, the essay does not treat
         Baldwin.

1965.75 Turpin, Waters. "The Contemporary American Negro Play-
         wright." CLAJ, 9 (September), 12-14.
              Cited in 1977.39; however, the essay contains nothing
         about Baldwin.

1969.35 Stanton, Robert. "Outrageous Fiction: Crime and Punish-
         ment and Native Son." Pacific Coast Philology, 4
         (April), 52-58.
              Listed in 1977.39; however, the essay includes no
         reference to Baldwin.

1970.45 Schatz, Walter, ed. Directory of Afro-American Resources.
         New York: R. R. Bowker Company, pp. 105, 186, 200, 209.
              Gives location of papers, speeches, recording, manu-
         scripts, etc., by Baldwin.

1972.68 ANON. "Books for Young Adults." Booklist (1 September),
         p. 40.
              Includes No Name as suitable for ages fourteen to
         eighteen as a fusion of personal history and the period
         of the 1960s and concludes that "the war between the
         blacks and whites is not likely to resolve itself soon."

1972.69 ANON. "SR Reviews Books." Sat R, 55 (2 December), 89.
              Contends that No Name reconsiders the American scene
         since The Fire and finds little "to relieve the anguish,
         gloom and despair" of the earlier book.

A Note about the Index

In addition to authors, titles of works, and names of people, this index also includes references to the thirty-nine subjects listed below:

Aesthetics
Africa
Afro-American literature
American literature
Bibliography
Biography
Black art
Black experience
Black/Jewish relations
Black power
Black/white relations
Characterization
Civil rights spokesman
Existentialism
Hate
Homosexuality
Humor
Identity quest
Literary criticism

Love
Manuscripts
Militancy
Movies
Music
Muslims
Negro folklore
Negro life
Plot and structure
Racial suffering
Racism
Religion
Sex
Style
Symbolism
Themes and motifs
Values
Violence
Voice of American consciousness

(N.D. refers to the No Date section at the end of the chapter, "Writings about James Baldwin, 1946-1978"; Add. refers to the Addenda.)

Index

Bulman, Leonard T., 1963.18
Burgess, Anthony, 1965.22, 23; 1967.5
Burke, William M., 1972.24
Burks, Mary Fair, 1976.22
Burroughs, William, 1963.37
Butcher, Margaret J., 1956.7
Butcher, Phillip, 1967.6
Butterfield, Stephen, 1974.22
Byam, Milton S., 1953.12; 1955.4

"CAAS Bibliography No. 5: James Baldwin," N.D.3
Cade Toni, 1969.10
Caldwell, Ben, 1970.35; 1973.19
"Caliban or Hamlet: An American Paradox," 1966.22
"The Call to Color Blindness," 1963.17
Campbell, Finley, 1962.18
Camus, Albert, 1964.15, 74; 1966.25; 1975.23; 1977.32
"Can You Go Home Again," 1974.35
Capote, Truman, 1973.22
Carey, Gary, 1976.23
Carlsen, G. Robert, Tony Manna, and Jan Yoder, 1976.24
Cartey, Wilfred, 1966.14; 1970.11
Cassidy, Claudia, 1964.20
Cassidy, T. E., 1953.13
"Cause My House Fell Down: The Theme of the Fall in Baldwin's Novels," 1972.23
Caute, David, 1972.25
"Celebrity and Boredom," 1972.2
"A Century of Negro Portraiture in American Literature," 1966.13; 1968.12
"A Change of Tune," 1964.41
"Channel X: Two Plays on the Race Conflict," 1964.65
Chapman, Abraham, 1973.15
Characterization, 1957.4; 1961.22; 1962.4, 6, 10, 13, 15, 20, 22, 27, 38, 40, 43, 48, 52, 53, 56; 1963.30, 55; 1964.20, 22, 24, 29, 51, 52, 56; 1965.20, 30, 32, 57, 71; 1966.8, 9, 14, 36; 1967.1, 4, 12, 13; 1968.21, 26, 29, 34, 37, 38, 43, 45; 1969.20, 24,

27, 29, 30; 1970.14, 25, 32, 37; 1971.8, 13, 15, 16, 22, 23, 29, 32, 33, 48, 52, 54; 1972.14, 27, 34, 45, 59, 67; 1973.19, 27, 29, 33; 1974.2, 7, 10, 16, 58, 59, 61; 1975.1, 9; 1976.22, 27, 33; 1977.1, 15, 16, 19, 20, 37, 41; 1978.12, 13
Charles, Ray, 1965.42
"'Charlie' Scored by London Critics," 1965.29
Charney, M., 1963.19
"A Checklist of Original Plays, Pageants, Rituals and Musicals by Afro-American Authors Performed in the United States from 1960-1973," 1974.36
Chesnutt, Charles, 1970.9
"Chicago City Council Delays Action on Novel by Baldwin," 1965.7
"Chicago School Panel Sets Hearing on Baldwin Book," 1965.8
"Children's Books," 1977.35
Childress, Alice, 1976.3
"Choose Something Like a Star," 1964.21
"Choosing One's Side with Care: The Liberating Repartee," 1975.28
The Chronological History of the Negro in America, 1969.8
"Church Sermon," 1953.29
Ciardi, John, 1963.20; 1964.21
"The Cities of Night: John Rechy's City of Night and the American Literature of Homosexuality," 1964.43
"The Cities of the Plain," 1956.9
Civil rights spokesman, 1963.2, 31, 36, 66, 69; 1964.5, 30, 38, 68; 1965.1, 74; 1966.19, 26, 30, 33; 1967.4, 12; 1968.3, 7, 42; 1969.13, 33; 1970.40; 1971.29, 31, 36; 1972.10, 49, 57, 65; 1974.41, 51; 1976.48
Clancy, T.H., 1963.21
Clark, Edward, 1960.2
Clarke, John Henrik, 1964.22; 1967.7; 1968.13; 1969.11; 1970.7, 43; 1971.40